Legal Implementation and Impacts of the European Green Deal

Moritz Reese · Romina Schaller · Till Markus ·
Kurt Faßbender
Editors

Legal Implementation and Impacts of the European Green Deal

Springer

Editors
Moritz Reese
Department of Environmental and Planning Law
Helmholtz Centre for Environmental Research – UFZ
Leipzig, Sachsen, Germany

Romina Schaller
Department of Environmental and Planning Law
Helmholtz Centre for Environmental Research – UFZ
Leipzig, Sachsen, Germany

Till Markus
Department of Environmental and Planning Law
Helmholtz Centre for Environmental Research – UFZ
Leipzig, Sachsen, Germany

Kurt Faßbender
Institute for Environmental and Planning Law
University of Leipzig
Leipzig, Sachsen, Germany

ISBN 978-3-032-17196-2 ISBN 978-3-032-17197-9 (eBook)
https://doi.org/10.1007/978-3-032-17197-9

This Springer imprint is published by the registered company Springer Nature Switzerland AG
The registered company address is: Gewerbestrasse 11, 6330 Cham, Switzerland

Preface

In 2019, the newly appointed European Commission proclaimed an epochal new political agenda: the European Green Deal (EGD). Conceived as the Union's overarching growth strategy, its ambition was nothing short of transformative, to reconfigure the European economy and society towards environmental sustainability and climate neutrality. It represented a paradigm shift in EU policymaking, moving beyond incremental environmental regulation to envision a comprehensive, cross-sectoral reconfiguration of core economic systems. The EGD's scope is vast, encompassing targeted policies for climate and energy, industry, building, pollution, biodiversity, agriculture, and mobility, while simultaneously addressing cross-cutting imperatives such as green finance, a just transition, social inclusiveness, and global responsibility.

Since its launch, the Commission has systematically elaborated this vision through a cascade of sectoral strategies and action plans. The process has now entered a decisive new phase: that of legal implementation. A plethora of legislative initiatives is currently reshaping the EU's legal landscape, affecting nearly every field of environmental law and extending far beyond its traditional boundaries to promote the greening of core economic sectors such as energy, agriculture, transport, and industry. This transformative wave of lawmaking raises profound questions for legal scholars, practitioners, and policymakers alike. How will these new legal instruments interact with the existing legal order? How effectively will they be transposed and applied by Member States? And ultimately, will they coalesce into a coherent and effective framework capable of delivering the sustainability transformation the EU envisions, within and beyond its borders?

This volume, based on contributions presented at the 10th European Environmental Law Forum, held in Leipzig in 2023, is dedicated to assessing these far-reaching legal developments. It provides a critical and timely examination of the European Green Deal's implementation and its expected impacts. The collected chapters adopt a multifaceted perspective, analysing both sectoral regulations and overarching constitutional and systemic themes from theoretical, technical, and practical viewpoints.

The volume is structured to guide the reader through the multi-layered challenge of implementing the European Green Deal. It begins with a foundational constitutional inquiry, as Christian Calliess questions the adequacy of the EU's primary law architecture for the challenges of the Anthropocene. The chapter focuses on the limitations of Article 11 TFEU and makes a compelling normative case for a deeper constitutional shift, including the potential establishment of justiciable environmental fundamental rights, to secure the necessary ecological transformation.

Subsequent chapters examine the dynamic interplay between EU and national legal frameworks. Delphine Misonne explores the role of national climate framework laws in fostering a sense of ownership over climate action, analysing how these domestic legal commitments interact with and complement the expanding body of EU climate legislation.

The relationship between international economic law and the Green Deal's objectives is explored by Daniela Muth, who delivers a compelling analysis of the EU's withdrawal from the Energy Charter Treaty. She argues that this step may have produced a counterintuitive outcome, reframing the debate to consider how future investment regimes could be recalibrated to support a decentralised energy transition.

The legal instruments underpinning the energy transition are further examined by Beatrice Bichi Ruspoli Forteguerri, who traces a paradigm shift in the EU's approach to long-term contracts. Her analysis suggests that while instruments such as Power Purchase Agreements are now promoted for decarbonisation, a carefully calibrated application of competition law remains crucial to safeguard the benefits of market liberalisation.

The analysis then turns to specific sectoral challenges. Jiri Vodicka provides a critical dissection of the EU's evolving legal strategy for aviation, a sector with persistently growing emissions. His chapter systematically assesses the revised regulatory framework across the aircraft lifecycle and offers a sharp critique of the complex interplay between the EU Emissions Trading System and the CORSIA scheme.

Inevitably, the accelerated pursuit of green objectives generates legal friction. Jan Darpö critically analyses the profound tensions between the EU's drive for renewable energy, accelerated by the REPowerEU Plan, and its foundational nature conservation laws, warning that the current emphasis on speed risks undermining key environmental safeguards.

The transition to a circular economy is addressed by Stéphanie van Gulijk and Jonas Voorter, who propose a holistic "Three P's" model (Products, Procurement, and Process) for the construction sector. They argue that a singular focus on any one element is insufficient, and call instead for a coordinated legal transformation across the entire value chain.

The marine and forest dimensions of the Green Deal are brought into sharp relief in the volume's closing chapters. Nikolaos Giannopoulos and Mathilde Hoarau critically assess the EGD's engagement with marine sustainability, concluding that its ambitious rhetoric has not yet translated into transformative action, with robust climate and energy targets overshadowing vague commitments to marine biodiversity. Complementing this, Gauthier Martens provides a comprehensive analysis of the EU's evolving forest protection framework, focusing on the new EU Deforestation Regulation and its significant extraterritorial implications.

Collectively, these chapters offer a nuanced and comprehensive portrait of European environmental law in a period of profound transformation. They shed light on the far-reaching legal ambitions of the European Green Deal, while critically examining its internal coherence, practical implementation, and capacity to achieve a just and effective transition. It is our hope that this volume will provide valuable insights and stimulate further debate among policymakers, legal professionals, and scholars dedicated to the pursuit of a climate-neutral and sustainable Europe.

Moritz Reese
Romina Schaller
Till Markus
Kurt Faßbender

Acknowledgments

This book stems from the 10th European Environmental Law Forum (EELF) Conference, held in Leipzig, Germany, from August 30 to September 1, 2023. The event was jointly organized by the European Environmental Law Forum, the project funded by the German Federal Ministry of Education and Research (BMBF) "KomUR – Competence Network 'Challenges of Environmental Law,'" the Helmholtz - Centre for Environmental Research-UFZ, and the University of Leipzig.

The primary aim of this volume is to bring together the diverse academic contributions presented during the conference. We would like to express our heartfelt appreciation to all participants, colleagues, collaborators, students, and external reviewers whose commitment and efforts made the realization of this book possible.

Contents

List of Authors and Editors

Beatrice Bichi Ruspoli Forteguerri is a Ph.D. candidate at Università degli Studi Roma Tre. She was awarded a doctoral position in the XXXVIII cycle (A.Y. 2022/2023) with a research project on the integration of environmental sustainability into European Union competition law. She graduated with honors in Law from Università degli Studi di Milano Statalein 2018, with a thesis in European Union Law. She has gained professional experience in public law, with a focus on competition, energy, and environmental law, at an international law firm in Rome and in public administrations, in particular at the Italian Competition Authority (AGCM) and the European Commission (DG COMP). She qualified as a lawyer in Italy in 2022.

Christian Calliess is Professor for Public, Environmental, and European Law at Freie Universität Berlin, Germany. In 2000 he finished his habilitation with a book on the rule of law, environmental law, the precautionary principle and fundamental rights ("Rechtsstaat und Umweltstaat"), which was awarded the prize of the German Gesellschaft für Umweltrecht (GfU). From 2008 till 2020, Christian Calliess served as a member of the Advisory Council on the Environment of the Federal Government of Germany (SRU). In 2013, he became a member of the Club of Rome, German branch. From 2015 till 2018, he was on leave from academia in order to work as Legal Adviser to the European Political Strategy Center (EPSC), the In-House-Think-Tank of the President of the European Commission.

Jan Darpö is an emeritus professor of environmental law. His research focuses on environmental procedure, water law, and nature conservation. He was a visiting professor at the University of Minnesota (2008) and UNSW in Sydney (2012). Between 2008 and 2021, he was a chair of the Task Force on Access to Justice under the Aarhus Convention. He has also worked as a lead consultant to the European Commission and the European Parliament and has been evaluator for several international research institutes. He is a member of the Avosetta Group and EELFs Advisory Board.

Kurt Faßbender is a professor of Public Law, with a specialization in Environmental and Planning Law, and serves as the executive director of the Institute for Environmental and Planning Law (Institut für Umwelt- und Planungsrecht, IUPR) at Leipzig University in Germany. His research focuses on European and German environmental law, particularly in the areas of water law, circular economy law, climate law, nature conservation law, and urban and infrastructure planning law. He is also the editor of the Zeitschrift für Umweltrecht (Journal of Environmental Law, ZUR).

Mathilde Hoarau is a jurist in environmental law and law of the sea. She is currently a French trainee lawyer at the Paris Bar Association Legal Training Centre. Her research interests include, amongst other, the adaptation of international law, more particularly the law of the sea, to the Anthropocene and the development of new legal tools such as the Rights of Nature/the Ocean.

Nikolaos Giannopoulos is an assistant professor of Public International and EU law at the Utrecht Centre for Water, Oceans, and Sustainability Law (UCWOSL) within the Law Faculty of Utrecht University. His research focuses on the legal and regulatory issues concerning the ongoing energy transition against the backdrop of the intertwined climate and biodiversity crises. He is also a qualified lawyer at the Athens Bar Association, where he has practised public administrative law for several years.

Stéphanie van Gulijk is a professor of Private Law at Tilburg Law School (currently also dean of Tilburg Law School) and deputy judge at the Court of Appeal in Amsterdam. She specializes in specific contracts law, with a strong focus on private construction law and the shift from a linear approach to a circular one. Stéphanie is also chair of the Dutch Association for Construction Law and senior lecturer construction law at the Dutch Grotius Academy."

Till Markus is Deputy Head of the Department of Environmental and Planning Law at the Helmholtz Centre for Environmental Research (UFZ), Leipzig, a position he has held since April 2024. He has been a Privatdozent at the Faculty of Law, University of Bremen, since February 2020. He serves as Co-Chief Editor of the Zeitschrift für Umweltrecht (Journal of Environmental Law, ZUR) and as Editor of the International Yearbook of Soil Law and Policy (Springer). His research and teaching focus on international and European law, environmental law, the law of the sea, comparative law, and legal theory.

Gauthier Martens is a PhD researcher at the Institut d'études européennes (IEE) and the Centre d'étude du droit de l'environnement (CEDRE) of UCLouvain Saint-Louis in Brussels, Belgium. His thesis deals with the translation in EU law of the Planetary boundaries framework in order to respond to the global ambit of contemporary ecological crises, using the EU Deforestation Regulation as a prototype of legislation embracing such planetary perspective.

Delphine Misonne is Senior Research Associate at the Belgian Fund for Scientific Research (FNRS) in Belgium and Professor at UCLouvain Saint-Louis Brussels, where she is also the head of the Environmental Law Center (CEDRE).

Daniela Muth is a lecturer of Law at the University of Westminster in London, where she teaches International Energy and Climate Change Law and is a member of the Climate Change, Energy Policy and Sustainability Research Group. She is dual-qualified to practise law in the UK and Germany and spent many years in private practice as a corporate lawyer specialising in mergers and acquisitions and corporate finance, with a particular focus on the energy sector. Before going into law, Daniela completed a Bachelor of Arts degree in History and Philosophy at Lancaster University and also holds a Master's degree in Philosophy from the University of Warwick.

Moritz Reese is Head of the Department of Environmental and Planning Law at the UFZ in Leipzig. He is also professor for European environmental law at the Faculty of Law of Leipzig University. His research focuses on European and national environmental law, particularly in the areas of water law, circular economy law, climate adaptation law, nature conservation law, immission control law, and urban and infrastructure planning law. In addition, his work addresses the theoretical foundations of environmental law and the overarching legal dimensions of the sustainability transformation. He is also a chair of the European Environmental Law Form (EELF), co-editor of the Zeitschrift für Umweltrecht (Journal for Environmental Law), and co-editor of the Journal for European Environmental & Planning Law (JEEPL).

Romina Schaller is Postdoctoral Researcher in the Department of Environmental and Planning Law at the Helmholtz Centre for Environmental Research-UFZ (Germany). She also coordinates the "Competence Network 'Challenges of Environmental Law' (KomUR)." Her work focuses on international and European environmental law, particularly in climate change mitigation (e.g. forest protection through REDD+) as well as on ecosystem services and sustainable development. Her current research explores the legal aspects for the regulation of carbon dioxide removal technologies (CDR) and the emerging challenges linked to their governance.

Jiri Vodicka is Assistant Professor at the Department of Environmental Law and Land Law at Masaryk University in Brno, Czechia. His work bridges academic research and policy practice, with a focus on environmental regulation in the automotive industry, climate policy, and the circular economy. Before entering academia, he worked at the Czech Competition Authority and completed a traineeship at the European Commission's Directorate General for Competition, gaining key insights into EU regulatory frameworks. He earned his PhD in Environmental Law from Masaryk University, where he now teaches. Dr. Vodicka has taught at institutions including Brno University of Technology, the University of Antwerp, National Tsing Hua University (Taiwan), the Academy of European Law, and the Czech Judicial Academy. He is also an active member of the Avosetta Group, a European network of legal scholars specializing in environmental law.

Jonas Voorter is working as Assistant Professor in Environmental Law at Hasselt University. He is both part of the Centre for Government and Law and the Centre for Environmental Sciences. He also is affiliated at Hasselt University as Postdoctoral Researcher working within the framework of the Flemish CE Center. His research focuses on facilitating the transition towards a circular and sustainable society using the full spectrum of legal instruments. He is mainly focused on the impact of this transition on the built environment.

The Constitutional and Governance Foundation

The European Green Deal and Its "Constitutional" Implications: Need for a "Greening of the Treaties"?

Christian Calliess(✉)

Faculty of Law, Freie Universität Berlin, Berlin, Germany
c.calliess@fu-berlin.de

Abstract. The EU's current legal framework might be regarded as insufficient to address the planetary crisis of the Anthropocene. This article evaluates whether the environmental integration principle (Article 11 TFEU) can serve as the primary tool for the ecological transformation envisioned by the European Green Deal, examining its application across key policy sectors. Finding significant limitations, the paper ultimately advocates for "greening the EU Treaties" itself through constitutional amendments, institutional reforms, and the establishment of new, enforceable environmental fundamental rights to secure an ecological minimum subsistence level for citizens.

1 Introduction: The Global Climate Crisis as a Challenge for the EU

1.1 Climate Change, the Anthropocene and Planetary Boundaries

Scientific analysis show that the earth is leaving its current geological epoch, the Holocene, behind, entering a new state, which is being described as the "*Anthropocene*"[1]. The Holocene is characterised by relatively stable and safe environmental conditions, which have allowed the social and economic development of humanity, while at the same time providing the basis for the preservation of peace and security.[2] The new geological epoch, defined by the significant human impact on the earth, the so-called Anthropocene, however, might become a state characterised by **instability, unpredictability and hostile conditions** for life on earth. Some even consider the possibility for the earth to enter a state that could be described as a "*wasteland Anthropocene*" (*Verwüstungsanthropozän*).[3] This transition to a new geological epochstresses the severity of changes which fundamental earth systems and processes are undergoing. These changes can be attributed to the significant influence that humankind is exerting on the Earth system. Against this background, it can be assessed that humanity has become a major "*geological force*".

[1] Crutzen and Stoermer (2000); Crutzen (2002).

[2] SRU (2019a), para 57 et seq.

[3] For the two varieties of the Anthropocene: "wasteland Anthropocene" and "Holocene-like Anthropocene" see SRU 2019a), para 64 et seq.

M. Reese et al. (Eds.): EELF 2023, *Legal Implementation and Impacts of the European Green Deal*, pp. 3–55, 2026.
https://doi.org/10.1007/978-3-032-17197-9_1

These observations are based on findings that derive from the research field of earth system science, which focuses on the dynamics of the entire earth system, illustrating the complexity of the earth's underlying processes and systems as well as their mutual interactions.[4] Relevant in this context is the scientific **concept of "*planetary boundaries*"**.[5] This concept identifies nine key processes and subsystems of the Earth, for which scientists have established and quantified boundaries that should not be transgressed. Planetary boundaries articulate a science-based concept for climate protection, biodiversity, nitrogen and phosphorus input into the environment, land use change, freshwater use, stratospheric ozone depletion, ocean acidification, as well as their interactions. The corresponding boundaries set the limits of the absorption capacity of ecological systems. Exceeding one or more of these boundaries may trigger large-scale and processes of unpredictable change, which can affect the functioning of the earth System as a whole, leading to the precipice of catastrophic environmental change.

In this context, the so-called ***tipping points*** pose a major challenge.[6] Exceeding them can lead to environmental damage that is irreversible and unfortunately their precise position cannot be determined with certainty. For instance, the 1.5 to 2 °C goal, as set in the 2016 Paris Agreement,[7] poses a threshold for such a tipping point.[8] Tipping points, if exceeded, are capable of altering Earth system functions in a non-linear or even abrupt manner, which could result in a kind of "*devastation scenario*". In light of these **catastrophic consequences**, the concept of planetary boundaries formulates a "*safe operating space*" and incorporates a **safety margin** when determining critical thresholds.[9]

With regard to legal implications, it is important to keep in mind that the core objective of the concept of planetary boundaries is to identify a "*safe operating space*" for humanity, in which it can likely exist under stable conditions of the Earth system.[10] Therefore, in order to achieve a sustainable Anthropocene, it is crucial to prevent further transgression of planetary boundaries. This may require a fundamental **realignment of European Environmental policies**. In terms of the climate-change boundary, in particular, greenhouse gas emissions must be substantially reduced, which in turn requires an immediate and drastic change of activities across all sectors.

1.2 The EU's Climate Protection Obligations, Particularly the European Green Deal

Over the decades, the Union has developed an extensive body of Environmental policy regulation and a wide range of European environmental law.[11] In legal literature, the

[4] See Schellnhuber (1998).

[5] Rockström et al. (2009); an updated version followed in 2015, see Steffen et al. (2015).

[6] Cf. SRU (2019a), para 43 et seq.

[7] Paris Agreement, United Nations, Treaty Series, vol. 3165 (2016), p. 79, Art. 2(1)(a).

[8] Intergovernmental Panel on Climate Change (IPCC) (2018), p. 11 et seq and 17 et seq; Paris Agreement, 3165 UNTS 79 (2016), Art. 2(1)(a).

[9] Rockström et al. (2009).

[10] Rockström et al. (2009).

[11] See for instance SRU (2020a) The historical development of European environmental policy. In SRU (2020b), para 693 et seq.

development of European environmental policy has even been described as "*an unparalleled success story*".[12] Articles 3(3) TEU, 191 TFEU and 37 EU Charta of Fundamental Rights point to the existence of an "Environmental Union" ("Umweltverbund"). Nevertheless, scientific findings show that previous efforts to limit climate change and the destruction of the environment have proved to be insufficient.[13] For instance, the European Environmental Agency noted in 2019 that more than half of the European sustainability targets set out by policy for 2020 might not be achieved[14] and its 2023 monitoring report of the 8th Environmental Action Programm (EAP) determines that 20 out of the 28 headline indicators included in the monitoring framework are not on track to reach their 2030 objectives.[15] Part of the reason lies in the **lack of adequate implementation and enforcement** of existing environmental legislation at member state level.[16] Additionally, environmental and climate-related concerns are not sufficiently taken into consideration in the context of other policy areas.[17]

The **need for urgent action** to combat these catastrophic risks associated with climate change has been recognized at the European level, and is particularly reflected in the European Commission's Communication on the ***European Green Deal***.[18] It was presented as the Commission's new growth strategy, and entails the EU's commitment to strive for carbon neutrality by 2050 at its core. A month earlier, the European Parliament had declared a global "*climate and environmental emergency*", and urged the EU to commit to the goal of reaching climate neutrality as soon as possible.[19] Previously, the need for a green transition had also been emphasised by the European Council in its Strategic Agenda for 2019 to 2024.[20]

The European Green Deal represents a growth strategy that aims to "*transform the EU into a fair and prosperous society, with a modern, resource-efficient and competitive economy*", and to make Europe greenhouse gas neutral by 2050.[21] Annexed thereto is a roadmap for measures that the European Commission intends to take in the coming years in order to implement the European Green Deal.[22] At the heart of this initiative was

12 Wegener (2009).

13 Among the many reports see the recent IPCC (2023).

14 EEA (2019)), p. 7.

15 Of these 20 indicators not on track, 15 are unlikely and 5 very unlikely to meet their 2030 targets, see EEA (2023), p. 7 et seq.

16 See SRU (2020b), para 732 et seq.

17 See SRU (2020b), para 728 et seq.

18 COM (2019) 640 final, European Commission (2019) Communication from the Commission: The European Green Deal. See European Commission Press Release (2019a); see Calliess and Dross (2020); cf. Also Köck and Markus (2020); see for further details SRU (2020c); Schmidt (2020); Schlacke (2020); Lösch (2020); Ammann (2020).

19 See European Parliament (2019a).

20 See European (2019).

21 COM (2019) 640 final, p. 2.

22 COM (2019) 640 final, European Commission (2019) Annex to the Communication from the Commission to the European Parliament, the Council, the European Economic and Social Committee and the Committee of the Regions, The European Green Deal.

the proposal for a "***European Climate Law***"[23], which has entered into force on 29 July 2021, stipulating the legally binding long-term objective of **greenhouse gas neutrality by 2050**. It aims to achieve this goal by ensuring that all EU policies contribute to the climate-neutrality objective and that responsibility for it is assumed across all sectors.[24] In July 2021, the European Commission also adopted a package of legislative proposals (**"*Fit for 55*"**), which aim at revising and updating EU legislation in order to cut the EU's net greenhouse gas emissions and reach climate neutrality.[25]

1.3 Greening the Treaty? An Old Debate in Light of the New Green Deal

The European Green Deal can be seen as a welcome signal that the EU is moving towards sustainability. Ecological transition requires far-reaching changes in various areas of society.[26] The envisaged fundamental orientation towards sustainability involves a task of transformation, which is primarily addressed to the legislator. However, the challenges associated with the consequences of the Anthropocene and the crossing of planetary boundaries emphasise the **urgency for the ecological transition** to be realised in the near future, creating immense time pressure. While this calls for immediate legislative and enforcement action, it also raises the question of whether the EU Treaties, as the Unions base, should be redesigned in an ecological sense.

The possibility of "*greening the Treaties*" is not an entirely new idea as it has already been debated in the context of negotiations for the Maastricht Treaty.[27] The topic arose as a result of the strategy of a global environmental protection policy drafted in Rio de Janeiro in 1992. However, in view of the European Green Deal, old debates become topical again, and the question of greening the EU Treaties or national constitutions arises once more. Most recently, in German scholarship, *Kersten* has analysed the German

---

23 Regulation (EU) 2021/1119 of the European Parliament and of the Council of 30 June 2021 establishing the framework for achieving climate neutrality and amending Regulations (EC) No 401/2009 and (EU) 2018/1999 ('European Climate Law'), OJ L 243, 9.7.2021; cf. Reese (2020); Schlacke et al. (2021); See also Frenz (2022).

24 Ibid, preamble paras 7, 10, 25.

25 COM (COM, 2021.a) 550 final, European Commission (2021) Communication for the Commission to the European Parliament, the Council, the European Economic and Social Committee and the Committee of the Regions. 'Fit for 55': delivering the EU's 2030 Climate Target on the way to climate neutrality. Among the proposals that have already been adopted and are in force are: The EU Emissions Trading System (ETS) reform, New EU Emissions Trading System for building and road transport fuels, the Social Climate Fund, Effort Sharing Regulation, Regulation on Land Use, Forestry and Agriculture, CO2 emissions standards for cars and vans, Carbon Border Adjustment Mechanism, see European Commission (2021a).

26 SRU (2020b), para 692.

27 See Calliess (1991), pp. 207–212; Calliess (1994); Arbeitskreis "Europäische Umweltunion" (1994); Report of the environmental organisations: WWF, CEAT, EEB, Greening the Treaty, Brüssel, November 1990; cf. Wilkinson (1992); Conference on "Wege zum ökologischen Rechtsstaat" of the Environmental Law Institute, Bremen, 6./7.2.1993, see the conference report, Reiter (1993); see also the different contributions in: Baumeister (1994); see the contributions in Calliess and Wegener (1992); Wolf (1996).

Constitution, the German Basic Law and developed proposals for greening its provisions.[28] According to him, if the citizens of the Global North intent to live up to their global responsibility for the catastrophic ecological developments, they need to ecologically transform their societies in a globally responsible manner.[29] In this ecological transformation, Constitutional Law is of central importance.[30] Most of the proposals analysed by *Kersten* are not entirely new, but have already been debated in the past decades under concepts such as "*Umweltstaat*" or "*Ökologischer Rechtsstaat*".[31] Taking up these arguments and concepts can help the design of an ecological constitutional order, that is ready to face the challenges of the Anthropocene.

Similarly, in the European Union context, and in light of the European Green Deal, it will be reflected on, whether and how the (Lisbon) treaties could be greened. This is embedded in the larger context regarding the question of the role that Law could play for realising an ecological transformation of the Union.

2 The Potential of Article 11 TFEU for an Ecological Transformation of the EU

A significant part of the debate about greening the Treaties, is the reflection on proposals which have already been debated by legal scholarship for years. Most of them can be applied in this new context regarding the ecological transformation, which is characterised in particular by the European Green Deal. Nevertheless, an analysis of some of the proposals raises the question of whether a greening of the Treaties truly has any added value as it can be argued that most of the suggestions may already be achieved by **simply applying Article 11 TFEU**, also referred to as the "***integration principle***" or "*cross-cutting clause*".[32] This gives rise to a brief examination of the provision.[33]

2.1 Content of Article 11 TFEU

Article 11 TFEU reads as follows: "Environmental protection requirements must be integrated into the definition and implementation of the Union's policies and activities, in particular with a view to promoting sustainable development." This article can be understood as a primary law requirement for conducting a **strategic environmental impact assessment,** which applies not only to individual measures, but also to policies, programs, plans and laws.[34] However, within the framework of Article 11 TFEU, the requirements of environmental protection must be balanced against **conflicting interests**

28 See Kersten (2022).

29 Kersten (2022), p. 5.

30 Kersten (2022), p. 5.

31 See for instance the proposals for an ecological transformation of the German Basic Law: Bosselmann (1994); Bosselmann (1992); Steinberg (1998); Kloepfer (1993). From 1988 to 1993 the Ladenburger Kolleg "Umweltstaat" took on these topics with an interdisciplinary view: see Kloepfer (1994) and on the final congress see the conference report by Lübbe (1994).

32 See already Calliess (1994a), p. 304.

33 On Article 11 TFEU see for instance Calliess (2022a); see Kahl (2018); Epiney (2018).

34 Appel (2018) § 2 para. 44.

(such as economic freedom and the principle of the welfare state). In this regard, politics, and in particular the legislator, have a political margin of discretion in implementing the provision.

When balancing environmental protection against conflicting interests, two specific aspects must be taken into account. Art.11's demands have to be implemented in conjunction with the precautionary principle of Art. 191(1) and (2) TFEU,[35], in addition to fundamental rights obligations that guarantee an "ecological minimum subsistence level" by respecting a "safe operating space"[36]. In the balancing process, this is further supplemented by a prohibition of insufficient means or actions ("Untermaßverbot") on part of the legislature.[37]

Secondly, the concept of integration implies that **environmental considerations** cannot simply be disregarded.[38] Instead, they **must be an integral part and visibly shape** the content of the individual EU measure.[39]

Apart from these substantive requirements, the integration clause also has a procedural dimension, that demands effective monitoring of the fulfilment of the substantive side in European decision making and the Member States' implementation process[40] by institutionally established scrutiny mechanisms or "watch dogs". Art. 11 TFEU has gained significance as environmental burdens have increased and the recognition has grown that environmental assets such as ecosystems, environmental media, and the climate are often closely interconnected, giving rise to strong interdependencies between various environmental sectors and issues.[41] The **legislative scope of discretion** in this respect is exceeded when a measure is visibly designed to the detriment of environmental protection. Such a measure, which is very likely to result in significant damage to the environment may not be adopted under Article 11 TFEU. A policy that crossed this boundary would be unlawful, as it would be in breach of Article 11 TFEU.[42]

2.2 Is Article 11 TFEU Legally Binding?

It is not entirely clear whether Article 11 TFEU merely represents a non-binding political program clause or comprises a legally binding rule.[43]

---

[35] Calliess (2022a), para 14.

[36] On the ecological minimum subsistance level, see Section 3.2.3.

[37] For a detailed discussion, Calliess (2001), p. 322 et seq, 451 et seq. And 566 et seq; similarly, Brönneke (1999), p. 272 et seq and 471 et seq; Sommermann (1997), p. 439 et seq.

[38] See Calliess (1998), pp. 565 et seq as well as Calliess and Dross (2020), p. 461.

[39] Hailbronner (1992), p. 20 et seq; Marin Durán and Morgera (2012); Epiney (1997), p. 162; Appel (2018) § 2 para. 4 et seq; Scheuing (1989), p. 176 et seq; Kahl (2018), para. 17; contra Nettesheim (2023), para 22, who also refers in para 23 et seq to European jurisdiction.

[40] On this already Calliess (1998), p. 566 et seq.

[41] Calliess and Dross (2020), p. 461.

[42] In contrast, AG Geelhoed argues that Article 6 EC (now Article 11 TFEU) can only serve as a criterion for the legality of Community acts if environmental concerns have obviously not been taken into account or completely disregarded, Opinion in Case C-161/04, ECLI:EU:C:2006:66, para 59 (no decision in this case due to withdrawal).

[43] Relativising Heselhaus (2017), para 12.

On the one hand the wording of Article 11 TFEU only prescribes general conditions for future measures of the Union without specifying the timeframe or form of realization. Furthermore, there are no limitations prescribed to the discretionary power of the Commission and the Council.[44] Finally, the lack of discernible legal consequences in the event of non-observance puts into question further if the clause is a legally binding rule or rather a mere principle.[45]

On the other hand, the use of the word "must" points to a clear obligation to incorporate environmental requirements.[46] Therefore, the requirement to "*include*" goes beyond a mere "*obligation of consideration*" in the weighing process.[47] This also corresponds to the purpose behind the two revisions of the cross-section clause which were aimed at making it more binding and more influential.[48] This means that Article 11 TFEU contains an "*imperativist mandate to act*"[49] which affords it more force than a mere political consideration dependent on the goodwill of the Union institutions.[50] Even though the manner of implementation is left to the discretion of the Union´s institutions, the commanding language clearly speaks to a legal imperative to realign all Union policy in accordance with the objectives and principles outlined in Article 191 TFEU.[51]

Confirming this assessment, Advocate General Jacobs in his opinion in the *PreussenElektra* case emphasized[52] that the cross-cutting clause is not merely programmatic but legally binding. Additionally, in the (legally non-binding) Declaration No. 20 to the Final Act of the Maastricht Treaty, the Intergovernmental Conference provided "that the Commission undertakes in its proposals, and that the Member States undertake in implementing those proposals, to take full account of the environmental impact and the principle of sustainable growth"[53] and the Commission has issued instructions to this effect to its Directorates-General in 1993.[54]

In conclusion, the requirement for environmental protection that Art. 11 TFEU poses is **binding for the legislator, the administration and the courts**. As the scientific concept of planetary boundaries can only indicate that measures are necessary, the choice of specific measures is up to the legislator (within the bounds of the prohibition of

---

[44] Jahns-Böhm (1994), 262.

[45] Krämer (1996); meanwhile differently Krämer (2013), p. 90 "policy objective"; Krämer (2015).

[46] Stroetmann (1993), p. 3; Kahl (1993), p. 58.

[47] Cf. Heselhaus (2017), para 14.

[48] Calliess (1992).

[49] Wiegand (1993), p. 536.

[50] Schmitz (1996), 151; critically Epiney and Furrer (1992), pp. 386 et seq, who do not see any changes in the legal situation in the new formulation, but probably already assumed a legal requirement under the EEA.

[51] In conclusion also Wiegand (1993), p. 536.; HYPERLINK "SPS:refid::bib107" Jahns-Böhm and Breier (1992), p. 52; Breier (1992), p. 181; Schmitz (1996), p. 151; Epiney (1995), p. 502; Calliess (1994a), p. 287; Scherer and Heselhaus (2017), para 53; Stroetmann (1993), p. 3; Breier (2008), para 10; Käller (2019), para 18, pp. 72 et seq.

[52] AG Jacobs Concluding Observations on ECJ Case C-379/98, PreussenElektra AG v Schhleswag AG, in the presence of Windpark Reußenköge III GmbH and Land Schleswig-Holstein (2000), ECLI:EU:C:2000:585, para 231.

[53] Treaty on the European Union, OJ C 191/1.

[54] Wägenbaur (1997) Europa-Report; EuZW (1997), p. 642.

insufficient means or actions). However, the legislator, is *de facto* obliged to deliver, in form of a "*guiding law*", a legally binding, coherent, and comprehensive concept of protection, including efficient monitoring, based on the balancing of conflicting interests as outlined above, in order establish a potent "*guard rail*" for all policy and to tackle the intertemporal problem of climate protection effectively.[55]

In addition to its significance as a legal requirement, Article 11 TFEU also serves as a **standard of interpretation** in relation to other norms of Union law.[56] This function particularly comes into play in the interpretation of indeterminate legal concepts and in the context of discretionary power. The requirement of environment-friendly interpretation of secondary Union law pursuant to Article 11 TFEU has also been emphasised in the *Concordia Bus* case,[57] where the CJEU confirmed that environmental considerations ought to be taken into account in EU public procurement law.

2.3 Article 11 TFEU as the Key Norm for Greening

Even though there is further room for unfolding the potential of Article 11 TFEU, it is evident that there are already instruments and tools, which provide for an operationalisation of environmental principles, such as the reversal of burden of proof in the context of the precautionary principle.[58]

As described above, the provisions of **Article 191(1) and (2) TFEU** and particularly the **precautionary principle** need to be taken into account in the balancing process, following Article 11 TFEU. The precautionary principle can be structured into two elements. The first is characterised by identifying and evaluating a **precautionary trigger**. The second refers to the **legal consequence** defined by the precautionary measure to be taken, supplemented by determining the addressee of the precautionary action. Precautionary considerations are triggered by an abstract potential for concern of the well-known situation of ***non liquet***, where the existing uncertainty cannot be resolved with the investigative means available. In this sense, the precautionary principle operates according to the legal pattern of a **rebuttable presumption of danger**. In its communication[59] on the precautionary principle, the Commission states that this can lead to a **reversal of the burden of proof**.[60] In order to challenge the presumption of danger, the party who creates the risk, is required to present facts and provide evidence based on a reasonable probability. This is based on the fact that the party, in whose sphere of influence the uncertainty arose has an **advantage of knowledge** due to its proximity to the subject matter.

---

[55] In-depth Calliess (2001), pp. 235 et seq; Calliess (2019), p. 386; similarly, SRU (2019), pp.182 et seq.

[56] Nettesheim (2023), para 31; Breier (2008), para. 15 et seq; Kahl (2018), para 29 et seq.

[57] Case C-513/99, Concordia Bus Finland (2002), para 57.

[58] See on the precautionary principle Calliess (2022c) Art. 191 TFEU, paras 28-37; see in detail Calliess (2001), p. 207 et seq.

[59] COM (2000) 1 final, Communication from the Commission on the precautionary principle.

[60] In detail Calliess (2013), pp. 3, 17; contra Arndt (2009), p. 290 et seq, 295 et seq, who considers only a reduction of the burden of proof as a direct consequence of the precautionary principle, but not a reversal of the burden of proof, which, however, he sees realized within the framework of the secondary legislative authorization procedures.

Article 11 TFEU, particularly in conjunction with the Preamble and Article 3(3) sentence 2 and 5(2) TEU, implies a **general principle of sustainability**. The EU's obligation to adhere to the principle of sustainable development is, therefore, beyond question.[61] According to the conception and intention of Article 11 TFEU, the integration clause is a significant instrument for implementing the principle of sustainable development in EU Law.[62] This leads to the assumption that Article 11 TFEU has great potential for realising the **ecological transformation of the Union**. Nevertheless, it can be said that the *explicit* inclusion of an ecological clause in highly complex areas, such as economic policy, could be beneficial, in particular, considering the difficulty regarding the implementation and legal enforcement of Article 11 TFEU[63]. The implementation of goals is too often entirely lost in the complexity of the political process. Therefore, it is very welcome that as part of the European Green Deal, the European Commission has announced that it will work to strengthen efforts to ensure that existing legislation and measures relevant to the European Green Deal are enforced and effectively implemented.[64] If the proclaimed strategy of the European Green Deal is not to be lost in everyday politics, Article 11 TFEU must fulfil its potential for realising the transformation towards an ecological legal system. The provision points the way to an ecologically sustainable and thus **future-oriented economic policy** that makes environmental policy one of its integral parts and is aligned with the sustainability and viability of ecological systems. Ultimately, the contribution of Article 11 TFEU to the realisation of an "*ecological Union*" depends on how it is handled in practice.

2.4 Greening the Union's Policies: Does Art. 11 TFEU Deliver What It Promises?

In order to meet the challenges of the Anthropocene, the **ecological dimension of policies**, especially financial and infrastructure-related ones, need to be strengthened.[65] To do so, *Kersten* (in the German context) suggests **including an "ecological reference"** within all relevant provisions, to ensure that environmental concerns are also integrated into policy of various sectors, preferably at an early stage, in order to promote sustainable development.[66]

Indeed, one of the main challenges for an ecological transformation relates to the, thus far, insufficient integration of environmental concerns into other policy areas, and in particular, those sectors, which are ecologically problematic.[67] Environmental pressures

[61] Regarding the previously existing uncertainties in this regard since the Treaty of Maastricht, see Calliess (1994), pp. 71, 77 et seq; Haigh and Kraemer (1996); for a general overview of the development in European law, see Monien (2013), p. 195 et seq.

[62] Fundamentally on this matter, see Calliess (1998); in this sense, probably also the Commission, see Wägenbaur B (Wägenbaur) Europa-Report. EuZW, 642; Calliess (2003), p. 73.

[63] Equally Kahl (2018); Calliess and Dross (2020), p. 461.

[64] COM (2019) 640 final, p. 4; On proposals for strengthening enforcement of European Environmental Law, see SRU (2020b), paras 753-754.

[65] Kersten (2022), p. 169.

[66] However, an integration of environmental concerns is already required by Article 11 TFEU and might not necessitate an amendment of the Treaties. See on Article 11 TFEU further below in Section C.

[67] SRU (2020b), paras 718, 728.

that are caused by activities in various economic sectors have so far not been effectively reduced.[68] However, an intact environment and the prevention of climate change are the foundation for all economic activity[69] and this pivotal importance needs to be reflected **in policy areas beyond traditional environmental protection.**[70]

In the context of the EU, the debate about greening the treaties, thus, also necessitates a reflection about a greening of the EU's Policies.[71]

2.4.1 European Semester

One greening option refers to the economic and budgetary coordination at the European level, specifically the "*European Semester*".[72] Indeed, President of the Commission *von der Leyen*, at the beginning of her term, stated that the *Sustainable Development Goals* (SDGs) will be incorporated into the European Semester[73] and has kept to that promise as the recent Commission's *Annual Sustainable Growth Survey 2024*, which launches the 2024 cycle of economic policy coordination, reiterated its commitment to monitor and promote the SDGs through the European Semester[74].

The European Semester is an annual cyclical process that is designed to coordinate the economic, fiscal, and labour market policies of the member states. Its establishment in 2011 was a response to the need for measures to stabilize the eurozone and the *Europe 2020 strategy*, providing a preventive mechanism for **monitoring national budgets at the European level**[75]. The main objective of the European Semester is to motivate member states to better coordinate their policies and **align them with the objectives agreed at the European level**. This is achieved by means of various reports, discussion processes and recommendations. It is important to note, however, that the European Semester is a non-binding process within the framework of economic policy coordination (Article 121 TFEU). Thus, only some of the recommendations are being implemented by the member states.

Traditionally, the economic and, at times, social aspects of sustainability play a significant role in this process.[76] The ecological dimension, in particular, has recently been

---

[68] EEA (2019), p. 8.

[69] SRU (2020b), para 738.

[70] SRU (2020b), para 738.

[71] Most of the suggestions have already been analysed elsewhere, see for instance Calliess (1994), p. 284; Calliess and Dross (2020). On the consideration of environmental protection within the Union's policies see the contributions in Rengeling (1993).

[72] See for the following, SRU (2020b), para 741.

[73] Von der Leyen (2019).

[74] COM (2015) 12, Communication from the Commission to the European Parliament, the Council, the European Central Bank, the Economic and Social Committee, the Committee of the Regions and the European Investment Bank, . Making the best use of the flexibility within the existing rules of the stability and growth pact, p. 10.

[75] Häde (2002) Art. 121 TFEU, para 25; Schulte (2015) Article 12 TFEU, para. 23.

[76] Commission Staff Working Document, Key European action supporting the 2030 Agenda and the Sustainable Development Goals. Accompanying the document COM(2016) 739 final, Communication from the Commission to the European Parliament, the Council, the European

strengthened.[77] This shift is a response to the observation of the increasing economic relevance of both ecological challenges and environmental policy measures. Moreover, environmental protection also presents economic opportunities. This expanded understanding of the economy is reflected, for instance, in the **renaming** of the "*Annual Growth Report*" at the beginning of the cycle to the ***"Annual Sustainable Growth Strategy"***.[78]

While this reform, to integrate environmental sustainability into the European Semester, represents a positive initiative towards mainstreaming environmental protection and sustainability, it should be noted that it does not serve as a substitute for a comprehensive EU sustainability policy. The European Semester, as a predominantly technical instrument, cannot advance the crucial implementation of SDGs at the European level by itself. This is due to the fact that the overall process is primarily focused on implementing SDGs within the member states. It has therefore been recommended that the European Semester should align with the yet-to-be-developed Sustainable Europe 2030 strategy, and in addition, include a sustainability check.[79] This measure has the advantage that it leverages existing EU instruments to achieve better integration of sustainability goals into the development of Union policies.[80]

2.4.2 Common Agricultural Policy (CAP)

In agriculture, persistent negative impacts on biodiversity, and air, water and soil pollution can continuously be witnessed.[81] It is thus evident that a greening is particularly crucial with regard to the ***Common Agricultural Policy* (CAP).**[82] The previous efforts to integrate environmental concerns into agricultural policy have proven insufficient to bring about the necessary ecological changes. While the CAP 2023–2027 already includes commendable adjustments by, for example, setting **more stringent environmental conditions** to be met by farmers who receive area- and animal-based CAP payments,[83] further decisive steps need to be taken to make CAP more environmentally sustainable. The SRU (*German Advisory Council on the Environment*) has consistently

Economic and Social Committee and the Committee of the Regions. Next steps for a sustainable European future: European Union action for sustainability.

[77] COM (2019) 650 final, Communication from the Commission to the European Parliament, the Council, the European Central Bank, the European Economic and Social Committee, the Committee of the Regions and the European Investment Bank, Annual Sustainable Growth Strategy 2020.

[78] COM (2019) 650 final.

[79] COM (2019) 22, Reflection Paper: Towards a sustainable Europe by 2030 , p. 31.

[80] European Parliament (2019b) Study, Europe's approach to implementing the Sustainable Development Goals.

[81] EEA (2019), p. 8.

[82] In the past, the Common Agricultural Policy (CAP) has been heavily criticised, including by the European Court of Auditors, see Opinion No. 7/2018 (pursuant to Article 322(1)(a) TFEU) concerning Commission proposals for regulations relating to the common agricultural policy for the post-2020 period, COM (2018) 392, 393 and 394 final. See on the consideration of ecological aspects in the agricultural production: Epiney (2009); see as well Götz (1993), pp. 173–203.

[83] European Commission (2019b), p. 5 et seq.

emphasised that public funds should be utilized exclusively for the **provision of public goods**, which encompass nature conservation, environmental protection, and the preservation of diverse and ecologically rich cultural landscapes.[84] Environmental considerations must be consistently taken into account in both the detailed European legislation, implementing the CAP and its application and enforcement by member states.

During the *Multiannual financial framework* (MFF) from 2014 to 2020, the European Union allocated 39% of its total budget under the heading of "*Sustainable Growth: Natural Resources*".[85] The CAP absorbed 97% of the funds allocated under this heading, making it a very sizeable MFF item.[86] Approximately EUR 239 billion of the CAP funds during the 2014–2020 period were directed towards direct payments,[87] which were primarily **based on agricultural land usage or production quantities**, rather than on the fulfilment of meeting sustainability criteria. Unfortunately, the greening measures implemented within the first pillar of the CAP have had limited success in safeguarding biodiversity.[88] In the future, it is crucial that public funds be allocated towards providing public goods in the field of environmental, climate, and biodiversity protection.[89] Furthermore, it is essential to enhance the ecological aspects of the ***Common Fisheries Policy*** (CFP), which originally was part of the CAP but has since evolved into a separate policy. Changes to the CFP should involve a more efficient implementation of sustainable stock management, as stock recovery of some fish stocks is still unacceptably slow,[90] and increased safeguarding of sensitive ecosystems and species, regarding which the Commission has recently taken a step by communicating its new action plan on restoring marine ecosystems[91].[92]

2.4.3 Economic Tools

Another greening option refers to an ecological realignment of taxes, duties and subsidies.[93] Environmentally hazardous products or manufacturing processes should be made more expensive through "***eco-taxes and levies***", in order to change the business

[84] Most recently SRU (2019b); SRU, WBBGR (2018).

[85] See SRU (2020a), para 742, referring to European Commission (2019) EU funding programmes 2014–2020. https://commission.europa.eu/strategy-and-policy/eu-budget/long-term-eu-budget/2014-2020/eu-funding-programmes_en. Accessed 25 Aug 2025.

[86] See SRU (2020a), para 742, referring to European Commission (2019) Rubrik 2 Nachhaltiges Wachstum: natürliche Ressourcen. https://commission.europa.eu/strategy-and-policy/eu-budget/long-term-eu-budget/2014-2020/eu-funding-programmes/heading-2-sustainable-growth-natural-resources_de. Accessed 25 Aug 2025.

[87] See SRU (2020c), para 742, referring to Heinrich Böll Foundation et al. (2019).

[88] SRU (2019b); SRU, WBBGR (2018).

[89] Ibid, p. 26.

[90] Schacht et al. (2019), p. 26.

[91] COM(2023) 102 final, Communication to the European Parliament, the Council, the European Economic and Social Committee and the Committee of the Regions, EU Action Plan: Protecting and restoring marine ecosystems for sustainable and resilient fisheries.

[92] SRU (2011); Schacht et al. (2019).

[93] See SRU (2019a), p. 14.

calculations of companies and **consumer habits** accordingly.[94] Products and processes causing the greatest damage or carrying the highest risks should be taxed the most. Instead of taxing added value, the "*diminished value*" – in terms of reducing the value of our environment through the consumption of natural resources – should be taxed.[95]

It has already been noted in the context of the Maastricht Treaty that, in the course of the internal market, indirect taxes such as *value-added tax* (VAT) and various consumption taxes must be harmonized.[96] The VAT has since been gradually standardized and is currently regulated by Directive 2006/112/EC (the VAT Directive), according to which the standard rate of VAT to be applied by all Member States to goods and services is at least 15%, with exceptions possible under certain conditions. However, harmonization reduces the scope for Member States to introduce "*eco-taxes*".[97] Furthermore, the reluctance to justify **competitive disadvantages for one's own industry** prevents many Member States from effectively using '*eco-taxes*' as a means in environmental policy. Further approaches that were suggested for environmental taxes at the EU level around the time of the Maastricht Treaty refer to a heavy goods vehicle levy, a waste disposal fee, and a levy for chlorine (CFCs).[98] The revenue from such environmental charges and taxes could be used to support investments in environmentally friendly substitutes in the respective areas. A portion of the revenue could also be deposited into a global environmental and climate protection fund.

Another economically effective instrument of environmental policy is to **reward production that is environmentally oriented**. In an ecological market economy, those who manufacture environmentally friendly products through environmentally sustainable production processes must be enabled to capitalize on the potential competitive advantage. They must be able to convey their '*more*' of environmental protection to consumers in order to influence their decision. A label, based on reliable and clear criteria of environmental compatibility, established through 'social consensus-building' and control, is in the interest of both the entrepreneur and the consumer. Keywords in this regard

---

94 See in the context of the Maastricht Treaty, Calliess (1994), pp. 301–302; see also Kloepfer (1991); Köck (1992).

95 For suggestions regarding additional criteria and starting points for the design, see European Environmental Bureau (1991), p. 13.

96 Calliess (1994), p. 301.

97 See Grabitz (1989).

98 As European environmental associations pointed out in the context of the Maastricht Treaty, see in European Environmental Bureau (1991), p. 15 et seq. Regarding heavy-duty vehicles, the Directive (EU) 2022/362 of the European Parliament and of the Council of 24 February 2022 amending Directives 1999/62/EC, 1999/37/EC and (EU) 2019/520, as regards the charging of vehicles for the use of certain infrastructures, OJ L 69, p.1, 4.3.2022 stipulates that starting in 2024, tolls and vignettes for heavy-duty vehicles must be varied based on a vehicle's CO_2 emission. While the Directive sets out specific standards, it however still applies to the tolls and levies set by the Member States and does not fully harmonize them at the Union level. The production and placing on the market of chlorofluorocarbons (CFCs) has been banned by Regulation (EC) No 2037/2000, OJ L 244/1, see current Regulation on the matter: Regulation (EU) 2024/590 of the European Parliament and of the Council of 7 February 2024 on substances that deplete the ozone layer, and repealing Regulation (EC) No 1005/2009, OJ L, 2024/590, 20.2.2024.

are '*trust and dialogue*'. In 1992, such a label – the *EU Ecolabel* – was established, then known as the "*Community Ecolabel*". It is a voluntary scheme and uses independent experts to determine whether products meet the strict required standards, yet it suffers from the general overcrowding of green labels that take away from its effectiveness[99] and its level of dissemination is limited[100].[101]

The Commission recognises in its communication the crucial role of tax policy in transitioning to a more environmentally friendly and sustainable growth in Europe, and calls for a better alignment of our tax systems with the EU climate goals.[102] Indeed, the Commission refers to their direct impact by sending appropriate price signals and offering incentives for sustainable practices among producers, users, and consumers. The European Green Deal mentions the **ambition** to establish a framework **for comprehensive tax reforms**, including the **elimination of subsidies for fossil fuels**, a shift in the tax burden from labor to pollution, and consideration of social factors. Within its package of proposals ("*Fit for 55*"), the Commission therefore proposes to **revise the *Energy Taxation Directive*** (ETD)[103] and to create a *Carbon Border Adjustment Mechanism* (CBAM). While the revision of the ETD seems to be stuck in talks between Member states,[104] the Regulation establishing CBAM entered into force on 17 May 2023, initiating a transitional phase (2023–2025) before the definitive regime will be applied starting in 2026.[105]

2.4.4 Ecology and Competition Law

In the Maastricht context, European environmental associations proposed in their 'Greening the Treaty' report to empower the Commission to **prohibit State aid (subsidies), if**

---

99 Marrucci et al. (2021), p. 575.

100 As of September 2023, only 2,584 licenses had been awarded for 88,921 products across different product groups, see European Commission (2023).

101 On further challenges of the EU Ecolabel, see Iraldo and Barberio (2017), p. 751.

102 According to the Commission, "well-designed tax reforms can boost economic growth and resilience to climate shocks and help contribute to a fairer society and to a just transition", see European Green Deal, p. 17.

103 The ETD lays down EU rules for the taxation of energy products and of electricity used as motor fuel or heating fuel. The Commission, in its 2021 revision proposal, set out to remove outdated exemptions from energy taxation, for example for intra-EU air transport and fishing, and to start taxing fuels according to their environmental performance rather than volume, see COM (2021) 563 final, Proposal for a Council Directive restructuring the Union framework for the taxation of energy products and electricity.

104 Implementation of the proposed revision has proved difficult as it requires unanimity in the Council of the EU but faces resistance from various Member States, particularly in Central and Eastern Europe – with talks only moving slowly, completing the reform before the 2024 elections thus seems out of reach, see Packroff and Kurmayer (2023).

105 As explained above, the CBAM aims at preventing the risk of "carbon leakage", which refers to the risk that EU-based companies move carbon-intensive production abroad to take advantage of less ambitious policies, see Regulation (EU) 2023/956 of the European Parliament and of the Council of 10 May 2023 establishing a carbon border adjustment mechanism, OJ L 130, p. 52, 16.5.2023. For the academic debate on the CBAM see for instance Trennt and Ulke (2023); Hench and Herdieckerhoff (2022); Geraets and Reins (2023); Mailänder (2023).

they have detrimental environmental effects.[106] In this regard, Article 107(1) TFEU could be supplemented with a provision stating that aid incompatible with environmental sustainability is inconsistent with the Treaty. However, it would be equally sensible to introduce a clear exception in Article 107(2) TFEU that allows for state aid within the framework of environmental policy measures.

Within the realm of competition law, it is necessary to **introduce an '*ecological cartel privilege*'** since environmental agreements between companies typically serve an important public interest. To address the currently limited scope for companies to make such agreements under competition law, an expansion of the exemption requirements in the value system of Article 101(3) TFEU to include an ecological component could be considered.[107] While Art. 101 TFEU has not been amended in this way thus far, the Commission published new guidelines on horizontal co-operation agreements between companies, clarifying, that the antitrust rules in general do not prevent sustainability agreements between competitors.[108] Lastly, it would be environmentally desirable to subject the allocation of financial resources from the Structural Funds, the European Investment Bank, or within the framework of EU research and development policy to a **verifiable environmental impact assessment (EIA)**.

Regarding the utilization of the allocation of state aid, in its European Deal Communication from 2019, the Commission referred to the ongoing assessments of applicable **State aid guidelines**, including environmental and energy State aid guidelines.[109] The Commission suggested to review these guidelines to accommodate the policy goals of the European Green Deal:[110] These revisions aim to facilitate a cost-effective shift towards climate neutrality by 2050, promoting the gradual phasing out of highly polluting fossil fuels and providing a **level-playing field** within the internal market. Finally, the Commission views these changes as an opportunity to address any market-related obstacles that hinder the introduction of clean products.[111]

---

[106] Revision of Articles 92-94 of the EC Treaty. On environmental protection and competition Law see as well Mehrländer (1993), pp. 35–46; Krämer (1993), p. 47-83.

[107] Based on Pernice (1992), p. 141.

[108] COM (2023) 3445 final, Annex to the Communication from the Commission, Approval of the content of a draft for a Communication from the Commission, Guidelines on the applicability of Article 101 of the Treaty on the Functioning of the European Union to horizontal cooperation agreement, , p. 146 et seq.

[109] COM (2019) 640 final, p. 18.

[110] In April 2023, the European Commission published updated State aid guiding templates to assist Member States in designing measures, see European Commission (2023) State aid: Commission updates guidance for measures to support the green transition; on the planned green state aid schemes see for instance Meyer and Hoffmann (2023).

[111] COM (2019) 640 final, p. 18.

2.4.5 Ecology and Monetary Policy

A rather innovative development refers to the discussion about what role central banks could play in mitigating climate change, and specifically, the possibilities for and limitations to the greening of the *European Central Bank's* (ECB) monetary policy.[112] The developments of recent years, suggest a gradual shift in the Eurosystem's role in addressing climate change. This is in contrast to the previously held view that climate aspects fall squarely out of the scope of the ECB's mandate, which is to promote and maintain price stability (Article 127(1) 1 TFEU).[113] However, considering the magnitude of the global climate crisis, it is clear that a green transition will not succeed without efforts in every sector including the financial institutions. The prospect of greening the treaties, therefore, gives rise to a reflection on an ecological transformation of the European Central Bank.

This could for instance be realised through an **extension of Article 127(1) TFEU by including an ecological reference** next to the primary objective of maintaining "price stability".[114] Yet this possibility poses the question of whether such an amendment of Article 127(1) TFEU might, have an adverse effect on the ECB's primary objective. Even though combatting climate change is a major priority of the EU, it is essential that within the ECB's monetary policy, the **primary objective of price stability** is not compromised for the pursuit of other goals. This limitation is the result of a longstanding guideline: The EC Treaty already made it made clear in its Art. 4(2) that among the goals of European monetary policy, price stability should take precedence above any other objectives due to the particular harmfulness of currency devaluation for the economy.[115] Any potential ecological reference in Article 127(1) TFEU would therefore need to comply with this hierarchy among the objectives.

Nevertheless, considering the evidence regarding the adverse effects that global warming could have on price stability, integrating climate-change factors may in some cases even be permissible in the pursuit of the primary goal. It follows that the ECB shall take climate-related aspects into consideration to the extent that climate change poses a threat to price stability. Against this background, it can be said that the legal framework provides for the possibility to formulate and design monetary policy in a way that contributes to the primary objective to maintain price stability, whilst at the same time, promoting an ecological transformation.[116]

Considering *Kersten's* proposal in the German context, **Article 127(1) could be amended** by way of **introduction of an ecological reference** in the third sentence of Article 127(1) TFEU, such that *"The ESCB shall act in accordance with the principles*

---

112 See Calliess and Tuncel (2022); Calliess and Tuncel (2023); for German scholarship see also Nees (2021), p. 119; Kaufhold (2022); Dietz (2022).

113 On the relation between climate considerations and the ECB's primary and secondary objectives see specifically, Calliess and Tuncel (2022).

114 In the German context, Kersten suggest to include in Article 88 GG a reference that the German Central Bank shall promote price stability "also with a view to its responsibility for the ecological well-being of the general public", p. 175-176.

115 Häde (2022).

116 On the ECB's Competence to pursue climate protection goals, see Calliess and Tuncel (2023), pp. 11–17.

of an open market economy with free competition, favouring an efficient allocation of resources ***[while taking into account its responsibility for the ecological well-being of the general public]****, and in compliance with the principle set out in Article 119."*

Moreover, taking into account the available operational framework, there are several monetary policy tools that could be subject to a greening.[117] One option is for instance to insert a consideration of climate-related factors into the ECB's existing **bond-buying programs** (APP). Among the several possibilities how climate aspects can be incorporated into the APP, one refers to the integration of climate factors into the **eligibility criteria** and **the rules about credit rating**. Another greening measure that could be considered, is the adoption of a new ***"Green Assets Purchase Programme***", which specifically focuses on the purchase of green bonds.[118] Indeed, the ECB has recently stepped up its climate-related ambitions, thereby moving into the right direction to make a crucial contribution to the green transition, but has yet to implement a number of those plans.[119]

3 Proposals for a Greening of the Treaties

Considering the above, this section analyses proposals for a greening of the Union's treaties. Greening options will be proposed for the Treaty on European Union (TEU), which contains general provisions that define the Union, and for the Treaty on the Functioning of the European Union (TFEU), which can be seen as containing specific provisions for the Union's institutions and policies. In doing so, on the one hand, the proposals issued by *Kersten* in the context of the German *Grundgesetz* will be taken into account.[120] On the other hand, proposals which have been developed within the greening-debate regarding the Maastricht Treaty might become relevant for the Treaty of Lisbon as well.[121] Overall, the aim is to sketch a broad picture of the main building blocks for creating a truly "*ecological Union*".

---

117 See in detail Calliess and Tuncel (2023), p. 18 et. Seq.

118 The main question is whether such a program may constitute a monetary policy measure, see Calliess and Tuncel (2023), pp. 24–25.

119 Among other initiatives, in 2022, the ECB set out to review its collateral framework and asset purchases to integrate climate change related disclosures as an eligibility requirement, see European Central Bank (2022), p. 4. However, in its "Climate and Nature Plan 2024-2025", the ECB plans for these climate-related disclosures to be included in the collateral framework only from 2026, see European Central Bank (2024), p. 5.

120 Kersten suggests greening options for several provisions of the German Basic Law. Among them, he considers a potential greening of the preamble, fundamental rights, constitutional principles, the governance system, legislation, policies and access to justice.

121 At the time of the Maastricht Treaty, two aspects have been described as fundamental for an ecological legal system, which are: 1) rights of nature and 2) enforcement of environmental legal norms, see Füks (1994), p. 13. Recently, the debate about rights of nature has become topical in view of global developments, see Sect. 3.3.3.

Beforehand, the **meaning of an "*ecological Union*"** should be defined.[122] As already elaborated in the context of the Maastricht Treaty:

> 'An ecological legal community can be understood as a legal system that is comprehensively ecologically oriented. This means, in particular, a legal system that consistently programmes economic action for environmental compatibility, that attempts to establish environmentally compatible behaviour from the outset, in particular environmentally compatible production processes, and that abandons the sectoral approach in environmental law in favour of an integrating, intermedial approach'[123].

Such a programmatic Union objective needs to be fleshed out and shaped further. Some elements can already be found in Union law, or are already inherent to it, so that they only require consistent further development. Other elements would have to be created anew.

3.1 Greening the Preamble, Article 2 and 3 TEU?

An ecological transformation of the Union may demand for a greening of the fundamental core provisions within the treaties.

In the context of German law, *Kersten* proposes to introduce a "*principle of ecological responsibility*" in the preamble to the German Basic Law.[124] In the Union context, the preamble to the TEU already mentions the "principle of sustainable development" and "environmental protection", while the preamble to the TFEU does not include any such reference. As far as the TEU is concerned, the ecological reference is made in the context of promoting economic and social progress. To strengthen the green outlook of the preamble, a possible modification, based on *Kersten*, that could be made is to **add "*ecological responsibility*"** to the list of principles that are confirmed at a previous point in the TEU's preamble, resulting in the heads of states of the member states *"confirming their attachment to the principles of liberty, democracy[,* ***ecological responsibility****] and respect for human rights and fundamental freedoms and of the rule of law"*.

Following the preamble, the TEU sets out the mission, values and goals of the European Union in its first provisions. **Article 2 TEU** pronounces a set of (liberal) core values, which define the basis of the Union.[125] While the founding treaties did not originally include an explicit reference to values but rather tacitly assumed their existence,[126] core

---

[122] In German scholarship, Bosselmann introduced the term "ökologischer Rechtsstaat", see Bosselmann (1992). There are, however, different legal understandings. According to Bosselmann, the "Ecologic State" describes the ongoing task of the state to strive for ecological balance, cf. Bosselmann (1994); see also Kloepfer (1994), pp. 3–40.

[123] Calliess (1994), p. 294. The definition is based on Murswiek (1992) Auf dem Weg zu einem ökologischen Recht? In FAZ from 26.10.1992, p. 38.

[124] See Kersten (2022), pp. 59–61.

[125] See Calliess (2004b); Calliess (2004a); on Article 2 TEU see Calliess (2022e) Art. 2 TEU.

[126] Calliess (2022e) Art. 2 TEU para 1. Generally speaking, values are basic attitudes of society or individuals that are characterised by a particular firmness or con-viction of correctness. Values are considered to be indeterminate, multi-layered, subjective and context-related. Values may

values were gradually explicitly enshrined in the treaties as the integration project progressed.[127] The Union thus developed to form a "*community of values*"[128] or a "*Union of values*".[129] Besides providing the basis of the Union, the core values also intend to have a unifying, legitimising and identity-building effect.[130] – Article 2 TEU thus constitutes a type of "***constitutional core***" of the European Union[131].

Considering the role of the provision as outlined above, it can be assumed that Article 2 TEU has to be the starting point of any ecological transformation of the treaties. So far, it contains no explicit ecological reference, and it is unclear whether a greening of Article 2 TEU would make a substantial contribution, or would be merely symbolic.

There are different possibilities for how Article 2 TEU could be enhanced by an "ecological value", and the wording might influence the exact content of such a value. One proposal, for example, is to include a **reference to "*ecological responsibility*"** or "*respect for nature*" after "*respect for human dignity*".[132]

The values articulated in Article 2 TEU so far have prescribed a human-centred approach.[133] Following the addition of such an ecological reference, respect for nature or ecological responsibility would be of equal importance as the other values. This could be emblematic of a shift from an "*anthropocentric*" (human-centred) to an **"ecocentric" approach**, and support the development towards the recognition of "rights of nature", which will be considered in detail further below.[134]

Moreover, in support of an ecological extension it should be considered that in order to reach a truly "*ecological Union*", ecological responsibility should not be left out of the list of values of Art. 2 TEU that form the very basis of the Union. An amendment to Art. 2 TEU goes beyond mere symbolism, as this explicit recognition would serve as a reminder to the Member States and Union institutions of the centrality of a green approach to all Union efforts. Nevertheless, considering that an increasing number of member states

---

change over time and adapt to social circumstances. In legal terms, they describe goods that a legal system recognises as given. Values, thus, convey legitimacy. Dogmatically, values operate like principles. They can also serve as a guideline for interpretation and as a standard for the control of norms, Calliess (2022e) Art. 2 TEU para 12.

127 Calliess (2004b), p. 1038.

128 Calliess (2009).

129 Calliess (2004b), p. 1038. Initially, the aim of the European integration process was the establishment of a common market. The economic community was, however, also intended to secure peace. Therefore, it can be said that the EC was based from the very beginning on the "magic triangle of values" of peace, economic freedom and integration, cf. Calliess (2022e) Art. 2 TEU para 2.

130 Calliess (2022e) Art. 2 TEU para 32; Terhechte (2021).

131 Jacqué (2015); Murswiek (2009), p. 483; Calliess (2004b), p. 1036; similarly, von Bogdandy et al. (2012), p. 45 et seq., who sees the "core" of Union citizen's rights guaran-teed by the essence of fundamental rights protected in Article 1 TEU. For further elaboration on the values of Art. 2 TEU, see Part II Constitutional Framework.

132 The wording of Article 2 TEU could be as follows: "The Union is founded on the values of respect for hu-man dignity, freedom, democracy, equality, the rule of law and respect for human rights, including the rights of persons belonging to minorities, [and respect for nature]."

133 Calliess (2022e) Art. 2 TEU para 11.

134 See Sect. 3.3.3.

have begun to challenge these liberal values as well as the Union's pursuit of them,[135] any amendment to Article 2 TEU has to be considered with caution. In the context of a politically charged environment, it might become subject to abuse by politically influenced interests, jeopardising its fundamental role within the Treaties.

Apart from Article 2 TEU, **Article 3 TEU** could also be considered for a potential greening. As a constitutional *Grundnorm* regarding the Union's integration programme, Article 3 TEU stipulates the Union's goals.[136] Over the course of the Union's history, its objectives have expanded and diversified considerably beyond its original focus exclusively on economic matters, particularly through the addition of social, environmental and cultural policy objectives.[137] Among its host of objectives, Article 3(3) TEU notably refers to "*sustainable development*" and "*a high level of protection and improvement of the quality of the environment*". Yet this ecological reference is only made within the context of the "*internal market*". This not only stresses the continued primarily economic orientation of the integration programme,[138] but also underlines that taking on ecological responsibility still does not constitute a Union objective in its own right. The ecological transformation of the Union therefore might necessitate a stronger reference, such as the inclusion of a principle of fulfilling "*ecological responsibility*" as an independent aim. However, according to Article 3(1) TEU, one of the Union's aims is to promote "*its values*". Therefore, if "*ecological responsibility*" was already introduced in Article 2 TEU, as proposed above, Article 3 TEU would not need any additional reference.

3.2 Greening at the Institutional Level

Next to amending programmatic clauses of the German Basic Law, *Kersten* also argues that an ecological transformation of society will only succeed if ecology, as a cross-cutting policy field, is **institutionally anchored at the crucial points of the parliamentary system of government.**[139] He stresses the importance of making the parliamentary system of government (at least also) an ecological system of government.[140] This is true not only in the national context but also for the EU and can be traced back to the fact that in everyday political life, short-term interests tend to dominate and the implementation of long-term interests prove to be difficult,[141] while however the appropriate **consideration of long-term (ecological) interests** lies at the core of the realisation of an Ecological Union. Supporting the integration of environmental sustainability in the political decision-making process and realising an Ecological Union therefore necessitates greening at the procedural and institutional level.

[135] On "The Crisis of liberal values" see for instance: Chalmers et al. (2019), pp. 52–56.

[136] See in detail Calliess C (2022f) Art. 3 TEU para. 1; for the predecessor norm of Article 2 ECT see Streinz (2003); similarly Terhechte (2021); Becker (2019); as well as Kotzur (2005), p. 322.

[137] Calliess (2022f) Art. 3 TEU, para 6.

[138] Calliess (2022f) Art. 3 TEU, para. 6.

[139] See Kersten (2022), pp. 133–134.

[140] Kersten (2022), p. 134.

[141] See the SRU's special report: SRU (2019a), where the SRU dealt with the obstacles and structural difficulties facing a policy of ecological sustainability at national level in detail. The SRU also developed recommendations on how environmental policy in Germany can be strengthened by institutional and organisational changes.

The EU has taken initial steps in this respect by establishing the ***Environmental Implementation Review*** **(EIR)** in 2016, which includes individual member state reports and aims to identify existing implementation gaps and enforcement deficiencies in EU environmental policy and to develop solutions for them.[142] In 2018, the EIR resulted in the adoption of an *action plan* for improved enforcement of environmental law and better environmental governance, which particularly focused on compliance and monitoring[143] and after its mandate was renewed as part of the European Green Deal, the most recent review was published in 2022[144].

Building on this idea, in order to more efficiently review ongoing efforts by giving it a more permanent form, an **independent institution to carry out monitoring and evaluation** should be introduced. This institution should be mandated to review upcoming political and legislative decisions in terms of their compatibility with the sustainability goals and should be able to raise objections if necessary.

Proposals within the academic debate of the early 1990s in this respect refer, for instance, to strengthening the ***European Environmental Agency***, the **introduction of an *"environmental ombudsman"*** or an *"ecological senate"/"ecological council"*.[145] Another measure envisages the introduction of **sustainability officers**[146]. The focus of these proposals is on the installation of institutions of long-term responsibility to make the democratic process truly sustainable.

3.2.1 Strengthening the European Environmental Agency

At the Union level, there is an increasing institutionalisation of administrative bodies under Union law.[147] These so-called *agencies* are established through regulations and are not provided for in primary law. They serve to support the enforcement of European

142 COM (2016) 316 final, Communication from the Commission to the European Parliament, the Council, the European Economic and Social Committee and the Committee of the Regions. Delivering the benefits of EU environmental policies through a regular Environmental Implementation Review. COM (2019) 149 final, Communication from the Commission to the European Parliament, the Council, the European Economic and Social Committee and the Committee of the Regions. Environmental Implementation Review: A Europe that protects its citizens and enhances their quality of life.

143 COM (2018) 10 final, Communication from the Commission to the European Parliament, the Council, the European Economic and Social Committee and the Committee of the Regions. EU actions to improve environmental compliance and governance.

144 COM (2022) 438 final, Communication from the Commission to the European Parliament, the Council, the European Economic and Social Committee and the Committee of the Regions. Environmental Implementation Review 2022: Turning the tide through environmental compliance.

145 Regarding these proposals and a detailed discussion, see Calliess (1994), p. 71; cf. Arbeitskreis "Europäische Umweltunion" (1994a), pp. 347, 350; Arbeitskreis "Europäische Umweltunion" (1994b); Calliess (1991), 207–212; Bosselmann refers to an "Ecological Council" ("Ökologischer Rat"), see Bosselmann (1994), pp. 66–67. See also Kahl (2018); however, Nettesheim expresses doubts in: Nettesheim (2024).

146 See Calliess and Dross (2020), p. 462.

147 Cf. Calliess (2022d) Art. 13 TEU, para. 31 et seq. And Art. 192 TFEU, para. 44.; cf. Wittinger (2008); see Priebe (2015).

law and the cooperation of the member states. In the area of environmental policy, the *European Environment Agency* (EEA)[148], located in Copenhagen, is responsible for the collection, evaluation, analysis, dissemination and provision of information for the Commission and the member states. In the context of the debate regarding the Maastricht Treaty, environmental organizations and the European Parliament were already holding expectations that the EEA should become an institution anchored in the EC Treaty, preferably an independent institution with its own executive and supervisory functions, following the model of the Federal *U.S. Environmental Protection Agency* (EPA).[149]

In order to enhance the enforcement of Union Law while **avoiding a centralistic "*super regulatory authority*,"** an EEA equipped with **control and executive powers** could be complemented by a **network of national environmental inspectorates.**[150] The European Parliament made a significant contribution in this regard by insisting on the introduction of **uniform environmental assessment criteria** in the Regulation that established the EEA,[151] which provides a solid foundation for the agency's work, as it would otherwise see itself confronted with fragmented assessment standards across Member States. The two Members of the EP, who are part of the EEA's governing body[152] ensure a limited democratic control. To complement the EEA's efforts, specialized departments for environmental issues could be established in all *Directorates-General* of the Commission, which would assess the environmental compatibility of proposed policy during the planning phase and propose appropriate modifications.[153]

In connection with monitoring standards, building on the *European Green Deal*, the 8th *Environment Action Programme* (EAP)[154] entered into force in May 2022: A framework for long-term environmental policy development which includes an obligation for the EU Commission to present a **new monitoring framework** for measuring progress towards its priority objectives.[155] This monitoring framework is to be based on a limited number of headline indicators, which are to be defined taking into account the 2024

[148] Established by Regulation (EEC) No. 1210/90/EWG, OJ No. L 120/1, amended by Regulation (EC) No. 933/1999, OJ 1999 No. L 117/1, and by Regulation No. 1641/2003, OJ 2003 No. L 245/1; in detail on the work of the Environment Agency von Lersner (1992), p. 81; on 10 years of its work: Runge (2005); Epiney (1997), p. 85 et seq; see Martens (2010).

[149] See Calliess (1994), p. 303 with reference to Petersen (1993); von Lersner (1992), p. 81.

[150] See Macrory (1992).

[151] European Parliament, Proposal for a Council regulation (EEC) on the establishment of the European Environment Agency and the European Environment Monitoring and Information Network, OJEC No. C 96/112.

[152] Regulation (EC) No 401/2009 of the European Parliament and of the Council of 23 April 2009 on the European Environment Agency and the European Environment Information and Observation Network (Codified version), Art. 8, OJ L 126 21.5.2009, p. 13.

[153] See already European Environmental Bureau (1991), p. 13.

[154] Decision (EU) 2022/591 of the European Parliament and of the Council of 6 April 2022 on a General Union Environment Action Programme to 2030, OJ L 114, p. 23, 12.4.2022.

[155] COM (2022) 357 final, Communication from the Commission to the European Parliament, the Council, the European Economic and Social Committee and the Committee of the Regions on the monitoring framework for the 8th Environment Action Programme: Measuring progress towards the attainment of the Programme's 2030 and 2050 priority objectives.

mid-term review[156] and the 2029 evaluation.[157] This framework is relevant to the EEA as pursuant to Article 4 EAP, the EEA supports the Commission in its obligation to monitor, assess and report annually on progress of the Union and the Member States on the priority objectives articulated in Article 2 EAP.

3.2.2 Environmental Ombudsman

A different proposal refers to the introduction of an environmental ombudsman.[158] In accordance with the Danish model[159], the European Parliament could appoint an *environmental ombudsman*, a position that is independent from the Commission, tasked with **reporting annually to the EP** on the state of environmental policy in the EU.[160] The ombudsman would conduct investigations on their own initiative, particularly at the suggestion of citizens and environmental associations. They could make use of the capacities of the EEA and national environmental inspectorates and could also act as a guardian of potential rights of nature.[161] The ombudsman's **administrative independence** would be a distinct feature that is based on the democratic legitimacy of the EP, as Parliament appoints the post. Accordingly, from a systematic point of view, the position would complement the Union's ecological control system in such a way that it would then function as a system of checks and balances under the rule of law in relation to environmental matters (Court of Justice, Parliament, Commission, and EEA).

3.2.3 Sustainability Officers

An alternative measure in this context is the appointment of sustainability officers **within the Directorates-General of the Commission**. They would be tasked with monitoring the implementation of the *European Green Deal* in line with the *European Climate Law* and the 8th *EAP* (the "*guiding laws*").[162] To ensure compliance, they would review all legislation and be equipped with a **suspensive veto right** that triggers a referral of the issue to the round of Directors-General and Cabinet Chiefs. This would allow for political conflicts regarding green implementation to be more transparent. If these conflicts then cannot be resolved at that level, they would need to be discussed within the College of Commissioners and, if necessary, decided upon by the President of the Commission in exercise of their directive powers, who has declared the European Green Deal a

[156] COM (2024) 123 final, Report from the Commission to the European Parliament, the Council, the European Economic and Social Committee and the Committee of the Regions, on the 8th Environment Action Programme Mid-Term Review.

[157] COM (2022) 357 final, p. 9.

[158] Cf. Calliess (1994), p. 304.

[159] See generally on the "Ombudsman", Schomerus (1989).

[160] This position would be modeled after the existing office of the (general) European Ombudsman, which has been opened in 1995 and is, as outlined in Art. 228 TFEU, tasked with identifying and investigating instances of maladministration of Union institutions and submits annual reports to the EP.

[161] See on the debate about rights of nature Sect. 3.3.3.

[162] See on this in Calliess and Dross (2020), p. 462; see as well SRU (2020b), para. 743.

priority of paramount importance[163]. Additionally, it could be considered to strengthen the responsible Commissioner through cross-sectoral initiative and veto rights.

3.2.4 Transforming the EESC to a Committee for Sustainable Development

Another proposal refers to the establishment of an *Ecological Senate*.[164] This institution would be detached from everyday political disputes and could develop socially viable concepts and strategies for solving future problems.[165] It is further envisioned to be an **independent monitoring institution** for the European sustainability and climate protection strategy and a watchdog for the "guiding laws". To ensure its independence, it should consist of representatives from science, technology, business, and environmental associations, elected in equal number by national parliaments and the EP. To ensure their independence from political parties and other interests, they should not be active members of parliament, public officials, or representatives of any organization holding public interests and would be elected for a one-time period of ten years.

If the Ecological Senate was to be created on the basis of an already existing institution in order to simplify its establishment, the ***European Economic and Social Committee*** (EESC) appears to be the most suitable of the existing European institutions for this task.[166] The European treaties envisage the EESC as an advisory body[167] and it currently advises the Council, the Commission, and the European Parliament on economic and social matters. Ecological issues, however, are not systematically included.[168] Therefore, the contemplated new task for the EESC would require a fundamental restructuring and a political reinforcement of this body. European Primary Law already provides some scope for strengthening the EESC's suggested role as a representative of environmental and sustainability interests. In the medium term, the EESC should be fully aligned with

---

163 Upon unveiling the European Green Deal, President of the Commission Ursula von der Leyen called its introduction "Europe's 'man on the moon' moment": European Commission (2019) Press remarks by President von der Leyen on the occasion of the adoption of the European Green Deal Communication. 11.12.2019.

164 Cf. Calliess (1994), p. 98 et seq.; Calliess (1994), p. 304 et seq.; Kloepfer et al. (1994), p. 346 et seq.

165 Partly based on the Ecological Council in Article 53b of the Constitutional Draft by the Board for a Democratically Constituted Federation of German States. From the Basic Law to the German Constitution, 1991, p. 45, 121, and the "Wissenschaftsparlament" ("Science Parliament") in Böhler (1991, pp. 999, 1015.

166 Calliess and Dross (2020); SRU (2020b), paras 747-752.

167 Article 300(1) TFEU; see for instance Hayder (2010); CESE (Conseil économique social et environnemental) (2020); Suhr (2022).

168 There have been proposals in the past regarding representatives of environmental conservation groups as members. Consequently, the EESC has taken up environmental protection as an issue, albeit as one among many, cf. Boisserée (2000). Gedenkschrift für Staatssekretär Dr. Günter Hartkopf anlässlich seines 10. Todestages am 19. September 1999, p. 287–297. Although the EESC has set up a Sustainable Development Observatory, it is evident that economic and labour interests are still shaping the approach in terms of content. Sustainable development is defined as "development that creates conditions for long term prosperity giving equal importance to the three pillars: economic, social and environmental", EESC, SDO work programme/roadmap 2018–2020, Brussels: EWSA. EESC-2018-03066-00-01-TCD-TRA, 2018.

the principle of sustainability and **renamed the "*European Sustainability Committee*"**. However, such a substantive realignment, renaming, and reinforcement of the current EESC would require an amendment to the European Treaties, making it only a medium- to long-term achievable goal.

As mentioned, the Committee would be tasked with promoting the **implementation and enforcement of the European sustainability and climate protection strategy**. This could be achieved through monitoring, in which progress in achieving sustainability goals and climate protection is regularly assessed and deficits are identified. In order to draw attention to long-term interests in day-to-day politics and to be able to influence the actual political decision-making process towards policy integration, the European Sustainability Committee should be allowed to give its opinion on specific political or legislative measures. It could maintain the existing mandatory consultation rights of the EESC. Furthermore, the *European Sustainability Committee* should be allowed to issue opinions on its own initiative regarding the future impact of current political and legislative decisions. Additionally, its current **consultation rights** in the legislative process would need to be complemented by a **suspensive veto right**, to be used in case the European Sustainability Council has serious concerns regarding the compatibility of a legislative proposal with the adopted European sustainability or climate protection strategy. Considering the principle of democracy, the veto would not have binding effects on the legislative bodies, the European Parliament and the Council, but it would nevertheless trigger a reassessment obligation. Consequently, these bodies would have to address the concerns raised by the Sustainability Council and publicly respond to them, which would prompt an "*ecological re-reading*" of the legislation, promote transparency and attract attention from the public and stakeholders involved in the decision-making process to the issue.

3.3 Greening Fundamental Rights

Greening the Union's treaties also leads to a reflection about the role of fundamental rights and their potential greening.[169] In the national context, *Kersten* views ecological fundamental rights as a key element of the "*anthropocenic transformation*" of the German Basic Law.[170]

In the Union context, pursuant to Article 6(1) TEU, the EU recognises the rights, freedoms and principles set out in the Charter of Fundamental Rights of the European Union (CFR). They thus have the same legal value as the treaties. **Article 37 of the Charter** already addresses "*environmental protection*". The provision reads: "*A high level of environmental protection and the improvement of the quality of the environment must be integrated into the policies of the Union and ensured in accordance with the principle of sustainable development.*" However, it's clear from the wording that Article 37 does not provide for a classic fundamental right: Article 37 does not contain an explicit and independent right to a healthy environment[171] and it does not grant individuals a right to

[169] See already Bosselmann (1998); Kloepfer (1978); on climate protection and fundamental rights see Kahl (2021), pp. 117–129; see for further references in the following subsection.

[170] Cf. For ecological rights in the German constitution, Kersten (2022), pp. 63–100.

[171] In detail Calliess (2022g).

a high level of environmental protection[172]. This design goes back to the drafting of the Charter by the Convention on Fundamental Rights established in 1999 – the Convention´s aim was to include only enforceable fundamental rights in the Charter which would not promise citizens more than they could actually redeem in court, yet an agreement could not be reached on a fundamental right to environmental protection.[173] Therefore, Art. 37 rather constitutes a **state objective-type provision**[174] **or a principle** that shall be observed[175] and can thus, in substantive terms, be viewed as a mere repetition of Art. 191 and Art. 11 TFEU[176]. There are different approaches that can be considered in the context of (ecological) fundamental rights: There are proposals for introducing an individual right to environmental protection, which will be analysed first.[177] In the course of this, the legal possibilities, including positive obligations derived from a duty to protect, and limits that (German and) European fundamental rights possibly provide in the context of climate policy will be considered. In conclusion, this part will advocate for an **enforceable procedural fundamental right to environmental protection**. Moreover, taking into account the planetary boundaries (especially, regarding the protection of the climate, the 1.5 to 2 °C target), a plea is made for the recognition of a fundamental right to the (individual) guarantee of an ecological minimum subsistence level, which entails a reversal of the burden of proof.

It can also be argued **that existing fundamental rights**, such as the right to life and the right to health, already encompass environmental protection (see Sect. 3.3.2). Finally, I will consider the possibility of **introducing independent rights of nature** (see Sect. 3.3.3).

3.3.1 Introducing a Human Right to a Healthy Environment?

Following the growing urgency of the climate crisis and the globally growing movement of the people's climate case[178], the debate about an individually justiciable "*fundamental right to environmental protection*" has gained new momentum. Such a right has been

---

172 Käller (2009), para 1; Frenz (2011), para 4319.

173 Calliess (2022g) Art. 37 CFR, para 1.

174 Calliess (2022g) Art. 37 CFR, para 4.

175 According to Article 52(5) of the Charter "The provisions of this Charter which contain principles may be implemented by legislative and executive acts taken by institutions, bodies, offices and agencies of the Union, and by acts of Member States when they are implementing Union law, in the exercise of their respective pow-ers. They shall be judicially cognisable only in the interpretation of such acts and in the ruling on their legality." See Dworkin (2013).

176 Calliess (2022g) Art. 37 CFR, para 4.

177 This section is based on the argument developed in Calliess (2021).

178 Courts in Germany and the EU are increasingly dealing with so-called climate lawsuits due to the lack of coherent and efficient action by the executive and legislative branches in Germany and at the EU level. In the context of climate lawsuits at the German and European levels, familiar difficulties of individual claims in environmental law are once again evident, see VG Berlin, judgement of 31.10.2019, 10K 412.18; see regarding the current discussion, Buser (2020); Groß (2020); Graser (2019); Winter (2019); critical Wegener (2019).

promoted and debated since the 1970s.[179] Most recently the debate has been reignited in the German context.[180] ***Von Schirach***, presented a **proposal**[181] for the modernization of the Charter of the Fundamental Rights of the European Union. Among other things, he advocates for the inclusion of a fundamental right to environmental protection with the following wording: "*Every person has the right to live in a healthy and protected environment.*"

The proposal has been enthusiastically welcomed by other scholars and lawyers[182]. Unfortunately, they do not contribute any (new) legal arguments to the debate of constitutional, European, and environmental lawyers, who have wrestled with this issue for the past 20 years.[183]

The fundamental right to environmental protection, as proposed by *Schirach*, is intended to be incorporated into the Charter of Fundamental Rights of the European Union. Since Article 37 of the Charter already contains a "right" under the heading of "*Environmental Protection*", *Schirach*'s proposal can only be understood as either an amendment to the provision or a replacement of its content. The fact that Article 37 of the Charter is, as examined above, merely a Union objective, corresponding to the provisions of Articles 11 and 191 TFEU, which cannot grant rights to Union citizens[184], speaks strongly in favour of understanding the proposal as a replacement of the provision as is.

3.3.1.1 The Substantive Content of a Fundamental Right to Environmental Protection

When considering the content of a fundamental right to environmental protection, a distinction must first be made between a defensive, performance-based, and procedural conception,[185] as fundamental rights can be designed as a right of defence, a right to benefit or a procedural right.

The conception of a fundamental right to environmental protection, focused on the **defence against environmental damage**, risks, and hazards[186] is at the centre of the current discussion on climate litigation and also implied by Ferdinand *von Schirach's* proposals. This conception, however, faces various difficulties.

---

179 Following an extensive discussion in the 1970s in German scholarship, the overwhelming majority shared the view that there is no fundamental environmental right: cf. Dellmann (1975), p. 589; Rauschning (1980), p. 178; Benda (1982), p. 242; Sendler (1983), p. 258; Schmidt (1999), p. 38 et. Seq; Ruffert (1996), p. 31 et. Seq. An instructive overview of the individual proposals can be found in Bock (1990), p. 54 et seq; cf. Also Kloepfer (1978), p. 31 et seq; Soell (1985); also, Karpen (1988), p. 9, 23; most recently Brönneke (1993), p. 153 et. Seq.

180 Von Schirach (2021); Klinger (2021).

181 Von Schirach (2021).

182 Klinger (2021)

183 Calliess (2001).

184 Calliess (2022g) Art. 37 CFR, para 4.

185 Similarly, Kloepfer (1978), p. 14 et seq; Bock (1990), p. 228 et seq; Brönneke (1993), p. 154 rightfully criticizes that in the discussion on an environmental fundamental right (incidentally), too little attention has been paid to "gradations".

186 See on this Lücke (1976), p. 291.

Apart from the legal problems associated with categorizing all environmental impairments (including those caused by private entities) as state infringements of fundamental rights[187], the main problem lies in determining the **scope of protection** of the fundamental right. As a part of that, it is necessary to determine who is entitled to the fundamental right. The crucial question is to what extent individuals can and should be granted individual subjective rights regarding natural environmental resources such as water, air, and landscapes. Even if the right was construed as a subjective one, since the state can only take steps to ensure the conditions for a healthy environment, but cannot guarantee the actual healthy environment itself, an intact environment cannot be the subject of an environmental fundamental right. Instead, the guarantee of protection can only pertain to "*human behaviour (including and especially that of public officials), in the form of obligations to act or refrain from acting, in order to preserve or restore a healthy environment.*"[188]

Yet, this means that in substantive terms, the right **would not provide more protection than what is already guaranteed** by the partial assurances derived from **Articles 2, 3(1), and 17 of the CRF**, protecting the right to life, to integrity of the person, and property respectively.[189]

Additionally, the difficult **determination of the infringement** of such a fundamental right would need to be considered and since it is closely connected to the question of who would be bound by a fundamental right to environmental protection, this aspect will be looked at first. Fundamental rights primarily serve as a defense against encroachments by state authority. As the defensive conception only applies to state-induced environmental burdens, the fundamental right does not protect against those caused by private entities. Even with a broad interpretation of the concept of infringement[190], the **majority of environmental impairments would still be excluded** from the scope of protection of an environmental fundamental right,[191] thus limiting its effectiveness.

Furthermore, the question of how to delineate between permissible and impermissible infringements of the environmental fundamental right, committed by state authorities, poses a problem. In the discussion, reference is partly made to established criteria, such as requiring a certain intensity of infringement to exclude negligible burdens or introducing the concept of the "***ecological minimum***" as an inviolable minimum level of protection.[192] Specific guidelines are also proposed, such as refraining from any state action that endangers the environment, choosing the most environmentally friendly

[187] See on this Calliess (2001), p. 307 et seq. And 423 et seq.

[188] Kloepfer (1978), p. 13 et seq; Bock (1990), p. 229.

[189] On this result in the context of German law (and assurance derived from Art. 2(2) of the German Basic Law protecting the right to life and physical integrity): Steinberg (1998), p. 425; Kloepfer (1978), pp. 17 et seq. And 35; Karpen (1988), p. 9, 17.

[190] In depth see Calliess (2001), p. 423 et seq. A different result can only be reached if one follows the approach of Murswiek (1985), p. 63 et seq, as well Bock (1990), p. 229 et seq. in conjunction with p. 143 et seq.

[191] Kloepfer (1978), p. 19.

[192] Kloepfer (1978), p. 20 et seq; Bock (1990), p. 231 et seq.

option among various state actions, and handling nature with the utmost care and preservation.[193] Despite certain precedents, both the protection afforded by an independent environmental fundamental right and by the partial assurances derived from already guaranteed rights, ultimately depend on **case-by-case balancing of conflicting interests**, for example economic freedom, in the multi-polar constitutional relationship[194]. The conflicting interests of the duty to protect the environment, to protect the right to health, and the duty to respect economic freedoms form a triangle that has to be resolved by means of a **multipolar proportionality test** in order to result in a fair distribution of freedom over time. As both variants – an independent right as well as partial assurances – are subject to the same balancing considerations, in conclusion, a fundamental right to environmental protection, conceptualised as a defensive right could not grant the affected party any more protection or an additional substantive legal position and an addition of such a right to the Charter thus proves to be unnecessary. The reasons presented against a substantive environmental fundamental right rightly outweigh in the current discussion.[195] A materially effective fundamental right to environmental protection can thus only be constructed as a partial assurance of environmental protection within another individual fundamental right (such as the right to life, health, or property), in conjunction with the recognized function of fundamental rights as containing positive obligations (*Schutzpflichten*) in the constitutional law of some member states.[196]

Nevertheless, it does not seem far-fetched to **further develop the presented approaches** for subjectivising environmental protection through a distinct fundamental or human right to environmental protection. The mentioned partial assurances of environmental protection, along with protective positive obligations, only cover the specific subset of the environment that must be protected for the sake of the human existence, even with a broad interpretation. However, animal welfare, species protection, and significant portions of nature and landscape conservation are not encompassed by these measures – subjectivised protection could be expanded in this direction. Currently, above all, an effective defense in a justiciable and enforceable manner against environmental impairments is not possible, unless these impairments, at least in part, directly affect individual legal, thus human, interests. Consequently, this also creates deficiencies in the enforcement of current environmental legislation in the form of EU secondary law and national law.

3.3.1.2 The Procedural Dimension

Given the difficulties outlined above in determining the substantive content of a fundamental right to environmental protection, it is therefore advisable to explore a procedural

[193] Pernthaler (1992), p. 1, 10.

[194] For a detailed discussion on this, see Calliess (2001), p. 373 et seq.

[195] Kloepfer (1978), p. 14 et seq, 27 et seq und 31 et seq; Bock (1990), p. 227 et seq; Benda (1982), p. 242; Dellmann (1975), p. 589; Rauschning (1980), p. 178; Sendler (1983), p. 258; Ruffert (1996), p. 31 et seq.

[196] In detail Calliess (2001), p. 298 et seq and 410 et seq.

conception of such a right. Through both national[197] and international[198] discussions, three components of a procedural environmental fundamental right have emerged: the right to **participation** (in environmentally relevant decisions), the right of adequate **access to justice**, and the right to **information** (as a necessary precondition for the exercise of the first two rights).

3.3.1.2.1 Impetus from International Law

Aspects of a human right to environmental protection play a significant role in recent, as well as older, environmental-specific declarations, resolutions, and agreements, including the principles of the 1992 Rio Declaration. Yet these documents are generally non-binding and, at best, have the character of "*soft law*".[199] The substantive and procedural dimensions of a human right to environmental protection have also been extensively discussed in international law literature, which, according to Article 38(1)(d) of the Statute of the International Court of Justice (ICJ), serves as a source of international law and can therefore help to determine existence and content of international legal norms.[200] However, overall, these approaches and considerations also encounter the problem of vagueness and indeterminacy regarding possible substantive contents, resulting in a prevailing opinion that focuses on the procedural dimensions of such an environmental fundamental right.[201]

The UNECE Convention on Access to Information, Public Participation in Decision-making and Access to Justice in Environmental Matters (known as the ***Aarhus Convention***), which was adopted in 1998 and has since been largely implemented in Union law, even **points toward a procedural environmental fundamental right**.[202] Article 1, in accordance with the Convention's name, states, that: "*In order to contribute to the protection of the right of every person of present and future generations to live in an environment adequate to his or her health and well-being, each Party shall guarantee the rights of access to information, public participation in decision-making, and access to justice in environmental matters in accordance with the provisions of this Convention*".

---

197 See for example Kloepfer (1978), p. 24 and 25 et seq, who (misleadingly) interprets this as a concept of participatory rights. More accurate in this regard is his reference to the "status activus processualism". Further, see Brönneke (1993), p. 157 et seq, whose approaches lead to the procedural concept of an environmental fundamental right.

198 See here only Ruffert (1996), p. 18 et seq.

199 For a detailed discussion on this, see Calliess (2000), p. 246 et seq.

200 See here only the overview provided by Ruffert (1996), p. 19 et seq; Taylor (1998), p. 234 et seq, each with numerous further references.

201 Regarding this, Krämer (1988), p. 291; Ruffert (1996), p. 23 et seq; in detail, Calliess (2000), p. 246 et seq, each with further references.

202 The Convention on Access to Information, Public Participation Published in AVR 38 (2000), pp. 253 et seq; see also Scheyli (2000), p. 217 et seq; Schlacke (2008), p. 233 et seq; on the origin and content of this agreement, Epiney (2019), p. 2 et seq.

3.3.1.2.2 Impetus from European Union Law

In implementing the Aarhus Convention at the EU and member state levels, an astonishing dynamic has been triggered in Germany, particularly regarding the mentioned procedural aspects of an environmental fundamental right, thanks in large part to the case law of the CJEU,[203] which primarily concerns access to justice.[204]

European law, similar to international law, is more cautious regarding substantive content rather than a procedural dimension. The right referred to as "*Environmental Protection*" in Article 37 of the Charter of Fundamental Rights of the European Union (GrCh) ultimately only represents a Union objective corresponding to Articles 11 and 191 TFEU.[205] **Partial guarantees to protect the environment** can be identified in Union law, which are linked to the subjective rights guaranteed by the Charter of Fundamental Rights, such as the rights to health, physical integrity, and property (see Articles 2, 3, and 17). According to Article 51(1) of the Charter, these rights bind not only the Union institutions when establishing Union law and exercising their administrative powers but also the member states in implementing Union law and within the scope of its application.[206]

These aforementioned partial guarantees of fundamental rights are applicable not only in their defensive dimension but, as suggested by Article 1 and 6 of the EU Charter of Fundamental Rights (CFR), in their **protective dimension**, too. However, the CJEU has so far only recognized a **duty of protection** by the member states within the framework of fundamental freedoms, specifically in the 1997 case of "*Spanish Strawberries*" concerning the free movement of goods.[207] Yet the obligations imposed by the European Convention on Human Rights (ECHR) – which, according to Article 6(3) TEU, must be taken into account in interpreting Union law – in conjunction with Articles 52(3) and 53 of the EU Charter of Fundamental Rights (CRF) – which guarantee that the provisions of the Charter do not fall behind or restrict levels of protection guaranteed by the ECHR – acknowledge protective duties, that are referred to as "***positive obligations***" by the European Court of Human Rights (ECtHR). These obligations, through the respect

[203] Regarding the implementation in Germany, see the Environmental Appeals Act (dated December 7, 2006) and the various amendments required as a result of ECJ decisions, most recently within the framework of the major amendment of 2017 (Act to adapt the Environmental Appeals Act and other provisions to European and international legal requirements, (Gesetz zur Anpassung des Umwelt-Rechtsbehelfsgesetzes und anderer Vorschriften an europa- und völkerrechtliche Vorgaben) dated 29.5.2017, BGBl. I p. 1298); most recently ECJ, C-752/18, Deutsche Umwelthilfe e. V v Freistaat Bayern; for a general overview of the case law, Kokott and Sobotta (2014), p. 132 et seq.; Sauer (2014), 195 et seq; Gärditz (2014), p. 1 et seq; Guckelberger (2020) p. 150 et seq; recent criticism by Ruffert (2019); in contrast, Berkemann (2020) with a response from Ruffert (2021), p. 309; for individual judgments, see among others Köck and Henn (2020), p. 504 et seq; Klinger (2018) p. 231 et seq; Wegener (2018); Franzius (2018); Sobotta (2018) Kment and Lorenz (2016); Siegel (2016).

[204] For further in-depth discussion, Calliess (2006a), p. 1 et seq; Schlacke (2008), p. 233 et seq; Guckelberger (2020), p. 150 et seq.

[205] For a detailed discussion, Calliess (2022g) Art. 37 CFR, para 1 et seq.

[206] For further in-depth analysis, Kingreen (2022), para. 7 et seq, as well as Calliess (2015), p. 17 et seq.

[207] Regarding this Calliess (2006b), § 44 para 4 et seq.

for private and family life under Article 8 of the ECHR, provide a partial guarantee of environmental protection encompassing both a defensive and protective dimension.[208] While in practice, this protection covers only evident cases of environmental pollution, ultimately ensuring only an "*ecological subsistence minimum.*",[209] the protective dimension of Article 8 ECHR, includes not only protection against significant environmental burdens but also, as a kind of procedural safeguard, a right to **environmental information.**[210]

3.3.1.3 Conclusion on a Procedural Fundamental Right to Environmental and Climate Protection

In conclusion, at the level of international and European law, there are at least some indications of both substantive and, above all, procedural fundamental rights to environmental protection.[211] While these indications often stem from non-binding, environment-specific declarations and agreements, whose nature as guaranteeing individual rights is not always entirely clear, they can be understood as a precursor to legal development and pioneers of legal evolution, consistent with their classification as "*soft law*". In this context, in substantive international law, a connection is established between environmental matters and existing human rights, such as the right to life, the right to health, or physical integrity.[212] In this way, these human rights are expanded as partial guarantees of environmental protection through broad interpretation. However, both in international and European law, the procedural dimensions of an environmental fundamental right take centre stage.[213]

From a **procedural environmental fundamental right**, specific procedural rights can be derived, which enable individuals to assert their interests and concerns in the field of environmental law in specific cases. For legislators and administrators, these procedural requirements contain certain mandates for structuring procedures. A procedural environmental fundamental right addresses the legitimate concerns raised against a substantive environmental fundamental right, that is formulated as a defensive or performance right, while effectively accounting for the limited legal subjectivisation of the public interest in the common good of environmental protection. In this way, a procedural concept helps address implementation and enforcement deficiencies in the field of environmental and climate policy.

---

208 Regarding this, Calliess (2000), p. 246 et seq.; further in-depth analysis by Schmidt-Radefeldt (2000).

209 ECtHR, Judgment of 9.12.1994, López Ostra v. Spain, No. 16798/90.

210 ECtHR, Judgment of 19.2.1998, Guerra and others v. Italy, No. 14967/89.

211 Calliess (2000), p. 246 et seq.

212 For a detailed discussion, Taylor (1998), p. 266 et seq; Hobe (1994), p. 18 et seq., with further references; see also the rare practice case of the Yanomami, which was decided by the Inter-American Commission on Human Rights, see Case No. 7615 of 5.3.1985, Annual Report of the Inter-American Commission on Human Rights, OAS Doc. OAE/Ser. L/VII. 66 Doc. 10 rev. 1 at 24 (1985); on this, see Schmidt-Radefeldt (2000), p. 51 et seq.

213 Ruffert (1996), p. 27; Rest (1997, p. 211; Hobe (1994), p. 18 et seq; Calliess (2000), p. 246 et seq.

Since the procedural dimension of the fundamental rights of the Charter of Fundamental Rights – mediated through the environment-related partial guarantees, particularly in Articles 3(1) and 17 of the CRF – can only partially convey rights to information, participation, and access to justice, the **addition of a procedural fundamental right to environmental protection** in the respective catalogue of fundamental rights is worth considering *de lege ferenda*. Against the background of the considerations outlined above, a judicially enforceable procedural fundamental right to environmental and climate protection in a new Article 37 of the Charter of Fundamental Rights could therefore be formulated as follows: "*Every person has the right to a clean and healthy environment, as well as its preservation and protection. This right is guaranteed through rights to information, participation in administrative proceedings, and effective access to justice*".

3.3.1.4 Ecological Subsistence Level

Does this mean that a fundamental right to environmental protection can have no material content that is legally enforceable? What about a right to an ecological subsistence minimum level? And would an amendment to the EU Charter of Fundamental Rights really be necessary in this regard?

To address this last question first: In EU law, prior to the binding inclusion of the Charter of Fundamental Rights through the Treaty of Lisbon (see Article 6(1) TEU), the entire protection of fundamental rights was based on unwritten fundamental rights, developed by the CJEU. They were derived from the legal understanding of the ECHR on one hand, and an evaluative comparison of the constitutional traditions of the Member States on the other.[214] The **possibility to develop "new" unwritten fundamental rights** on this basis of general legal principle is still provided for in Article 6(3) TEU.[215]

3.3.1.4.1 Foundations of an Ecological Subsistance Minimum in German Constitutional Law

The *German Federal Constitutional Court* (BVerfG) serves as an example for making use of its possibility for judicial development of fundamental rights, as it has developed "new" fundamental rights with a view to current challenges. In the present context, the German fundamental right to the *guarantee of a* ***(social) subsistence minimum***,[216] established in 2010, is particularly groundbreaking.

Similar to the German fundamental right to a minimum subsistence level, it is not clearly defined, in detail, what standard an "*ecological minimum subsistence level*" demands. In principle, individuals must be enabled to lead a life that is in keeping with **human dignity – the central basis** of the subsistence level. Based on this foundation, found in the German social subsistence minimum, the fundamental right of an ecological subsistence minimum grants a claim to freedom from extremely environmentally harmful state interventions. Moreover, it encompasses a duty for the state to maintain a minimum state of natural resources: The state must ensure that all necessary natural environmental elements exist and are maintained in a sufficiently adequate condition for human health and life.

---

[214] Schorkopf (2024).

[215] Schorkopf (2024).

[216] Established by BVerfG judgement of 9.2.2010 - 1 BvL 1/09, paras 1-220.

Elements considered part of the ecological minimum standard include breathable air, drinkable water, edible food, and, as an essential environmental condition, the ozone layer[217]. However, especially when anchoring the fundamental right in human dignity, its guarantees go beyond the preservation of a viable environment but also encompass the preservation of an environment that is worth living in:[218] "*It is not sufficient if human beings could only survive with the help of technical support or aids, for example, under a glass dome, because otherwise they would become mere objects of the technological-industrial world.*"[219] State authorities have to take action to ensure that their population is provided with ecologically acceptable conditions to live in, even though this standard does not have to be met comprehensively without any gaps.[220]

It is important to note that the ecological minimum standard can be affected not only when these minimum conditions are no longer present but also when there is serious risk of extreme ecological distress, particularly a risk of irreversible environmental damage by surpassing the **planetary boundaries** in the form of tipping points.[221] Given the comparable fundamental rights in Articles 1, 2, 3, and 37 of the Charter of Fundamental Rights, the approach outlined can be transferred to the European level, with an ecological minimum subsistence level anchored in Article 1 of the CFR.

3.3.1.5 Coupling with Planetary Boundaries and the Precautionary Principle

Crossing tipping points can lead to irreversible environmental damage, resembling a "*devastation scenario*", which can endanger the survival of humans and the environment. Given the uncertainties and potentially catastrophic risks associated with irreversible critical changes of the Earth system, the concept of planetary boundaries incorporates a safety margin, particularly in quantifying critical thresholds, when determining the "***safe operating space***".

The concept of planetary boundaries, particularly through this safety margin, includes a normative component that corresponds to the constitutional objective of environmental protection in Article 20a of the German Basic Law (Grundgesetz) and the **precautionary principle** inherent[222] in that norm. In EU law, the precautionary principle is explicitly mentioned as a guiding principle in **Article 191 TFEU** and is linked to the principle of sustainability through the integration clause of **Article 11 TFEU**. The precautionary principle aims to establish a "*precautionary reserve*" in situations of abstract concern which does not reach the threshold of danger, because there is only a possibility of harm, that can neither be confirmed nor denied with certainty.[223] It is particularly applicable

[217] Cf. Murswiek and Rixen (2018).

[218] The German Constitutional Court, in its famous climate protection ruling from 2021, in this regard contemplated that the ecological subsistence minimum could be violated, if "participation in social, cultural and political life" were no longer meaningfully possible as a result of drastic climate change that leads to a hostile environment – however, it left the question of violation in the specific case unanswered in the end, see BVerfGE judgement of 24.3.2021 - 1 BvR 2656/18, para 113 et seq; Hillgruber (2024), para 51a.

[219] Buser (2021), p. 8; cf. Steiger (1975), p. 35. (translated).

[220] Buser (2021), p. 8.

[221] See Calliess (2019).

[222] Calliess (2001), p. 114 et seq, 181 et seq.

[223] Calliess (2019), p. 386.

where scientific evidence is insufficient, does not allow for clear conclusions, or is uncertain, but when a preliminary and objective scientific risk assessment gives rise to abstract concerns.[224] Therefore, in both European law and German constitutional law, the precautionary principle replaces the requirement of concrete, sufficient probability with the mere possibility and abstract concern of potential harm. In this context of abstract concern or "***non liquet***", where existing uncertainty cannot be resolved with available investigation means, the precautionary principle operates as a **rebuttable presumption of danger**, which can, as rightly confirmed by the European Commission[225], lead to a **reversal of the burden of proof**.[226] However, for the sake of the rule of law, the requirements of burden of proof must not reach the level of requiring positive proof or disproof of the possibility of harm.[227]

Based on the precautionary principle, there are significant normative guidelines for dealing with ecological boundaries. Both dimensions of the precautionary principle – risk prevention and resource conservation – aim to avoid critical loads or tipping points that could lead to severe and irreparable damage to environmental goods. From the legal standpoint, the concept of not exhausting ecological boundaries can be derived from the precautionary principle. These boundaries establish a threshold that should be carefully avoided by taking measures that steer away from it.[228]

If, in the event of crossing tipping points, there is a risk of irreversible environmental damage that can lead to a kind of '*devastation scenario*,' then, from a legal perspective, the constitutionally derived claim of every citizen to the ecological minimum subsistence level is violated. This claim is derived from **human dignity**, the fundamental rights to life and health, and the environmental objective of **Articles 119 and 11 TFEU**. In any case, the protected right is always affected, if there is a high probability that the planetary boundaries will be exceeded. Moreover, with a view to future generations and thus taking into account the sustainability principle, including the precautionary principle, the ecological subsistence level is affected not only if these minimum levels are no longer met, but – because it concerns irreversible environmental damage – already in case **extreme ecological distress** in the form of the aforementioned 'scenario of devastation' is to be feared.

In this respect, the planetary boundaries and their tipping points, in particular the 1.5–2° target, as mentioned above, formulate a rebuttable presumption. Thus, the applicants claiming the right to an ecological subsistence minimum are not required to present evidence and substantiation – rather, the defendants, i.e., the state institutions as addressees of the fundamental right, must prove that they have taken all necessary measures in their

224 See on the precautionary principle: Köck (2023).

225 COM (2000) 1 final, p. 24; critical in this regard Rengeling (2000), p. 1479 et seq; contra Appel (2001), pp. 396, 398.

226 For a detailed discussion, Calliess (2001), p. 223 et seq; contra Arndt (2009), pp. 290 et seq, 295 et seq, who considers only a reduction in the bur-den of proof as a direct consequence of the precautionary principle, but not a reversal of the burden of proof, which he sees realized within the framework of the secondary regulatory authorization procedures.

227 Rehbinder (1989), p. 9 et seq; Ritter (1992), p. 648 et seq; for further details (2001), p. 223 et seq.

228 Calliess (2001), p. 176 et seq; see also Appel (2005), p. 299 et seq.

concept of protection in form of a "*guiding law*" to effectively steer away ('keeping a safe distance') from the planetary boundaries and that they thus can effectively guarantee the minimum ecological existence.

Beyond the defined ecological minimum subsistence level, the substantive Union objective of Articles 191 and 11 TFEU, in conjunction with the fundamental right to life and health of Articles 2 and 3 of the EU Charter, establish an absolute minimum limit through the mentioned **prohibition of insufficient means or actions** (*Untermaßverbot*).[229] This demands a suitable environmental protection concept and in this regard, the scope for action of state institutions in specifying the protection concept – for example, through environmental quality objectives[230] – is greater (than within guaranteeing only the ecological subsistence minimum). They have, in this respect, an optimization task (*Optimierungsauftrag*)[231] that is subject to balancing. However, the more serious the foreseeable consequences of exceeding the planetary stress limits are, the more weight should be given to the requirement of keeping a safe distance from the planetary boundaries in the political consideration process.[232]

This has implications for the extent of **judicial review**. Similar to decisions regarding the social minimum subsistence level, first the legislature must further sufficiently define and describe the objective of guaranteeing this level.[233] Furthermore, the legislature has leeway to determine a suitable calculation method. And finally, it must ensure that all facts, especially relevant needs, that are necessary for calculation, are ascertained and that all calculation steps are within reasonable bounds, while disclosing the methods and calculation steps that were used for constitutional court review.[234]

Measured against these normative requirements, the right to an ecological minimum subsistence level entails a judicially enforceable mandate, within which the institutions of the EU must steer far clear of the planetary boundaries and prevent the Earth system's ecological boundaries to be exceeded (further) by way of a suitable and effective, thus meaning coherent, long-term, and legally binding protection concept.[235] In particular regarding climate protection, there is already a legal framework with the *Paris Agreement* and the European climate targets for 2030, to which Germany and the EU are bound and must adhere to in their climate protection policies.[236] In this context, the *European Climate Law*[237] represents a promising approach. Its establishment of an institutional

229 For a detailed discussion, Calliess (2001), p. 322 et seq, 451 et seq. And 566 et seq; similarly, Brönneke (1999), p. 272 et seq and 471 et seq; Sommermann (1997), p. 439 et seq.

230 Reese (2010).

231 Brönneke (1999), p. 269 et seq; Sommermann (1997), p. 360 et seq.

232 Calliess (2019); in agreement Meyer (2020), p. 897 et seq.; Buser (2020), p. 1392.

233 As a reference, the German social minimum subsistence level guarantees a dignified minimum existence, covering the means absolutely necessary for securing both one's physical existence and a minimum of participation in social, cultural and political life (cf. BVerfGE 125, 175 <223>; 132, 134 <160, para. 64>, judgement of 9.2.2010 - 1 BvL 1/09,) but details are left for the legislature to determine.

234 BVerfG judgement of 9.2.2010 - 1 BvL 1/09, Rn. 144; in principle, the following Calliess (2001), p. 125 et seq.

235 In-depth discussion on this can be found in Calliess (2001), p. 125 et seq and 235 et seq.

236 Saurer (2017).

237 Regulation (EU) 2021/1119.

monitoring process is necessary to fulfill the European Green Deal's objectives, not least to meet the requirements of the environmental policy integration clause of Article 11 TFEU.[238] However, the law is still too weak, especially with regard to the required monitoring of the implementation of the agreed goals, as the independent "*Expert Council on Climate Issues*", which performs a mere notarial function rather than a genuine control function, is rather toothless. Therefore, effective monitoring, as a form of "climate protection through procedure" must additionally be installed.

3.3.1.6 Interim Conclusion

If the proposal by *von Schirach* for a fundamental right to environmental protection, is meant to be more than programmatic symbolism in face of the climate crisis, then the lack of determinability of the content of the fundamental right and its enforceability before the courts pose unresolved problems. For these reasons, a substantively effective fundamental right to environmental protection can only be constructed as a protective partial guarantee of an existing individual fundamental right (e.g., to life, health, property) in connection with the recognized function of fundamental rights as containing positive obligations of protection. However, this does not cover protection of species and animals, as well as large parts of nature and landscape protection. Consequently, these omissions also apply to existing enforcement deficits in the applicable environmental law.

Moreover, the introduction of a **procedural fundamental right to environmental protection** is recommended, which could read as follows: "*Every person has the right to a clean and healthy environment, as well as its preservation and protection. This is ensured through rights to information, participation in administrative procedures, and effective access to justice.*" In substantive terms, the enforceable fundamental right to the ecological minimum subsistence level can be fruitfully utilized, which, mediated through the planetary boundaries defined by Earth system sciences, sets an absolute minimum level of protection. These boundaries, with their tipping points, establish an evidence-based threshold for the burden of proof and a rebuttable presumption, requiring the state institutions as addressees of the fundamental right to demonstrate and prove in court that they have taken all necessary measures by means of their concepts of protection to effectively steer away from the planetary boundaries and thereby ensure the ecological minimum subsistence level.

3.3.2 Greening Existing Fundamental Rights

In the context of the "*greening the treaties*" debate, proposals also suggest a potential greening of existing fundamental rights.[239] These proposals are not entirely new, and have already been invoked in the past.[240] According to *Kersten* and as already mentioned in the context of partial guarantees, when it comes to the ecological transformation of the German Basic Law, central fundamental rights are the right to property, the right to life and physical integrity.

[238] See on this, Calliess and Dross (2020), p. 461 et seq.

[239] Cf. in the German context, Kersten argues for a greening of Articles 1, 2(1) and (2), 9(3) and 14, and the introduction of a new Article 2a, p. 63-100.

[240] See for instance Bosselmann (1998).

Kersten suggests the **introduction of the principle of "*ecological responsibility*"** into Article 1 of the German Basic Law.[241] In the European context, such a principle could accordingly be introduced into Article 1 of the Charter of Fundamental Rights, which reads: "*Human dignity is inviolable. It must be respected and protected*". The dignity of the human person constitutes the real basis of all other fundamental rights.[242] Introducing "*ecological responsibility*" in Article 1 would place the principle at the very beginning of the Charter and could, hence, stress its central position. In addition, anchoring ecological responsibility next to "*human dignity*" may, at the same time, benefit a potential approach to "*rights of nature*", which will be discussed below.

Furthermore, Art. 2(1)'s right to life ("*Everyone has the right to life.*") could be supplemented by the "right to ecological integrity".[243]

Article 17 of the Charter anchors the "right to property". According to Article 17(1) of the Charter "*Everyone has the right to own, use, dispose of and bequeath his or her lawfully acquired possessions. No one may be deprived of his or her possessions, except in the public interest and in the cases and under the conditions provided for by law, subject to fair compensation being paid in good time for their loss. The use of property may be regulated by law in so far as is necessary for the general interest.*" The right to property is a relative right that may be limited in accordance with public interest. In order to green Article 17(1) of the Charter, one option would be to introduce a special "ecological limitation" ("*ökologische Grundrechtsschranken*") to the fundamental right.[244] This could serve to establish an "***ecologically responsible concept of property***".[245]

3.3.3 Rights of Nature

Greening fundamental rights also gives rise to a reflection rights of nature.[246] The introduction of rights of nature, by recognising for instance the legal personality and legal capacity of ecological entities may contribute to an ecological transformation of society.[247] The surrounding discussion has its origin in the 1970s,[248] and has intensified

[241] For an amendment of Article 1 of the Basic Law see Bosselmann (1998), p. 94.

[242] Cf. Explanations relating to the Charter of Fundamental Rights, 2007/C303/02/, p. 17.

[243] Cf. Kersten (2022), p. 68-71. For an amendment of Article 2(1) of the Basic Law, see Bosselmann (1986), p. 20; Bosselmann (1994), p. 15; Bosselmann (1998), p. 96.

[244] See Bosselmann (1998), pp. 19–30, 65–79.

[245] See Kersten (2022), pp. 92–99; for an amendment of Article 14 of the Basic Law, see Bosselmann (1998), p. 124; Bosselmann (1992), p. 204 et seq.

[246] See my analysis: Calliess (2022h) Art. 20a GG, para. 56-66.

[247] See Kersten (2022), pp. 100–109, who suggests a recognition of ecological people in Article 19(3) of the Basic Law; see also Kersten (2020), p. 30 et seq; Kersten (2020), pp. 87, 109 et seq.; see as well Buser and Ott (2021), pp. 159, 169.

[248] Stone (1972), p. 450 et seq; Bosselmann (1992); Leimbacher (1988); as early as the debate on the constitutional objective provision of Article 20a of the German Basic Law, it has been discussed whether the natural foundations of life should be linked to humans as the reference point and thus protected in an anthropocentric manner or eco-centrically protected for their own sake, see BT-Drucks. 12/6000, p. 65 et seq: "Verfassungspolitisch blieb vor al-lem umstritten, ob der Schutz der natürlichen Lebensgrundlagen anthropozentrisch formuliert und mit einem

since the mid-1980s concerning the differences between anthropocentric and ecocentric environmental protection.[249] The debate centrally revolves around the rationale of environmental protection, namely the question of whether the environment should be protected based on human purposes, as in the **anthropocentric approach**, or for its intrinsic value and own sake, as in the **ecocentric approach**. While the neutral term "*environmental protection*" does not necessarily imply an anthropocentric approach, as it refers to nature as a whole, encompassing the surroundings and the basis of human life,[250] the understanding that environmental protection is, at least in part, in the self-interest of humans has accompanied the concept of environmental protection since its inception.[251] The question of whether nature should have independent rights has recently gained renewed attention.[252] In various jurisdictions, there is a growing tendency of judicially recognising natural entities as a subject of rights or constitutionalising rights of nature.[253]

Against this background, the question arises as to whether strengthening environmental protection could be achieved by explicitly anchoring the ecocentric approach in the treaties or in the Charter of Fundamental Rights. As described above, scholarly proposals have been made to liberate nature from its vulnerability through the construction of inherent rights combined with representative actions by trustee environmental organizations.[254] Another proposal suggests dissociating the ecocentric approach from the inherent rights of nature and further developing it in a comprehensive sense throughout the entire legal system with the goal of ecologicalising the law. In this way, a correlating

---

Gesetzgebungsvorbehalt versehen werden soll oder nicht"; see on this as well Uhle (1993), p. 949; Müller-Bromley (1990), p. 108 et seq; an overview at Calliess (2001), p. 106 et seq.

249 See the overview by Heinz (1988), pp. 181, 192 et seq; Bock (1990), p. 211 et seq.; Kloepfer (1995), p. 7 et seq, each with further references.

250 However, see Kloepfer (1995), p. 3.

251 See also: Benöhr (1994), p. 145 et seq.

252 See for instance: Johns (2023); Wolf (2022); Mührel (2022); Gutmann (2021); Köck and Markus (2018); Calliess (2023), p. 4; Schröter and Bosselmann (2018); Fischer-Lescano (2018); Krämer (2020); Boyd (2017); Burger and den Outer (2023); Kersten (2020); Kersten (2020), p. 87; Adloff and Busse (2022); Kaufmann and Martin (2021).

253 The Constitution of Ecuador has adopted the rights of nature in 2008, see Gutmann (2019); see Gutmann (2021). New Zealand declared the legal personality of a national park and a river, see New Zealand, Te Urewera Act 2014, no.51 (Te Urewera Park); Te Awa Tupua Act 2017, no.7 (Whanganui River). Legal personality was also recognised for the Ganges and Yamuna rivers in India, see Süddeutsche Zeitung from 4./5./6.6.2022, p. 49. In 2022, Spain adopted the "Mar Menor Act", granting legal personality to the Mar Menor lagoon and its basin, see Krämer (2023). Most recently, indigenous leaders from the Cook Islands and New Zealand signed a treaty (He Wha-kaputanga Moana) which recognises the legal personhood of whales, see: Evans (2024).

254 Stone (1992), p. 25 et seq (this is the German translation of an article published in the Southern Californian Law Review 45 (1972), p. 450 etseq); also Tribe (1980), p. 20 et seq (previously published in Yale Law Journal 83 (1974), p. 1315 et seq.); von Lersner (1988), p. 988 et seq; Kloepfer (1990), p. 55 et seq.; Bosselmann (1986), p. 1 et seq; Pernthaler (1992), pp. 1, 8 et seq; Häberle (1988), pp. 19 et seq, 85; on corresponding trends in international law: Emmenegger and Tschentscher (1994), p. 550 et seq.

subjectivity would be attributed to nature as an inherent limitation on individual freedom of the human being, who has been the sole bearer of fundamental rights so far.[255] While the legal contours and implications of the latter concept remain comparatively vague from a doctrinal perspective, proposals for specific wording have been put forward regarding the inherent rights of nature as part of constitutional reform.[256]

However, the ecocentric approach tends to entail an inherent contradiction that is difficult to resolve. If its necessity is justified by arguing that, in accordance with the anthropocentric approach, humans have thus far viewed nature merely as an object of disposal, consumable for their own benefit, it is not readily apparent why and how this same human being would be entrusted to be a **trustee of nature** in an ecocentric-oriented environmental protection framework, considering that nature, unable to assert its inherent value autonomously, relies on human intervention.[257] Additionally, equating the rights of humans with those of animals, plants, and inanimate nature, as proposed by *Pernthaler*, presents a solution that, irrespective of the ethical problems associated with such a construction, would be incompatible with the human-centred conception of the European Convention on Human Rights[258].

On the other hand, the legal controversy between anthropocentric and ecocentric environmental protection appears to be primarily theoretical in nature. While there are indeed interdependencies between philosophy (morality and ethics), law, politics, and society, in the sense that philosophy can convey ethical guidelines, for human behaviour towards the environment, to society through the law as a fundamental pattern of political design, and can initiate collective learning processes through continuous interactions[259], this realization cannot ignore the fact that ecocentrism, at least in the legal realm, ultimately refers back to anthropocentric foundational structures[260]. In any case, the prevailing literature correctly states that, from a purely legal perspective, following either an ecocentric or anthropocentric approach in environmental law results in no difference in practice.

With an increasing understanding of the complexity of the natural ecosystem, it is now widely presumed that environmental protection always benefits humans. Consequently, it can be assumed that the integrity of every aspect of nature ultimately has significant implications for human livelihoods. If one follows this broad interpretation, for example also implied by the Article 20a of the German Basic Law, which obliges the state to protect the natural foundations of life as a whole, the theoretical dichotomy

255 Bosselmann (1998), p. 18 et seq and p. 54 et seq.

256 For instance, the proposal introduced in the discussion on Article 20a of the Basic Law, which suggests a protection of nature "for its own sake," reflects an ecocentric tendency (see in detail Brönneke (1999, p. 164 et seq). Additionally, noteworthy are the proposals for constitutional reform in Austria developed by Pernthaler in the early 1990s (see Pernthaler (1992), p. 1, 10 et seq. According to these proposals, human rights should be understood as part of the rights of nature, alongside the rights of animals, plants, and inanimate nature.

257 Kloepfer (1995), p. 25 et seq; similarly, Appel (2005), p. 65.

258 In-depth analysis on this matter can be found in Bergmann (1995), p. 119 et seq and 264 et seq

259 Ritter (1992), p. 648 et seq.

260 This is not made clear in the ecocentric approach by Bosselmann (1998), pp. 47 et seq, which struggles to explain the legal (not ethical) novelty of its conception.

between anthropocentric and ecocentric environmental protection becomes practically insignificant in the realm of law.[261] This is particularly true when considering the possibility of introducing **class actions**. In practical legal terms, the primary function of the inherent rights of nature would be to ensure access to the courts through **representative actions** (e.g., in the case of constructing a road in a nature reserve) where there is a lack of individuals whose subjective rights have been affected.[262] As a result, it can be concluded that existing law does not need to be exposed to the still unexplored implications and potential frictions of an ecocentric legal system in order to strengthen environmental protection.[263] Taking into account the existence of class actions, it can be said that rights of nature would not have any added value.

References

Adloff, F., Busse, T.: Welche Rechte braucht die Natur? Campus Verlag, Frankfurt, Wege aus dem Artensterben (2022)

Ammann, N.: Was kann die Wirtschaft gegen den Klimawandel tun (– und was nicht)? In: Schmidt, C., et al. European Green Deal – Bottlenecks bis 2030, ifo Schnelldienst 6/2020, pp. 35–37 (2020). https://t1p.de/akkkk. Accessed 25 Aug 2025

Appel, I.: Anwendbarkeit des Vorsorgeprinzips. NVwZ **20**(4), 395–398 (2001)

Appel, I.: Staatliche Zukunfts- und Entwicklungsvorsorge - Zum Wandel der Dogmatik des Öffentlichen Rechts am Beispiel des Konzepts der nachhaltigen Entwicklung im Umweltrecht. Mohr Siebeck, Tübingen (2005)

Appel, I.: § 2 Europäisches and nationales Umweltverfassungsrecht. In: Koch, H.J. et al. (eds.) Handbuch Umweltrecht, 5th edn. C.H. Beck, München (2018)

Arbeitskreis "Europäische Umweltunion" (1994a) NuR:346

Arbeitskreis: "Europäische Umweltunion" Umweltpolitische Ziele und Grundsätze für die Europäische Union. GAIA **3**(1), 11–17 (1994b)

Arndt B (2009) Das Vorsorgeprinzip im EU-Recht, Mohr Siebeck, Tübingen

Baumeister, H. (ed.): Wege zum ökologischen Rechtsstaat. Blottner Verlag, Taunusstein, Umweltschutz ohne Öko-Diktatur (1994)

Becker, U.: Art. 3 EUV. In: Schwarze, J. et al. (eds.) EU-Kommentar, 4th ed. Nomos, Baden-Baden (2019)

Benda, E.: Verfassungsrechtliche Aspekte des Umweltschutzes. UPR **2**(8), 241–247 (1982)

Benöhr, H.P.: Arbeitsbereich: Umweltrecht in Deutschland im 19. Jahrhundert. In: Kloepfer, M. (ed.) Umweltstaat als Zukunft: juristische, ökonomische und philosophische Aspekte, pp. 145–170. Economica Verlag, Bonn (1994)

Bergmann, J.M.: Das Menschenbild der Europäischen Menschenrechtskonvention, 1st ed. Nomos, Baden-Baden (1995)

Berkemann, J.: Replik: Rufferts Suche nach methodischen Grundlagen im EuGH-Umweltrechtsschutz. DVBl **23**, 1516–1523 (2020)

Bock, B.: Umweltschutz im Spiegel von Verfassungsrecht und Verfassungspolitik. Duncker u. Humblot, Berlin (1990)

[261] Similarly, Murswiek (2021); Waechter (1996), p. 324; Kloepfer (1995), pp. 25 et seq; Kuhlmann (1995), p. 3.

[262] See in this regard the approach of Brönneke (1999), p. 396 et seq; also see Calliess (2001), p. 522 et seq.

[263] In this context refer to Waechter (1996), p. 324.

Böhler, D.: Mensch und Natur: Verstehen, Konstruieren, Verantworten. Deut Z Philos **39**(9), 999–1019 (1991)
Boisserée, K.: Europäische Umweltpolitik im Wirtschafts- und Sozialausschuss der Europäischen Union. In: von Köller, H. (ed.) Umweltpolitik mit Augenmaß. Gedenkschrift für Staatssekretär Dr. Günter Hartkopf anlässlich seines 10. Todestages am 19. September 1999, pp. 287–297. Erich Schmidt, Berlin (2000)
Bosselmann, K.: Eigene Rechte für die Natur? Ansätze einer ökologischen Rechtsauffassung. KJ **19**(1), 1–22 (1986)
Bosselmann, K.: Im Namen der Natur – Der Weg zum ökologischen Rechtsstaat, 1st ed. Wiss. Buchges., Darmstadt (1992)
Bosselmann, K.: Der Ökologische Rechtsstaat – Versuch einer Standortbestimmung. In: Baumeister, H. (ed.) Wege zum Ökologischen Rechtsstaat. Umweltstaat ohne Öko-Dikatur, pp. 53–69. Blottner, Taunusstein (1994a)
Bosselmann, K.: Vom Umweltrecht zum Ökorecht – Skizze eines grundlegenden Wandels. In: Jahrbuch des Umwelt- und Technikrechts 1994, pp. 3–22. E. Schmidt, Berlin (1994)
Bosselmann, K.: Ökologische Grundrechte. Zum Verhältnis zwischen individueller Freiheit und Natur, 1st ed. Nomos, Baden-Baden (1998)
Boyd, D.: The Rights of Nature: A Legal Revolution that Could Save the World. ECW Press (2017)
Breier, S.: Die Bedeutung der umweltrechtlichen Querschnittklausel des Art. 130r II S. 2 EWGV für die Verwirklichung des europäischen Binnenmarktes. NuR, 174–181 (1992)
Breier, S.: Article 11 AEUV. In: Lenz, C.O., Borchardt, K.D. (eds.) EU-Verträge, 4th ed. Bundesanzeiger Verlag, Köln (2008)
Brönneke, T.: Vom Nutzen einer einklagbaren Umweltverfassungsnorm. ZUR **153** (1993)
Brönneke, T.: Umweltverfassungsrecht, 1st ed. Nomos, Baden-Baden (1999)
Burger, L., den Outer, J.: Das Meer klagt an! Der Kampf für die Rechte der Natur, 1st edn. S. Hirzel Verlag, Stuttgart (2023)
Buser, A.: Ein Grundrecht auf Klimaschutz? Möglichkeiten und Grenzen grundrechtlicher Klimaklagen in Deutschland. DVBl **21**, 1389–1396 (2020)
Buser, A.: Klimaziel 2020 erreicht – Klimaklagen erledigt? Zur Bedeutung eines Grundrechts auf ein ökologisches Existenzminimum für aktuelle Klimaklagen in Deutschland. BOB No. 127 (2021). https://t1p.de/303dp. Accessed 25 Aug 2025
Buser, A., Ott, H.: Zur Ökologisierung des Rechts: Rechte der Natur als Paradigmenwechsel. In: Adloff, F., Busse, T. (eds.) Welche Rechte braucht die Natur? Wege aus dem Artensterben, pp. 159–177. Bundeszentrale für politische Bildung, Bonn (2021)
Calliess, C.: "Greening the Treaty"? Perspektiven europäischer Umweltpolitik und europäischen Umweltrechts. Informationsdienst Umweltrecht **4**, 207–212 (1991)
Calliess, C.: Europäisches Umweltrecht als Chance: Die Umweltpolitik der EG und die Einflussmöglichkeiten der Umweltverbände. Blottner, Taunusstein (1992)
Calliess, C.: Perspektiven für eine Weiterentwicklung der Europäischen Union zu einer ökologischen Rechtsgemeinschaft. KJ, 284–305 (1994a)
Calliess, C.: Ökologisierung des EWG-Vertrages – Schritte auf dem Wege der Europäischen Gemeinschaft (EG) zu einer ökologischen Rechtsgemeinschaft unter Berücksichtigung des Vertrages über die Europäische Union (EU) von Maastricht. In: Baumeister, H. (ed.) Wege zum ökologischen Rechtsstaat, pp. 71–100. Eberhard Blottner Verlag (1994b)
Calliess, C.: Die neue Querschnittsklausel des Art. 6 ex 3c EGV als Instrument zur Umsetzung des Grundsatzes der nachhaltigen Entwicklung. DVBl, 559–568 ((1998))
Calliess, C.: Ansätze zur Subjektivierung von Gemeinwohlbelangen im Völkerrecht – Das Beispiel des Umweltschutzes. ZUR **11**, 246–257 (2000)
Calliess, C.: Rechtsstaat und Umweltstaat – Zugleich ein Beitrag zur Grundrechtsdogmatik im Rahmen mehrpoliger Verfassungsrechtsverhältnisse. Mohr Siebeck, Tübingen (2001)

Calliess, C.: Verwaltungsorganisationsrechtliche Konsequenzen des integrierten Umweltschutzes. In: Ruffert, M. (ed.) Recht und Organisation, pp. 73–106. Duncker und Humblot, Berlin (2003)
Calliess, C.: Die Werte in der Europäischen Union: Der europäische Staaten- und Verfassungsverbund als Wertebund. BOB No. 18 (2004a). https://ssrn.com/abstract=3750382. Accessed 25 Aug 2025
Calliess, C.: Europa als Wertegemeinschaft – Integration und Identität durch europäisches Verfassungsrecht? JZ **59**(21), 1033–1045 (2004b)
Calliess, C.: Feinstaub im Rechtsschutz deutscher Verwaltungsgerichte, Europarechtliche Vorgaben für die Klagebefugnis vor deutschen Gerichten und ihre dogmatische Verarbeitung. NVwZ **25**(1), 1–7 (2006)
Calliess, C.: Schutzpflichten, § 44. In: Merten, D., Papier, H. (eds.) Handbuch der Grundrechte in Deutschland und Europa. Grundrechte in Deutschland, vol. 2, pp. 964–991. Allgemeine Lehren. C.F. Müller, Heidelberg (2006)
Calliess, C.: Europe as transnational law – the transnationalization of European values. German Law J. **10**(10), 1367–1382 (2009). https://doi.org/10.1017/S2071832200018277
Calliess, C.: Rechtsstaat und Vorsorgestaat. In: Byrd, S. et al. (eds.) Annual Review of Law and Ethics, pp. 3–22. Duncker & Humblot Berlin (2013)
Calliess, C.: Kooperativer Grundrechtsschutz in der Europäischen Union – Überlegungen im Lichte der aktuellen Rechtsprechung von EuGH und deutschem Bundesverfassungsgericht. BOB No. 101 (2015). https://t1p.de/vtqzl. Accessed 25 Aug 2025
Calliess, C.: Abstand halten: Rechtspflichten der Klimaschutzpolitik aus planetaren Grenzen. ZUR **30**(7–8), 385–386 (2019)
Calliess, C.: Klimapolitik und Grundrechtsschutz. ZUR **32**(6), 323–332 (2021)
Calliess, C.: Art. 11 TFEU. In: Calliess, C., Ruffert, M. (eds.) EUV/AEUV, 6th edn., pp. 533–541. C.H. Beck, München (2022a)
Calliess, C.: Art. 13 TEU. In: Calliess, C., Ruffert, M. (eds.) EUV/AEUV, 6th edn., pp 237–255. C.H. Beck, München (2022b)
Calliess, C.: Art. 191 TFEU. In: Calliess, C., Ruffert, M. (eds.) EUV/AEUV, 6th edn., pp. 1854–1876. C.H. Beck, München (2022c)
Calliess, C.: Art. 192 TFEU. In: Calliess, C., Ruffert, M. (eds.) EUV/AEUV, 6th edn., pp. 1877–1901. C.H. Beck, München (2022d)
Calliess, C.: Art. 2 TEU. In: Calliess, C., Ruffert, M. (eds.) EUV/AEUV, 6th edn., pp 34–47 C.H. Beck, München (2022e)
Calliess, C.: Art. 3 TEU. In: Calliess, C., Ruffert, M. (eds.) EUV/AEUV, 6th edn., pp. 48–59. C.H. Beck, München (2022f)
Calliess, C.: Art. 37 CFR. In: Calliess, C., Ruffert, M. (eds.) EUV/AEUV, 6th edn., pp. 2827–2830. C.H. Beck, München (2022g)
Calliess, C.: Art. 20a GG, para. 56–66. In: Dürig, G. et al. (eds.) Grundgesetz-Kommentar, 99th supplement September 2022 (2022h)
Calliess, C.: Umweltpolitik im Grundgesetz. JuS **63**(1), 1–9 (2023)
Calliess, C., Dross, M.: Umwelt- und Klimaschutz als integraler Bestandteil der Wirtschaftspolitik. ZUR **31**(9), 456–464 (2020)
Calliess, C., Tuncel, E.: Greening the Euro? The impact of the Environmental Integration Clause (Art. 11 TFEU) on the European Central Bank's Primary and Secondary Objectives. BOB No. 136 (2022). https://t1p.de/jltdz. Accessed 25 Aug 2025
Calliess, C., Tuncel, E.: The role of Article 11 TFEU in the greening of the ECB's monetary policy. German Law J. **24**(5), 796–824 (2023)
Calliess, C., Wegener, B.: Europäisches Umweltrecht als Chance: Die Umweltpolitik der EG und die Einflussmöglichkeiten der Umweltverbände. Blottner Verlag, Taunusstein (1992)
Chalmers, D., et al.: European Union Law, 4th edn. Cambridge University Press (2019)

Crutzen, P., Stoermer, E.: The "Anthropocene". Global Change Newslett. **41**, 17–18 (2000). https://t1p.de/ieafo. Accessed 25 Aug 2025

Crutzen, P.: Geology of mankind. Nature **415**, 23 (2002). https://doi.org/10.1038/415023a

Dellmann, H.: Zur Problematik eines "Grundrechts auf menschenwürdige Umwelt". DÖV, 588–592 (1975)

Dietz, S.: Die Finanzmärkte in der Klimakrise: Zur Grünen Geldpolitik der EZB und den Maßnahmen für ein nachhaltiges Finanzsystem der Kommission. EuR **57**(4), 443–460 (2022)

Dworkin, R.: Taking Rights Seriously, 1st edn. Bloomsbury, London (2013)

Emmenegger, S., Tschentscher, A.: Taking nature's rights seriously: the long way to biocentrism in environmental law. Georgetown Int. Environ. Law Rev. **6**(3), 545–592 (1994)

Epiney, A.: Umweltrechtliche Querschnittsklausel und freier Warenverkehr: Die Einbeziehung umweltpolitischer Belange über die Beschränkung der Grundfreiheit. NuR, 497–504 (1995)

Epiney, A.: Umweltrecht der Europäische Union, 4th ed. Nomos, Baden-Baden (1997)

Epiney A (2018) Art. 11 TFEU. In: Vedder C, Heintschel von Heinegg W (eds) Europäisches Unionsrecht, 2nd ed. Nomos, Baden-Baden

Epiney, A.: Schwerpunkt: 20 Jahre Aarhus-Konvention. EurUP **17**(1), 2–17 (2019)

Epiney, A., et al.: Zur Berücksichtigung umweltpolitischer Belange bei der landwirtschaftlichen Produktion in der EU und in der Schweiz: ein Vergleich unter besonderer Berücksichtigung der Implikationen eines Freihandelsabkommens im Agrar- und Lebensmittelbereich. Schulthess Juristische Medien AG, Zürich (2009)

Epiney, A., Furrer, A.: Umweltschutz nach Maastricht – Ein Europa der drei Geschwindigkeiten? EuR, 369–408 (1992)

Fischer-Lescano, A.: Natur als Rechtsperson. ZUR **29**(4), 205–217 (2018)

Franzius, C.: Genügt die Novelle des Umwelt-Rechtsbehelfsgesetzes den unionsrechtlichen Vorgaben? NVwZ **37**(4), 219–222 (2018)

Franzius, C.: Der "Green Deal" in der Mehrebenenordnung. KlimR **1**(1), 2–5 (2022)

Frenz, W.: Handbuch Europarecht. Springer, Heidelberg (2011)

Frenz, W.: Klimaschutz nach BVerfG-Beschluss und EU-Klimagesetz. EnWZ **10**(6), 201–208 (2021)

Frenz, W.: EU-Klimagesetz. In: Frenz, W. (ed.) Klimaschutzrecht: EU-Klimagesetz, KSG Bund und NRW, BEHG, Steuerrecht Querschnittsthemen, Gesamtkommentar, 2nd ed. Erich Schmidt Verlag GmbH & Co. KG, Berlin (2022)

Füks, R.: Eröffnung. In: Baumeister, H. (ed.) Wege zum ökologischen Rechtsstaat. Umweltschutz ohne Öko-Diktatur, pp. 11–15. Blottner, Taunusstein (1994)

Gärditz, K.: Verwaltungsgerichtlicher Rechtsschutz im Umweltrecht. NVwZ **33**(1–2), 1–10 (2014)

Geraets, D., Reins, L.: EU einigt sich auf CBAM und EU-EHS-Reform. EnK-Aktuell **2**(1), 01010 (2023)

Götz, V.: Agrarumweltrecht der Europäischen Gemeinschaften. In: Rengeling, H.W. (ed.) Umweltschutz und andere Politiken der Europäischen Gemeinschaft, pp. 173–203. Carl Heymann, Köln, Berlin, Bonn, München (1993)

Grabitz, E.: Handlungsspielräume der EG-Mitgliedstaaten zur Verbesserung des Umweltschutzes – Das Beispiel der Umweltabgaben und Umweltsubventionen. In: Breuer, R. (ed.) Jahrbuch des Umwelt- und Technikrechts. E. Schmidt, Berlin (1989)

Graser, A.: Vermeintliche Fesseln der Demokratie: Warum die Klimaklagen ein vielversprechender Weg sind. ZUR **30**(5), 271–278 (2019)

Groß, T.: Die Ableitung von Klimaschutzmaßnahmen aus grundrechtlichen Schutzpflichten. NVwZ **39**(6), 337–342 (2020)

Guckelberger, A.: Aarhus-Konvention und Unionsrecht als Prägende Faktoren für die Verbandsklage im UmwRG. NuR **42**(3), 149–157 (2020)

Gutmann, A.: Pachamama als Rechtssubjekt? Rechte der Natur und indigenes Denken. ZUR **30**(11), 611–618 (2019)

Gutmann, A.: Hybride Rechtssubjektivität – Die Rechte der "Natur oder Pacha Mama" in der ecuadorianischen Verfassung von 2008, 1st ed. Nomos, Baden-Baden (2021)

Häberle, P.: Das Menschenbild im Verfassungsstaat. Duncker & Humblot, Berlin (1988)

Häde, U.: Art. 121 TFEU. In: Calliess, C., Ruffert, M. (eds.) EUV/EGV, 2nd edn. (2002)

Häde, U.: Art. 127 TFEU. In: Calliess, C., Ruffert, M. (eds.) EUV/AEUV, 6th edn. (2022)

Haigh, N., Kraemer, R.A.: "Sustainable Development" in den Verträgen der Europäischen Union. ZUR **11** (1996)

Hailbronner, K.: Stand und Perspektiven der EG-Umweltgesetzgebung. In: Calliess, C., Wegener, B. (eds.) Europäisches Umweltrecht als Chance: die Umweltpolitik der EG und die Einflussmöglichkeiten der Umweltverbände, pp. 15–28. Blottner, Taunusstein (1992)

Hayder, R.: Der Europäische Wirtschafts- und Sozialausschuss (EWSA) – eine unterschätzte EU-Institution. EuZW **21**(5), 171–176 (2010)

Heinz, H.: Die Problematik des Staatszieles Umweltschutz im Lichte der Unterscheidung von subjektiven Rechten und objektivem Recht. In: Heckmann, D., Meßerschmidt, K. (eds.) Gegenwartsfragen des Öffentlichen Rechts, pp. 181–212. Duncker & Humblot, Berlin (1988)

Hench, P., Herdieckerhoff, E.: Beitragsreihe Politische Maßnahmen: Was ist der Carbon Border Adjustment Mechanism – CBAM? EnK-Aktuell **1**(7), 01113 (2022)

Heselhaus, S.: Article 11 TFEU. In: Pechstein, M. et al. (eds.) Frankfurter Kommentar EUV/GRC/AEUV, pp. 90–110. Mohr Siebeck, Tübingen (2017)

Hillgruber, C.: Art. 1 GG. In: Epping, V., Hillgruber, C. (eds.) BeckOK Grundgesetz, 58th ed. Nomos (2024)

Hobe, S.: Menschenrecht auf Umweltschutz? Bestand und Begründungsmöglichkeiten. ZUR **1**, 15–19 (1994)

Intergovernmental Panel on Climate Change (IPCC) (2018) Global Warming of 1,5°C. See Summary for Policymakers. https://www.ipcc.ch/sr15/chapter/spm/. Accessed 25 Aug 2025

IPCC: Climate Change 2023 – Synthesis Report. A Summary for Policymakers (2023). https://www.ipcc.ch/report/ar6/syr/downloads/report/IPCC_AR6_SYR_SPM.pdf. Accessed 25 Aug 2025

Iraldo, F., Barberio, M.: Drivers, barriers and benefits of the EU ecolabel in European companies' perception. Sustainability **9**(5), 751 (2017). https://doi.org/10.3390/su9050751

Jacqué, J.P.: Art. 2 EUV. In: von der Groeben, H. et al. (eds.) Europäisches Unionsrecht, 7th ed. Nomos, Baden-Baden (2015)

Jahns-Böhm, J.: Umweltschutz durch europäisches Gemeinschaftsrecht am Beispiel der Luftreinhaltung. Duncker & Humblot, Berlin (1994)

Jahns-Böhm, J., Breier, S.: Die umweltrechtliche Querschnittsklausel des Art. 130 r II 2 EWGV. EuZW **2**, 49–55 (1992)

Johns, L.: Eigenrechte der Natur im internationalen Kontext. KlimR **2**(4), 98–103 (2023)

Kahl, W.: Umweltprinzip und Gemeinschaftsrecht. Müller, Heidelberg (1993)

Kahl, W.: Art. 11 TFEU. In: Streinz, R. (ed.) EUV/AEUV, 3rd ed. C.H. Beck, München (2018)

Kahl, W.: Klimaschutz und Grundrechte. Juristische Ausbildung **43**(2), 117–129 (2021)

Käller, A.: Art. 37 GRCh. In: Schwarze, J. et al. (ed.) EU-Kommentar, 2nd ed. Nomos, Baden-Baden (2009)

Käller, A.: Article 11 TFEU, para. 18. In: Schwarze, J. et al. (eds.) EU-Kommentar, 4th ed. Nomos, Baden-Baden

Karpen, U.: Zu einem Grundrecht auf Umweltschutz. In: Thieme, W. (ed.) Umweltschutz im Recht, pp. 9–24. Duncker & Humblot, Berlin (1988)

Kaufhold, A.K.: Grüne Geldpolitik. In: Kahl, W., Mager, U. (eds.) Verwaltungsaufgaben und Legitimation der Verwaltung, 1st ed. Nomos, Baden-Baden, pp. 135–166 (2022)

Kaufmann, C., Martin, P.: The Politics of Rights of Nature: Strategies for Building a More Sustainable Future. MIT Press (2021)

Kersten, J.: Die Rechte der Natur und die Verfassungsfrage des Anthropozäns. In: Soentgen, J. et al. (eds.) Umwelt und Gesundheit, 1st ed., pp. 87–120. Nomos, Baden-Baden (2020)
Kersten, J.: Natur als Rechtssubjekt. ApuZ **11**(2020), 27–32 (2020)
Kersten, J.: Das Ökologische Grundgesetz. C.H. Beck, München (2022)
Kingreen, T.: Art. 51 CFR. In: Calliess, C., Ruffert, M. (eds.) EUV/AEUV, 6th edn. (2022)
Klinger, R.: Klagerecht von Umweltverbänden gegen Verschlechterung des Zustands von Wasserkörpern. NVwZ **37**(4), 231–232 (2018)
Klinger, R.: Ein Grundrecht auf Umweltschutz. Jetzt. ZUR **32**(5), 257–258 (2021)
Kloepfer, M.: Zum Grundrecht auf Umweltschutz. Lecture given to the Berlin Law Society (Juristische Gesellschaft) on 18 January 1978, Berlin/New York (1978)
Kloepfer, M.: Umweltschutz als Aufgabe des Zivilrechts – aus öffentlich-rechtlicher Sicht. Jahrbuch des Umwelt- und Technikrechts 1990. E. Schmidt, Berlin (1990)
Kloepfer, M.: Zu den neuen umweltrechtlichen Handlungsformen des Staates. JZ **46**(15–16), 737–744 (1991)
Kloepfer, M.: Langzeitverantwortung im Bundesstaat. In: Gethmann, C. et al. (eds.) Langzeitverantwortung im Umweltstaat, pp. 22–41. Economica, Bonn (1993)
Kloepfer, M.: Das Ladenburger Kolleg Umweltstaat – Resultate und Perspektiven. In: Kloepfer, M. (ed.) Umweltstaat als Zukunft – Studien zum Umweltstaat, pp. 3–40. Economica, Bonn (1994)
Kloepfer, M.: Interdisziplinäre Aspekte des Umweltstaats. DVBl **12** (1994)
Kloepfer, M.: Anthropozentrik, Freiheit und Umweltschutz in rechtlicher Sicht (1995). Economica Verlag, Bonn
Kloepfer, M., et al.: AK Europäische Umweltunion. NuR **346** (1994)
Kment, M., Lorenz, C.: Eckpfeiler des deutschen Verwaltungsrechts auf europäischem Prüfstand. EurUP **14**(1), 47–57 (2016)
Köck, W.: Umweltrechtsentwicklung und ökonomische Analyse. NuR **12**, 412–420 (1992)
Köck, W.: Das Vorsorgeprinzip im Umweltrecht. In: Köck, W. et al. (eds.) Zukunftsfähiges Umweltrecht I: Umweltrecht im Anthropozän – Das Vorsorgeprinzip vor neuen Herausforderungen, pp. 69–98. Nomos, Baden-Baden (2023)
Köck, W., Henn, E.: Die Rechte der Wasserversorger bei der Grundwasserressourcenbewirtschaftung. NVwZ **39**(8), 504–511 (2020)
Köck, W., Markus, T.: 30 Jahre "Robbenklage": on the relevance of rights of nature. ZUR **29**(4), 193–194 (2018)
Köck, W., Markus, T.: Der europäische "Green Deal" – Auf dem Weg zu einem EU-"Klimagesetz." ZUR **31**(5), 257–258 (2020)
Kokott, J., Sobotta, C.: Rechtsschutz im Umweltrecht – Weichenstellungen in der Rechtsprechung des Gerichtshofs der Europäischen Union. DVBl **3**, 132–137 (2014)
Kotzur, M.: Die Ziele der Union: Verfassungsidentität und Gemeinschaftsidee. DÖV **8**, 313–322 (2005)
Krämer, L.: Grundrecht auf Umwelt und Gemeinschaftsrecht. EuGRZ **15**(11), 285–294 (1988)
Krämer, L.: Die Integrierung umweltpolitischer Erfordernisse in die gemeinschaftliche Wettbewerbspolitik. In: Rengeling, H.W. (ed.) Umweltschutz und andere Politiken der Europäischen Gemeinschaft, pp. 47–83. Carl Heymann, Köln, Berlin, Bonn (1993)
Krämer, L.: EC Treaty and Environmental Law. Sweet & Maxwell, London (1996)
Krämer, L.: Giving a voice to the environment by challenging the practice of integrating environmental requirements into other EU policies. In: Kingston, S. (ed.) European Perspectives on Environmental Law and Governance, 1st edn., pp. 83–101. Routledge, Londo (2013)
Krämer, L.: Article 11 TFEU. In: von der Groeben, H., et al. (eds.) Europäisches Unionsrecht, 7th edn. Nomos, Baden-Baden (2015)
Krämer, L.: Planning for climate and the environment: the European green deal. JEEPL **17**(3), 267–306 (2020)

Krämer, L.: Rights of nature and their implementation. JEEPL **17**(1), 47–75 (2020)
Krämer, L.: Rights of nature in Europe: the Spanish Lagoon Mar Menor becomes a legal person. JEEPL **20**(1), 5–23 (2023)
Kuhlmann, H.: Der Mittelweltschutz im gesamtdeutschen Grundgesetz. NuR, 1–10 (1995)
Leimbacher, J.: Die Rechte der Natur. Helbing u. Lichtenhahn, Basel (1988)
Lösch, H.: Smart Deal – Klimapolitik in Krisenzeiten neu denken. In: Schmidt, C., et al. European Green Deal – Bottlenecks bis 2030, ifo Schnelldienst 6/2020, pp. 32–34 (2020). https://t1p.de/akkkk. Accessed 25 Aug 2025
Lübbe, A.: Tagungsbericht: Ladenburger Kolleg “Umweltstaat.” ZUR **1994**, 42 (1994)
Lücke, J.: Das Grundrecht des einzelnen gegenüber dem Staat auf Umweltschutz. DÖV:289 et seq (1976)
Macrory, R.: The enforcement of community environmental laws: some critical issues. Common Market Law Rev. **29**(2), 347–369 (1992)
Mailänder, M.: CO2-Grenzausgleichsmechanismus – Hintergründe des CBAM als neuer “Klimazoll” und Herausforderungen für Unternehmen in 2023. EnK-Aktuell **2**(2), 01028 (2023)
Marin Durán, G., Morgera, E.: Environmental Integration in the EU’s External Relations: Beyond multilateral dimensions. Hart Publishing, Oxford, Portland (2012)
Marrucci, L., et al.: Investigating the management challenges of the EU Ecolabel through multistakeholder surveys. Int. J. Life Cycle Assess. **26**, 575–590 (2021)
Martens, M.: Voice or loyalty? The evolution of the European environment agency (EEA). JCMS **48**(4), 881–901 (2010)
Mehrländer, H.: (1993) In: Rengeling, H.W. (ed.) Umweltschutz und andere Politiken der Europäischen Gemeinschaft, pp. 35–46. Carl Heymann, Köln, Berlin, Bonn (1993)
Meyer, S.: Grundrechtsschutz in Sachen Klimawandel? NJW **73**(21), 894–902 (2020)
Meyer, S., Hoffmann, C.: Die grüne Transformation des europäischen Beihilferechts. EuZW **34**(9), 413–417 (2023)
Momsen, C., Sandbrink, A.: Umweltschutz und Klimaschutz – Der “Europäische Grüne Deal”. ZRP **56**(3), 76–79 (2023)
Monien, J.: Prinzipien als Wegbereiter eines globalen Umweltrechts? Nomos, Baden-Baden (2013)
Mührel, J.: Welche Natur? ZUR **33**(9), 464–472 (2022)
Müller-Bromley, N.: Staatszielbestimmung Umweltschutz im Grundgesetz? E. Schmidt, Berlin (1990)
Murswiek, D.: Die Staatliche Verantwortung für die Risiken der Technik. Duncker & Humblot, Berlin (1985)
Murswiek, D.: Die heimliche Entwicklung des Unionsvertrages zur europäischen Oberverfassung – Zu den Konsequenzen der Auflösung der Säulenstruktur der Europäischen. NVwZ **28**(8), 481–486 (2009)
Murswiek, D.: Art. 20a. In: Sachs, M. (ed.) GG, 9th edn. C.H. Beck, München (2021)
Murswiek, D., Rixen, S.: Art. 2. In: Sachs, M. (ed.) GG, 8th edn. C.H. Beck, München (2018)
Nees, D.: Klimaschutz durch die EZB? Reichweite und Grenzen des Mandats der EZB in Bezug auf den Erwerb sogenannter “grüner” Anleihe. EuR **56**(2), 119–137 (2021)
Nettesheim, M.: Art. 11 TFEU. In: Grabitz, E., et al. (eds.) Das Recht der Europäischen Union, 78th supplement January 2023 (2023)
Nettesheim, M.: Art. 11 TFEU, para. 26. In: Grabitz, E., et al. (eds.) Das Recht der Europäischen Union, 81st supplement January 2024 (2024)
Pernice, I.: Rechtlicher Rahmen der europäischen Unternehmenskooperation im Umweltbereich unter besonderer Berücksichtigung von Art. 85 EWGV. EuZW, 139–143 (1992)
Pernthaler, P.: Reform der Bundesverfassung in Sinne des ökologischen Prinzips. In: Pernthaler, P., et al. (eds.) Umweltpolitik durch Recht – Möglichkeiten und Grenzen, pp. 1–48. Manz, Wien (1992)

Petersen, L.: Zwischen Mythos und Misere: Die amerikanische Umweltbehörde EPA. KJ **26**(3), 351–364 (1993)
Priebe, R.: Agenturen der Europäischen Union – Europäische Verwaltung durch eigenständige Behörden. EuZW **26**(7), 268–273 (2015)
Rauschning, D.: Staatsaufgabe Umweltschutz. In: VVDStRL. De Gruyter, **38**, 168–385 (1980)
Reese, M.: Leitbilder des Umweltrechts – Zur Zukunftsfähigkeit leitender Schutzkonzepte. ZUR **21**(7–8), 339–346 (2010)
Reese, M.: Das EU-Klimagesetz – Nachhaltigkeit durch Umweltpolitikplanungsrecht? ZUR **30**(12), 641–642 (2020)
Rehbinder, E.: Grenzen und Chancen einer ökologischen Umorientierung des Rechts. IKO-Verlag, Frankfurt (1989)
Rengeling, H.W.: Bedeutung und Anwendbarkeit des Vorsorgeprinzips im europäischen Umweltrecht. DVBl **20**, 1473–1483 (2000)
Rest, A.: Europäischer Menschenrechtsschutz als verbesserter Katalysator für ein verbessertes Umweltrecht. NuR **209** (1997)
Ritter, E.H.: Von den Schwierigkeiten des Rechts mit der Ökologie. DÖV **45**, 641–649 (1992)
Rockström, J., et al.: A safe operating space for humanity. Nature **461**, 472–475 (2009). https://doi.org/10.1038/461472a
Ruffert, M.: Subjektive Rechte im Umweltrecht der Europäischen Gemeinschaft – unter besonderer Berücksichtigung ihrer prozessualen Durchsetzung. V. Decker, Heidelberg (1996)
Ruffert, M.: Umweltrechtsschutz ohne methodische Grundlage? – Zur neueren Rechtsprechung des EuGH und ihren Folgen für Deutschland. DVBl **16**, 1033–1040 (2019)
Ruffert, M.: Schlußwort: Umweltrechtsbehelfe, europarechtliche Methoden und Kompetenzen. DVBl **5**, 309–311 (2021)
Runge, T.: Zehn Jahre Umweltinformationsmanagement für Europa – die Tätigkeit der Europäischen Umweltagentur. DVBl **9**, 542–551 (2005)
Sauer, M.: Rechtsschutz in Umweltangelegenheiten im Umbruch? ZUR **25**(4), 195–202 (2014)
Saurer, J.: Klimaschutz global, europäisch, national – Was ist rechtlich verbindlich? NVwZ **36**(21), 1574–1579 (2017)
Schellnhuber, H.J.: Discourse: earth system analysis – the scope of the challenge. In: Schellnhuber, H.J., Wenzel, V. (eds.) Earth System Analysis. Springer, Heidelberg (1998)
Scherer, J., Heselhaus, S.: O. Umweltrecht. In: Dauses, M., Ludwigs, M. (eds.) Handbuch des EU-Wirtschaftsrechts, 43th Supplement, C.H. Beck (2017)
Scheuing, D.: Umweltschutz auf der Grundlage der Einheitlichen Europäischen Akte. EuR **34**(3), 152–192 (1989)
Scheyli, M.: Die Aarhus-Konvention über Informationszugang, Öffentlichkeitsbeteiligung und Rechtsschutz in Umweltbelangen. AVR **38**(2), 217–252 (2000)
Schlacke, S.: Überindividueller Rechtsschutz. Mohr Siebeck, Tübingen (2008)
Schlacke, S.: European Green Deal – Bottleneck bis 2030 – eine rechtswissenschaftliche Perspektive. In: Schmidt, C., et al. (2020) European Green Deal – Bottlenecks bis 2030, pp. 28–31. ifo Schnelldienst 6/2020 (2020). https://t1p.de/akkkk. Accessed 25 Aug 2025
Schlacke, S., et al.: Das "Europäische Klimagesetz" und seine Konsequenzen. EuZW **32**(14), 620–626 (2021)
Schmidt, C.: Globale Klimapolitik: Welchen Beitrag sollten Deutschland und Europa leisten. In: Schmidt C., et al (2020) European Green Deal – Bottlenecks bis 2030, pp. 3–6. ifo Schnelldienst 6/2020 (2020). https://t1p.de/akkkk. Accessed 25 Aug 2025
Schmidt, R.: Einführung in das Umweltrecht, 5th edn. C.H. Beck, München (1999)
Schmidt-Radefeldt, R.: Ökologische Menschenrechte – Ökologische Menschenrechtsinterpretation der EMRK und ihre Bedeutung für die umweltschützenden Grundrechte des Grundgesetzes, 1st edn. Nomos, Baden-Baden (2000)

Schmitz, S.: Die EU als Umweltunion: Entwicklung, Stand und Grenzen der Umweltschutzkompetenzen der EU. Rhombos, Berlin (1996)
Schomerus, T.: Ein Ombudsmann mit Klagebefugnis statt Verbandsklage im Naturschutzrecht? NuR **11**(4), 171–175 (1989)
Schorkopf, F.: Art. 6 TEU. In: Grabitz, E., et al. (eds.) Das Recht der Europäischen Union, 81 supplement. C.H. Beck, München (2024)
Schröter, M., Bosselmann, K.: Die Robbenklage im Lichte der Nachhaltigkeit. ZUR **29**(4), 195–205 (2018)
Schuelken, T., Sichla, B.: Das Europäische Klimagesetz – Inhalt, Rechtsfragen und Ausblick. UPR **1** (2021)
Schulte, D.: Article 12 TFEU. In: von der Groeben, H., et al. (eds.) Europäisches Unionsrecht,7th ed. Nomos, Baden-Baden (2015)
Sendler, H.: Grundprobleme des Umweltrechts. JuS:255 (1983)
Siegel, T.: Die Präklusion im europäisierten Verwaltungsrecht. NVwZ **35**(6), 337–342 (2016)
Sobotta, C.: New cases on article 9 of the Aarhus convention. JEEPL **15**(2), 241–258 (2018)
Soell, H.: Umweltschutz, ein Grundrecht? NuR **205** (1985)
Sommermann, K.P.: Staatsziele und Staatszielbestimmungen. Mohr Siebeck, Tübingen (1997)
SRU: Fischbestände nachhaltig bewirtschaften – Zur Reform der Gemeinsamen Fischereipolitik. Stellungnahme No. 16 (2011). https://t1p.de/pw52x. Accessed 25 Aug 2025
SRU: Democratic government within environmental limits – on the legitimation of environmental policy (2019a). https://t1p.de/y2qh3. Accessed 25 Aug 2025
SRU: Demokratisch regieren in ökologischen Grenzen – Zur Legitimation von Umweltpolitik (2019b). https://t1p.de/iq7k2. Accessed 25 Aug 2025
SRU: The historical development of European environmental policy. In: SRU (2020) Environmental report 2020. The future of European environmental policy, pp. 7–8 (2020a). https://t1p.de/ys9y7. Accessed 20 Aug 2025
SRU: Environmental Report 2020. Towards an ambitious environmental policy in Germany and Europe (2020b). https://t1p.de/l89p3. Accessed 25 Aug 2025
SRU: Die Zukunft der europäischen Umweltpolitik. In: SRU (2020) Umweltgutachten 2020: Für eine entschlossene Umweltpolitik in Deutschland und Europa, pp. 469–521 (2020c). https://t1p.de/a0zl. Accessed 25 Aug 2025
SRU: WBBGR Für einen flächenwirksamen Insektenschutz – Stellungnahme (2018). https://t1p.de/vumn5. Accessed 25 Aug 2025
Steffen, W., et al.: Planetary boundaries: Guiding human development on a changing planet. Science **347**, 1259855 (2015). https://doi.org/10.1126/science.1259855
Steiger, H.: Mensch und Umwelt: Zur Frage der Einführung eines Umweltgrundrechts. E. Schmidt, Berlin (1975)
Steinberg, R.: Der ökologische Verfassungsstaat. Suhrkamp, Frankfurt (1998)
Stone, C.: Should trees have standing? toward legal rights for natural objects. Southern California Law Rev. **45**, 450–501 (1972)
Stone, C.: Umwelt vor Gericht. Trickster Verlag, München (1992)
Streinz, R.: Art. 2 EGV. In: Streinz, R. (ed.) EUV/EGV, 1st edn. C.H. Beck, München (2003)
Stroetmann, C.: Introduction. In: Rengeling, H.W. (ed.) Umweltschutz und andere Politiken der EG, pp. 1–14. Carl Heymanns (1993)
Suhr, O.: Art. 301–304 TFEU. In: Calliess, C., Ruffert, M. (eds.) AEUV/EUV, 6th edn. (2022)
Taylor, P.: International Human Rights and the Environment. In: Bosselmann, K. (ed.) Ökologische Grundrechte, pp. 234–334. Nomos, Baden-Baden (1998)
Terhechte, J.: Art. 3 EUV. In: Grabitz, E., et al. (eds.) Das Recht der Europäischen Union. C.H. Beck, München (2021)
Terhechte, J.: Präambel EUV. In: Grabitz, E., et al. (eds.) Das Recht der Europäischen Union. C.H. Beck, München (2021)

Trennt, M., Ulke, S.: Das CO2-Grenzausgleichssystem (CBAM). EuZW **34**(10), 452–460 (2023)
Tribe, L.H.: Was spricht gegen Plastikbäume? In: Birnbacher, D. (ed.) Ökologie und Ethik, pp. 20–71. Reclam, Stuttgart (1980)
Uhle, A.: Das Staatsziel "Umweltschutz" im System der grundgesetzlichen Ordnung – Zu dem von der Verfassungskommission empfohlenen neuen Art. 20 a GG. DÖV, 947–954 (1993)
von Bogdandy, A., et al.: Ein Rettungsschirm für europäische Grundrechte – Grundlagen einer unionsrechtlichen Solange-Doktrin gegenüber Mitgliedstaaten. ZaöRV **72**, 45–78 (2012)
von Lersner, H.: Gibt es Eigenrechte der Natur? NVwZ **7**(11), 988–992 (1988)
von Lersner, H.: In: Calliess, C., Wegener, B. (eds.) Europäisches Umweltrecht als Chance: Die Umweltpolitik der EG und die Einflussmöglichkeiten der Umweltverbände, pp. 81–89. Blottner Verlag, Taunusstein (1992)
von Schirach, F.: Jeder Mensch, 1st edn. Luchterhand, München (2021)
Waechter, K.: Umweltschutz als Staatsziel. NuR:321 et seq (1996)
Wägenbaur, B.: Europa-Report. EuZW **642** (1997)
Wegener, B.: Zukunftsfähigkeit des europäischen Umweltrechts. ZUR **20**(10), 459–464 (2009)
Wegener, B.: Der Braunbär lernt schwimmen – Die "Protect"-Entscheidung des EuGH stärkt den Rechtsschutz im Umweltrecht. ZUR **29**(4), 217–222 (2018)
Wegener, B.: Urgenda – Weltrettung per Gerichtsbeschluss? ZUR **30**(1), 3–13 (2019)
Weidemann, A.: Die Bedeutung der Querschnittsklauseln für die Kompetenzen innerhalb der europäischen Gemeinschaft aus deutscher Sicht. Peter Lang, Frankfurt, Berlin (2007)
Wiegand, B.: Bestmöglicher Umweltschutz als Aufgabe der Europäischen Gemeinschaften. DVBl **10**, 533–543 (1993)
Wilkinson, D.: Maastricht and the environment: the implications for the EC's environment policy of the treaty on European union. J. Environ. Law **4**(2), 221–239 (1992)
Winter, G.: Armando Carvalho et alii versus Europäische Union: Rechtsdogmatische und staatstheoretische Probleme einer Klimaklage vor dem Europäischen Gericht. ZUR **30**(5), 259–271 (2019)
Wittinger, M.: "Europäische Satelliten": Anmerkungen zum Europäischen Agentur(un)wesen und zur Vereinbarkeit Europäischer Agenturen mit dem Gemeinschaftsrecht. EuR **43**(5), 609–627 (2008)
Wolf, R.: Der ökologische Rechtsstaat als prozedurales Programm. In: Roßnagel, A., Neuser, U. (eds.) Reformperspektiven im Umweltrecht – Dokumentation der "Haydauer Hochschul-Gespräche 1995", 1st edn., pp. 57–95 Nomos, Baden-Baden (1996)
Wolf, R.: Eigenrechte der Natur oder Rechtsschutz für intertemporalen Freiheitsschutz? ZUR **33**(9), 451–464 (2022)

Cases

BVerfGE judgement of 9.2.2010 - 1 BvL 1/09, ECLI:DE:BVerfG:2010:ls20100209.1bvl000109
BVerfG, judgement of 24.3.2021 - 1 BvR 2656/18, ECLI:DE:BVerfG:2021:rs20210324.1bvr265618
ECJ: ECJ, C-379/98, PreussenElektra AG v Schhleswag AG, in the presence of Windpark Reußenköge III GmbH and Land Schleswig-Holstein (2000), ECLI:EU:C:2000:585
ECJ: ECJ, C-513/99, Concordia Bus Finland Oy Ab, formerly Stagecoach Finland Oy Ab v Helsingin kaupunki and HKL-Bussiliikenne (2002). ECLI:EU:C:2002:495
ECJ: ECJ, C-752/18, Deutsche Umwelthilfe eV v Freistaat Bayern (2019). ECLI:EU:C:2019:1114
ECtHR, Judgment of 9.12.1994, López Ostra v. Spain, No. 16798/90
ECtHR, Judgment of 19.2.1998, Guerra and others v. Italy, No. 14967/89
VG Berlin, judgement of 31.10.2019, 10K 412.18, ZUR **31**(3), 160–170 (2019)

EU Documents

COM: 1 final, Communication from the Commission on the precautionary principle, 2.2.2020 (2000)

COM: 12, Communication from the Commission to the European Parliament, the Council, the European Central Bank, The Economic and Social Committee, the Committee of the Regions and the European Investment Bank. Making the best use of the flexibility within the existing rules of the stability and growth pact, 13.1.2015 (2015)

COM: 316 final, Communication from the Commission to the European Parliament, the Council, the European Economic and Social Committee and the Committee of the Regions. Delivering the benefits of EU environmental policies through a regular Environmental Implementation Review, 27.6.2016 (2016)

COM: 739 final, Communication from the Commission to the European Parliament, the Council, the European Economic and Social Committee and the Committee of the Regions. Next steps for a sustainable European future: European Union action for sustainability, 22.11.2016 (2016)

COM: 10 final, Communication from the Commission to the European Parliament, the Council, the European Economic and Social Committee and the Committee of the Regions. EU actions to improve environmental compliance and governance, 18.1.2018 (2018)

COM: 22, Reflection Paper: Towards a sustainable Europe by 2030, 30.1.2019 (2019)

COM: 149 final, Communication from the Commission to the European Parliament, the Council, the European Economic and Social Committee and the Committee of the Regions. Environmental Implementation Review: A Europe that protects its citizens and enhances their quality of life, 4.4.2019 (2019)

COM: 640 final, Annex to the Communication from the Commission to the European Parliament, the Council, the European Economic and Social Committee and the Committee of the Regions, The European Green Deal, 11.12.2019 (2019)

COM: 650 final, Communication from the Commission to the European Parliament, the Council, the European Central Bank, the European Economic and Social Committee, the Committee of the Regions and the European Investment Bank, Annual Sustainable Growth Strategy 2020,17.12.2019 (2019)

COM: 102 final, Communication from the Commission to the European Parliament, the European Council, the Council, the European Economic and Social Committee and the Committee of the Regions,. A New Industrial Strategy for Europe, 10.3.2020 (2020)

COM: 98 final, Communication from the Commission to the European Parliament, the Council, the European Economic and Social Committee and the Committee of the Regions. A new Circular Economy Action Plan. For a cleaner and more competitive Europe, 11.3.2020 (2020)

COM: 380 final, Communication for the Commission to the European Parliament, the Council, the European Economic and Social Committee and the Committee of the Regions, EU Biodiversity Strategy for 2030. Bringing nature back into our lives, 20.5.2020 (2020)

COM: 381 final, Communication for the Commission to the European Parliament, the Council, the European Economic and Social Committee and the Committee of the Regions, A Farm to Fork Strategy for a fair, healthy and environmentally-friendly food system, 20.5.2020 (2020)

COM: 662 final, Communication from the Commission to the European Parliament, the Council, the European Economic and Social Committee and the Committee of the Regions. A Renovation Wave for Europe - greening our buildings, creating jobs, improving lives, 14.10.2020 (2020)

COM: 350 final, Communication from the Commission to the European Parliament, the Council, the European Economic and Social Committee and the Committee of the Regions, Updating the 2020 Industrial Strategy: Building a stronger Single Market for Europe's recovery, 5.5.2021 (2021)

COM: 550 final, Communication for the Commission to the European Parliament, the Council, the European Economic and Social Committee and the Committee of the Regions. 'Fit for 55': delivering the EU's 2030 Climate Target on the way to climate neutrality, 14.7.2021 (2021)
COM: 563 final, Proposal for a Council Directive restructuring the Union framework for the taxation of energy products and electricity, 14.7.2021 (2021)
COM: 357 final, Communication from the Commission to the European Parliament, the Council, the European Economic and Social Committee and the Committee of the Regions on the monitoring framework for the 8th Environment Action Programme: Measuring progress towards the attainment of the Programme's 2030 and 2050 priority objectives, 26.7.2022 (2022)
COM: 438 final, Communication from the Commission to the European Parliament, the Council, the European Economic and Social Committee and the Committee of the Regions. Environmental Implementation Review 2022: Turning the tide through environmental compliance, 8.9.2022 (2022)
COM: 102 final, Communication to the European Parliament, the Council, the European Economic and Social Committee and the Committee of the Regions, EU Action Plan: Protecting and restoring marine ecosystems for sustainable and resilient fisheries, 21.2.2023 (2023)
COM: 3445 final, Annex to the Communication from the Commission, Approval of the content of a draft for a Communication from the Commission, Guidelines on the applicability of Article 101 of the Treaty on the Functioning of the European Union to horizontal cooperation agreement, 1.6.2023 (2023)
COM: 123 final, Report from the Commission to the European Parliament, the Council, the European Economic and Social Committee and the Committee of the Regions, on the 8th Environment Action Programme Mid-Term Review, 13.3.2024 (2024)
European Central Bank: ECB climate agenda 2022 (2022). https://t1p.de/9d9ts. Accessed 25 Aug 2025
European Central Bank: Climate and Nature Plan 2024–2025. https://t1p.de/nfr32. Accessed 25 Aug 2025 (2024)
European Commission: Press remarks by President von der Leyen on the occasion of the adoption of the European Green Deal Communication. Brussels, 11.12.2019, SPEECH/19/6749 (2019)
European Commission: The European Green Deal sets out how to make Europe the first climate-neutral continent by 2050, boosting the economy, improving people's health and quality of life, caring for nature, and leaving no one behind, Press Release, 11.12.2019 (2019a). https://t1p.de/79lxk. Accessed 20 Aug 2025
European Commission: The post-2020 Common Agricultural Policy: Environmental Benefits and Simplification (2019b). https://t1p.de/x9lty. Accessed 25 Aug 2025
European Commission: Fit for 55: Delivering on the proposals (2021a). https://t1p.de/f14id. Accessed 25 Aug 2025
European Commission: Sustainable & Smart Mobility Strategy: Putting European transport on track for the future, 20.07.2021 (2021b). https://transport.ec.europa.eu/document/download/be22d311-4a07-4c29-8b72-d6d255846069_en?filename=2021-mobility-strategy-and-action-plan.pdf. Accessed 25 Aug 2025
European Commission: EU Ecolabel key figures (2023). https://t1p.de/0ti90. Accessed 25 Aug 2025
European Commission: State aid: Commission updates guidance for measures to support the green transition. Press Release, 3.4.2023 (2023). https://ec.europa.eu/commission/presscorner/detail/en/ip_23_2090. Accessed 25 Aug 2025
European Council: A new strategic agenda for the EU 2019–2024 (2019). https://t1p.de/0ti90. Accessed 25 Aug 2025
EEA: The European environment – state and outlook 2020. Executive summary (2019). https://t1p.de/c1xlr. Accessed 25 Aug 2025

EEA: European Union 8th Environment Action Programme. Monitoring report on progress towards the 8th EAP objectives (2023). https://t1p.de/r2chq. Accessed 25 Aug 2025

European Environmental Bureau: White Paper of European Environmental Associations. EU Internal Market and Environment, Brussels (1991)

European Parliament: The European Parliament declares climate emergency, Press Release, 29.11.2019 (2019a). https://www.europarl.europa.eu/news/en/press-room/20191121IPR67110/the-european-parliament-declares-climate-emergency. Accessed 25 Aug 2025

European Parliament: Directorate-General for External Policies – Policy Department, Study, Europe's approach to implementing the Sustainable Development Goals: good practices and the way forward (2019b). https://t1p.de/p0aa3. Accessed 25 Aug 2025

Opinion No. 7/2018 (pursuant to Article 322(1)(a) TFEU) concerning Commission proposals for regulations relating to the common agricultural policy for the post-2020 period, COM(2018) 392, 393 and 394 final, (OJ C, C/41, 01.02.2019, p. 1. https://op.europa.eu/en/publication-detail/-/publication/6b6b2b8c-25b3-11e9-8d04-01aa75ed71a1/language-en. Accessed 25 Aug 2025

Others

CESE (Conseil économique social et environnemental): L'Histoire du CESE (2020). https://www.lecese.fr/decouvrir-cese/historique. Accessed 25 Aug 2025

Evans, R.: What if whales took us to court? A move to grant them legal personhood would include the right to sue. Greenpeace, 15.04.2024 (2024). https://www.greenpeace.org/aotearoa/story/whales-legal-personhood-would-include-right-to-sue/. Accessed 24 Aug 2025

Foundation, H.B., et al.: Agrar-Atlas 2019 – Daten und Fakten zur EU-Landwirtschaft (2019)

Murswiek, D.: Auf dem Weg zu einem ökologischen Recht? In FAZ from 26.10.1992, p. 38 (1992)

Packroff, J., Kurmayer, N.: Energy Taxation Directive: Europe's key climate law stuck in a quagmire. Euractiv, 20.05.2023 (2023). https://t1p.de/4lj8f. Accessed 25 Aug 2025

Schacht, K., et al.: 5-year review (2014–2019) of the EU Common Fisheries Policy. Deutsche Umwelthilfe, Bundesamt für Naturschutz (2019). https://t1p.de/lnl3w. Accessed 25 Aug 2025

von der Leyen, U.: Eine Union, die mehr erreichen will – Meine Agenda für Europa. Politische Leitlinien für die künftige Europäische Kommission 2019–2024. Brüssel: Europäische Kommission (2019). https://t1p.de/vtbju. Accessed 25 Aug 2025

National Climate Framework Laws in Europe - How Do They Relate to National Ownership?

Delphine Misonne(✉)

UCLouvain Saint-Louis Brussels, Brussels, Belgium
delphine.misonne@uclouvain.be

Abstract. The contribution reflects on the importance and specificities of law-making on the climate challenge at the level of Member States, in the specific context of today and in due regard of the new legislative developments and targets adopted by the European Union. It discusses the possible appraisals and declinations of ownership in relation to the climate challenge. It also observes how the content of climate laws has recently evolved in Europe and tries to explain the reasons but also consequences of the quite large margin of appreciation left to Member States on the very question of adopting new laws and possibly new targets at their own level on the climate challenge.

1 Introduction

The present contribution discusses national framework climate laws in the European Union in the context of today[1] through the prism of "ownership" of the climate challenges by individual States. It also observes how the structure and content of national climate framework laws are evolving, together with the transformation of ideas and priorities.

How do you "own" the climate challenge and say, as a State, "this is mine and I will run for it"? And why is this question focused on the national level, in a European Union (EU) where lawyers tend rather to discuss the need for new harmonization measures, to assess the *implement*ation of secondary law and to highlight the trumps and inadequacies of primary law?

The chosen entry route in the subject matter is related to the novel features of the recent collective commitments on climate issues, either at global or European levels. In each of these arenas, policy-making tends to entrust "Parties" or "Member States" – the national level – with the responsibility to decide at their own level on their own ambition – even if more indications were given recently at EU level –, but also on the way to anchor such ambition in their own legal regime.

One hypothesis we would like to discuss here is whether the climate challenge might be better "owned" at national level when it is framed through a set of coherent legislative provisions, in a "framework law" installing dedicated governance dynamics. Answers will vary according to the degree of foreseeability, performance, inclusivity, objectivity and transparency a sovereign State wants to dedicate to the climate challenge, in due respect of the supranational collective goals and related procedural requirements.

[1] March 2024.

M. Reese et al. (Eds.): EELF 2023, *Legal Implementation and Impacts of the European Green Deal*, pp. 56–70, 2026.
https://doi.org/10.1007/978-3-032-17197-9_2

The contribution is structured in two parts. First, the contribution explores contextual elements showing how climate and regulation intersected in Europe in the recent years, in a changing atmosphere, made of trust but also distrust in the very need to regulate on climate issues. Second, the contribution observes the current offer of framework climate laws on various national scenes in Europe and they possibly build or show national ownership, from a lawyer's point of view, not so much around targets setting but most importantly on better governance issues.

2 Setting the Scene

2.1 Trust in Regulation

2.1.1 National Framework Climate Acts as Pioneering Approaches (from 2008 Onwards)

Where the reader might expect an analysis drawing links between the "sky" (new EU harmonized measures) and the "bottom" (how are they applied or translated, where applicable, at Member State level), the history of the adoption of framework climate laws at national level do – to a certain degree – justify a less classical approach.

The first framework climate law in Europe surged in the United Kingdom, in 2008[2], at a time where the UK was still a Member of the European Union but also at a time where discussions were still raging of the future of the Kyoto Protocol and when the negotiation of the Paris Agreement was not even pointing on the horizon. A true pioneer moment, emanating from suggestions made by civil society, the initiative was meant to meet the challenge of providing direction, clarity but also consensus in society around the future of climate policies at a broad economy-wide level. Most importantly, it transformed the governance of the climate challenge in a comprehensive manner, by setting a long-term emission goal and requiring the identification of interim targets, translated into five-year carbon budgets. It imposed new accountability mechanisms benefiting from the support of a new independent Climate Change Committee with advisory and monitoring powers on climate governance at UK-economy wide level[3]. The Committee is mandated to advise the government and devolved governments on emissions targets and to report in Parliament on progress made by competent authorities. It regularly publishes letters to the public authorities with its recommendations on climate change policies.

The broader dissemination of the new concept (the statutory incorporation of a long-term transformation of society, trajectories based upon the notion of carbon budget) became one of the recurring requests of climate protesters or associations initiating legal actions in the climate field.

As observed by the OECD, the UK Act soon "served as a model for the development of climate legislation in a number of countries, including Denmark, France, Germany, Ireland, Mexico, New Zealand and Sweden. The specifics of these laws vary between countries, but in all cases the laws involve setting interim targets on the pathway to a long-term goal and independent evidence-based advice"[4].

---

2 Climate Change Act 2008. See Macrory R (2012); Stallworthy M (2009).

3 https://www.theccc.org.uk.

4 OECD (2021). See also Averchenkova et al. (2017); Scotford E and Minas S (2019); Nash S and Steurer R (2019).

2.1.2 The EU Climate Law (2021)

In the meantime, States did also manage to revitalize the way they wanted to cooperate on the climate challenge at the global level, with the Paris Agreement, its collective goals and procedural obligations to produce regularly updated nationally determined contributions – a decision taken at Party level in due consideration of its own specificities and capacities.

The European Union took some years to profile itself but did it *urbi and orbi* in 2019 with its proposal for a *Green Deal*, initiated as a main promise and project for the new Commission "We want to be the first climate neutral continent by 2050"), at a pivotal moment where revendications and protests in the streets – by young people in particular – were clearly expressing an expectation for States to do much more on the climate urgency. Two years later, in 2021 – and with the COVID-crisis in between –, in order to better convince both the word outside and the world inside (not all Member States were fully aligned on the new societal project), the European Union enshrined its own new long-term collective target on emissions mitigation in a new "*European Climate Law*" in 2021, based upon the environmental chapter of the Treaty: a long-term binding collective target of climate neutrality and a harmonized mi-term target of -55% by 2030 by comparison to 1990.

The European Climate "law" is a strange name for a Regulation.[5] One might certainly see there another emanation of the template pioneered in the United Kingdom more than a decade earlier (long-term targets, mid-term targets, independent bodies, trajectories, even if new elements were added like on the stakeholders dialogue) and another answer to the youth and other people that took the streets in 2019, expressing their trust in an intervention of the legislative power: "We want a Climate Law, Now".

The protests in Brussels, including by young people opting for school-strikes and by NGOs requiring a modification of the Belgian Constitution in order to ease the adoption of an economy-wide climate law including common targets on mitigation (to no avail[6]), certainly did not escape the eyes and ears of civil servants working in the European institutions nearby, even if these demands were by priority dedicated to the Belgian federal government.

The EU Climate law mimicks, at the scope of a territory including 27 Member States, the same systemic approach that was promoted in pre-existing national framework climate laws: long-term (2050) and mid-term (2030) objectives at Union level, the identification of a dedicated scientific advisory board on climate change, provisions on public participation and on the need to install a broad multilevel climate and energy dialogue, both at Commission and Member States levels. The long-term climate neutrality objective imposes that Union-wide greenhouse gas emissions and removals regulated in Union law shall be balanced within the Union at the latest by 2050, thus reducing emissions to net zero by that date, and the Union shall aim to achieve negative emissions thereafter (article 2.1). The binding 2030 climate target at Union level shall be a domestic reduction of net greenhouse gas emissions (emissions after deduction of removals) by at least 55% compared to 1990 levels by 2030 (article 4), imposing the relevant

[5] Peeters M and Misonne D (2022).

[6] Orsini A, Cobut L and Gaborit M (2021); Davio V (2021).

Union institutions and the Member States shall prioritise swift and predictable emission reductions and, at the same time, enhance removals by natural sinks.

In order to achieve its own goal, the European Union decided to overhaul a very large number of existing legislative acts (to make them "fit-for-55") and even to transform new ideas and necessities (like a carbon-adjustment border mechanism or a social fund) into new legislation. Targets multiplied in 2023, with different characteristics – some of them are mechanisms-wide (like for the emissions trading scheme), others remain collective at EU level – and this is partly due to the division of competences as established under the Treaties – and a few of them are already individualized at the level of member States.

This is the case with the effort sharing Regulation, as amended inn 2023,[7] for sectors that are not included in the European trading scheme. By 2030 and by comparison to its emissions in 2005, Germany must for instance reduce its emissions by at least 50%, The Netherlands 48%, Belgium 47%, Spain 37.7%, Poland 17.7%, Bulgaria 10%, etc. Such targets are binding and directly applicable to the Member State.

2.1.3 Framework Climate Laws

In parallel or even before, many Member States – but not all – had adopted their own framework climate laws, either economy-wide or at the level of some of their own institutional entities (like at the level of the Region, in Belgium), ahead of a harmonization process at European level.

This was made dramatically necessary by an oddity in the way European legislation progressed between the Paris Agreement and the Green deal: a Regulation of 2018 on the governance of the Energy Union and Climate Action[8] had indeed imposed on Member States a requirement to intensively *plan* their efforts in an integrated way on five dimension, including decarbonation, and at very frequent intervals (every ten years with an update after five years), without fixing yet the shared and quantified collective targets to be reached at the scale of the European Union.

The so-called national energy and climate plans (NECPs) forced several States in fixing their own share of the contribution to the collective goals of the Paris Agreement, with an eye on the content of the EU nationally determined contribution then announcing a reduction goal of −40% by 2030. It also prompted them to proceed to a fitness-check of their own governance process for making sure they will be apt to deliver such integrated plans, a process that might be facilitated where national frameworks law organize procedures and accountability (Table 1).

[7] Regulation (EU) 2023/857 of the European Parliament and of the Council of 19 April 2023 amending Regulation (EU) 2018/842 on binding annual greenhouse gas emission reductions by Member States from 2021 to 2030 contributing to climate action to meet commitments under the Paris Agreement, and Regulation (EU) 2018/1999, OJ L 111, 26.4.2023.

[8] Regulation (EU) 2018/1999 of the European Parliament and of the Council of 11 December 2018 on the Governance of the Energy Union and Climate Action, OJ L 328, p. 1, 21.12.2018.

Table 1. Framework climate laws in Europe (2023)

Before the Paris Agreement	Date	Name
UK (now non-EU)	2008/2019	Climate Change Act 2008
Belgium (partim) – Walloon Region	2014/2021	Climate Change Decree 2014 (cancelled)
After the Paris Agreement (2015)		
Finland	2015	Climate Act (cancelled)
Ireland	2015/2021	Climate Act 2015
Sweden	2017	Climate Act 2018
Norway (non-EU)	2017	Climate Act 2017
France	2018	Energy and Climate Law 2019
The Netherlands	2019	Climate Act 2019
Germany	2019/2021	Climate Action Law 2019
Luxembourg	2020	Climate Law 2020
Denmark	2020	Climate Act 2020
After the EU Climate Law (2021)		
France	2021	Climate and resilience Act 2021
Portugal	2021	Framework climate Law
Spain	2021	Law on Climate Change and Energy Transition
Belgium (partim) – Brussels Region	2021	Amendment to the Air, Climate and Energy Code
Greece	2022	National climate law 2022
Finland	2022	New Climate Act 2022
Belgium (partim) – Federal State	2023	Federal Climate Law
Switzerland (non-EU)	2023	Climate and Innovation Act 2023
Belgium (partim) – Walloon Region	2023	Decree on Carbon Neutrality 2023

@Misonne2024

2.2 Distrust in Regulation

Adopting legislation on the climate challenge had never been easy but a new kind of resistance arose in 2022–2023 as a direct consequence of the war in Ukraine and the related energy crisis Europe did go through, at the sight of rising prices, scarcity of energy resources and possible impact on competitiveness.

This was also related to the lack of level-playing field induced by supranational obligations. Only days after influential reports were published, like in France[9], denouncing

[9] France Stratégie Website (2023).

the weakness of the current EU climate governance package, pointing to its lack of sticks and carrots - "a soft coordination whose effectiveness is uncertain"[10] -, calls for a regulatory break surged at the highest political level in May 2023[11], that crystallized around the draft regulation on nature restoration and on measures potentially impacting the agricultural sector.

In the meantime, climate change itself has become tangible and perceptible everywhere, while the very capacity of the Paris Agreement to deliver in due time on its own promises and ambition started being questioned, in the light of the most recent reports on the status of mitigation efforts in the world.[12]

3 National Climate Laws

3.1 Anti-Climate Laws

Framework climate laws at national level are not the only legislative acts to look at when assessing the role of the lawmaker in relation to climate ambition. This is because law intersects with climate in many ways, sometimes less easily expected by the environmental lawyer, but quite present in the real world.

For instance, dedicated laws happen sometimes not to enable mitigation efforts but, on the contrary, for barring the way to the possibility to move in such direction.

A sample of such odd attitude was revealed in the case *Held v. Montana* in 2023[13], across the Atlantic in the United States, where the Energy Policy Act contained a limitation. It did impose that the environmental review of projects may not include an evaluation of greenhouse gases emissions and corresponding impacts to the climate in the state or beyond the state's borders. In that landmark lawsuit where the plaintiffs were young people, a judge found that such limitation was unconstitutional, because the state must actively protect, in a preventative manner, the constitutional right to a clean and healthful environment. Therefore, the State must not deprive citizens or decision-makers from the possibility to rely on remedies and adequate procedures, like impact assessment.

The district judge recalled how the mere content of a law can have a profound influence on climate-related policies and decisions, within and beyond the borders of a state. It also shed light on the fact that effective climate protection needs an appropriate toolbox, including on procedural instruments, like prior impact assessment inclusive of climate change issues.

The judgment also stigmatized the importance and necessity never to forget the hierarchy of norms. Like primary law, national constitutional rights matter, also for the

---

[10] "The division of labour between EU and domestic policies must be revisited. Currently, the EU sets the objectives but leaves a large part of the corresponding political and financial costs to Member States, while relying on soft coordination whose effectiveness is uncertain. The EU cannot afford to put forward a grand climate strategy while remaining vague about its actual implementation. It needs to define and implement a new climate governance framework that matches its ambition" (France Stratégie (2023), p. 18 at Nr. 17 of the executive summary).

[11] Tonnelier A et al. (2023), Le Monde (2023).

[12] UNEP (2023).

[13] Held v. Montana, No. CDV-2020-307, Mont. 1st Dist. Ct. Mont., 14.8.2023.

lawmaker, and their meaning is dynamic, in due consideration of the specificities of each legal order.

3.2 Lawmaking, Ownership and the Climate Challenge

It might be interesting to insist on some features that can contribute to draw tighter links between the notion of ownership and the existence of dedicated climate laws. Pledges remain to no avail if domestic institutional frameworks are too weak to materialize them. In that kind of exercise, the implication of the domestic lawmaker is a necessity, for many reasons, both substantial and procedural, if one wants to guarantee the robustness of the new societal project.

First of all, the mere existence of a climate law is by itself an achievement and the successful end of a long process, the roots of which can be found in various fora, like academic discussions or civil society proposals, be they spontaneous (such as the Swiss Glacier initiative) or organized (such the French citizen convention on climate, as an answer to the yellow vests protests that started in 2018[14]). The political backing (see Table 2) to adopt the final version of the text, whatever was lost on the way, is as such meaningful: the required majority to move the climate challenge from the stage of "policy" to the stage of "law" was there. Recent research results show that "debate around the adoption of climate framework laws can help consolidate political consensus on climate change, while implementation requires sustained political pressure and public participation"[15].

A climate law, when adopted, is also the launch of a new governance process (see Table 2), in which elements are foreseen that shall create better conditions for enabling ownership. The content of framework climate laws in European countries vary but present the common feature to clarify and specify decision-making processes. Like on the adoption of climate plans or on public participation. For instance, in the Walloon Decree on Climate Neutrality of 16 November 2023 - a true legislative act that can be assimilated to a framework climate law, a provision is dedicated to the possible creation of a group of citizens, on a voluntary basis but also by drawing lots and with requirements of balanced representativity based upon sex, age, geography, income, level of education, with a mandate to advise public authorities.

Inserting the climate ambition in a legislative act is also tremendously important on the side of legitimacy (see Table 2) and assimilation to the public interest. Conflicting rights and interest will often be judged and balanced on basis of whether or not they are guaranteed by the law. "Be ready for the fight", it somehow indicates, as the objective is settled by the lawmaker and will bear on related matters, like the assessment of proportionality and of legitimate expectations.

A last, moving from a policy to a law means opening all paths to scrutiny (see Fig. 1), both upstream and downstream, including though judicial control. Upstream, a law shall only be valid if it meets constitutional guarantees. Downstream, the implementation measures shall themselves be tested against the choices made by the lawmaker and become justiciable. A climate law is a possible avenue for new kind of court cases (even

[14] See Girard Ch (2021).

[15] Averchenkova A, et al. (2024). See also Nash S and Steurer R (2021).

if the absence of climate law, as demonstrated in the landmark case *Urgenda* in The Netherlands, already opened avenues on the basis of civil law and the supranational protection of human rights).

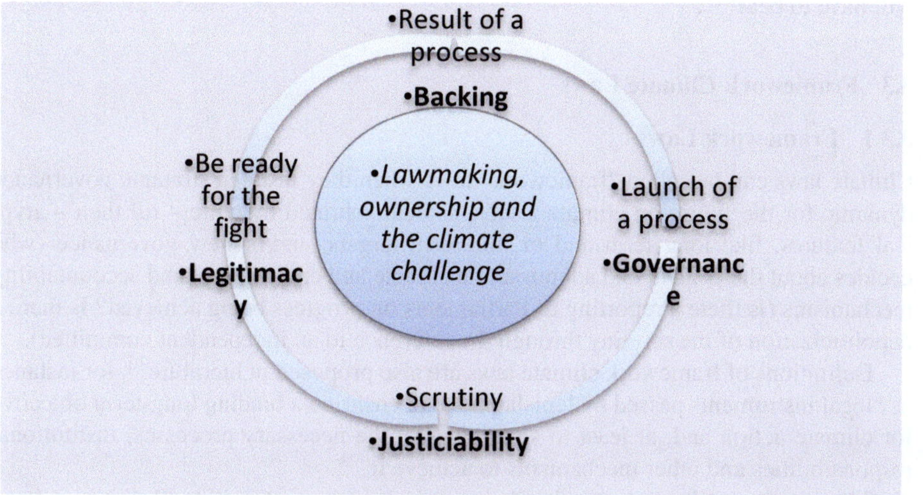

Fig. 1. The importance and effects of lawmaking on the climate challenge. @Misonne2024

Proceeding through the adoption of laws instead of keeping it to policy makes a huge difference, as it opens doors to justiciability.

In Ireland, the Supreme court judged in July 2020 that a climate plan was to be approached as a law rather than as a policy. What might well have been a non-justiciable question of policy clearly became justiciable because the need to specify how the policy was to be achieved became matter of law by virtue of the 2015 Irish Climate Act[16].

The German Constitutional Court found in 2021 that provisions of the German Climate Act violated the freedoms of the plaintiffs, because the Act offloaded major emission reduction burdens onto periods after 2030, with consequences on freedoms protected by fundamental rights. The statutory provisions on adjusting the reduction pathway for greenhouse gas emissions from 2031 onwards were not sufficient to ensure that the necessary transition to climate neutrality was achieved in time[17].

In the case *Grande Synthe*, the French Council of State decided that the French Government had a problem with its trajectory and implementation of carbon budgets[18].

In Belgium, the Constitutional Court, about a regional decree restricting the replacement of oil-fired heating systems, admitted that "by restricting the installation of oil-fired

[16] Friends of the Irish Environment v. The Government of Ireland and ors., IESC 49, 31 July 2020.

[17] Neubauer et al. v Germany, Case No. 1 BvR 2656/18, 1 BvR 78/20, 1 BvR 96/20, 1 BvR 78/20, 24 March 2021

[18] C.E., 19 November 2020, Commune de Grande-Synthe et Damien Carême (maire), No 427301 (Grande-Synthe); C.E., 12 February 2021, Commune de Grande-Synthe, No 428177 (Grande-Synthe); C.E., 10 May 2023, Commune de Grande-Synthe e.a. (Grande-Synthe III), No 467982.

heating systems now, the decretal lawmaker takes due account of the consequences of its policy for future generations"; the contested measure is in the general interest. It is efficient and aligned on the new EU obligations at 2030 and 2050, said the Court, adding that the duty to pursue a sustainable development "includes the climate change others will have to bear"[19].

3.3 Framework Climate Laws

3.3.1 Framework Laws

Climate laws can be called "framework" laws when they install a strategic governance dynamic for the future on climate issues, as demonstrated by quite – till then – atypical features, like long term and or mid-term targets, and/or new governance (who decides about the content and adoption of a climate and energy plan) and accountability mechanisms (is there a reporting to Parliaments on progress being achieved? Is there a depoliticization of the scrutiny through the reference to an independent committee).

Definitions of framework climate laws are also proposed in literature[20], for instance as "legal instruments passed by legislatures that enshrine a binding long-term objective for climate action and, at least to some degree, the necessary processes, institutional responsibilities and other mechanisms to achieve it"[21].

There is a general acceptance that the concept does thus not include all climate-related laws[22], but encapsulates a novelty in governance and law-making. The main purpose in adopting climate laws is to create a new legal narrative, a systemic approach fixing the conditions of predictability and legal certainty (climate neutrality becomes a legitimate but also required expectation), to ease decision-making and planification processes, to guarantee an optimal coordination between the various competent authorities and to organize transparency and accountability, under the rule of law, in relation to climate governance at national or devolved level.

It might be naïve[23], but it expresses a need to *de-soft-alize* climate governance and make it more trustable, even if the option of establishing a stable goal in a changing world, through a mere legislation, is a challenge to history.

In a recent report commissioned by the European Environmental Agency[24], Evans & al. Affirmed that the added value of climate laws is *evident* if they contain a core of good governance elements: "*at a bare minimum, well-formulated framework laws provide a normative foundation for climate action, facilitating the integration and mainstreaming of climate priorities across governmental agencies and ministries. Not only can they formally establish a coherent system of goals (targets) and means of achievement (cycles*

[19] Federation of Oil v. Flemish Region, case 147/2022, Belgian Constitutional Court, 10 November 2022.

[20] See inter alia: Muinzer T (2020); J. Huang (2021), p. 285.

[21] Evans N et al. (2023), p.1.

[22] For the larger picture, see the data bank of the Grantham Institute, UK, totalizing more than 5000 documents, all available in open access via https://www.lse.ac.uk/granthaminstitute/climate-change-laws-of-the-world-/. See also Nash S et al (2021).

[23] Macrory R (2012).

[24] Evans N and Duwe M (2021)

of action and planning), but they often lead to a professionalization of political structures by clearly assigning roles and responsibilities within government and creating new coordinating institutions or advisory bodies, composed of external scientific experts, stakeholders and public officials"[25].

National climate laws are very much praised in some societal networks, like those advocating the serious consideration of the climate challenge[26]. Therefore, many interesting reports were published recently, drawing "global lessons in climate law-making". Databanks are also available in open access, on "Climate Change Laws of the Word", or national framework climate laws in Europe[27].

3.3.2 A Patchwork

There are currently different types of framework climate laws in Europe. The impression that emerges is that of patchwork: an assembly of different pieces that nevertheless seem to make sense together.

National framework laws in Europe vary as to their institutional scope (are they state-wide or sub-state wide, for reasons of institutional structure and type of federalism, like in Belgium), adoption processes (are they the (far) result of a popular initiative, like in Switzerland where a demand by civil society to include a net zero target in the federal Constitution landed, after many *peripeties* and difficulties, in a new Act) and kind of content (Are the targets binding? How does the Act revitalize citizen participation?).

Putting the data on a map reveals an uneven situation. There is an East-West divide on the existence or absence of framework climate laws at national level. An absence does not mean there were no attempts for adopting so-called framework climate laws. The adoption of framework climate laws remains conditioned by the institutional and constitutional peculiarities of each legal order, in addition to political contingency[28].

---

25 Ibid, p.12.

26 See CAN Europe (2022)

27 Ecologic Institute (2023).

28 On that aspect, see in Belgium the difficulty to find an appropriate institutional "space" to fix shared common goals, and discussions around a modification of the Constitution, as synthetized in Rolland G and Romainville C (2020); Davio V (2021).

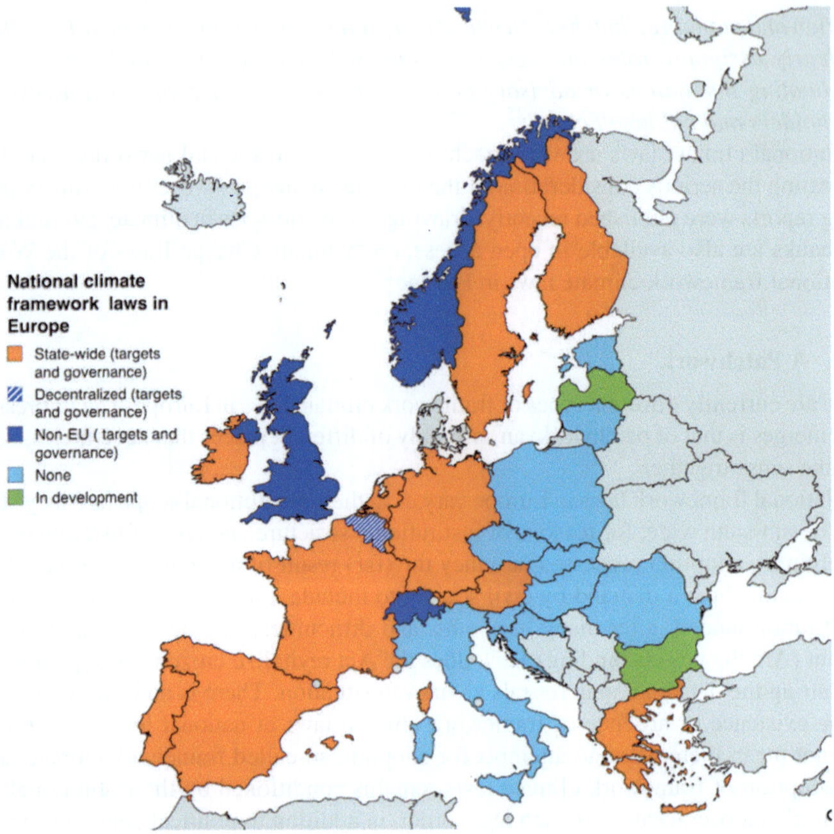

Fig. 2. National climate framework laws in Europe. @Misonne2023

3.3.3 Generations of Framework Climate Laws

We can observe also that several "generations" of framework climate laws have already emerged.

The framework laws that surged after the adoption of the European Climate Law, or around the same moment, are quite different in content by comparison to the first framework laws, that were already different from preexisting more 'classical' and EU-derived climate laws (on specific instruments, like emissions trading). It is therefore interesting to compare national framework climate laws according to the moment they were adopted, before or after the Paris Agreement, before or after the new European collective legislative targets, as enshrined in the EU climate law, and the individual targets set in other texts like the effort sharing regulation. One more recent aspect characterizing the newest framework climate laws is their endorsement of an explicit goal of climate neutrality, also called net zero, sometimes already endorsed for 2035 (Finland) or 2045 (Sweden) (Fig. 2).

Another specificity of the more recent framework laws is the attention paid to sectoral goals, like when imposing a target for the land use sector concerning stronger carbon sinks, or when the lawmaker wants to address the very concrete implications of the general approach on governance and global national targets, at the cost of increasing "the strain on political consensus"[29].

Participation requirements are becoming more explicitly inclusive in certain framework climate laws. In the Walloon and Brussels regions, the consultation of groups of citizens is organized by the new framework climate legislations. In Finland, according to the new Climate Act, the rights of the Sámi must be taken into account and negotiations with the Sámi Parliament are required in the processes to prepare climate policy plans.

Local authorities have also become part of the story, when the framework law imposes an obligation for municipalities to draw up climate plans and with provisions on requests for review concerning the climate policy plans (Finland), or where funding is foreseen for hiring coordinators in charge of a municipal plan or climate and energy (Walloon Region).

3.4 Are Framework Climate Laws Consistent with the EU Climate Law and Related Regulation?

One newly arising question is whether those framework laws are (still) aligned on the newly adopted package of EU harmonized legislative acts, in due regard of the principle of primacy and of the possibility for a member State, where the legal basis of the EU act allows, to enhance the level of protection.

Some aspects might also become *surabondant*. For instance, where framework climate laws tended to be necessary to encapsulate targets, several individualized targets applicable to member States have already been enshrined, as a minimum, in a directly applicable EU regulation. But, of course, due to the legal basis of the targets on the effort sharing of mitigating greenhouse gases, such targets can be enhanced at national level and are therefore justified, as far as they do not lower the EU binding requirements.

On the other side, some aspects remain unregulated at EU level, like the legal status of the Climate and Energy plans, and justify the need for Member States to fill the gaps.

The Governance regulation of 2018 imposes the production of energy and climate plans by Member States, which must contain certain elements and fit within certain deadlines, which must also be very sophistically integrated and made publicly available, but the regulation does not elaborate at all on the legal status or expected legal status of the national plan themselves and on how enforceable they should be. The mechanic is more about provoking a brainstorming and developing foresight, less about legality, bindingness or even accountability at national level.

No harmonization of an ideal climate law template nor governance modus is anyhow proposed in the EU Climate law.

On the role and importance of independent high committees on climate issues, the EU climate law only contains an invitation to Member State to have their own national climate advisory body, responsible for providing expert scientific advice on climate

[29] Bailey I et al. (2024), mentioning that The Irish Act also draws attention to the importance of cross-party involvement in decision-making as a way of maintaining trust and cooperation on supporting policies. Conversely, CCA negotiations may trigger a longer-lasting convergence in how different political parties discuss climate policy that reduces contestation over future supporting policies".

policy to the relevant national authorities[30]. But there is a carrot: the European Scientific Advisory Board may take into account, "where available", the work of national advisory bodies[31]. There is no indication on the optimal independence that should characterize such bodies.

One observes also that several recent national climate laws tend to be more "laws" than "frameworks". The French Climate Law of 20 July 2021 called "climat et resilience"[32] is the fruit of an innovative process involving a citizen assembly and contains many detailed measures like: the obligation to promote the education to the climate and environmental challenges at all levels, from schools to Universities; veggie menus once a week in schools; a ban on the advertisement for fossils fuels and even for buying new cars (the list of which must be adopted); an ecoscore; the possibility for a local authority to ban or restrict energy-consuming advertisement devices; ban of greenwashing and false allegations like carbon-free; restrictions on the expansion of malls and commercial buildings on agricultural land; no heating on terraces; etc.

In June 2023, Swiss voters backed by a referendum a new climate and innovation law, seeking a gradual reduction of imported fossil fuels in favour of Swiss-made renewables to improve energy security and proudly using a "carrot-not-stick" approach: financial support – CHF3.2 billion ($3.2 billion) over ten years – is foreseen for homeowners to replace electric, gas or oil heating systems with more climate-friendly systems like heat pumps and businesses will also be stimulated to draw transition plans and invest in green technologies.

In the recent Walloon Decree of 2023, the concept of "carbon communities" is created to designate groups of enterprises that want to enter into "carbon convention", the new name of agreements concluded between the Region and a sector or part of it, with a commitment for the public authority not to regulate any further than the carbon convention (except if required under EU law)[33]. It seems to revisit the notion of sectoral agreement ("accord de branche"), under a trendier name.

The new Portuguese climate framework Act of December 2021 contains a set of interesting principles and definitions: it declares the climate emergency, promotes the guarantee of climate justice and wants to combat energy poverty. It also contains a right to climate balance - defined as "the right to defend oneself against the impacts of climate change, as well to demand that public and private entities comply with their duties and obligations regarding climate change".

4 Conclusion

Climate law is for sure in transformation, including at national level, where the landscape if changing under the impetus of the Green Deal but also based upon own dynamics and necessities. Nothing new under the sun: "laws cannot themselves ensure effectiveness if the political commitment to deliver is either not present or is weakened, and the

[30] European Climate Law, art.3.4.

[31] Ibid, art.3.3.

[32] Law No 2021-1104 portant lutte contre le dérèglement climatique et renforcement de la résilience face à ses effets, 22 August 2021.

[33] See art. 31 of the Walloon Decree.

resources needed to implement actions are not available[34]", but without framework climate laws, the tasks might even be more daunting. The global impression given by national framework climate laws is that of a patchwork, even a patchy patchwork, with many different patterns and colors. The mere existence of such framework laws can be seen as an achievement – they are not found everywhere – but the proof of the pudding is of course in the eating. Framework climate laws will really translate national ownership not only if they truly deliver on mitigating emissions but most importantly if they succeed in creating a proactive and up-to-the-challenge dynamic in decision-making on such sensitive issues as climate mitigation and adaptation.

References

Averchenkova, A., et al. (eds.): Trends in Climate Change Legislation. Edward Elgar Publishing, Cheltenham (2017)

Averchenkova, A., et al.: Impacts of climate framework laws: lessons from Germany, Ireland and New Zealand (2024). https://www.lse.ac.uk/granthaminstitute/publication/impacts-of-climate-framework-laws/. Accessed 18 Aug 2025

Bailey, I., Nutkins, R., Inderberg, T.H.J.: The anchoring effect of climate change acts: a policy streams analysis of Ireland's climate act reform. Climate Policy **24**(3), 396–409 (2023). https://doi.org/10.1080/14693062.2023.2261886

CAN Europe, Climate Laws in Europe. Essential for Achieving Climate Neutrality (2022). https://caneurope.org/content/uploads/2022/05/2022_04_Climate-laws-briefing-ENG.pdf. Accessed 18 Aug 2025

Davio, V.: La loi climat: une errance législative face à l'urgence? Amén, pp. 6–20 (2021)

Ecologic Institute, Climate Framework Laws Info-Matrix. Ecologic Institute, Berlin (2023). https://www.ecologic.eu/19320. Accessed 18 Aug 2025

Evans, N., Duwe, M.: Climate governance systems in Europe: the role of national advisory bodies (2021). https://www.iddri.org/en/publications-and-events/report/climate-governance-systems-europe-role-national-advisory-bodies. Accessed 18 Aug 2025

Evans, N., et al.: The landscape of national climate framework laws in Europe: a status update (2023). https://www.ecologic.eu/19399. Accessed 18 Aug 2025

Girard, C.: Lessons from the French Citizens' Climate convention: on the role and legitimacy of citizens' assemblies. In: VerfBlog, 28 July 2021 (2021). https://verfassungsblog.de/lessons-from-the-french-citizens-climate-convention/. Accessed 18 Aug 2025

Huang, J.: Exploring climate framework laws and the future of climate action. Pace Environ. Law Rev. **38**(2):285–326 (2021). https://doi.org/10.58948/0738-6206.1849

Macrory, R.: Towards a brave new legal world? In: Backer, I., Fauchald, O., Voigt, C., Pro Natura, Universitetsforlaget, Oslo, pp. 306–322 (2012)

Muinzer, T. (ed.) National Climate Change Acts: The Emergence, Form and Nature of National Framework Climate Legislation. Bloomsbury Publishing (2020)

Nash, S., Steurer, R.: Taking stock of climate change acts in Europe: living policy processes or symbolic gestures? Climate Policy **19**(8), 1052–1065 (2019). https://doi.org/10.1080/14693062.2019.1623164

Nash, S., Steurer, R.: Climate change acts in Scotland, Austria, Denmark and Sweden: the role of discourse and deliberation. Climate Policy **21**(9), 1120–1131 (2021)

Nash, S., Torney, D., Matti, S.: Climate change acts: origins, dynamics, and consequences. Climate Policy **21**(9), 1111–1119 (2021). https://doi.org/10.1080/14693062.2021.1996536

34 Averchenkova A et al. (2024).

OECD, The United Kingdom's pioneering climate change act – case study (2021). https://www.oecd.org/climate-action/ipac/practices/the-united-kingdom-s-pioneering-climate-change-act-c08c3d7a/. Accessed 18 Aug 2025

Orsini, A., Cobut, L., Gaborit, M.: Climate change acts non-adoption as potential for renewed expertise and climate activism: the Belgian case. Climate Policy **21**(9), 1205–1217 (2021). https://doi.org/10.1080/14693062.2021.1978052

Peeters, M., Misonne, D.: The European Union and its rule-creating force at the European continent for moving to climate neutrality in 2050. In: Reins, L., Verschuuren, J. (eds.), Research Handbook on Climate Change Mitigation Law, 2nd edn. Edward Elgar Publishing, pp. 59–102 (2022)

Rolland, G., Romainville, C.: Voyage au coeur de la notion de loi spéciale. Propositions de loi spéciale climat. Administration publique **2**, 286–309 (2020)

Scotford, E., Minas, S.: Probing the hidden depths of climate law: analysing national climate change legislation. RECIEL **28**(1), 67–81 (2019). https://doi.org/10.1111/reel.12259

Stallworthy, M.: Legislating against climate change: a UK perspective on a sisyphean challenge. Mod. Law Rev. **72**(3), 412–436 (2009). https://doi.org/10.1111/j.1468-2230.2009.00752

Others

France Stratégie Website, The economic implications of climate action, May 2023, Report to the Prime Minister (2023). https://www.strategie-plan.gouv.fr/en/publications/economic-implications-climate-action. Accessed 18 Aug 2025

Le Monde, le premier ministre belge, Alexander De Croo, favorable, comme Emmanuel Macron, à une «pause» réglementaire européenne. In: Le Monde (2023), 24 May 2023. https://www.lemonde.fr/planete/article/2023/05/24/environnement-le-premier-ministre-belge-alexander-de-croo-emboite-le-pas-a-emmanuel-macron-sur-une-pause-reglementaire-europeenne_6174551_3244.html. Accessed 18 Aug 2025

Tonnelier, A., et al.: Industrie: Macron appelle à une pause dans la réglementation environnementale européenne. In: Le Monde (2023). 11 May 2023. https://www.lemonde.fr/politique/article/2023/05/12/industrie-macron-appelle-a-une-pause-dans-la-reglementation-environnementale-europeenne_6173001_823448.html. Accessed 18 Aug 2025

UNEP, Emissions Gap Report 2023 (2023). https://www.unep.org/resources/emissions-gap-report-2023. Accessed 18 Aug 2025

Energy and Climate Transitions

The Rise and Fall of a Treaty: Is the EU's Withdrawal from the Energy Charter Treaty in Line or at Odds with Its Ambitions to Achieve a Locally Driven Energy Transition?

Daniela Muth(✉)

University of Westminster, London, UK
D.Muth@westminster.ac.uk

Abstract. In order to meet the EU's climate goals, the Clean Energy Package envisages a fundamental transformation of the energy sector, a decentralisation away from fossils fuels towards renewable sources of energy with local energy communities playing a significant role in making the transformation publicly acceptable. But in a decentralised energy system – do we still need a multilateral energy treaty?

As of 28th June 2025, the EU is no longer a party to the Energy Charter Treaty (ECT). This chapter explores the impact of the EU's withdrawal on the protection of energy investments. It addresses the main criticisms of the ECT and takes a fresh look at the extent to which investment protection provisions in a multilateral energy treaty might contribute to a just energy transition by supporting a flow of private finance towards local communities. By doing so it provides a new perspective from which to judge the strengths and weaknesses of the ECT and argues that there is still a valuable discussion to be had about what lessons we can learn from this treaty and how these lessons can feed into a new investment regime that is in line with the EU's climate goals.

1 Introduction

It has been called a "climate wrecking treaty"[1], a "fossil fuel dinosaur"[2] and many things besides. As international treaties go, the Energy Charter Treaty ("ECT") has had more than its fair share of controversy. In yet, when the Energy Charter Conference finally adopted an amended treaty text on 3rd December 2024[3], following intense debate and a long, drawn-out modernisation process, it felt somewhat like an anti-climax. The Conference proceedings in December 2024 marked the end of the negotiations to modernise the ECT, which had begun in 2017 and had culminated in an Agreement in Principle being reached in 2022.[4] Whereas the negotiation process and immediate aftermath of

[1] For example, Friends of the Earth Europe (2024).
[2] European Parliament, Plenary Session, Press Releases, 24.4.2024 (2024).
[3] Energy Charter Secretariat (2024).
[4] Energy Charter Secretariat (2022).

M. Reese et al. (Eds.): EELF 2023, *Legal Implementation and Impacts of the European Green Deal*, pp. 73–94, 2026.
https://doi.org/10.1007/978-3-032-17197-9_3

the Agreement in Principle were accompanied by fierce discussion around the potential dangers of the ECT, the actual decision to adopt the amendments more or less in line with the Agreement in Principle went ahead without much fanfare. The lack of media attention was probably due to the fact that most of the discussion and negotiations had already taken place and many parties, including Germany, the EU and the UK had already made the decision to withdraw.[5] The fact that here, for the first time, there was a multilateral agreement which included a phase out mechanism for protection of investments in fossil fuels went largely unnoticed. Or might there have been an element of embarrassment that here was a treaty which allowed for a phase out of protection for existing fossil fuel investments after 10 years to which the EU, Germany and others were no longer Contracting Parties and who might now instead be locked into a protection mechanism for fossil fuel investors for twice as long under the ECT's sunset provision? As we shall see, the impact of the decision on those countries whose withdrawal has already become effective or whose withdrawal will soon become effective is not entirely clear. According to Article 47.3 of the ECT, the provisions of the treaty will apply for 20 years following the date that withdrawal becomes effective. But will the amended version of the ECT apply or the old version? And what of the newly worded Annex NI which specifically refers to a termination of investment protection for fossil fuel investments made on or after 3rd September 2025 for the EU and the UK? Will this annex be applicable, seeing that neither the EU nor the UK will be Contracting Parties to the ECT come September 2025? The interpretation of the treaty wording is ambiguous on this and will no doubt be the subject of deliberation in years to come when arbitrators try to determine which level of protection is afforded fossil fuel investors during the 20-year sunset period by those who decided to withdraw after the Agreement in Principle but before the amended text comes into force. The irony is that those countries who justified their withdrawal with the argument that the ECT was too protective of fossil fuel investors may find that they are locked into continued investment protection for existing fossil fuel investments during the sunset period, whilst others who remained in the ECT have the opportunity to end that protection.

2 Exodus from an Unpopular Treaty

On the 24 April 2024, about 9 months after the European Commission had announced that it was preparing for a coordinated withdrawal from the ECT, the European Parliament voted 560 to 43 in favour of exiting the treaty.[6] This came after 11 states, including Spain, France, Germany and the UK, had already indicated that they intended to leave the ECT.

Broadly speaking, the majority of observers seems to have welcomed these announcements, following the number of high-profile cases of fossil fuel investors invoking the investor state dispute settlement (ISDS) provisions in Article 26 of the ECT. This Article gives foreign investors the right to make claims in international tribunals against

[5] See Table 1 for the list of Contracting Parties that have notified the Energy Charter Secretariat of withdrawal since June 2022.

[6] European Parliament, Plenary Session, Press Release (2024).

the host state for breaches of the ECT. Prominent examples of such claims are the Rockhopper case against Italy[7], RWE and Uniper's claims against the Netherlands.[8] Many critical voices amongst academics, campaigners, politicians and experts had concluded that the ECT is no longer fit for purpose and is unduly protecting fossil fuel investors. The general consensus has certainly been that the ECT has at least the potential to slow down the energy transition.[9] Judging from the response to the Agreement in Principle that was concluded in 2022, many held the view that the Agreement in Principle to modernise the ECT had not adequately addressed these concerns and that on balance an exit from the treaty was preferable to staying in the ECT as amended by the Agreement in Principle. There followed a spate of notifications of withdrawal which will reduce the total number of Contracting Parties to the ECT from 53 to 42 come September 2025. The following countries (see Table 1) have now withdrawn from the ECT or have notified the Secretariat of the intention to withdraw:[10]

Now that the EU's position has been decided and some of the heat has been taken out of the debate, it is worth taking a step back and engaging in a spot of treaty soul-searching. Is it possible that the controversial investor state disputes between fossil fuel investors and states and the general stir they have understandably created have clouded our judgment as to whether a withdrawal from the ECT is in fact the greenest option? It is suggested here that this is not necessarily the case. The purpose of this chapter is not to advocate a revival of the ECT negotiations or to suggest that those countries that have decided to withdraw should remain in the ECT or rejoin. It is a little late for that and would not be feasible given the high threshold of mistrust that has developed around the ECT over the past few years. The aim is rather to demonstrate that the content and format of the current debate about investment in the energy transition is not bearing any fruit but instead is leading us into blind alleys. The perceived failings of the modernisation process are evidence that a different approach to investment protection may lead to a better outcome. The urgent need for private capital to finance the energy transition towards renewable energy sources has not dissipated and global investment in the energy sector is currently not flowing to where it should be. According to the World Energy Outlook compiled by the International Energy Agency (IEA), investment in oil

[7] Rockhopper Exploration PLC, Rockhopper Italia S.P.A. and Rockhopper Mediterranean Ltd v Italy, ICSID Case No ARB/17/14

[8] RWE AG and RWE Eemshaven Holding II B.V. v Netherlands, ICSID Case No ARB/21/4 and Uniper SE, Uniper Benelux Holding B.V. and Uniper Benelux N.V. v Netherlands ICSID Case No ARB/21/22

[9] Many commentators have made well-reasoned and convincing arguments as to why the Energy Charter Treaty in its old form had the potential to hinder the energy transition. See in particular N. Bernasconi-Osterwalder of the International Institute for Sustainable Development, M. Brauch from the Columbia Centre on Sustainable Investment, K. Tienhaara (Queen's University) & C. Downie (Australian National University) and Amandine van den Berghe, a lawyer for Client Earth.

[10] According to Art. 47(2) of the Energy Charter Treaty, withdrawal takes effect one year after the date of a Contracting Parties notification of withdrawal. The list of countries is taken from Written Notification of Withdrawal from the Energy Charter Treaty Secretariat's website: <http://www.energycharter.org/media/news/article/written-notifications-of-withdrawal-from-the-energy-charter-treaty/. Accessed 14 April 2025.

Table 1. Contracting Parties that have notified the Energy Charter Secretariat of withdrawal since June 2022

Country	Effective Date of Withdrawal
France	8 December 2023
Germany	20 December 2023
Poland	29 December 2023
Luxembourg	17 June 2024
Slovenia	14 October 2024
Portugal	2 February 2025
Spain	17 April 2025
United Kingdon	27 April 2025
European Union and Euratom	28 June 2025
Netherlands	28 June 2025
Denmark	4 September 2025

and gas in 2023 was almost double what it should be if we are to reach our global net zero targets.[11] At the same time, the IEA estimates that there is a current shortfall of USD 4.7 trillion needed to finance the energy transition to clean sources of energy.[12] Furthermore, the current investment climate with high interest rates is increasing the costs for investors which poses challenges for investors in capital intense clean energy technology. This is particularly a problem for lower income countries with insufficient home-grown capital looking for foreign direct investment just at the time when the current international investment regime as formulated by the 1000s of bilateral investment treaties and trade agreements is coming under increasing scrutiny.

There is currently an additional challenge in that the majority of investment treaties but especially the Energy Charter Treaty are built upon the foundations of the global trading system and the WTO Agreements established since the creation of the WTO in 1995. This system is experiencing considerable strain with a stymied WTO dispute resolution mechanism following the inability to maintain a functioning Appellate Body, as well as recent volatility and uncertainty in international trade following the US Administration's trade and tariff policies.

As the incumbent investment treaty regime crumbles and the numerous withdrawals of countries leaves the ECT weakened and limited in its applicability, we need to look afresh at these issues and formulate a new legal framework that governs foreign investment in the energy sector. Whilst recent geopolitical developments on the global stage seem to be rewriting the rule book on international trade and investment, particularly in the energy sector, calling into question our prevailing assumptions and certainties, it may be a good time to reimagine what a new set of rules might look like. This chapter

[11] International Energy Agency (2023), p. 19.

[12] Ibid, p. 49.

does not seek to map out the shape of such a new framework but rather seeks alternative foundations upon which we can build a new and solid energy investment structure.

Where should we look for such foundations? When the Energy Charter Treaty was originally negotiated in the first half of the 1990s, the backdrop and context of the negotiations was the collapse of the Soviet Union and the urgent need to shore up the (mainly fossil fuel) energy infrastructure in the old Soviet block, and to bring Russia and the old Soviet satellite states into the emerging WTO trading system.[13] 30 years later, the modern day backdrop to any formulation of a new investment regime is the climate crisis and the need for a transformation of our energy system. Our starting point in any endeavour to find new ground from which a new investment framework might emerge should therefore be the international climate obligations of the EU and its member states most notably under the Paris Agreement and the targets and goals of EU energy policy as formulated by the European Green Deal. One of the pillars of the EU's current energy policy is the decentralisation of the energy sector and the development of local energy communities[14], it therefore makes sense to examine the potential benefits a reformed ECT may have had on investment in local energy projects. It is proposed that ISDS provisions in an international treaty could be made to facilitate the flourishing of community energy projects, if anchored within a regulatory regime that enables cooperation of public and private investment at local level.

However, it would not be worth replicating key provisions of a treaty that is hindering a phase out of fossil fuels simply to allow for a possible future benefit that has not yet quite materialised. Therefore, if we want to explore the possible impact of investment protection and ISDS on a decentralised, locally driven energy transition, we first need to examine whether there is more or less scope for a phase out of protection for fossil fuel investors for those countries who have withdrawn or are about to withdraw from the ECT.

3 The Impact of Withdrawal on Investment Protection for Fossil Fuel Investors

The EU's goal is to reduce net greenhouse gas emissions by at least 55% by 2030 compared to 1990 levels and to be the first climate neutral continent by 2050.[15] This requires a deep-rooted transformation of the energy sector. The rationale for exiting the ECT was, therefore, that it is slowing down the energy transition because it restricts the EU's policy space to implement the Green Deal. From this, it would follow that it is the EU's goal to deal with fossil fuel investors in such a way that would represent a breach of the provisions of the ECT, perhaps suggesting that there is a clear policy to phase out or at least restrict fossil fuel investment protection in the immediate future.

In order to assess whether a withdrawal from the ECT is in line with the EU's climate ambitions, it is necessary to compare investment protection that will be afforded

[13] The Uruguay Round of talks that culminated in the formation of the WTO were being conducted at the same time as the negotiations around the Energy Charter Treaty and there is specific reference and alignment to the WTO Agreements in the ECT.

[14] European Commission (2019), 'Clean Energy for All Europeans'.

[15] European Commission, Energy, Climate Change, Environment (2024).

to fossil fuel investments after a withdrawal with a possible scenario of phasing out such protection by remaining in a reformed ECT. The conclusion drawn here is that currently there would be more scope for restricting investment protection for fossil fuels if the "Exiteers" had stayed in a reformed treaty than withdraw from it. Once we have dealt with the legitimate concern that an ECT, even in its modernised form, would slow down a phase out of protection for fossil fuel investments, we can then move on to ask the question what else might be lost by withdrawing from the ECT. The findings suggest that some of the disputed provisions of the ECT could still be aligned with the EU's ambitions under the Green Deal by encouraging private investment in local energy projects and that attempts to establish a decentralised energy sector, in which communities play a more active role would be helped rather than hindered by the possibility of investor state dispute resolution. It is proposed that more research is needed to determine whether larger stumbling blocks might not in fact be found elsewhere, such as within the definitions of 'renewable energy communities' and 'citizen energy communities' contained in the latest Electricity and Renewable Energy Directives[16] and within some of the provisions of the WTO rules on local content requirements and EU restrictions on state aid.

3.1 The Agreement in Principle to Modernise the Energy Charter Treaty

To those who had been following the negotiations for the modernisation of the ECT closely, it had come as quite a surprise when, on 24 June 2022, the ECT Secretariat announced that the Contracting Parties to the Energy Charter Treaty had settled on an agreement in principle to modernise the treaty. Contrary to what everyone had expected, it seemed as if most proposals of the EU had been adopted. Most notably, there was reference to alignment to the goals of the Paris Agreement, tighter definitions of 'Investment', 'Investor', 'Fair and Equitable Treatment' and 'Indirect Expropriation' with a carve out for non-discriminatory measures adopted with respect to climate change mitigation and adaptation. The parties had also agreed on a new article confirming the right to regulate in the interests of public policy objectives, including climate change mitigation and adaptation, a new article on sustainable development and corporate social responsibility and an obligation on Contracting Parties to ensure responsible business conduct of investors in their area. Furthermore, as well as a duty to declare third party funding and tightening the valuation of damages, the EU had negotiated a release from Article 26 for intra member states disputes by forming a Regional Economic Integration Area within which the controversial ISDS provisions would not be applicable, thereby putting to rest the recent Achmea / Komstroy upheaval in EU investment law and the question of how intra EU disputes between member states of the EU would fare, at least within the realms of the Energy Charter Treaty. And then, maybe most promising, a flexibility mechanism that gave states the option of phasing out investment protection for fossil fuels – the first time there has ever been an attempt within a treaty to target

[16] See Art 2(11) Directive (EU) 2019/944 of the European Parliament and of the Council of 5 June 2019 on common rules for the internal market for electricity and amending Directive 2012/27/EU (recast), OJ L 158, p. 125, 14.6.2019 and Art 2(16) EU 2018/2001 of the European Parliament and of the Council of 11 December 2018 on the promotion of the use of energy from renewable sources (recast), OJ L 328, p. 82, 21.12.2018.

fossil fuel investments directly. Whilst there would be no immediate stop to investment protection, Contracting Parties would have the option to carve-out protection for fossil fuel investments in their territory. The EU and UK had already indicated that they would opt for a carve-out of protection for new investors in fossil fuels after one year and for existing investors after 10 years.[17]

It seemed like a genuine breakthrough with the proposals put forward by the EU adopted almost in their entirety – that is until the notifications of withdrawals started coming in to spoil the party.

As mentioned above, the reasons given for the withdrawals mainly centre around the continued protection of fossil fuel investors. The German Ministry for the Economy and Climate Protection states that Germany left the ECT because it is a barrier to climate protection and the energy transition and because the Agreement in Principle falls short of Germany's climate goals.[18]

In a statement on 7 July 2023, the European Commission said:

> "Despite fulfilling all the requirements of the negotiating mandate given by the Council, Member States did not find the necessary majority to ratify the modernised Treaty, as proposed by the European Commission in October 2022. Given this situation, a coordinated withdrawal by the EU, Euratom and all EU Member States is now the most consistent approach from a legal and policy perspective."[19]

Anna Cavazzini, rapporteur for the Trade Committee is quoted as saying:

> "Finally, the fossil dinosaur treaty is no longer standing in the way of consistent climate protection, as we no longer have to fear corporate lawsuits demanding billions of Euros in compensation brought before private arbitration tribunals."[20]

To many campaigners the EU's withdrawal from the ECT seems like a fitting and successful conclusion to a long campaign to end the powerful protection mechanisms for the fossil fuel industry that emanate from the Articles of the ECT.

But before we heave a sigh of relief at the thought that at least one barrier to a successful and speedy energy transition has been removed, we should be clear that following the Agreement in Principle, the choice was no longer between the old and tired ECT with its whiff of 90s neoliberal optimism. The choice is between an ECT amended as per the proposed Agreement in Principle or not being in the ECT altogether. This changes the goal posts, and the discussion should now also shift to account for the new circumstances in which it finds itself.

Whilst the arguments given to justify an exit would have been valid against the old version, they now have to stack up against a modernised version.

Much of the debate around the modernisation of the ECT has circled around potential dangers, the fact that there is at least a possibility that policy changes will not happen

---

[17] Energy Charter Secretariat (2022), Decision of the Energy Charter Conference, CCDEC 22, 10 Gen, 24.6.2022.

[18] Bundesministerium für Wirtschaft und Klimaschutz (2022a).

[19] European Commission Announcement, DG Energy (2023).

[20] European Parliament, Plenary Session, Press Releases (2024).

because there is the threat of claims made by fossil fuel investors against governments trying to commit to their climate goals. These are very plausible concerns. But rather than look at the theoretical impact, let us look at the actual impact on the level of fossil fuel protection that we can in fact measure:

Let us compare two scenarios:

Scenario 1:

The Agreement in Principle was implemented as planned by all parties in November 2022 and the UK and EU did decide to take advantage of the flexibility mechanism in Pillar 2 of the Energy Charter Conference decision to phase out investment protection for fossil fuel, as they had indicated that they would.

Outcome:

UK and EU investment protection (and any other country who would have decided to join the phase out – presumably this would have included those countries who have now chosen to withdraw due to the fact that the phase out is currently not quick enough, so Germany, Belgium, France, Luxembourg, Netherlands, Poland, Portugal, Slovenia, and Spain) would have stopped on 15th August 2023 for any new investments in fossil fuels. For existing investments in fossil fuels, protection would have ended 10 years later, i.e. August 2033.[21]

Scenario 2 – The current scenario

The ECT is modernised on 3 December 2024 after some withdrawals have already taken effect (e.g. France, Germany and Poland) whilst others will take effect before the proposed adoption of the amended treaty text in September 2025.

Outcome:

For those countries whose withdrawal had already been effective before the decision of the Energy Charter Conference on 3 December 2024 (France, Germany, Poland, Luxembourg and Slovenia) the date on which investment protection under the ECT for existing investments in all energy sources (fossil fuels and renewables) will end is 2043/2044, due to the 20-year sunset provision in Article 47(3), for fossil fuel investments 10 years later than if they had remained party to the ECT and opted for the phase of investment protection. Italy, who withdrew from the Energy Charter Treaty in 2016 has since been subject to 7 claims,[22] 4 of which were still pending at the time of writing.[23] Furthermore, any future claims brought by existing fossil fuel investors before the end of the sunset period are dealt with under the old, unamended treaty text.

Investment protection for new investments in all sources of energy under the ECT ceased from the effective date of withdrawal, so only a few months later than if they had remained party to the ECT, although now, of course, the investment protection for investments in renewable energy under the ECT has also been lost for any new investments in renewable energy.

For those countries who are still party to the ECT but have given notification of their withdrawal (eg the EU and the UK), the situation is more complicated.

---

[21] Energy Charter Secretariat (2022).

[22] Ekardt et al. (2022), p. 353

[23] Energy Charter List of Cases. In: https://www.energychartertreaty.org/cases/list-of-cases/. Accessed 25 Aug 2025.

The modifications to Annex NI, which lists Energy Materials and Products that are excluded from the provisions of the treaty, make specific reference to an exclusion by the EU and the UK of protection for fossil fuel investments made on or after 3 September 2025 and an exclusion of protection for investments in fossil fuels that are made before 3 September 2025 in 10 years from the date of entry into force of the approval to modify Annex NI (i.e. 3 September 2025).[24]

The modifications of Annex NI relating to the exclusion of future fossil fuel investments will enter into force on 3 September 2025. The modifications relating to fossil fuel investments made before 3 September enter into force in the same way as the amendments to the main treaty text, i.e. 90 days after they have been ratified or approved by 3/4ths of the Contracting Parties amongst those CPs that have ratified or approved and for any other CP 90 days after it has ratified or approved the modifications. However, both the amendments to the treaty text as well as the modifications to Annex NI will apply provisionally from 3. September 2025 until they come into force.[25]

For the EU and the UK this means that the amendments and modifications' provisional application begins after the effective date of withdrawal and within the sunset period.

The full wording of the sunset provision in Art. 47(2) is as follows:

> "The provisions of this Treaty shall continue to apply to Investments made in the Area of a Contracting Party by Investors of other Contracting Parties or in the Area of other Contracting Parties by Investors of that Contracting Party as of the date when the Contracting Party's withdrawal takes effect for a period of 20 years from such date."

There is considerable uncertainty on how the approved amendments and modifications to the ECT will apply to those that are about to withdraw. Law firms are advising their clients to carefully consider the impact of the amendments and modifications on current and planned investments. Eversheds Sutherlands concludes that the effect of the changes to Annex NI on the UK and the EU are yet to be seen.[26] Oliver Hailes in his recent examination of environmental clauses in investment arbitration assumes that the amendments and modifications of the ECT will not apply to those who are to withdraw before the 3 September 2025.[27] Yet, whether they do or don't, no one can plausibly argue that the EU or the UK have fewer obligations towards fossil fuel investors now than if they had remained in the ECT. In fact, there is a very real possibility that by withdrawing they have extended protection for fossil fuel investments rather than shortened it.

3.2 Recent Investment Activity in the Fossil Fuel Sector

We can already see the impact of the decision not to remain in a modernised ECT. There are a number of large new coal, oil and gas projects that have recently received funding.

[24] Decision of the Energy Charter Conference (2024), CCDEC 2024 13 GEN, Section B and C.

[25] Decision of the Energy Charter Conference (2024), CCDEC 2024 15 GEN.

[26] In: https://www.eversheds-sutherland.com/en/united-kingdom/insights/modernisation-of-the-energy-charter-treaty-approved-what-investors-need-to-know. Accessed 25 Aug 2025

[27] Hailes (2024), p. 25

It is difficult to determine just how many but an analysis by the German NGO Urgewald claims that 96% of exploration and extraction production companies have expansion plans and that short term expansion plans have increased by 20% since 2021.[28]

Despite the International Energy Agency warning in 2021 that no new fossil fuel projects should be approved if we want to tackle climate change[29], there are numerous large projects that have received the green light since then, although not all within the territory of the Contracting Parties of the ECT. The biggest projects are apparently being planned by Saudi Aramco, Quatar Energy and Abu Dhabi National Oil Co, followed by Exxon, Mobil, TotalEnergies and Chevron.[30] According to Urgewald's figures, Shell has invested nearly £10bn into oil and gas projects (as opposed to the £3bn it has invested in renewables).[31] Of its planned oil and gas field developments 57% are incompatible with the 1.5 degree model scenario mapped out by the IEA in 2021. If we believe the figures, Equinor has spent USD 1.139 billion and BP USD 858 million since 2021 on searching for new oil and gas reserves.[32]

The Guardian reported in March 2023 that the UK had supported the fossil fuel industry with £20bn more investment than renewables since 2015. Between 2020 and 2021, the UK government's support for fossil fuels showed a 10.7% increase.[33] And a UK Government analysis from April 2022 has indicated that the North Sea Transition Authority intended to launch a licensing round with a view to extracting the estimated 7.9 billion barrels of oil that remain under the sea and 560 billion cubic meters of gas.[34]

One concrete example is the oil exploration project under the Rosebank Field Development Plan for which Norwegian investor Equinor received the final go ahead from the North Sea Transition Authority on 27th September 2023.[35]

Had the Agreement in Principle been adopted as planned in November 2022 and had the UK made use of the flexibility mechanism as it has announced that it would, this investment would not have fallen under the protection provisions of the ECT, it having been approved one month after the phase out of protection for new fossil fuel investments would have taken effect. Equinor claims that the project will generate a total of £8.1bn direct investment in its lifetime.[36] Even though the UK has recently announced its intention to withdraw, this investment will now be protected under the ECT for at least 10 years (20 years if the unamended version of the treaty applies).

The Rosebank licence is unlikely to be the only example of recent investment activity in fossil fuels in the UK. In July 2023 Rishi Sunak, the prime minister at the time said that the UK government intended to 'max out' the UK's fossil fuel reserves when he

---

28 Carrington (2022).

29 International Energy Agency (2023), p. 212

30 Urgewald Media Briefing (2023).

31 European Commission Announcement, DG Energy (2023).

32 Urgewald Global Oil and Gas Exit List, in: https://gogel.org/. Accessed 25 Aug 2025.

33 Horton (2023).

34 UK Government Policy Paper, British Energy Security Strategy (2022).

35 Equinor Announcement 27 September 2023, in: https://www.equinor.com/news/20230927-rosebank-field-to-progress-in-the-uk. Accessed 25 Aug 2025

36 Ibid.

unveiled plans to authorise more than 100 new North Sea licences in July of 2023.[37] The current Labour government has since backtracked on this policy. But in January 2024, the UK's North Sea Transition Authority announced it had issued another 24 oil and gas licences to a total of 17 companies, including Shell, BP, Equinor, Total and NEO Energy. These licences only cover 74 out of a total of 900 blocks that have been made available. The rest are still subject to environmental evaluations,[38] but it is possible that some of these licences will have already resulted in some initial foreign investments and / or legitimate expectations of future profits.

According to a news report from Euronews in 2021, the UK was planning at least 40 fossil fuel projects, including a new coal mine in Cumbria, and extracting oil in Surrey. If these reports are accurate, then companies were seeking approval for 30 offshore oil and gas projects, 7 onshore and 3 coal mines during the years 2021 to 2025.[39] Although it was unclear at the time of writing which of these had received licences and to what extent any foreign investor interests have been created before the UK's effective withdrawal date in April 2025.

Within the EU there have also been some eye-catching new developments following the Russian invasion of Ukraine and the resulting worries about energy supply. The EU Agency for the Cooperation of Energy Regulators (ACER)'s opinion on the Hydrogen and Natural Gas TYNP 2022 highlights that in 2022 there was around 30bn worth of planned investment into new gas infrastructure, at least 40% of which was in conventional natural gas or infrastructure projects.[40] Investment into any of these planned projects coming to fruition since August 2023 would have fallen outside of the ECT's investment protection provisions had the Agreement in Principle been adopted and if the countries adopting these plans had taken the opportunity to phase out the investment protection provisions for fossil fuels.

Particularly in Germany, heavily depended on the import of Russian gas at the time of the invasion of Ukraine, the newly elected coalition government was faced with difficult choices about how to secure its energy supply. As a result, Germany called on G7 states to work with third countries to develop new gas fields and according to the Financial Times pushed for a watering down on commitments to end financial support for fossil fuels in order to tackle the energy crisis. The 2022 G7 statement said publicly supported investment in the gas sector can be appropriate as a temporary response to the exceptional circumstances created by the war in Ukraine[41] At the same time as asking for a delay in the planned phase out of financial support for fossil fuels at the G7 summit, Germany indicated its intention to withdraw from the ECT claiming that it was slowing down the energy transition because the phase out of support for fossil fuel investors was too slow.[42]

---

[37] BBC 6 o'Clock News (2025).

[38] North Sea Transition Authority (2024).

[39] Euronews (2021).

[40] European Network of Transmission System Operators for Gas (2022) and ACER Opinion on TYNDP (2022).

[41] Mooney et al. (2023).

[42] Bundesministerium für Wirtschaft und Klimaschutz Eckpunktepapier (2022b).

Even after a withdrawal from the Energy Charter Treaty, there are still a large number of bilateral investment treaties in place that would cover those fossil fuel investments that are no longer protected by membership of the ECT. Staying with Germany for the moment, Germany has investment treaties in place with all non-EU countries that are also signatories of the ECT, except for Japan and Iceland, which are covered by other trade agreements. The investment protection provisions may not all be as strong as those found in the ECT, but most will contain standard investment protection provisions, including ISDS.[43] A withdrawal from the ECT will not affect any protection afforded fossil fuel investments under those treaties. However, there is an argument that any amendments to the ECT that are incompatible with those BITs would prevail pursuant to Article 30 of the Vienna Convention, thereby potentially limiting those BITs for those countries who remain party to the treaty[44] - so not for Germany.

There may have been very good reasons for the many decisions to withdraw from the ECT. However, withdrawing in order to achieve a quicker phase out of investment protection for fossil fuel investors does not seem to be one of them. If we look at the question purely from the point of view of ending protection for fossil fuels, then it would seem that staying party to the ECT and adopting the Agreement in Principle would have allowed for a speedier end to protection in fossil fuels than withdrawing.

Remaining a Contracting Party would also have paved the way for tribunals to adopt the amended, more climate focused interpretation of the drafting in future claims brought by existing fossil fuel investors against governments seeking to honour their obligations under the Paris Agreement, which those who withdrew before the modernised version comes into force will no doubt face during the 20 years 'sunset' period. Any such claims are now likely to be considered under the old wording rather than the modernised one. And just at a time when investors in renewable energy are facing an increasingly uncertain international investment climate the investment protection the ECT afforded investors in renewable energy is no longer applicable.

To conclude, the withdrawal from the ECT by the EU cannot therefore be said to be in line with its policy to phase out fossil fuels and implement a speedy energy transition towards renewable sources of energy.

3.3 Moving on from the Fossil Fuel Debate

The protection for fossil fuel investors has, understandably, dominated the discussion. However, it has also obscured some of the other aspects of the ECT and has invalidated any arguments that point to its potential benefits - because what is the point of any benefit when there is the large elephant of fossil fuel protection blocking the way in the middle of the room. A treaty that stops governments from implementing a phase out of fossil fuels is a hindrance, no matter what its other benefits may be. But having now moved the elephant along, we can get a clearer view on what investment protection provisions, including ISDS can offer.

[43] See UNCTAD Investment Policy Hub. In: https://investmentpolicy.unctad.org/international-investment-agreements/countries/78/germany. Accessed 25 Aug 2025

[44] Vienna Convention on the Law of Treaties, United Nations, Treaty Series Vol 1155, p. 331, 235.1969, art. 30.

It is often cited as a counter argument to its critics, that in fact the ECT also protects renewable energy investors and therefore has the potential to support the energy transition. Here, we can cite the many awards that have already been granted in favour of renewable investors. These exceed those of the fossil fuel industry, if not in the overall amount (mainly due to the large award granted in the Yukos case), then at least in the number of awards.[45]

But is this a valid argument? As we recalibrate the parameters of the international investment framework is there still room for ISDS? To argue convincingly that there is, we would need to show that ISDS and investment protection for foreign investment is useful in the context of current EU energy policy. In other words, can investment protection provisions help establish an energy transition based on a decentralised energy infrastructure and community participation in energy production?

This is an angle that has not yet been considered in any detail, if at all, and that is whether the ECT, has any relevance on investment in local energy communities, one of the pillars of EU energy policy. It is argued here, that even if, de facto, the ECT is in it's dying days, there may yet be an argument to develop some of the principle provisions for a new and improved energy treaty, possibly in the form of a strengthened and legally binding implementation of the International Energy Charter – which is currently a non-binding statement of political will made by 90 countries. To explore this potential, we need to take a closer look at EU energy policy.

4 EU Energy Policy and the Decentralisation of the Energy Sector

The EU has set itself the target to achieve carbon neutrality by 2050.[46] There are currently two main obstacles to achieving this goal: lack of finance and local opposition.[47] Furthermore, the energy transition requires a fundamental change in the way we produce, distribute and consume energy, in other words an energy sector shake up that, ideally, would be built on renewable energy sources, tackle fuel poverty and that is widely accepted by the public. Local energy communities are central to achieving this goal. The EU's Clean Energy Package set out a number of policy initiatives that firmly places community energy at the heart of the coming energy revolution.[48] It is easy to see why this appears to be a promising pathway. The Commission for the Environment, Climate Change and Energy 2018 concluded that in order to implement the EU climate and energy policy objectives there would need to be a move towards a decentralised energy system and a change in the roles of energy producers and consumers.[49]

45 International Energy Chapter News (2023).

46 Rockhopper Exploration PLC, Rockhopper Italia S.P.A. and Rockhopper Mediterranean Ltd v Italy, ICSID Case No ARB/17/14.

47 European Committee of the Regions Commission for the Environment, Climate Change and Energy (2018).

48 See EU Clean Energy Package 2019. In: https://energy.ec.europa.eu/topics/energy-strategy/clean-energy-all-europeans-package_en. Accessed 25 Aug 2025.

49 European Committee of the Regions. Commission for the Environment, Climate Change and Energy (2018).

This in turn will be hard to achieve if local communities do not accept this very visible change to their local landscapes. Research shows that local acceptance of energy infrastructure – wind turbines, solar panels etc. is strongest when there is a tangible benefit in the form of some kind of participation, both financially and democratically.[50] According to a number of studies and surveys, there is a positive correlation between the development of community energy projects and support for local renewable energy[51] This is particularly true of communities of place.[52] In a comparison of acceptance levels among 320 residents of Zschadrass in Germany who formed a citizens renewable energy (CRE) initiative and the neighbouring town of Nossen, where a traditional corporation built a wind farm, Musall and Kuik found that the CRE project in Zschadrass led to a higher rate of acceptance not only to the local wind farm but also of wind energy in general.[53] Bauwens & Devine Wright[54] and Schumacher[55] have also shown that CRE projects with local citizen participation make citizens more supportive, not just of local renewable energy infrastructure but more generally of public policies and trends in favour of renewable energy and climate action.

This suggests a possible way out of the conundrum that although the majority of the population are in favour of an expansion of renewable energy (in Germany, for example, 93% are in favour of scaling up production of energy from renewable sources[56]), when it comes to agreeing to such installations within their locality there is an element of Nimbyism at play, i.e. that people support the energy transition, so long as it is not happening in their back yard.

A decentralised approach in which citizens can participate in the shaping of their local energy transition might also allow for different approaches and views of the energy transition to emerge. Some communities that are currently heavily reliant on fossil fuels or whose livelihoods currently depend on the production of fossil fuels will take a different approach, a rural community will not have the same priorities and approaches as an urban centre. Different communities will have a variety of diverging attitudes and cultures and there may be different things that they are keen to protect or nurture, as well as differing levels of ability or willingness to participate.[57]

And then, of course, there is the key factor that community energy can make energy cheaper. In Feldheim, just over an hour's drive from Berlin, the electricity grid is run by a 100% renewable energy community. 150 citizens raised 3000 Euros to participate in the acquisition of the grid from private company E.on. The grid is now owned by Feldheim Energie GmbH & Co Kg. Energiequelle GmbH is the general partner. Since the takeover of the grid energy bills have been reduced by 31% and citizens have a

50 See for example studies by Bauwens and Devine-Wright (2018); Bauwens (2016) and Roberts et al. (2014).

51 Musall and Kuik (2011).

52 Fast (2013).

53 See UNCTAD Investment Policy Hub.

54 Devine-Wright and Bauwens; Bundesministerium für Wirtschaft und Klimaschutz Eckpunktepapier (2022b).

55 Schumacher (2019).

56 Staab (2016).

57 Velasco-Herrejon et al. (2022).

say in price regulation.[58] On Energiequelle's website, a spokesperson from the John Laing Group in London, an international investor in infrastructure projects, provides an endorsement for the Energiequelle's investor page, an example of how international investment can be successfully married up with local energy communities.[59]

EU energy policy has taken this on board and has provided policy space to enable citizen participation in energy projects to flourish, most notably in the provisions of the Renewable Energy Directive II[60] and the recast Electricity Directive.[61] Great importance is placed on the development of the prosumer and in building local energy communities where citizens are encouraged to participate in the production and distribution of energy. Local authorities and sub national and regional authorities are called upon here to develop and facilitate these. In the words of the RESCoop EU website: "Regional and national authorities as well as their support networks have a crucial role to play in developing and communicating tools and approaches to designing procedures in support of community ownership."[62]

There is a great opportunity here to direct the energy transition towards more energy democracy and to create value for local communities, rather than extracting value from them.

One challenge, however, is that more investment is needed than citizens and local authorities or even governments are likely to be able to raise from the public purse. As we have seen at both global and EU level, access to funding for the energy transition remains a challenge, whether at national or local level. If funding is an issue for the EU and its member states with its relatively full public coffers and the political motivation to direct funds towards the energy transition, it will pose an even greater challenge for countries with a smaller wallet.

A 2022 study by Broska et al. concluded that a citizen-driven energy transition is unlikely to be successful unless access to finance can be improved.[63] The study envisages more public funding in the form of subsidies, feed-in tariffs etc. But given the funding gap, this will be expensive. However, private finance is often also difficult to raise. Because energy communities are usually geared towards community interest rather than profit and operate on a 'one member one vote' system of governance, they are not necessarily attractive to a private investor.

This may be the reason why investment treaties are not seen as relevant to community owned enterprises. There is currently no literature that draws a connection between the investment protection provisions in the ECT and local energy communities. Likewise local authorities and managers of local energy communities on the whole do not see the ECT as relevant to their local enterprise. In fact, even 2 years ago interviews with stakeholders in local energy were rarely aware of the existence of the ECT, although

---

58 Roberts et al. (2014), p. 75; UNCTAD Investment Policy Hub.

59 Energiequelle GmbH. In: https://www.energiequelle.de/en/investors/. Accessed 25 Aug 2024

60 Directive (EU 2018/2001.

61 Directive (EU) 2019/944.

62 European Federation of Renewable Energy Cooperatives (2018).

63 Broska et al. (2022).

this has changed in recent years due to the increased media attention the treaty has attracted.[64]

Does that mean then, that an international investment treaty is not relevant to local energy communities? - far from it. Pursuant to Article 23 of the ECT, the ISDS provisions already apply to local energy infrastructure projects to the extent that they involve foreign direct investment.

5 Article 23 of the Energy Charter Treaty

The link between the Energy Charter Treaty and local energy systems lies in Article 23 which makes Contracting Parties responsible for making sure that regional and local governments within their area comply with the ECT. Article 23(3) states that:

> "The dispute settlement provisions in Parts II, IV and V of this Treaty may be invoked in respect of measures affecting the observance of the Treaty by a Contracting Party which have been taken by regional or local governments or authorities within the Area of the Contracting Party."[65]

Pursuant to Article 23 therefore, the dispute resolution provisions in Article 26, including the controversial investor-state dispute resolution mechanism, would bite in the event that a local authority takes measures that are in breach of the ECT for the duration of a state's membership of the ECT and for a further 20 years after any date of withdrawal due to the sunset provision. At first glance this may be a worrying prospect. Although under international law, Article 23 is not a novel provision. It mirrors similar provisions in the GATT adopted in 1994 and follows customary international law rules on attribution as codified in the UN International Law Commission Articles on State Responsibility.[66]

A decentralisation of energy production and a greater role of local municipal authorities in shaping energy policy has the potential of widening the reach of the ECT to local energy communities. There is not much commentary on this Article, although it was one of the more controversial treaty provisions during the original negotiations between the contracting parties. The US, in particular, found this Articles problematic due to its federal system of government.[67] Within the EU governance structure, sub national authorities also play a significant role as they are closest to the citizen and therefore, following the principle of subsidiarity defined in Article 5 of the Treaty on the EU, decisions should be taken by municipalities wherever this is possible.[68]

Article 23 could have far-reaching implications for current EU energy policy. If we are giving local authorities more responsibility in shaping the energy transition, then there will be more scope for breaches of the ECT at local level.

---

[64] These preliminary findings are part of an ongoing study being conducted by the author on the legal framework governing local energy communities in Germany, which due to be completed in 2025.

[65] Art 23(3) The Energy Charter Treaty 1994.

[66] Hober (2020).

[67] Grasso C (2018).

[68] Ibid, 23.10.

Some may plausibly argue, that this should not be a problem, as surely there are no foreign investors in local energy communities. Broadly speaking, this is indeed currently the case. In Germany, as at December 2022, only 4% of investors in local energy communities were companies and an even smaller percentage were foreign investors.[69] This is most likely due to several reasons. Most foreign investors are currently invested in larger, possibly more profitable enterprises. And of course, it is likely that most community owned energy projects will have been set up using some form of not-for-profit organisational structure.

6 EU Definitions of Community Energy

At this stage it helps to clarify what the EU defines as a local energy community. There are currently two different definitions of energy communities in circulation. The first can be found in Article 2(11) of the new Electricity Directive which defines "citizen energy communities" as a legal entity that is controlled by natural persons, local authorities and small enterprises and "has for its primary purpose to provide environmental, economic or social community benefits to its members or shareholders or to the local areas where it operates rather than to generate financial profits".[70]

The second is the definition of "renewable energy communities" in Art 2(16) of the Renewable Energy Directive which, unlike the definition of "citizen energy communities" ties the community to its locality and requires a legal entity that is effectively controlled by shareholders or members "that are located in the proximity of the renewable energy projects that are owned and developed by that legal entity", which can include natural persons, local authorities and small and medium sized enterprises. The definition also stipulates the same required purpose as being one that is primarily not for profit but adds that it needs to benefit the shareholders, members or the local area.[71] There is thus rightly a focus on creating value for the community. On the other hand, these definitions do not leave much room for private investors.

In yet, as we have seen, private investment is needed to fill the funding gap. Not only are private investors well placed to provide finance, they also bring valuable technical expertise. Whilst local communities might be understandably wary of inviting foreign investors to invest in their local energy infrastructure, particularly if they are protected by ISDS in international treaties, there is also a great opportunity here. Investors will be investing in local communities with some form of citizen participation. And therefore, community interest will be a determining factor in formulating the conditions for their investment and shape their legitimate expectations. These will limit the amount of claims that they will be able to successfully make which are pitched against community interests, whilst at the same time, having protection at treaty level will provide at least some insurance against the apparent risks of investing in local community projects. But why would investors invest in these projects? Because, if we play our cards right, investors will have no choice if they want to do business. The EU guidance for Public Procurement allows authorities to put limitations and requirements on renewable energy

69 Dannemann (2022).

70 Directive (EU) 2019/944.

71 Directive (EU 2018 /2001).

developments,[72] and municipalities are increasingly making use of these powers. In 2020, Strasbourg for example, only allowed organisations taking the form of "citizen energy communities" to participate in the tender process for the development of a wind park.[73] Therefore, if private investors and developers in renewable energy infrastructure want to have a presence in local energy, they would need to set up business models that include community participation and ownership. However, in return they will need to be able to generate a profit, which would disqualify the project from falling under the definitions of renewable or citizen energy communities. On the other hand, operating on a profit basis puts such communities in danger of falling within the remit of the WTO rules and fall foul of the local content requirement restrictions as well as making it harder for the EU to circumvent its own rules on state aid, subsidies and competition.

7 Klixbuell – a Profitable Energy Community

These matters require further research, but if these difficulties could be overcome, it would make for a happier marriage between private and public ownership of energy infrastructure. One example of how this might operate in practice is the small local community of Klixbuell in the North of Germany close to the Danish border. The village produces 100% of its energy needs from renewables and local citizens part-own the two local wind farms. Klixbuell is now working on positioning itself as the energy 'powerhouse' of the North. A look at the company structure reveals that not only are local citizens investors in the wind parks but there is also foreign investment involved. The wind park is run by a GmbH & Co KG, a limited liability partnership owned by the local community who enjoy limited liability and a management company who takes a share of the profit and is fully liable. Involved in this management company is Euro Wind Energy A/S, a Danish enterprise. Setting aside for a moment the developments around intra EU investment dispute settlement, we here have a clear format where the ECT could be directly relevant to a local energy community. This business model has the advantage of enabling citizen participation and also facilitating investment. Furthermore, it is being run by a company that has specialist technological expertise resulting in innovative new technology currently being piloted to produce more efficient wind turbines, as well as developing a new energy storage hub in an old Second World War bunker. The aim is to become what the coal producing Ruhr area became for Germany after the previous energy revolution – an engine that powers Germany's industry. Whilst the Ruhr could provide the necessary natural resource for the first fossil fuel era, before the age of oil put coal on the backburner, the northern climes of Klixbuell can offer the resources for the next energy transition – not very much sun – but copious amounts of wind and sea. From suffering years of depopulation, Klixbuell has recently bucked the trend and is seeing an increase in people moving into the area, attracted by the clean air, the proximity to the sea and the newly created opportunities economically but also in terms of quality of life and wellbeing. This corporate model shows a path away from large multinationals managing our common resources to creating a stable investment climate that enables smaller businesses working in tandem with local communities. And it also

[72] European Federation of Renewable Energy Cooperatives (REScoop) (2023).

[73] Ibid, p. 28

points towards a role for investment treaties that facilitate investment and create value for local communities. It creates a possible path towards what Jeremy Rifkin termed the Third Industrial Revolution.

8 Conclusion

In his book The Third Industrial Revolution, Jeremy Rifkin set out a vision for a new way of doing business, one that places social capital on an equal footing with financial capital.[74] In yet, we always seem to have a tendency towards ignoring one when pursuing the other. Pitching community interest against financial interest often leads to conflict in which finance frequently has the upper hand. The energy transition will be harder to achieve and less palatable if we cannot mobilise private investment. Article 2 of the Paris Agreement 2015 obliges countries to "make finance flows consistent with a pathway towards low greenhouse gas emissions and climate resilient development".[75] If we decide that granting a central role for community energy is key to achieving the energy transition, then this is where the finance flows should go. Public funds are limited and dependent on the political will and ability to spend them. Our best option is therefore to look towards private capital to lend a helping hand. However, this will not be possible unless there is sufficient financial incentive as well as sufficient investment protection. Investing in local energy projects with citizen participation is inherently risky and requires considerable up-front costs.

On 16th April 2025, the Trump administration ordered an immediate stop to the construction of a wind farm off the coast of Long Island as part of a policy change away from renewable energy back to oil, gas and coal. The Norwegian company Equinor had acquired a lease for the site in 2017 and construction had begun in 2024.[76] Despite being a key negotiator of the ECT in the 1990s, the US never signed the treaty. The move against the wind park will therefore not result in a potential claim against the US under the ECT. However, it illustrates the dangers that investors face when the political winds change direction. Therefore, particularly in the energy sector, reassurance in the form of investor-state dispute resolution, within an investment treaty can still fulfil a useful role. There is still more research needed into how ISDS can be made a more transparent, fair and speedy judicial process and how foreign direct investment can be best embedded into the structure of a community enterprise. The provisions of the newly modernised Energy Charter Treaty, may prove to be a good starting point after all, if not as a way of keeping alive a tired old treaty of the 1990s but to formulate a more sustainable international investment framework for the next decade and beyond.

References

Bauwens, T.: Explaining the diversity of motivations behind community renewable energy. Energy Policy **93**, 278–290 (2016). https://doi.org/10.1016/j.enpol.2016.03.017

[74] Rifkin (2011).

[75] Article 2.1c of the Paris Agreement to the United Nations Framework Convention on Climate Change, 12 Dec 2015, T.I.A.S. No 16-1104

[76] McGeehan (2025)

Bauwens, T., Devine Wright, P.: Positive energies? An empirical study of community energy participation and attitudes to renewable energy. Energy Policy **118**, 612–625 (2018). https://doi.org/10.1016/j.enpol.2018.03.062

Bernasconi-Osterwalder, N., Dietrich Brauch, M.: Redesigning the Energy Charter Treaty to Advance the Low-Carbon Transition (February 1, 2019). TDM 1 (2019)

Broska, L.H., et al.: On the future(s) of energy communities in the german energy transition: a derivation of transformation pathways. Sustainability **2022**, 14 (2022)

Dannemann, B.: Energie gemeinsam nutzen. Deutscher Genossenschafts- und Raiffeisenverband (2022). https://www.dgrv.de/energie-gemeinsam-nutzen-2/. Accessed 25 Aug 2025

Ekardt, F., Roos, P., Barenwaldt, M.: Energiecharta-Vertrag, Paris Abkommen und die Menschenrechte. Zeitschrift fuer Neues Energierecht. **26**(4), 347–355 (2022)

Fast, S.: Social acceptance of renewable energy: trends, concepts, and geographies. Geogr. Compass **2013** (2013)

Grasso, C.: Observance by sub-national authorities. In: Leal-Arcas, R. (ed.) Commentary on the Energy Charter Treaty, pp 322–332. Edward Elgar Publishing Ltd. (2018)

Hailes, O.: Environmental clauses in investment arbitration: deep roots, green shoots, and dead wood. LSE Law, Society and Economy Working Papers 17/2024 (2024). https://doi.org/10.1093/icsidreview/siaf003

Hober, K.: The Energy Charter Treaty: A Commentary. Oxford University Press, Oxford (2020)

Musall, D., Kuik, O.: Local acceptance of renewable energy – a case study from southeast Germany. Energy Policy **39**(6), 3252–3260 (2011)

Rifkin, J.: The Third Industrial Revolution: How Lateral Power is Transforming Energy, the Economy and the World. Palgrave Macmillan, London (2011)

Roberts, J., et al.: Community Power: model legal framework for citizen-owned renewable energy. Client Earth. London (2014). https://papers.ssrn.com/sol3/papers.cfm?abstract_id=4637691

Schumacher, K.: Public Acceptance of renewable energies and energy autonomy: a comparative study in the French, German and Swiss Upper Rhine region. Energy Policy **126**, 315–332 (2019)

Staab, J.: Erneuerbare Energien in Kommunen: Energiegenossenschaften gründen, führen und beraten. 3rd edn. Springer Gabler (2016)

Tienhaara, K., Downie, C.: Risky business? The energy charter treaty, renewable energy and investor-state disputes. Glob. Gov. **24**, 451–471 (2018)

Velasco-Herrejon, P., Bauwens, T., Friant, M.C.: Challenging dominant sustainability worldviews on the energy transition: lessons from Indigenous communities in Mexico and a plea for pluriversal technologies. World Dev. **150** (2022). https://doi.org/10.1016/j.worlddev.2021.105725

Government, Agencies and International Organisations Publications

ACER (European Union Agency for the Cooperation of Energy Regulators) Opinion on TYNDP (2022). https://www.acer.europa.eu/news-and-events/news/acer-calls-improvements-entsogs-draft-gas-and-hydrogen-ten-year-network-development-plan. Accessed 25 Aug 2025

Bundesministerium für Wirtschaft und Klimaschutz (2022a), Klimawende Direkt, Ausgabe 11. https://www.bmwk-energiewende.de/EWD/Redaktion/Newsletter/2022/11/Meldung/direkt-erklaert.html. Accessed 25 Aug 2025

Bundesministerium für Wirtschaft und Klimaschutz. Weiterentwicklung des Eckpunktepapiers, Handelspolitik der Bundesregierung (2022b). https://www.bundeswirtschaftsministerium.de/Redaktion/DE/Downloads/E/eckpunktepapier-weiterentwicklung-des-eckpunktepapiers-handelspolitik-der-bundesregierung.html. Accessed 25 Aug 2025

Energy Charter Secretariat, Decisions of the Energy Charter Conference, CCDEC 22 10 GEN, 24.6.2022. https://www.energycharter.org/fileadmin/DocumentsMedia/CCDECS/2022/CCDEC202210.pdf. Accessed 25 Aug 2025
Energy Charter Secretariat, Decisions of the Energy Charter Conference, CCDEC 2024 12 GEN, CCDEC 2024, 13 GEN & CCDEC 2024 15 GEN, 3.12.2024. https://www.energycharter.org/media/news/article/the-energy-charter-conference-adopts-decisions-on-the-modernisation-of-the-energy-charter-treaty/. Accessed 25 Aug 2025
European Commission. Clean Energy for All Europeans. Publications Office of the European Union 2019 (2019). https://wayback.archive-it.org/12090/20241209144917/https://energy.ec.europa.eu/topics/energy-strategy/clean-energy-all-europeans-package_en. Accessed 25 Aug 2025
European Commission, Energy, Climate Change, Environment (2024) https://climate.ec.europa.eu/eu-action/climate-strategies-targets/2030-climate-targets_en. Accessed 25 Aug 2025
European Committee of the Regions. Commission for the Environment, Climate Change and Energy. Models of Local Energy Ownership and the Roles of Local Energy Communities in Energy Transition in Europe (2018). https://data.europa.eu/doi/10.2863/603673. Accessed 25 Aug 2025
European Federation of Renewable Energy Cooperatives (REScoop) (2018). https://www.rescoop.eu/toolbox/the-rescoop-municipality-approach. Accessed 25 Aug 2025
European Federation of Renewable Energy Cooperatives (REScoop). EU Procurement Guide for Community Energy (2023). https://www.rescoop.eu/toolbox/procurement-guide-for-community-energy. Accessed 25 Aug 2025
European Network of Transmission System Operators for Gas. Ten Year Network Development Plan (TYNP) (2022). https://www.entsog.eu/sites/default/files/2023-05/ENTSOG_TYNDP_2022_Executive_Summary.pdf. Accessed 25 Aug 2025
European Parliament, Plenary Session, Press Release. MEPs consent to the EU withdrawing from the Energy Charter Treaty, 24.04.2024 (2024). https://www.europarl.europa.eu/news/en/press-room/20240419IPR20549/meps-consent-to-the-eu-withdrawing-from-the-energy-charter-treaty. Accessed 25 Aug 2025
International Energy Agency (2023) World Energy Outlook 2023. https://www.iea.org/reports/world-energy-outlook-2023. Accessed 25 Aug 2025
North Sea Transition Authority (2024), Press Release, 31.1.2024, https://www.nstauthority.co.uk/news-publications/24-licences-offered-in-second-tranche-of-33rd-oil-and-gas-licensing-round/. Accessed 25 Aug 2025
UK Government Policy Paper (2022), British Energy Security Strategy, 7.4.2022. https://www.gov.uk/government/publications/british-energy-security-strategy/british-energy-security-strategy. Accessed 25 Aug 2025

Cases

RWE AG and RWE Eemshaven Holding II B.V. v Netherlands, ICSID Case No ARB/21/4
Uniper SE, Uniper Benelux Holding B.V. and Uniper Benelux N.V. v Netherlands, ICSID Case No ARB/21/22
Rockhopper Exploration PLC, Rockhopper Italia S.P.A. and Rockhopper Mediterranean Ltd v Italy, ICSID Case No ARB/17/14

News Sources

BBC 6 o'Clock News (2023), 31.7.2023. https://www.bbc.co.uk/sounds/play/m001p7df. Accessed 22 April 2025

Carrington, D.: Oil and Gas firms planning frightening fossil fuel growth, report finds. The Guardian (2022). https://www.theguardian.com/environment/2022/nov/10/oil-and-gas-firms-planning-cop27-climate-crisis-frightening-fossil-fuels-growth-report-finds. Accessed 25 Aug 2025

Euronews (2021). https://www.euronews.com/green/2021/10/28/the-uk-has-40-new-fossil-fuel-projects-in-the-pipeline-what-does-this-mean-for-cop26-credi. Accessed 25 Aug 2025

Friends of the Earth Europe (2024). https://friendsoftheearth.eu/press-release/win-eu-parliament-votes-for-exiting-the-climate-wrecking-energy-charter-treaty/. Accessed 25 Aug 2025

Horton, H.: Fossil Fuels received £20bn more UK support than renewables since 2025. The Guardian (2023). https://www.theguardian.com/environment/2023/mar/09/fossil-fuels-more-support-uk-than-renewables-since-2015. Accessed 25 Aug 2025

McGeehan, P.: Trump Administration Halts Building of Giant Wind Farm Off N.Y. Coast. The New York Times (2025)

Mooney, A., Chazan, G., Inagaki, K., et al.: Financial Times, Germany sets stage for G7 clash with push to endorse gas (2023)

Unlocking the Potential of Long-Term Contracts in the EU Energy Landscape

Beatrice Bichi Ruspoli Forteguerri(✉)

Università Degli Studi Roma Tre, Rome, Italy
beatrice.bichiruspoliforteguerri@uniroma3.it

Abstract. On 14 December 2023 the European Parliament and the Council reached an agreement on a reform to improve the European Union's electricity market design within the framework of the 2019 Green Deal. Historically, the Commission has regarded long-term contracts as barriers to energy market liberalization, launching proceedings to terminate them under State aid rules or for abuse of dominant position. However, the European Union (EU) now intends to incentivize the use of long-term contracting in the form of power purchase agreements to advance decarbonisation. This chapter delves into the evolving role of long-term contracting in the EU energy landscape, arguing that competition still has an important role to play in energy markets.

1 Introduction

The aim of the EU's common rules for the internal market for electricity is to ensure affordable and transparent energy prices for consumers, while preserving a high degree of security of supply and promoting a smooth transition towards a sustainable low-carbon energy system[1]. This balance between energy security, equity, and environmental sustainability is often referred to as 'Energy Trilemma'[2]. However, as proved by the extraordinary surge in energy prices experienced in 2022, more is needed to safeguard this balance.

Experts concur that the underlying reason for the extraordinary price hikes can be attributed to the effective operation of the current wholesale electricity market, rather than to anticompetitive behaviours[3]. During the crisis, the correct functioning of the market failed to provide energy security and equity to consumers, and the Commission had to implement a series of measures to soften the impact of high prices. Among these, it has proposed to improve the electricity market design, including by increasing the role of long-term contracts. The challenge lies in striking the right balance between short-term and long-term considerations in energy markets, ensuring that the gains achieved through liberalization are not lost in the reform.

[1] Article 1(2) of Directive (EU) 2019/944 of the European Parliament and of the Council of 5 June 2019 on common rules for the internal market for electricity and amending Directive 2012/27/EU (recast), OJ 2019 L 158, 14.6.2019, pp. 125-199.

[2] Popkostova (2022), p. 1.

[3] Zachmann et al. (2023). The authors report that there is no evidence so far that anti-competitive behaviors punishable under EU competition law played a role in driving up prices, p. 24.

M. Reese et al. (Eds.): EELF 2023, *Legal Implementation and Impacts of the European Green Deal*, pp. 95–116, 2026.
https://doi.org/10.1007/978-3-032-17197-9_4

After briefly introducing the shortcomings of the current market design revealed by the recent energy crisis (Sect. 2), this chapter looks into the evolution of long-term contracts (as defined in Sect. 3) in the EU energy landscape, exploring how they have transitioned from an instrument to maintain market power (Sect. 4) to a crucial tool for renewable energy investment (Sect. 5). It is argued that in the ongoing reform long-term contracts play a pivotal role to achieve decarbonisation and improve energy security and affordability, ultimately restoring a more favourable balance within the Energy Trilemma (Sect. 6). Lastly, the chapter offers some brief conclusions on how competition enforcement and advocacy could be essential in complementing the regulatory reform to preserve the benefits of liberalisation (Sect. 7).

2 The Electricity Market Design in the Energy Crisis

In the wholesale market, electricity is sold in bulk to suppliers, who then provide it to consumers in the retail market[4]. Wholesale procurement operates on a system of marginal pricing, in accordance with the so-called 'merit-order' principle[5]. In marginal pricing, electricity producers bid into the market by establishing their price according to their marginal cost of production (essentially, the cost to operate for a given period) and electricity is bought according to a merit-order from the cheapest to the most expensive. Marginal pricing ensures that energy is supplied to consumers at the lowest price possible, while the merit-order promotes investment in decarbonisation, since renewables are always dispatched by the market[6].

According to the Commission, one of the main causes of the price peaks of energy in 2022 has been the reduction in gas supply, especially after the start of the war in Ukraine[7]. It is true that the present market design has successfully fulfilled its purpose by conveying to consumers that energy is a limited resource, encouraging them to reduce their energy consumption during a period of scarcity[8]. However, this also meant that the

4 OECD (2022). The electricity supply chain involves five main stages: generation, high-voltage transmission, low-voltage distribution, trading (i.e., selling and buying on the wholesale market), and retail supply to final customers (id. at p. 11).

5 SWD (2023) 58 final, Commission Staff Working Document, Reform of Electricity Market Design, p. 7. Marginal pricing is not a rule imposed by EU legislation, but simply the way in which prices emerge in free markets (see Zachmann et al. (2023), pp. 22-23). Also, the merit-order is not an instruction to market players, but only a description of free market outcomes (id.).

6 SWD(2023) 58 final, pp. 3-7. Unlike conventional plants, where ongoing operating costs play a significant role, the cost of renewable energy production (particularly for solar and wind power) is primarily tied to the initial investment. Consequently, renewable energy typically carries a lower price and is consistently prioritized in market dispatch at the rate set by the last plant required to meet demand. However, given that renewable energy sources (RES) constitute only 17% of the EU energy mix, as per the latest Eurostat data (https://ec.europa.eu/eurostat/web/interactive-publications/energy-2023. Accessed 15 Aug 2025), fossil-fuel operating plants often become essential to meet demand. As a result, energy bills remain notably influenced by fossil fuel prices.

7 SWD (2023) 58 final, p 3. Other causes identified by the Commission were the pick-up of economy after the Covid-19 pandemic and shortfalls in nuclear and hydropower.

8 Meeus et al. (2022).

exceptionally high prices for fossil fuels in 2022 saw energy bills triple or quadruple for many consumers[9], leading to windfall profits for renewable energy producers[10].

In response, the Commission enacted a series of measures to soften the impact of high prices in the short-term. Most notably, a temporary State aid regime[11] and price limiting interventions to prevent windfall profits for energy producers[12] were implemented. Most of these measures were adopted in the framework of the special legislative procedure provided by Article 122(1), TFEU, to bolster solidarity between Member States. These regimes could only be temporary to avoid the risk of altering competition in the internal market[13].

In this framework, in 2022 the Commission adopted the REPowerEU plan[14] to boost energy efficiency and renewable energy production. Closely aligned with the Green Deal Industrial Plan[15], it aims to phase out Europe's dependency on Russian energy imports as soon as possible by accelerating the deployment of renewable energy sources (RES), not only to reach decarbonisation targets but also to increase security of supply and lower prices for consumers.

---

[9] Popkostova (2022), pp. 2-4.

[10] COM/2023/148 final, Commission's Proposal for a Regulation of the European Parliament and of the Council amending Regulations (EU) 2019/943 and (EU) 2019/942 as well as Directives (EU) 2018/2001 and (EU) 2019/944 to improve the Union's electricity market design, p. 1.

[11] Communication from the Commission, Temporary Crisis Framework for State aid measures to support the economy following the aggression against Ukraine by Russia, OJ 2022 CI 131/1.

[12] To avoid distortions between generators in the Union, the Council implemented a coordinated temporary cap on market revenues from electricity produced from generators with lower marginal costs, such as renewables (see Articles 6-7 of Council Regulation (EU) 2022/1854 of 6 October 2022 on an emergency intervention to address high energy prices, OJ 2022 LI 261/1).

[13] Hancher (2023). The author observes that large sums of public money were spent on national subsidies to contain the effects of the crisis on consumers, and this raised the issue of how effectively Treaty rules on State aid have been applied (id. at pp. 156-157).

[14] COM(2022)230, Communication from the Commission to the European Parliament, the European Council, the Council, the European Economic and Social Committee and the Committee of the Regions, REPowerEU Plan..

[15] COM(2023) 62 final, Communication from the Commission to the European Parliament, the European Council, the Council, the European economic and social committee and the Committee of the Regions, A Green Deal Industrial Plan for the Net-Zero Age.

REPowerEU was followed in March 2023 by the Commission's proposal to reform to the electricity market design[16]. At the time of writing (February 2024), the European Parliament and the Council have reached an agreement on the text of the reform (Provisional Agreement)[17], but it has not yet been formally adopted[18].

The reform would amend various regulations and directives that currently shape the EU electricity market, including Regulation (EU) no. 943 of 2019 (Electricity Regulation)[19]. Specifically, it aims to provide a buffer between short-term markets (also known as 'spot-markets')[20] and consumers' electricity bills through a significant expansion of the role of long-term contracting in the form of contracts for difference and power purchase agreements[21].

3 Understanding Power Purchase Agreements and Contracts for Difference

The energy crisis brought the reform of the electricity market to the forefront of the EU's political agenda, with long-term contracting emerging as a pivotal element in the Commission's proposal, also in the form of power purchase agreements (PPAs).

PPAs are private commercial bilateral agreements, freely negotiated by the parties, with some common characteristics. Typically spanning 10 to 20 years, PPAs enable buyers to procure electricity from producers directly, offering fixed or minimum prices and volumes[22].

[16] COM/2023/148 final, Commission Proposal to improve the Union's electricity market design. More details on the reform are provided in section 6.

[17] This consensus was achieved through interinstitutional negotiations, commonly known as 'trilogues'. See General Secretariat of the Council (2023), Proposal for a Regulation of the European Parliament and of the Council amending Regulations (EU) 2019/943 and (EU) 2019/942 as well as Directives (EU) 2018/2001 and (EU) 2019/944 to improve the Union's electricity market design - Analysis of the final compromise text with a view to agreement, Interinstitutional File 2023/0077(COD).

[18] Widuto (2024). Since the submission of this chapter, the reform was formally adopted on 21 May 2024 as Directive (EU) 2024/1711, published in OJ L 2024/1711, 26.6.2024, and Regulation (EU) 2024/1747, published in OJ L 2024/1747, 26.6.2024. Both acts entered into force on 16 July 2024. The final text includes some changes in article numbering, which have been updated accordingly in this chapter.

[19] Regulation (EU) 2019/943 of the European Parliament and of the Council of 5 June 2019 on the internal market for electricity, OJ 2019 L 158/54, 14.6.2019.

[20] More details on different timeframes for energy trading are provided in section 3.

[21] COM/2023/148 final, Commission Proposal to improve the Union's electricity market design, p. 2.

[22] Harada and Coussi (2020). Indeed, in PPAs prices are generally fixed, but may also be indexed to the zonal price or set a cap and floor (id. at p. 201). As for the volumes of purchase electricity there are two main options: (i) pay as produced, in which 100% of the energy produced is purchased at the price set in the PPA (i.e., the buyer bears the risk of intermittent production); (ii) the producer commits to a given volume and/or production profile (i.e., the producer and third-party intermediary bear the risk of intermittent production) (id. at p. 201). The single possible clauses of the contracts will not be examined in detail, since it goes beyond the scope of the present contribution, but for an in-depth analysis please refer to Wallace (2019).

These are one of several kinds of instruments available in wholesale energy trading, which takes place on forward markets (where energy is traded several years in advance), day-ahead markets (spot or short-term markets for the next day), and intraday markets (for same-day delivery)[23]. Transactions occur either on organised and standardised marketplaces (power exchanges) or bilaterally over-the-counter (OTC)[24]. Long-term contracts, such as PPAs, are characterised by the extended timeframe, even compared to forward markets, and the negotiation OTC[25]. Indeed, their primary purpose is to hedge against price and quantity risks over an extended duration[26]. This approach benefits generators by securing returns on investments, simultaneously shielding consumers from the volatility of prices in the short-term spot market.

There are three primary types of contractual arrangements used in PPAs[27]: (i) on-site or local PPA, in which the plant is built and operated in an area close to the supplied facility and the electricity is directly consumed at the price agreed in the PPA; (ii) physical or sleeved PPA, in which the electricity produced is fed into the grid (i.e., there is no direct connection between the production site and the point of consumption) and delivered to the consumer at the price set into the contract; (iii) financial, virtual or synthetic PPAs, which are financial instruments used for managing risks, with no physical delivery of electricity, directly fed into the grid at market price. The main category of virtual PPAs are the contracts for difference (CfDs), in which the consumer sources energy from its usual supplier at market price. However, if the market price is higher than a strike price set in the PPA, the producer will pay the buyer the difference ('one-way'); conversely, if the market price falls below the strike price, the buyer will pay the producer the difference ('two-way')[28].

Generally, the buyer will also receive a guarantee proving the renewable origin (guarantees of origin or GOs[29]) of its electricity, showing that the PPA is directly financing a specific renewable energy plant. In case of on-site or physical PPAs, the buyer will need

---

[23] SEC(2006) 1724, DG Competition Report on Energy Sector Inquiry, 2007, Part 2, pp. 120-121 (hereinafter, the "Energy Sector Inquiry"). Also, Zachmann (2023), p. 20, Figure 4.

[24] SEC(2006) 1724, Energy Sector Inquiry, pp. 120-121.

[25] Zachmann (2023), p. 20, Figure 4. The Electricity Regulation allows the trading of long-term hedging products on power exchanges and the negotiation of long-term electricity supply contracts OTC, subject to compliance with Union competition law (Regulation (EU) 2019/943 of the European Parliament and of the Council of 5 June 2019 on the internal market for electricity, OJ 2019 L 158, p. 54, 14.6.2019,Article 3(o)).

[26] De Hauteclocque (2009), p. 96.

[27] Harada and Coussi (2020), pp. 198-202.

[28] Another type of financial PPA are options: the put-option gives the producer the possibility to sell the electricity produced at a set price if the wholesale price falls below that price; the call-options enable a customer to buy electricity at a given price (Harada and Coussi(2020), p. 199).

[29] Guarantees of origin are electronic documents which enable an electricity supplier to prove that a given share of the energy sold was produced from renewable energy sources (see Article 2(2) no. 12, and Article 19 of Directive (EU) 2018/2001, Directive (EU) 2018/2001 of the European Parliament and of the Council of 11 December 2018 on the promotion of the use of energy from renewable sources (recast) (Text with EEA relevance.), OJ L 328, p. 82, 21.12.2018). GOs enable corporates to provide stakeholders with proof of their commitment to green energy.

to enter into an additional contract with a supplier for the part of its power consumption not covered by the PPA and balancing services. Furthermore, the producer will need to ensure that it has a market for any production excess not covered by the PPA.

Given these complicated contractual links, it may be easier to keep the same supplier throughout the term of the PPA, which could be seen as an obstacle to competition between suppliers[30]. This is one of the reasons that the Commission has been historically suspicious of long-term contracts in the energy market due to possible competition concerns, and even launched several proceedings to terminate them in the wake of the liberalisation of energy markets in the 1990s[31].

4 Long-Term Contracts as an Obstacle to Liberalisation

Concerns over the anti-competitive effect of long-term energy contracts have come to the fore over the past years. Pre-liberalisation, vertically integrated companies were responsible for carrying out all the key functions of the electricity supply chain and prices were regulated by either government institutions or regulatory agencies[32]. After liberalisation the electricity market was split up into regulated (transmission and distribution[33]) and competitive (generation, supply, and trading) segments[34]. In addition, the unbundling of generation and transmission from its distribution required the introduction of a wholesale market for electricity[35].

The passage from natural monopolies, integrated both horizontally and vertically, to market-based competition redefined the role of the State in energy markets[36]. This model, termed an 'energy-only market', operates without the need for extensive State intervention, as competitive short-term prices should optimize cost-effective usage and dispatch in the short run, while also steering optimal long-term investments and shutdowns[37].

The Commission perceived long-term contracts as standing in the way of these efforts towards market liberalisation. The Energy Sector Inquiry of 2007[38] revealed that a small number of incumbent suppliers continued to control a significant portion of electricity generation assets, either directly or indirectly through PPAs[39]. The vertical

30 Harada and Coussi(2020), p. 201.

31 The liberalisation process began with Directive 96/92/EC of the European Parliament and of the Council of 19 December 1996 concerning common rules for the internal market in electricity, OJ 1997 L 27/20.

32 See OECD (2022), pp. 11-15.

33 Indeed, the existing network is considered a natural monopoly that cannot be duplicated in an economic manner and/or in a reasonably short time frame OECD (2022).

34 Ibid

35 Ibid

36 De Hauteclocque (2013), p. 10.

37 Keppler et al. (2022). The authors recall how in the 1980-90s technological and institutional changes held out the hope that competition based on short run marginal costs, rather than tariffs set by a regulated monopolist, could achieve 'optimal capacity levels' (id. at pp. 8-9).

38 SEC(2006) 1724, Energy Sector Inquiry.

39 Del Vecchio et al. (2021). According to the authors, in 'traditional' PPAs the buyer was often a vertically integrated company, which then sold the power to retail customers in its service area, closed to competition.

tying of markets through long-term downstream contracts by dominant firms posed a risk of foreclosure for more or as efficient competitors[40] Addressing the issue of vertical foreclosure, primarily stemming from inadequate unbundling of networks and supply, became imperative to fully exploit the advantages of liberalisation[41] In subsequent years, various enforcement proceedings were launched to terminate such contracts under EU competition law (State aid rules as well as Article 101 and 102, TFEU).

The State aid cases involving Hungary[42] and Poland[43], related to long-term electricity purchase contracts between State-owned companies[44] and specific power generators, have been among the most notorious involving PPAs. These long-term contracts were meant to achieve public policy goals, specifically the modernization of the electricity sector and advancements in environmental protection and security of supply, with a view to entering the European Union.

Despite being in force at the time of accession, these contracts were categorized as 'new aid' and treated as post-accession support[45]. Scholars have criticized this decision, contending that it reflects a lack of due consideration by the Commission for the circumstances prevailing at the time when the PPAs were originally signed, which could have led to considering them compatible with the internal market in consideration of long-term efficiencies[46].

However, the Commission found that the PPAs constituted unlawful operating State aid[47], incompatible with the internal market, and demanded their termination[48]. The

[40] SEC(2006) 1724, Energy Sector Inquiry, at Executive Summary, p. 13.

[41] See SEC(2006) 1724, Energy Sector Inquiry, at Part 1, p. 4.

[42] 2009/609/EC: Commission Decision on the State aid C 41/05 awarded by Hungary through Power Purchase Agreements, OJ 2009 L 225, p. 53, 27.8.2009. The Decision was ultimately confirmed by the European Court of Justice in Case C-357/14 P, Electrabel SA et Dunamenti Erőmű Zrt. v. European Commission (2015), ECLI:EU:C:2015:642.

[43] 2009/287/EC: Commission Decision on the State aid awarded by Poland as part of Power Purchase Agreements and the State aid which Poland is planning to award concerning compensation for the voluntary termination of Power Purchase Agreements, OJ 2009, L83, p.1, 28.3.2009.

[44] Respectively, Magyar Villamos Művek Zrt. (MVM) and Polskie Sieci Elektroenergetyczne S.A. (PSE).

[45] Commission Decisions 2009/609/EC at para 381 and 2009/287/EC at para 288.

[46] Hancher (2010), pp. 292 and 302, considers that the Commission should have assigned more relevance to the disadvantages for buyers relying on spot markets and short-term contracts (*i.e.*, exposure to volatility and liquidity risk) when the contracts were entered into. Also, Tóth (2016) p. 314, observes how without long-term contracts foreign companies would have been less incentivised to buy Hungarian electricity generators shortly after the collapse of its socialist regime.

[47] According to the Commission, PPAs could not be considered an investment aid since they covered not only investment costs but also most operating costs (Commission Decisions 2009/609/EC at para 396 and 2009/287/EC at para 302). Operating aid could be allowed under specific circumstances, but none were deemed applicable to the specific cases of Hungary and Poland (Commission Decisions 2009/609/EC at para 409 and 2009/287/EC at para 315).

[48] At the same time, the Commission authorised the Polish State aid for the compensation of the termination of PPAs, deeming it compatible with the internal market under 107(3)(c) on the basis of the so-called 'stranded costs methodology', i.e. Commission Communication relating

Commission highlighted that these agreements could distort merit-based competition, bestowing a selective advantage and restricting a significant portion of the market from new entrants[49].

Indeed, PPAs shielded selected generators from the commercial risk related to changes in electricity prices and demand for a significant portion of the lifetime of the assets[50]. The responsibility for operating the plant and the associated risks were shifted to the public buyer, providing economic benefits to the generators beyond what they would have received in a typical market scenario[51]. The timeframe of the agreements, market shares of the involved plants, guaranteed sales volumes, and price-setting mechanisms were crucial factors in the Commission's assessments[52].

Similar considerations were involved in other well-known cases against the incumbent companies in Belgium[53] and France[54] for alleged abuse of dominant position through long-term contracts in the markets for the supply to industrial customers, respectively, of gas and of electricity. Both these cases ended with commitments[55] to return to the market significant volumes of gas/electricity[56], to provide a maximum duration for

---

to the methodology for analysing State aid linked to stranded costs, IP/01/1077 (Commission 2009/287/EC at Article 2).

49 Commission Decisions 2009/609/EC at para 326 and 2009/287/EC at para 254.

50 Commission Decision 2009/609/EC at paras 211 and 334 and 2009/287/EC at paras 189-192.

51 Ibid.

52 MVM entered into PPAs ranging from 15 to 27 years agreeing to purchase a specific minimum quantity of electricity from power generators covering a substantial portion (80/60%) of Hungary's electricity demand. Notably, these agreements were designed to ensure profitability by stipulating fixed prices covering both fixed and variable costs. Similarly, PSE concluded long-term PPAs spanning from 7 to 20 years, concerning plants with a very important share of the market, procuring a fixed minimum volume of electricity at a price covering both fixed and variable costs plus a reasonable margin. De Hauteclocque (2009), p. 98, contends that the Commission's first decisions on PPAs offer a methodology for the analysis of long-term energy contracts, identifying key elements that inform individual competition assessments.

53 2008/C 9/05 Commission Decision relating to a proceeding pursuant to Article 82 of the EC Treaty, Distrigas, OJ 2008 C 9/8, 15.1.2008. Distrigaz S.A. / Distrigas N.V. (Distrigaz) concluded a series of contracts with customers in the relevant markets for varying durations (indefinite or with tacit renewals), which required customers to purchase certain volumes of gas (alternatively covering all the customer's demand or fixing an annual contractual quantity and an annual minimum quantity). The proportion of the market already tied to Distrigaz under the contracts in force on 1 January 2005 was 50-60%.

54 2010/C 133/05, Summary of Commission Decision relating to a proceeding under Article 102 of the TFEU and Article 54 of the EEA Agreement, Long-term contracts France, OJ 2010 C 133/5, 22.5.2010. EDF S.A. (EDF) was investigated for abusing its dominant position by concluding in France contracts with large industrial customers of electricity which, by their scope, duration and nature, could foreclose the market.

55 Annexed to the respective Commission Decisions 2008/C 9/05 and 2010/C 133/05.

56 For EDF 65% of its portfolio on average throughout the duration of commitments and at least 60% per calendar year, for Distrigaz a minimum of 65 % for each calendar year and a minimum of 70% on average for all calendar years.

new contracts of not more than five years[57], and to delete any resale restriction clauses from future and existing contracts.

Some literature has suggested that the Commission had to resort to antitrust enforcement because the transition towards a liberalised market had been incomplete[58]. The author argues that this limitation was caused by the Commission's inability, under Article 295 EC (now, 345 TFEU), to restructure industries and alter property rights in Member States, as well as by the governance structure of EU energy policy[59]. Consequently, the Commission resorted to antitrust laws as 'quasi-ex ante regulatory tool' to shape the liberalised market[60]. This chapter does not delve into the extensive debate on the goals of competition or evaluate the appropriateness of utilizing competition enforcement as a tool for achieving broader policy objectives[61]. However, it is noteworthy that EU competition has historically served a dual, occasionally contradictory, role: functioning both as a system of rules and as a tool to pursue diverse policy objectives[62].

Ultimately, long-term energy purchase contracts are far from being unlawful *per se* under EU competition law[63]. When concerns for liberalization became less pressing, they evolved in the EU energy policy, taking on a new role regarding renewable energy[64].

5 Long-Term Contracts as a Tool to Promote Renewables in Current EU Legislation

State aid was indispensable for the renewables industry at an early stage when it was too expensive to compete with fossil fuels-based generators[65]. The Commission recognized this market failure and allowed Member States considerable freedom in choosing support schemes to promote the adoption of RES, also in the form of long-term contracting[66]. Nowadays the conditions under which State aid in the form of long-term energy purchasing with a public counterparty is considered compatible with the internal market are detailed in EU legislation and soft law on renewable energy and State aid.

The promotion of use of energy from RES is disciplined by the recently amended Directive (EU) 2018/2001, i.e. the Renewable Energy Directive (RED III)[67]. According

[57] Distrigaz, in particular, agreed to a maximum duration of contracts with industrial customers and electricity generators (apart from new installations) of five years and with gas resellers of two years.

[58] De Hauteclocque (2013), pp. 53-57; 66-72; 169-174.

[59] ibid, p. 55 et seq. Energy falls under competence shared between the EU and Member States, as stipulated in Article 4(2), TFEU. Most importantly, Union energy policy may not affect a Member State's choice of energy mix and general structure of supply (Article 194(2), second subpara, TFEU).

[60] Ibid.

[61] Whish and Bailey (2021), p. 17 et seq.

[62] Amato (1998), p. 89.

[63] Hancher (2023), p. 173. De Hauteclocque (2013), p. 82.

[64] Del Vecchio et al. (2021).

[65] OECD (2022), p. 36.

[66] Ibid.

[67] Directive (EU) 2018/2001 of the European Parliament and of the Council of 11 December 2018 on the promotion of the use of energy from renewable sources, OJ 2018 L 328/82, 21.12.2018

to the RED III, State support may include direct price support schemes, such as feed-in tariffs (or FITs) and sliding or fixed premium payments (feed-in premiums or FIPs)[68]. Except for small-scale plants, direct price support may be granted exclusively as a fixed or sliding FIP, which ensure that producers are market responsive and maximise integration of electricity from RES[69].

All support schemes generally involve a long-term agreement. However, while in FITs volumes and relevant prices are fixed and tied to the cost of production, in FIPs energy is typically sold on the spot market. The producer is then entitled to receive from the State either a fixed premium on top of the market price ('fixed' FIP) or a sliding premium ('sliding' FIP), equal to the difference between the market price and a fixed strike price[70]. In other words, a sliding FIP is another term used to refer to a CfD[71].

State support schemes for RES must in any case comply with State aid rules[72]. Hence, they are subject to the notification obligation under Article 108(3) TFEU, unless they fulfil the conditions of the general block exemption regulation (GBER)[73]. Specifically, operating aid for the promotion of electricity from RES may be deemed compatible with the internal market ex Article 107(3), TFEU, *inter alia*, if the aid is granted only over the lifetime of the project, at the end of a competitive bidding process, and in the form of a fixed FIP or CfD[74]. Even if such conditions are not met, an aid notified to the Commission could still be deemed compatible with Article 107(3)(c), TFEU, if it meets the conditions set out in the guidelines on State aid for environmental protection and energy, which expressly mentions CfDs among categories of admissible aid for decarbonisation[75]. Ultimately, State aid to support decarbonisation is still an exception to the general prohibition set out in Article 107(1), TFEU, which must be interpreted

---

which was recently amended by Directive (EU) 2023/2413 of the European Parliament and of the Council of 18 October 2023, OJ L 2023/2413, 31.10.2023. For the purposes of this chapter, the term 'RED III' refers to Directive (EU) 2018/2001, as amended by Directive (EU) 2023/2413.

68 The RED III (Directive (EU) 2023/2413) at Article 2(2), no. 5, provides for the definition of 'support scheme'.

69 RED III at Article 4(3). Only small-scale installations can be exempted from this paragraph and can still receive direct support in the form of feed-in tariffs.

70 SWD (2023) 58 final, p. 28.

71 Ibid.

72 RED III at Article 4(9).

73 Commission Regulation (EU) 651/2014 declaring certain categories of aid compatible with the internal market in application of Articles 107 and 108 of the Treaty, OJ 2014 L 187, 26.6.2014, recently amended by Commission Regulation (EU) 2023/1315, OJ 2023 L 167, 30.6.2023. In particular, the conditions for compliance of operating aid for the promotion of electricity from RES are laid down in Article 42 and, in general, Chapter I.

74 A CfD is defined as an instrument 'which entitles the beneficiary to a payment equal to the difference between a fixed "strike" price(s) and a reference price – such as a market price, per unit of output' - GBER, Regulation (EU) 2023/1315 at Article 2(114b)).

75 Communication from the Commission – Guidelines on State aid for climate, environmental protection and energy, OJ 2022 C 80, 18.2.2022. Specifically, Chapter 4, Section 4.1.4., paras 121-123. The aid should be designed in a way to prevent any undue distortion of the efficient functioning of the markets and preserve efficient operating incentives and price signals.

restrictively, as State aid should drive (never substitute) private investment so as to avoid any distortion of competition in the internal market[76]. Indeed, over-reliance on State aid could potentially result in a green transition at varying speeds within the EU, favouring less-indebted countries[77].

PPAs offer a key alternative to public support for renewable projects, reducing pressure on public budgets. In the legislative framework of the EU, 'renewables' PPAs are already mentioned in the RED III, as contracts through which a consumer sources renewable electricity directly from an electricity producer[78]. Most importantly, the RED III mandates Member States to remove any unjustified regulatory and administrative barriers and to promote the uptake of long-term renewables PPAs[79]. Member States must explore how to reduce the financial risks associated with them, also through credit guarantees, and ensure that any associated GOs can be transferred to the buyer. Apart from legislation, the Commission adopted a recommendation to Member States to promote the uptake of renewables PPAs in 2022 as part of the REPowerEU package[80].

Unlike CfDs, the Commission has not developed a specific competition policy about long-term contracts in the energy sector between private parties. In principle, even renewables PPAs could pose competition concerns, especially when concluded between market players with significant market shares[81], and must comply with Articles 101 and 102, TFEU. As observed in literature, long-term contracts carry the risk of foreclosure of more efficient players if a significant part of the demand is locked-in in the long-term, precluding customers from switching to a more efficient supplier[82], and may also have indirect exclusionary effects by drying out spot markets[83]. Renewables PPAs could still present

---

[76] Baratta (2022), pp. 527; 529.

[77] Cornago and Springford (2023).

[78] The RED III at Article 2, n. 17, defines 'renewables power purchase agreement' as 'a contract under which a natural or legal person agrees to purchase renewable electricity directly from an electricity producer'.

[79] The RED III at Article 15(8).

[80] Opinion of the European Economic and Social Committee on Communication from the Commission to the European Parliament, the Council, the European Economic and Social Committee and the Committee of the Regions — EU Solar Energy Strategy (COM(2022) 221 final) and Commission recommendation on speeding up permit-granting procedures for renewable energy projects and facilitating Power Purchase Agreements (C(2022) 3219 final), OJ 2023 C 75, p. 178, 28.2.2023.

[81] The risks highlighted in general by De Hauteclocque (2013), pp. 51, 78 and 80, could still be relevant. The Commission should intervene when a long-term contract is entered into by a company with market power, and market shares can be used to approximate the level of dominance. A big corporate costumer or a consortium of small-medium costumers signing a long-term contract for a major share of its demand with an incumbent, a dominant firm or collectively dominant firms can be considered out of the market for the duration of the contract, creating a possible impediment to entry.

[82] De Hauteclocque (2009), p. 101.

[83] De Hauteclocque (2013), p. 38; indeed, long-term contracts, similarly to vertical integration, diminish the volumes to be traded on spot markets, increasing price volatility. Spot markets deliver a better outcome than bilateral contracting only if sufficiently liquid. The drying out of spot markets is what prompted to intervene in its earlier cases on PPAs (see section 4).

strong anti-competitive effects, for example, because of an exclusivity clause[84]. They also lack transparency as they are generally negotiated OTC, thus potentially increasing information asymmetry in the market, and the opportunity for dominant agents to abuse their market power[85].

If an agreement falls within the scope of Article 101(1), the Commission and national competition authorities may have to carry a delicate balancing operation under Article 101(3), TFEU[86]. The recent guidelines on vertical restraints[87], as well as those on horizontal cooperation[88], generally mention the pursue of 'sustainability objectives' among efficiencies that the Commission would consider when balancing pro- and anti-competitive effects to allow an agreement under 101(3) TFEU[89] In recent years, there has been a vigorous debate on green antitrust, with many authors advocating for an update of the conditions under which an agreement may be exempted under Article 101(3) TFEU for environmental reasons[90]. While a comprehensive discussion of this topic is beyond the scope of this chapter, it is worth noting that the notion of 'sustainability' remains somewhat ambiguous[91]. More guidance would be needed to understand what sources of electricity are considered 'sustainable' for the purpose of antitrust enforcement, specifically if limited to RES[92].

Ultimately, the EU seems aware of possible competition concerns stemming from the integration of long-term contracts in the electricity market design and includes various safeguards to preserve market dynamics in the ongoing reform.

---

[84] Ibid, pp. 44; 81. In general, all clauses leading to significant switching costs, unclear termination rights, fidelity rebates and tacit renewal would be subject to sever competition scrutiny, especially when concluded by dominant firms.

[85] Ibid, p. 38. The price negotiated in a long-term contract depends on the information available on market conditions.

[86] Such balancing shall be carried out according to the conditions set out in the Commission's Guidelines on the application of Article 81(3) of the Treaty, OJ 2004 C 101/97.

[87] 2022/C 248/01, Communication from the Commission, Guidelines on vertical restraints, OJ 2022 C 248.

[88] 2023/C 259/01, Communication from the Commission – Guidelines on the applicability of Article 101 of the Treaty on the Functioning of the European Union to horizontal cooperation agreements, OJ 2023 C 259.

[89] Provided, of course, that all other requirements set by Article 101(3) TFEU are met. Hence, for e.g., Article 101 TFEU may be declared inapplicable to long-term non-compete obligations essential for facilitating investments in RES (Guidelines on vertical restraints, supra, note 87 at para 316). Similarly, joint purchase of energy is mentioned among possible efficiency gains of an horizontal agreement to be assessed under Article 101(3), TFEU (Guidelines on horizontal cooperation agreements, supra, note 88 at para 305).

[90] Many scholars advocate for a greener competition law, among which: Holmes (2020); Monti (2020); Nowag (2016).

[91] 2022/C 248/01, at para 8 and 2023/C 259/01, para 516 et seq.

[92] Indeed, the concept of 'decarbonisation' could encompass other sources of low-carbon electricity (see note 102, below).

6 Long-Term Contracts in the Ongoing Reform of the Electricity Market Design

As seen, the European Parliament and the Council have recently reached an agreement on the content of the electricity market reform. The goal is to significantly advance the deployment of RES, increasing the role of long-term contracting in the form of PPAs and CfDs. Overall, the reform appears to privilege the development of a market for PPAs to reach decarbonisation, to limit pressure on public budgets, while introducing further limits to State aid for more mature technologies to avoid any distortions in the internal market[93].

The diffusion of renewables PPAs in the EU has so far been significantly different from one Member State to another, even for more mature technologies[94]. The market remains accessible only to large credit-worthy companies[95]. In contrast, the barriers to participating in corporate PPAs for small and medium-size businesses are still very high[96].

The main barriers to the diffusion of PPAs, as identified by the Commission[97], fall into several categories: (i) regulatory and administrative issues, including lengthy permitting procedures and obstacles to direct contracting, aggregation, and guarantee of origin issuance; (ii) political barriers, as policies often favour public support schemes over PPAs; (iii) economic challenges, particularly associated with the long contract duration, posing risks related to uncertain future electricity prices, RES production intermittency, and credit risk; (iv) awareness issues, since many small businesses lack the expertise needed to recognize and leverage PPA benefits due to the absence of standardized conditions, leading to significant transaction costs. Another barrier can be consumers' limited engagement in energy markets and reliance on interventions by the State in case of price spikes[98].

Some of these barriers have been addressed in the recent reform of the RED III in relation to renewables PPAs. The reform of the Electricity Regulation will support long-term investments in general, not only to increase renewable energy generation, but also to enable consumers to make their energy bills affordable and less dependent from fluctuations of short-term electricity market prices[99].

---

93 SWD (2023) 58 final, Commission Staff Working Document, p. 32, 'it is crucial that all possible investments from the private sector are mobilised first, in order to limit the pressure on the public budget'; see also Provisional Agreement, supra, note 17 at Annex I, recital 45; now adopted as recital 44 of Regulation (EU) 2024/1747.

94 Harada and Coussi (2020), p. 195.

95 SWD (2023) 58 final, Commission Staff Working Document p. 19.

96 SWD(2022) 149 final, Commission Staff Working Document on Guidance to Member States on good practices to speed up permit-granting procedures for renewable energy projects and on facilitating Power Purchase Agreements,.

97 SWD(2023) 58 final, Commission Staff Working Document .p 20. See also Commission Staff Working Document, supra, note 96, pp. 36 et seq.

98 Keppler et al. (2022), p. 5. Also, Batlle et al. (2023), p. 198.

99 General Secretariat of the Council (2023), Provisional Agreement, at Annex I, Article 1(1)(b); now adopted as Article 2(1)(b) of Regulation (EU) 2024/1747.

The Electricity Regulation will now include a definition of two-way CfDs and PPAs[100]. Both definitions will be technologically neutral (i.e., not limited to renewables) and the purchase of PPAs shall be 'on a market basis'[101]. A new chapter on incentives to reach decarbonization will then provide for more detailed provisions on these type of contractual arrangements[102].

Most notably, Member States must generally promote PPAs, including with respect to renewable energy, while preserving 'competitive and liquid electricity markets'[103]. Member States are bound to implement two measures to spread the use of PPAs: allow producers to cumulate to some extent renewables PPAs with public support schemes for renewable energy, provided this does not negatively affect competition in the market[104]; and provide instruments to reduce financial risks linked to the off-takers' payment default (e.g., guarantee schemes at market prices), either market driven or publicly supported[105]. Also, PPAs must specify exit conditions for customers and producers (such as any applicable exit fees and notice periods), in compliance with Union competition law[106].

The reform includes obligations related to PPAs for the Commission and the EU Agency for the Cooperation of Energy Regulators (ACER). The former is mandated to assess the possibility to implement in the future one or several EU market platforms for PPAs, to be used on a voluntary basis, and to monitor persisting barriers and transparency in PPA markets, for which it may draw specific guidelines[107]. ACER, on the other hand, will publish an annual assessment of the PPA market and assess the need to develop standard PPAs for voluntary use, adapted to the needs of the different categories of parties[108].

---

[100] Ibid, Article 1(2); now adopted as Article 2(2)(76) and (77) of Regulation (EU) 2024/1747. While PPAs were already defined in legislation (in particular, RED III, supra, note 67 at Article 2), even if specifically referred to renewables, CfDs were so far only defined in a delegated act (GBER, at Article 2(114b).

[101] General Secretariat of the Council (2023), at Annex I, Article 1(2); now adopted as Article 2(2) of Regulation (EU) 2024/1747.

[102] The decarbonisation dimension encompasses both the target on the reduction of greenhouse gas emissions and on the share of energy from renewable sources in gross final consumption of energy, as referred to in Regulation (EU) 2018/1999 of the European Parliament and of the Council of 11 December 2018 on the Governance of the Energy Union and Climate Action, OJ 2018 L 328, at Article 4(a) (General Secretariat of the Council (2023), at Annex I, Article 1(9); now adopted as Article 2(9) of Regulation (EU) 2024/1747).

[103] General Secretariat of the Council (2023), at Annex I, Article 1(9), now adopted as Article 2(9) of Regulation (EU) 2024/1747 introducing Article 19a(1) in the Electricity Regulation.

[104] Regulation (EU) 2024/1747, introducing Article 19a(5) and (6) in the Electricity Regulation.

[105] Ibid, introducing Article 19a(3) and (4) in the Electricity Regulation. If a guarantee scheme is backed by a Member State it shall comply with State aid rules, include provisions to avoid lowering the liquidity in electricity markets and not provide support to the purchase of generation from fossil fuels. It is left to the discretion of Member States to decide to limit those guarantee schemes to the exclusive support of the purchase of new renewable generation.

[106] Ibid, introducing Article 19a(8) in the Electricity Regulation.

[107] Ibid, introducing Article 19a(2) and (10) in the Electricity Regulation.

[108] Ibid, introducing Article 19b, in the Electricity Regulation. The Article then enumerates the elements that ACER should consider in the possible design of such standard contracts.

As for two-way CfDs, or equivalent schemes, according to the reform they will become the only form of direct public support scheme applicable to investments in 'new power-generating facilities' for the generation of electricity from the following sources: wind energy, solar energy, geothermal energy, hydropower without reservoir, as well as nuclear energy[109]. The provision also details design principles for such schemes, which the Commission will have to consider when assessing compliance with State aid rules[110]. The revenues generated by two-way CfDs must also be distributed to final customers[111].

This provision will set up a special discipline in relation to support schemes for RES, generally regulated by the RED III[112]. Only for the RES listed above, considered technologically more mature, the Commission intends that support schemes should limit remuneration to avoid any overcompensation using public funding. Indeed, different forms of direct price support schemes may be better placed to incentivise the development of innovative technologies, which do not yet benefit from the necessary economies of scale to limit investment costs.

In conclusion, regulatory and political discussions in the EU appear to reflect recent insights from energy economics scholars who argue that relying exclusively on energy-only markets, even with additional policies, isn't sufficient to ensure a secure energy supply and to achieve deep decarbonization 'as economically as possible and on schedule'[113].

Energy policy has always been struggling over the optimal mix of long-term contracting, vertical integration, and spot trading, to support both investment and entry[114]. The challenge is to balance the interest of ensuring free competition in the short-term, but at the same time guarantee sufficient investment in infrastructure to improve competition in

[109] Ibid, introducing Article 19d(1) and (4) in the Electricity Regulation. The initial version proposed by the Commission mentioned direct price support schemes for 'new investments', which to a certain extent also included investments on existing facilities, rather than 'new generation'. Indeed, the inclusion of existing facilities has been subject of controversy (Hancher (2023), p. 172; Zachmann et al (2023), p. 39). The compromise reached between Parliament and Council 'keeps CfDs as mandatory only for investments in new power-generating facilities' (General Secretariat of the Council (2023), at Section III). Anyhow, the possibility for Member States to grant support by way of two-ways CfDs or equivalent schemes for new investments aimed at substantially repowering existing power generation facilities, or at substantially increasing their capacity or prolonging their lifetime, is preserved in the recitals (General Secretariat of the Council (2023), at Annex I, recital 35; now adopted as recital 35 of Regulation (EU) 2024/1747,).

[110] General Secretariat of the Council (2023), at Annex I, now adopted as Article 2 of Regulation (EU) 2024/1747, introducing Article 19d(2) and (3) in the Electricity Regulation.

[111] Regulation (EU) 2024/1747., introducing Article 19d(5) in the Electricity Regulation.

[112] Indeed, an amendment to Article 4(3) of the RED III will ensure that the form of direct price support schemes for these sources will be regulated by the Electricity Regulation (General Secretariat of the Council (2023), at Annex II, Article 2; now adopted as Article 1 of Directive (EU) 2024/1711).

[113] Keppler et al. (2022), p. 1. Batlle et al. (2023), p. 197. Finon (2023), p. 32. Also, Genoese et al. (2016), p. 4.

[114] Already in 2013, De Hauteclocque (2013), p. 44, mentioned the need for regulators and competition authorities to find a middle path 'where spot contracting would combine with a satisfactory share of long-term contracts and vertical integration'.

the long-term[115]. With this reform, the EU seems to be transitioning towards a 'hybrid' market model, combining elements of both long- and short-term approaches[116]. This shift doesn't signify a return to the highly regulated systems of the pre-liberalization era, but it also marks a departure from a market focused exclusively on competition based on short-run marginal costs[117].

However, competition still has an important role to play in electricity markets to ensure that energy policy goals do not hinder the benefits of liberalisation. In this respect, scholars urge regulators to preserve at least competition for the market in long-term contracting, through transparent and competitive procurement[118], which currently represents an established principle only for CfDs[119].

7 Concluding Remarks

The recent energy crisis, characterized by soaring prices for fossil fuels, exposed the risks of an electricity market design primarily centred on short-term markets. To address this, the EU wishes to improve the market design by matching spot-markets with long-term contracting, also to advance decarbonisation.

Long-term contracting can take on various shapes in business practice, from on-site and physical PPAs, to financial instruments like CfDs. Their common characteristics rely on the very long duration, fixed prices and volumes, and negotiation OTC. These features have raised concerns in past antitrust and State aid cases in gas and energy markets, as the Commission considered PPAs as potential factors contributing to market foreclosure, hindering the liberalisation process.

Yet, as mentioned, long-term contracting for the purchase of electricity is not *per se* unlawful under EU competition law. Indeed, long-term contracts could be pro-competitive when indispensable for investment in RES, having the potential to increase the number of market players in electricity generation[120] and prevent revenue cannibalization in a market dominated by RES with zero marginal costs[121].

The EU has recognized the positive contribution that long-term contracts could give to the promotion of renewable energy and detailed the conditions under which Member States could directly finance renewable energy projects. To lower the pressure on public

[115] De Hauteclocque (2013), p. 64.

[116] Keppler et al (2022), pp. 2-4, argue that so far prices have remained below levels that could spur innovation and investment in decarbonisation.

[117] Keppler et al. (2022), p, 7.

[118] Ibid.

[119] Batlle et al. (2023), p. 199, remark how CfD markets are transparent by nature and an equal transparency should be required for PPAs.

[120] As argued by De Hauteclocque (2013), p. 34, long-term contracts have positive effects on social welfare in the medium to long-term primarily because they facilitate entry and 'thus contribute to market building when spot prices are volatile'. Batlle et al. (2023), p. 198, observe how the risk-hedging provided by long-term contracts is especially important for independent project developers, who must compete with vertically integrated incumbents, naturally hedged by their retail portfolio.

[121] Hancher (2023), p. 170. Also, OECD (2022), p. 30.

budget, the EU and its Member States are now stepping in to create a PPA market, which so far struggled to emerge spontaneously[122].

The amendments to the Electricity Regulation will insert PPAs and CfDs in the central legislation shaping the EU electricity market, directly applicable in Member States. The main difference compared to the provisions of the RED III relies on the technical neutrality of PPAs contemplated by the reform and on the novel legal basis for State financing of new and (to some extent) existing nuclear plants[123].

However, the EU acknowledges the persistent competition risks associated with long-term contracting and incorporates safeguards in the reform to protect competition[124]. Ultimately, the reform does not wish to diminish competition in the market, which will be crucial in ensuring the right balance between short and long-term considerations.

The key role assigned to long-term contracting in the reform should not bring the Commission and national competition authorities to treat these contracts differently in the enforcement of competition law. While the merits of green antitrust are beyond the scope of this chapter for in-depth discussion, it is noteworthy that competition enforcement and advocacy emerge as complementary tools in achieving the objectives of energy regulation[125]. In other words, preserving competition would help maintain a balance in the Energy Trilemma.

Hence, competition enforcement and advocacy in energy markets should remain a high priority for competition authorities. Their role will be fundamental in ensuring that the electricity market reform preserves the benefits that liberalisation has brought in terms of cost-effectiveness and innovation. A case-by-case approach, considering the specifics of the single contract, appears as the best solution[126]. In this framework, the

---

122 Keppler et al. (2022), p. 5. Furthermore, Glanchant (2023).

123 Regulation (EU) 2024/1747.

124 Most notably, (i) Member States shall promote the uptake of PPAs 'while preserving competitive and liquid electricity markets and cross-border trade'; (ii) if a guarantee scheme for PPAs is backed by a State, it shall include provisions 'to avoid lowering the liquidity in electricity markets'; (iii) in the design of support schemes for electricity from RES, Member States shall allow the participation of projects which reserve part of the electricity for sale through a renewables PPA 'provided this does not negatively affect competition in the market', and facilitate the access of customers that face entry barriers to the PPA market 'provided this does not negatively affect competition in the market'; (iv) PPAs shall specify exit-conditions 'in compliance with Union competition law'; (v) the Commission shall assess whether there is 'sufficient transparency' in PPA markets; (vi) all direct price support schemes in the form of two-way CfDs and equivalent schemes shall avoid 'distortions to competition and trade in the internal market'; (vii) the distribution of revenues from two-way CfDs to final customers shall be designed 'not to undermine competition between electricity suppliers' (see General Secretariat of the Council (2023), at Annex I, now adopted as Article 2 of Regulation (EU) 2024/1747, introducing Articles 19a and 19d in the Electricity Regulation).

125 To use the term coined by Holmes (2020), competition could be used as a 'sword' to tackle energy policy issues.

126 As observed by De Hauteclocque (2013), p. 40, the economic analysis of long-term contracts in decentralized markets shows that 'anti- and pro-competitive effects are highly context specific' and it is impossible to conclude that the 'net competition effect' of these contracts will be in general positive or negative. Hence, a case-by-case approach is the best path possible, allowing

provisions on State aid appear more detailed, clearly identifying the criteria which make a support scheme compatible with the internal market[127].

Conversely, the Commission and national competition authorities enjoy wider discretion under Article 101 and 102, TFEU, enforcement. Hence, they bear the key responsibility of ensuring that, when PPAs may affect competition, any anti-competitive effect is truly and proportionally outweighed by efficiencies in terms of security and sustainability and, crucially, that PPAs do not eliminate competition in respect of a substantial part of the market[128]. Indeed, PPAs should increase competition between generators in the long-term, without compromising competition in the short term.

From this point of view, more guidance would be welcome, to enhance legal certainty and boost private investments[129]. The Commission could intervene by clarifying the vague notion of 'sustainability', helping identify in what cases long-term contracts for decarbonisation would fall outside the scope of antitrust enforcement, and defining the hierarchy among elements to be considered during the balancing exercise when they don't[130]. Such guidance, perhaps through non-binding guidelines on acceptable contract forms, would improve clarity and predictability[131].

In the reform, the EU explicitly reserves the right to intervene in the future by establishing one or more EU-wide PPA market platforms and providing guidance on contract design[132]. The delay in implementation can be attributed to the imperative to adhere to the principle of subsidiarity (Article 5, TEU)[133]. Ultimately, the reform adds more fire to the current debate on the division of competences in EU energy policy prompted by the energy crisis, advancing the fundamental question of who is better

the Commission and national competition authorities to tailor competition enforcement, taking into account long-term efficiencies.

127 Commission Regulation (EU) 651/2014 declaring certain categories of aid compatible with the internal market in application of Articles 107 and 108 of the Treaty, OJ 2014 L 187, recently amended by Commission Regulation (EU) 2023/1315, OJ 2023 L 167, p.1. In particular, the conditions for compliance of operating aid for the promotion of electricity from RES are laid down in Article 42 and, in general, Chapter I. Communication from the Commission – Guidelines on State aid for climate, environmental protection and energy, OJ 2022 C 80. Specifically, Chapter 4, Section 4.1.4., paras 121-123.

128 De Hauteclocque (2013), pp. 97-101, notes how the requirement under Article 101(3)(b) will constitute the biggest hurdle for long-term contracts.

129 Ibid, p. 174, advocates for better complementarities between sector regulation and antitrust enforcement.

130 Ibid, pp 97-101. EU guidance on market design is also advocated by Genoese et al. (2016).

131 De Hauteclocque (2013), pp. 97-101.

132 Batlle et al. (2023), p. 199, argue that guidance at EU level will be needed to avoid fragmentation within the internal electricity market. The main challenge in contract design is to ensure that long-term contracts remain to some extent market responsive, sending appropriate price signals to producers and consumers, favouring energy conserving behaviour and energy-efficiency investments while minimising market distortions.

133 The French Sénat in its Avis politique relatif aux propositions de règlement du Parlement européen et du Conseil portant réforme du marché de l'électricité de l'Union of 1st June 2023, meaningfully recalls Member States' competence to define their energy mix, to ensure complete technological neutrality for nuclear energy and hydrogen; it also calls for the competence of Member States to define scope and modalities of PPAs and CfDs.

placed to guide the energy transition[134]. A revision of the current division of competences in the energy sector may soon be necessary, as the increasing imperative to ensure the correct balance of the Energy Trilemma emphasizes the need for intervention at EU level.

References

Amato, G.: Il Potere e l'Antitrust: il Dilemma della Democrazia Liberale nella Storia del Mercato. Il Mulino, Bologna (1998)

Baratta, R.: Aiuti di stato e fragilità ambientali: i nuovi orientamenti della Commissione. Diritto e Società 3 (2022)

Batlle, C., et al.: The EU commission's proposal for improving the electricity market design: treading water, but not drowning. Curr. Sustain./Renew. Energy Rep. **10**, 197–205 (2023). https://doi.org/10.1007/s40518-023-00223-4

Cornago, E., Springford, J.: Europe needs both fiscal and energy solidarity. Centre for European Reform (2023). https://www.cer.eu/publications/archive/policy-brief/2023/europe-needs-both-fiscal-and-energy-solidarity. Accessed 15 Aug 2025

De Hauteclocque, A.: Legal uncertainty and competition policy in European deregulated electricity markets: the case of long-term exclusive supply contracts. World Compet. **32**(1), 91–112 (2009). https://doi.org/10.54648/woco2009006

De Hauteclocque, A.: Market Building Through Antitrust: Long-Term Contract Regulation in EU Electricity Markets. Edward Elgar Publishing, Cheltenham (2013)

Del Vecchio, P., et al.: The Power Purchase Agreement in Transition (2021). https://www.powermag.com/the-power-purchase-agreement-in-transition/. Accessed 15 Aug 2025

Finon, D.: The central trader model: a solution to strengthen the low-carbon transition and to protect consumers in the European union. The Oxford Institute for Energy Studies. Oxford Energy Forum: Q. J. Debating Energy Issues Policies **136**, 31–35 (2023)

Genoese, F., Drabik, E., Egenhoffer, C.: The EU power sector needs long-term price signals. CEPS Special Report No. 135 (2016). https://www.ceps.eu/ceps-publications/eu-power-sector-needs-long-term-price-signals/. Accessed 15 Aug 2025

Glanchant, J.M.: Reforming the EU internal electricity market will not suffice to deliver EU aims. The Oxford Institute for Energy Studies. Oxford Energy Forum: Q. J. Debating Energy Issues Policies **136**, 43–45 (2023)

Hancher, L.: Long-term contracts and state aid – a new application of the EU state aid regime or a special case? Eur. State Aid Law Q. **9**(2), 18 (2010). https://doi.org/10.21552/ESTAL/2010/2/176

Hancher, L.: The challenges of energy market reform: what can the Spanish presidency achieve? Anales Derecho **40**(2), 153–176 (2023). https://doi.org/10.6018/analesderecho.590401

Harada, L.N., Coussi, M.: Power purchase agreements: an emerging tool at the center of the European energy transition – a focus on France. Eur. Energy Environ. Law Rev. **29**(5), 195–2025 (2020). https://doi.org/10.54648/eelr2020043

---

[134] Hancher (2023), p. 169. Also, Glanchant (2023), pp. 43-44, argues that the allocation of core decision-making powers to Member States, rather than the EU, in key areas needed for success in the reform of the electricity market (namely, long-term contracts for price hedging, energy delivery, and capacity building, as well as grids and infrastructure adequacy), represents an indirect constraint to the success of the reform. Hence, strong coordination at EU level will be necessary to coordinate the new web of long-term contracts, since many core results will affect the EU as a whole and appear at EU level.

Holmes, S.: Climate change and competition law. J. Antitrust Enforce. **8**(2), 354–405 (2020). https://doi.org/10.1093/jaenfo/jnaa006

Keppler, J.H., Quemin, S., Saguan, M.: Why the sustainable provision of low-carbon electricity needs hybrid markets. Energy Policy **171**, 113273 (2022). https://doi.org/10.1016/j.enpol.2022.113273

Meeus, L., et al.: The 5th EU electricity market reform: a renewable jackpot for all Europeans package? European university institute (2022). https://op.europa.eu/en/publication-detail/-/publication/ec0cb355-9618-11ed-b508-01aa75ed71a1/language-en. Accessed 15 Aug 2025

Monti, G.: Four options for a greener competition law. J. Eur. Compet. Law Pract. **11**(3–4), 124–132 (2020). https://doi.org/10.1093/jeclap/lpaa007

Nowag, J.: Environmental Integration in Competition and Free-Movement Laws. Oxford University Press, Oxford (2016)

OECD. Competition in Energy Markets. OECD Competition Policy Roundtable Background Note (2022). https://www.oecd.org/en/publications/competition-in-energy-markets_e2e1b9be-en.html. Accessed 15 Aug 2025

Popkostova, Y.: Europe's energy crisis conundrum – origins, impacts and way forward. Publications Office of the European Union Luxembourg (2022). https://www.iss.europa.eu/sites/default/files/EUISSFiles/Brief_2_Energy%20Crisis.pdf. Accessed 15 Aug 2025

Tóth, T.: Evaluation of pre-accession state aid in the energy sector. Yearb. Antitrust Regulatory Stud. **9**(14), 299–316 (2016). https://doi.org/10.7172/1689-9024.YARS.2016.9.14.16

Wallace, P.: Long-term power purchase agreements: the factors that influence contract design. In: Djakhongir, S. (ed.) Research Handbooks in Private and Commercial Law, pp. 305–333. Edward Elgar Publishing, Cheltenham (2019)

Whish, R., Bailey, D.: Competition Law, 10th edn. Oxford University Press, Oxford (2021)

Widuto, A.: Improving the design of the EU electricity market, Briefing EU Legislation in Progress 2024 (2024). www.europarl.europa.eu/thinktank/en/document/EPRS_BRI(2023)745694. Accessed 15 Aug 2025

Zachmann, G., et al.: The Design of the European Electricity Market. Publication for the Committee on Industry, Research and Energy, Policy Department for Economic, Scientific and Quality of Life Policies, European Parliament, Luxembourg (2023). https://www.europarl.europa.eu/thinktank/en/document/IPOL_STU(2023)740094. Accessed 15 Aug 2025

Cases

C-357/14 P, Electrabel SA et Dunamenti Erőmű Zrt. v. European Commission (2015), ECLI:EU:C:2015:642

Others

2008/C 9/05, Commission Decision relating to a proceeding pursuant to Article 82 of the EC Treaty, Distrigas, OJ 2008 C 9/8, 15.1.2008

2010/C 133/05, Summary of Commission Decision relating to a proceeding under Article 102 of the TFEU and Article 54 of the EEA Agreement, Long-term contracts France, OJ 2010 C 133/5, 22.5.2010

2022/C 80/01, Communication from the Commission – Guidelines on State aid for climate, environmental protection and energy, OJ 2022 C 80, 18.2.2022

2022/C 248/01, Communication from the Commission, Guidelines on vertical restraints, OJ 2022 C 248, p.1, 30.6.2022

2023/C 259/01, Communication from the Commission – Guidelines on the applicability of Article 101 of the Treaty on the Functioning of the European Union to horizontal cooperation agreements, OJ 2023 C 259, 21.7.2023

Opinion of the European Economic and Social Committee on Communication from the Commission to the European Parliament, the Council, the European Economic and Social Committee and the Committee of the Regions — EU Solar Energy Strategy (COM(2022) 221 final) and Commission recommendation on speeding up permit-granting procedures for renewable energy projects and facilitating Power Purchase Agreements (C(2022) 3219 final), OJ 2023 C 75, p. 178, 28.2.2023

COM (2022) 230, Communication from the Commission to the European Parliament, the European Council, the Council, the European Economic and Social Committee and the Committee of the Regions, REPowerEU Plan

COM/2023/148 final, Commission's Proposal for a regulation of the European Parliament and of the Council amending Regulations (EU) 2019/943 and (EU) 2019/942 as well as Directives (EU) 2018/2001 and (EU) 2019/944 to improve the Union's electricity market design, Explanatory Memorandum

COM (2023) 62 final, Communication from the Commission to the European Parliament, the European Council, the Council, the European economic and social committee and the Committee of the Regions, A Green Deal Industrial Plan for the Net-Zero Age

Communication from the Commission, Temporary crisis framework for State aid measures to support the economy fol-lowing the aggression against Ukraine by Russia, OJ 2022 CI 131/1, 24.03.2022

SEC (2006) 1724, DG Competition Report on Energy Sector Inquiry, Commission staff working document accompanying the Communication from the Commission - Inquiry pursuant to Article 17 of Regulation (EC) No 1/2003 into the European gas and electricity sectors (Final Report) {COM(2006) 851 final}, 10.1.2007. https://www.astrid-online.it/static/upload/protected/Tech/TechnicalReport_Energy_part1.pdf. Accessed 15.8.2025

SWD: 149 final. Commission Staff Working Document on Guidance to Member States on good practices to speed up permit-granting procedures for renewable energy projects and on facilitating Power Purchase Agreements **18**(5), 2022 (2022)

SWD (2023) 58 final, Commission Staff Working Document, Reform of electricity market design accompanying the documents proposal for a Regulation (EU) of the European Parliament and of the Council amending Regulations (EU) 2019/943 and (EU) 2019/942 as well as Directives (EU) 2018/2001 and (EU) 2019/944 to improve the Union's electricity market design Proposal for a Regulation (EU) of the European Parliament and of the Council amending Regulations (EU) No 1227/2011 and (EU) 2019/942 to improve the Union's protection against market manipulation in the wholesale energy market

General Secretariat of the Council (2023) Proposal for a Regulation of the European Parliament and of the Council amending Regulations (EU) 2019/943 and (EU) 2019/942 as well as Directives (EU) 2018/2001 and (EU) 2019/944 to improve the Union's electricity market design - Analysis of the final compromise text with a view to agreement, Interinstitutional File 2023/0077(COD). www.consilium.europa.eu/en/press/press-releases/2023/12/14/reform-of-electricity-market-design-council-and-parliament-reach-deal/. Accessed 26 Feb 2024. Accessed 15 Aug 2025

New Regulatory Framework for Air Pollution and Greenhouse Gas Emissions in the Aviation Sector under the Green Deal

Jiri Vodicka(✉)

Masaryk University, Brno, Czech Republic
Jiri.Vodicka@law.muni.cz

Abstract. The transport sector is one of the few sectors that has not yet been significantly affected by regulatory changes connected to the reduction of air-polluting substances and GHG in the EU. As opposed to "traditional" EU ETS sectors, the emissions from the transport sector have been experiencing steady growth over the past decade. Even though the aviation transport sector is a part of EU ETS, the scheme was not as successful as it should have been. However, under the Green Deal, the transport sector faces reduction challenges as it has never before. All these challenges are connected to the aim of the European Green Deal to make the EU climate-neutral by 2050, and the transport sector is a crucial aspect of achieving this goal. This chapter explores the current regulatory framework for air pollution and GHG emissions from aviation in the EU, with a focus on the legal instruments related to the Green Deal. The research draws on a systematic review of relevant academic literature, legislation, and policy papers. Through this review, the chapter identifies the key features of the regulatory framework for air pollution and GHG, including the role of the ICAO, as well as the EU's own policies and initiatives.

1 Introduction

Since the Wright brothers' inaugural flight in 1903, the aviation sector has experienced rapid and dynamic evolution. It ranks among the fastest-growing transportation sectors globally, not just within the EU. The possibility of traveling vast distances at reasonable prices within reasonable time has made the aviation sector one of the most popular transport sectors. These combined factors have contributed to the massive expansion that manifests itself in growing numbers of passengers and cargo transported every year. However, the darker side of this rapid expansion is the increase in greenhouse gas (GHG) emissions from aircraft.

Relative to other modes of transport, international and EU (domestic) flights contribute a minor share of total GHG emissions. Data indicate these flights account for approximately 4.6% (4.2% for international aviation and 0.4 % for domestic aviation) of all GHG emissions in the EU, in contrast to the broader EU transport sector's contribution of roughly 24.7% to the region's GHG emissions in 2023.[1] The COVID-19

[1] EEA greenhouse gases—data viewer. (16.4.2025). European Environment Agency's Home Page. https://www.eea.europa.eu/en/analysis/maps-and-charts/greenhouse-gases-viewer-data-viewers. Accessed 20 Aug 2025

M. Reese et al. (Eds.): EELF 2023, *Legal Implementation and Impacts of the European Green Deal*, pp. 117–132, 2026.
https://doi.org/10.1007/978-3-032-17197-9_5

pandemic's impact, which precipitated significant losses in the aviation sector due to travel restrictions, raises questions about the appropriateness of stringent regulatory measures. According to the European Environment Agency, aviation traffic surged by 24% in 2021 and 48% in 2022, with projections suggesting a return to pre-pandemic levels by 2025.[2] Contrarily, Transport & Environment forecasts this rebound might occur as early as 2024.[3]

Moreover, the European Commission (Commission) has projected that by 2040, the transport sector will account for 60% of the residual fossil fuel energy consumption (this includes phase-out of coal and the persistence of oil use in road, maritime and aviation transport).[4]

Furthermore, the necessity for robust EU regulation is evident given the leniency of Member States towards aviation regulation, as revealed by the analysis of National Energy and Climate Plans submitted to the Commission.[5] Approved plans typically feature a 134% increase in aviation references following Commission feedback[6], yet often propose few, if any, substantial national measures to mitigate aviation-related GHG emissions.[7]

These insights underscore the urgent need for the aviation sector to adopt a more sustainable trajectory.[8] Without such a gradual shift, we risk encountering resistance similar to that observed in the automotive industry, where stringent regulations, like the Euro 7 standards, faced formidable opposition from manufacturers and lobbying groups.

The sector's century-long expansion has significantly impacted the environment, affecting air quality, the atmosphere through GHG emissions, ecosystems, waste production, and human health. This chapter explores legal regulation of air quality and GHG emissions, noting recent studies and Commission statements that highlight the greater climate risk posed by non-CO_2 emissions (for example PM, NOx, oxidised sulphur species, and water vapour) compared to CO_2 emissions alone.[9]

---

[2] Greenhouse gas emissions from transport in Europe. (31.10.2024). European Environment Agency's Home Page.https://www.eea.europa.eu/en/analysis/indicators/greenhouse-gas-emissions-from-transport?activeAccordion=. Accessed 20 Aug 2025.

[3] Green recovery necessary after airline pollution fell 64% last year. (31.5.2024). T&E. https://www.transportenvironment.org/discover/green-recovery-necessary-after-airline-pollution-fell-64-last-year/. Accessed 20 Aug 2025.

[4] COM/2024/63 final, Communication from the commission to the European parliament, the council, the European economic and social committee and the committee of the regions: Securing our future Europe's 2040 climate target and path to climate neutrality by 2050 building a sustainable, just and prosperous society.

[5] Schmidt et al. (2022).

[6] ibid, p. 5.

[7] ibid

[8] This is further supported by Andrejiová et al. (2020).

[9] COM/2020/747 final, Report from the Commission to the European Parliament and the Council Updated analysis of the non-CO2 climate impacts of aviation and potential policy measures pursuant to EU Emissions Trading System Directive Article 30(4). Airplane pollution. (31.5.2024). T&E. https://www.transportenvironment.org/topics/planes/airplane-pol lution. Accessed 20 Aug 2025.

This chapter outlines the main elements of the EU's current legal framework concerning aviation's environmental impacts, specifically addressing regulatory responses to air pollution and GHG emissions as articulated under the EU Green Deal strategy.

Achieving this goal involves scrutinising pertinent EU policy documents and legislation related to air quality and climate change.

The chapter begins with an examination of policies that integrate aviation with GHG emission reduction strategies, focusing specifically on relevant policies and legislative documents. It then segments into discussions on various topics aligned with the aircraft lifecycle, proposing a foundation for GHG reduction efforts. Initial discussions centre on aircraft design innovations that could reduce emissions, followed by an exploration of aviation fuels, highlighting legal measures that promote the adoption of sustainable aviation fuels (SAF) to minimise carbon footprints. Further, the chapter addresses the responsibilities of aircraft operators, emphasizing the current EU ETS Directive[10] and international carbon offsetting schemes. Finally, it considers consumer behaviour, underscoring the influential role consumers play in driving GHG emission reductions through lifestyle adjustments.

Subsequently, the chapter shifts focus to legal mechanisms relevant to managing local air quality impacts of aviation, acknowledging that pollution is most pronounced in vicinities surrounding airports. This segment briefly considers specific EU-level instruments.

Conclusively, the chapter emphasises substantive legal mandates derived from existing legislation, deliberately omitting detailed discussions on enforcement and litigation cases.[11]

2 Curbing the Aviation Carbon Footprint

The mitigation of carbon footprints significantly depends on two pivotal factors: technological advancements and legislative frameworks. These elements are deeply interconnected; effective legislation can catalyse technological innovation, while laws must also evolve in tandem with technological capabilities to remain practical and attainable.

Technologically, the aviation sector has at its disposal several innovative solutions aimed at reducing GHG emissions. Noteworthy among these are the open rotor engine design[12], the adoption of alternative fuels (including biofuels and liquid hydrogen), the

[10] Directive 2003/87/EC of the European Parliament and of the Council of 13 October 2003 establishing a scheme for greenhouse gas emission allowance trading within the Community and amending Council Directive 96/61/EC, OJ L 275, p. 32, 25.10.2003.

[11] For litigation in the aviation sector see Balounová (2023).

[12] The engine is not yet commercially viable. It has been developed haphazardly since the 1940s with some use cases in military aviation, but it was never used in commercial aviation. However, there has been some news about Airbus considering this engine design (Niles 2025).

implementation of more efficient air traffic management systems[13], and the optimisation of flight paths to minimise environmental impact.[14]

Legislatively, various measures can be employed to curb GHG emissions, each targeting a different phase of the aircraft lifecycle and reliant upon technological support:

- Design of the aircraft.
- Types of aviation fuels used.
- Regulations governing aircraft operators.
- Influencing consumer behaviour.

2.1 Design of the Aircraft

The first strategy to reduce GHG emissions involves introducing stricter technical standards for aircraft seeking entry into the internal market. Aircraft manufacturers aiming to enter the EU market would need to adhere to more stringent emission criteria as part of the type-approval process, subsequently leading to certification under Regulation (EU) 2018/1139[15].

Article 87(1) of this Regulation establishes a foundational environmental framework for product design, stating:

> "… [it] shall aim to prevent significant harmful effects on climate, environment and human health caused by the civil aviation products concerned, giving due consideration to the international standards and recommended practices, environmental benefits, technological feasibility and economic impact."

[13] The modernisation of the air traffic system has been in development for over 20 years in the USA (based on Next Generation Air Transportation System Integrated Plan created by Federal Aviation Administration). The gradual changes in the uptake of new technologies such as precise aircraft tracking, software, and automation are already yielding cost savings and GHG reductions (Overton, 2025). In the EU similar action (with similar benefits as the US plan) is taking place. In 2024 SESAR joint undertaking published European ATM Master Plan that focuses on: trajectory-based operations, greater data volumes through better air–ground and ground–ground communication, higher levels of automation between the flight deck and the ground, human–machine teaming and dynamic airspace. https://www.sesarju.eu/MasterPlan2025. Accessed 20 Aug 2025

[14] Grewe (2020), p. 11.

[15] Regulation (EU) 2018/1139 of the European Parliament and of the Council of 4 July 2018 on common rules in the field of civil aviation and establishing a European Union Aviation Safety Agency, and amending Regulations (EC) No 2111/2005, (EC) No 1008/2008, (EU) No 996/2010, (EU) No 376/2014 and Directives 2014/30/EU and 2014/53/EU of the European Parliament and of the Council, and repealing Regulations (EC) No 552/2004 and (EC) No 216/2008 of the European Parliament and of the Council and Council Regulation (EEC) No 3922/91, OJ L 212, 22.8.2018.

This principle is further detailed in Annex III of the Regulation, which specifies essential requirements for environmental compatibility related to products. A similar approach is employed within the automotive industry[16], where the EU has adopted stringent CO_2 regulations for new vehicles, ultimately aiming for a 100% reduction in CO_2 emissions from new vehicles from 2035.[17]

However, adopting such an approach would necessitate new legislation mandating manufacturers or distributors to progressively reduce emissions from aircraft. Unlike the vehicle sector, this obligation may prove unfeasible due to challenges associated with transitioning to non-fossil fuels in aviation. Moreover, the aviation sector is tightly integrated with standards established and adopted by the International Civil Aviation Organization (ICAO). Within the international legislative framework, the ICAO specifies particular standards for CO_2 emissions and other environmental requisites.[18] The ICAO's CO_2 standards apply to new aircraft designs from 2020 and to aircraft types already in production as of 2023.[19] Yet, some experts argue that the effectiveness of these standards is undermined by the overall growth of the aviation market, which offsets the benefits of new standards.[20]

These requirements are then implemented through the Commission's delegated acts (for example, Regulation No. 748/2012[21]) and the European Union Aviation Safety Agency (EASA)[22]. Indeed, Regulation No. 748/2012 was notably amended in

[16] Regulation (EC) No 715/2007 of the European Parliament and of the Council of 20 June 2007 on type approval of motor vehicles with respect to emissions from light passenger and commercial vehicles (Euro 5 and Euro 6) and on access to vehicle repair and maintenance information, OJ L 171, 29.6.2007 and Regulation (EU) 2024/1257 of the European Parliament and of the Council of 24 April 2024 on type-approval of motor vehicles and engines and of systems, components and separate technical units in-tended for such vehicles, with respect to their emissions and battery durability (Euro 7), amending Regulation (EU) 2018/858 of the European Parliament and of the Council and repealing Regulations (EC) No 715/2007 and (EC) No 595/2009 of the European Parliament and of the Council, Commission Regulation (EU) No 582/2011, Commission Regulation (EU) 2017/1151, Commission Regulation (EU) 2017/2400 and Commission Implementing Regulation (EU) 2022/1362, OJ L 1257, 8.5.2024.

[17] Regulation (EU) 2019/631 of the European Parliament and of the Council of 17 April 2019 setting CO2 emission performance standards for new passenger cars and for new light commercial vehicles, and repealing Regulations (EC) No 443/2009 and (EU) No 510/2011, OJ L 111, p. 13, 25.4.2019.

[18] Annex 16 – Environmental Protection, Volume III to the Convention on International Civil Aviation.

[19] Fichert et al. (2020), p. 51.

[20] ibid

[21] Commission Regulation (EU) No 748/2012 of 3 August 2012 laying down implementing rules for the airworthiness and environmental certification or declaration of compliance of aircraft and related products, parts and appliances, as well as for the capability requirements of design and production organisations, OJ L 224, 21.8.2012.

[22] CS-CO2 Issue 2 - Implementation of the latest CAEP amendments to ICAO Annex 16 Volumes I, II, and III — CAEP/11. EASA. (14.7.2021). EASA. https://www.easa.europa.eu/en/document-library/certification-specifications/cs-co2-issue-2. Accessed 20 Aug 2025.

2019[23] to include modified and updated environmental requirements for aircraft EASA certification in the EU.

Given the international legislative framework imposes binding standards on aircraft, the EU's leverage in this domain is limited, and its discretion is narrow, thereby presenting a challenge to the EU's ambitious climate goals targeting the aviation sector.

2.2 Types of Aviation Fuels Used

Another approach to reducing the carbon footprint in the aviation sector focuses on sustainable aviation fuels. SAF represent a highly promising future for the aviation industry, offering a significant potential for GHG reduction. However, several challenges could impede their widespread adoption. Firstly, the approval process for new fuels can be lengthy, taking up to five years and requiring an investment of up to €5 million.[24] Moreover, as a new fuel type, SAF will initially face high production costs, which are expected to decrease as production scales up. Another challenge is the current lack of production capacity, stemming from underdeveloped infrastructure and the producers' focus on other sustainable fuels for different sectors.[25]

The EU views SAF as a feasible and promising solution, incorporating them into its policies and initiatives. A notable example is the RefuelEU initiative, part of the Fit-for-55 package, which has evolved into Regulation 2023/2405[26].

This Regulation targets key areas to not only facilitate the reduction of GHG from aviation fuel but also to ensure that all EU stakeholders have equal opportunities to transition to SAF. It mandates fuel suppliers to the aviation industry to include a minimum percentage of SAF in the fuel offered at EU airports starting from 2025, with this requirement extending to synthetic fuels from 2030. The mandated proportions will incrementally increase, reaching 70% SAF by 2050 of which a minimum share of 35% is to be synthetic aviation fuels.

Aircraft operators are also required to ensure that the annual volume of aviation fuel uplifted at any EU airport covers at least 90% of their yearly needs, a measure aimed at reducing emissions linked to tankering practices.

The Regulation defines eligible sustainable and synthetic aviation fuels as those that meet the sustainability and emissions reduction criteria of the Renewable Energy Directive (2018/2001[27]). Low-carbon aviation fuels, including low-carbon hydrogen, are also recognised for meeting the minimum quotas.

---

23 Commission Delegated Regulation (EU) 2019/897 of 12 March 2019 amending Regulation (EU) No 748/2012 as regards the inclusion of risk-based compliance verification in Annex I and the implementation of requirements for environmental protection, OJ L 144, 3.6.2019.

24 Sustainable Aviation Fuels (SAF). EASA. (n.d.). EASA. https://www.easa.europa.eu/en/domains/environment/sustainable-aviation-fuels-saf. Accessed 20 Aug 2025.

25 SAF volumes growing but still missing opportunities. (6.12.2023). IATA. https://www.iata.org/en/pressroom/2023-releases/2023-12-06-02/. Accessed 20 Aug 2025.

26 Regulation (EU) 2023/2405 of the European Parliament and of the Council of 18 October 2023 on ensuring a level playing field for sustainable air transport (ReFuelEU Aviation), OJ L, 2023/2405, 31.10.2023.

27 Directive (EU) 2018/2001 of the European Parliament and of the Council of 11 December 2018 on the promotion of the use of energy from renewable sources, OJ 2018 L 328.

Member States must appoint competent authorities to enforce these regulations and impose penalties for non-compliance. The Regulation 2023/2405 also introduces a Union-wide labelling system to rank the environmental performance of aircraft operators using SAF, guiding consumer choices towards greener flight options.

Additionally, it requires fuel suppliers and aircraft operators to collect and report data to evaluate the impact of these measures on the competitive landscape of EU aviation.

Lastly, the Regulation imposes data collection and reporting duties on both fuel suppliers and aircraft operators. These requirements are intended to assess the impact of this Regulation on the competitive positioning of EU aviation operators and infrastructure.

Complementing RefuelEU Regulation, Regulation 2023/1804[28] mandates airports within the TEN-T core networks and comprehensive networks to provide access to external electricity supplies for stationary aircraft, with specific deadlines for implementation at contact and remote stands.[29]

A critical challenge with SAF and the decarbonisation of the aviation industry is the availability of fuels. Despite EU legislation mandating the provision and use of SAF, meeting the industry's demand depends on the capacity to produce enough SAF, which may prove challenging in the future.[30]

2.3 Regulations Governing Aircraft Operators

The EU can take pride in its Emission Trading System (ETS), which has played a crucial role in decarbonising several sectors (notably electricity generation, energy-intensive industries) over the past two decades.

In its first three phases, the ETS covered 40% of GHG emission production in the EU[31], significantly reducing carbon emissions by 6% in the first phase and by 15% in the second phase, while companies maintained stable profit margins and employment rates.[32] Since its commencement, the ETS has managed to reduce carbon emissions by 37.3% in the sectors of electricity and heat production, along with industrial production.[33]

Subsequent amendments aim to extend the ETS to cover almost 62% of all GHGs produced in the EU. This expansion includes additional flights and the maritime sector and introduces ETS 2, which covers buildings, small industries, and fossil fuels in the road transport sector.[34]

---

28 Commission Delegated Regulation (EU) 2019/897.

29 Sustainable Aviation Fuels (SAF). EASA. (n.d.). EASA. https://www.easa.europa.eu/en/domains/environment/sustainable-aviation-fuels-saf. Accessed 20 Aug 2025

30 SAF volumes growing but still missing opportunities. (6.12.2023). IATA. https://www.iata.org/en/pressroom/2023-releases/2023-12-06-02/. Accessed 20 Aug 2025.

31 Regulation (EU) 2023/2405.

32 Directive (EU) 2018/2001.

33 Regulation (EU) 2023/1804 of the European Parliament and of the Council of 13 September 2023 on the deployment of alternative fuels infrastructure, and repealing Directive 2014/94/EU, OJ 2023 L 234.

34 ibid, Article 12.

The EU ETS serves as a pioneering example for other countries, such as China.[35] However, the ETS distinguishes itself from other systems through the specific inclusion of the aviation sector.

The aviation sector within the ETS has undergone significant changes over the years. From receiving almost all allowances for free until the end of phase III (2020), there is a planned phase-out of free allocations by 2026 and an emphasis on promoting SAF.

2.3.1 EU ETS Directive

The ETS Directive, as amended by Directive 2023/959, introduces new challenges for the aviation sector. However, with proper implementation and enforcement, it could significantly address GHGs from aviation.

Non-CO_2 Aviation Effects

Historically, the non-CO_2 effects of aviation have been underrecognised. Nonetheless, the Directive now includes a definition in Article 3(v), establishing a foundational framework for related obligations. Until now, the Directive's focus has been on the monitoring and reporting of these substances (Article 14). This article requires the Commission to implement acts for detailed monitoring and reporting of emissions, including non-CO_2 emissions, specifically from aviation activities as detailed in Annex I of the Directive. A key aspect is the introduction of measures for tracking and reporting the global warming potential of various greenhouse gases, integrating the latest scientific findings on the impact of non-CO_2 aviation emissions.

Furthermore, Article 14(5) outlines obligations for Member States and aircraft operators regarding the monitoring and reporting of non-CO_2 emissions. It mandates that each Member State ensure aircraft operators monitor and report the non-CO_2 effects from each aircraft they operate over each calendar year, beginning January 1, 2025. Aircraft operators are required to annually report on the non-CO_2 aviation effects from the same start date as the Member States.

The monitoring of non-CO_2 aviation emissions is scheduled for a two-year period, and by the end of 2027, the Commission, if necessary, based on the reports, shall prepare a legislative proposal to mitigate non-CO_2 aviation emissions.

Linear Reduction Factor

The quantity of allowances allocated to the aviation sector is now subject to a linear reduction factor, as specified in Article 9, aligning it with the approach for stationary installations.[36] This factor was set at 2.2% starting from the year 2021. However, between 2024 and 2027, the linear reduction factor will increase to 4.3%, and from 2028 onwards, it will rise slightly to 4.4%.[37] This adjustment marks a significant advancement in EU regulation, as such a provision did not exist before the enactment of Directive 2023/958.[38] The reduction factor has a direct impact on the aviation cap detailed in

[35] Shehab et al. (2023).

[36] Article 3c(5) of Directive 2003/87.

[37] ibid, Article 9.

[38] Directive (EU) 2023/958 of the European Parliament and of the Council of 10 May 2023 amending Directive 2003/87/EC as regards aviation's contribution to the Union's economy-wide emission reduction target and the appropriate implementation of a global market-based measure, OJ L 130, p. 115, 16.5.2023.

Article 3c(5), which the Commission calculates. This cap is formalised through a Commission decision. For instance, the cap for the year 2024 was established at 28,866,578 allowances.[39]

Promotion of SAFs

The Directive provides incentives for the use of SAF from 2024 to 2030, as outlined in Article 3c. This is facilitated through the allocation (reservation) of 20 million allowances from the ETS. Operators utilising sustainable or non-fossil aviation fuels are eligible for these incentives. The revenue generated from these reserved allowances is designed to offset part or the entirety of the cost disparity between conventional fossil kerosene and SAF. This financial support takes into account the carbon price and any existing taxes on fossil fuels, thereby rendering SAF a more economically attractive option for airlines. The Directive delineates the proportion of the price difference to be covered for various types of sustainable fuels, promoting the adoption of hydrogen derived from renewable sources, advanced biofuels, renewable fuels of non-biological origin, and other qualified non-fossil aviation fuels.

Moreover, these initiatives align with the RefuelEU policy and Regulation 2023/2405, thereby establishing a comprehensive legal framework that supports the adoption of SAF.

Allocation of Allowances

Article 3d marks a pivotal change in the allocation of allowances for the aviation sector, introducing stricter regulations and set deadlines. This means that operators will no longer benefit from freely allocated allowances to the extent they did before 2023. Specifically, this provision establishes a reduction framework for 2024 and 2025, wherein 15% of the total quantity of allowances designated for aircraft operators (as per Article 3c(5)) will be auctioned.

This adjustment is compounded by a further reduction in the freely allocated allowances: a 25% reduction in 2024 and a 50% reduction in 2025 from the remaining 85%.

Crucially, starting from January 1, 2026, the number of freely allocated allowances will be reduced to zero, with almost all allowances slated for auction. Exceptions are made for circumstances outlined in Article 3c(6), related to SAF, and Article 10a(8), fourth paragraph, which pertains to innovation and support measures.

Despite these significant changes, the EU ETS continues to cover only intra-EEA flights, along with flights to Switzerland and the United Kingdom from EEA territory.[40] This means the EU ETS still accounts for only about 40% of the EU's greenhouse gas emissions from the aviation sector, as flights entering and exiting the EEA territory are not included and are expected to be addressed by a different offsetting scheme.[41]

[39] Article 1. Commission Decision (EU) 2023/2440 of 27 October 2023 on the Union-wide total quantity of allowances to be allocated in respect of aircraft operators under the EU Emissions Trading System for 2024, C/2023/7164.

[40] Annex I of Directive 2003/87.

[41] EU aviation deal will see another lost decade in tackling emissions. (7.12.2022). T&E. https://www.transportenvironment.org/discover/eu-aviation-deal-will-see-another-lost-decade-in-tackling-emissions. Accessed 20 Aug 2025.

2.3.2 CORSIA and ETS Coexistence

Since its inception in 2016, the Carbon Offsetting and Reduction Scheme for International Aviation (CORSIA) has aimed to introduce an international market-based mechanism for reducing aviation emissions, a concept that predates CORSIA itself.[42] In 2019, the ICAO finalised its implementation plan, introducing three phases of implementation. States' participation in the pilot phase (2021–2023) and the first phase (2024–2026) is voluntary.

Various studies have highlighted the shortcomings of CORSIA, particularly its ineffectiveness in significantly reducing GHG. One critical issue is the prevalence of low-integrity offsets within the CORSIA system, offering airlines a cost-effective but ultimately insufficient solution for truly addressing GHG emissions. The lack of rigorous oversight to verify the effectiveness and performance of these offsets poses a risk, potentially misleading the public and legislators into believing in their efficacy and encouraging their continued use.[43] Additionally, some analyses suggest that even with mandatory implementation, CORSIA would only provide partial environmental benefits compared to the full application of the EU ETS. The compensation rate under CORSIA, ranging from 11.5% in 2027 to 23.4% in 2039, falls short of what is needed to address the current climate crisis.[44]

The EU has been meticulously monitoring CORSIA's development to evaluate its potential to replace the ETS for aviation. The EU's approach has been one of caution and hesitancy, driven by uncertainties about CORSIA's ability to deliver meaningful GHG reductions. Various scenarios for CORSIA's implementation are under consideration, supported by studies aiming to guide the EU in selecting the most appropriate approach.

Integrating CORSIA with the EU ETS could jeopardise the EU's ambitious goal of reducing GHG by 55% by 2030. A commissioned study – Assessment of ICAO's global market-based measure (CORSIA) pursuant to Article 28b and for studying cost pass-through pursuant to Article 3d of the EU ETS Directive, in 2020 concluded that CORSIA might not lead to a sufficient decrease in GHG.[45] The study pointed out significant variations in the quality of offsets (even among approved ones[46]) and raised concerns about the pricing and motivational impact of offsets.[47]

Recent studies have explored various policy scenarios concerning the scope of the EU ETS in relation to international aviation emissions. Specifically, these studies assess whether the EU ETS should encompass all intra-EEA flights, including both outgoing from and incoming to the EEA, or limit its coverage to only outgoing flights.[48] Another scenario considers the Commission's official proposal, which recommends retaining the EU ETS for intra-EEA flights while applying CORSIA to both incoming and outgoing international flights. The findings indicate that fully implementing the EU ETS to cover

[42] Maertens et al. (2020), pp. 117-118.

[43] Wozny et al. (2022).

[44] Scheelhaase and Maertens (2020), p. 111.

[45] European Commission: Directorate-General for Climate Action, Air Transportation Analytics, Cambridge Econometrics, HFW, ICF, NewClimate Institute & Sven Starckx. (2022), p. 22.

[46] ibid, p. 18-21.

[47] ibid, p. 20.

[48] van Velzen (2022).

intra-EEA flights, along with both incoming and outgoing flights, would lead to a 113% increase in GHG reductions compared to the Commission's proposal. A partial implementation, including intra-EEA and outgoing flights, would result in a 53% increase in GHG reductions compared to the Commission's approach.[49]

A significant challenge with CORSIA is its baseline for offsetting requirements, which was set using data from 2019—a pre-COVID year when air traffic was significantly higher. This baseline means that only operators exceeding these high, pre-pandemic numbers are required to offset their emissions.[50]

Despite these considerations, in 2023, the European Parliament and the Council of the EU opted for what is perceived as the least favourable option for mitigating GHG from the aviation sector.[51]

To date, the EU ETS has been engaged in a Monitoring, Reporting, and Verification (MRV) phase concerning CORSIA. This phase is crucial for determining the scope of emissions CORSIA can potentially cover in the future.

CORSIA's implementation within the EU ETS Directive includes key provisions outlined in Article 12(6)–(9), addressing aspects such as offsetting Requirement Calculation, CORSIA compliance periods, notification conditions, exemptions for specific (non-commercial) flights, calculation methodology, and the cancellation of units. These provisions are expanded in Article 28a, which restricts the EU ETS's scope to only intra-EEA flights and flights to the United Kingdom and Switzerland, leaving other flights under CORSIA's purview.

Additionally, Article 28b mandates a Commission report by July 1, 2026, to the European Parliament and the Council, assessing CORSIA's environmental integrity, including its alignment with the Paris Agreement and various operational and compliance factors (for example enforceability, transparency, the penalties for non-compliance, the processes for public input, the quality of offset credits). Should this assessment reveal shortcomings, the EU may consider extending the EU ETS to cover flights from the EEA to third countries, as stipulated in Article 28b(3).

Article 28b(3) specifies conditions critical for evaluating CORSIA's effectiveness and its alignment with global climate goals, notably those established in the Paris Agreement. These conditions mandate that CORSIA must demonstrate substantial progress toward its long-term global aspirational goal to mitigate aviation emissions. Moreover, the scheme needs to be embraced and implemented by states representing at least 70% of total international aviation emissions for it to be deemed satisfactory by the EU.

A list of countries applying CORSIA for the ETS Directive, as per Article 25a(3), will be adopted by the Commission. Moreover, Article 25a(7) seeks to protect operators holding certificates from an EU Member State or registered in a Member State who might be adversely affected by a third state's improper CORSIA application, exempting them from certain offsetting requirements under Article 12(9).

[49] ibid, p. 20.

[50] CORSIA Fact sheet. (n.d.). IATA. https://www.iata.org/en/iata-repository/pressroom/fact-sheets/fact-sheet-corsia. Accessed 20 Aug 2025

[51] Decision (EU) 2023/136 of the European Parliament and of the Council of 18 January 2023 amending Directive 2003/87/EC as regards the notification of offsetting in respect of a global market-based measure for aircraft operators based in the Union, OJ L 19. 20.2.2023.

2.4 Influencing Consumer Behaviour

The potential for GHG reduction significantly lies in a challenging area to regulate: consumer behaviour. States have various strategies to modify or influence such behaviour. They can either introduce legal regulations that directly impact consumers or target companies and their products, which, in turn, may influence consumer choices. For instance, Regulation 2019/631, which effectively bans the sale of new vehicles with combustion engines from 2035, targets manufacturers. Although this regulation primarily targets manufacturers, it also indirectly affects consumers by limiting their choices, hence demonstrating the indirect effect of regulation.

In the aviation sector, there are multiple possible legal and non-legal instruments aimed at consumers, both directly and indirectly. Non-legal instruments often encourage consumers to prefer alternative modes of transport when viable, such as trains. This encouragement can come through educational campaigns or incentives for public transportation.

Legal instruments might include measures like bans on short-haul flights (for example France[52]) a solution feasible in countries with sufficient train capacity and railroad networks but not addressing long-haul flights. Another approach is to internalise the environmental costs of aviation by increasing flight ticket prices, through mechanisms like raising emission allowance prices, properly taxing aviation fuel, or introducing a new carbon tax. This could lead to higher consumer prices and deter from flying, although it could disproportionately affect low-income households.

For several years, airline operators have offered voluntary carbon-offset payments. While commendable, this approach presents several issues. One major concern is its social impact: by promoting environmental responsibility, it shifts the primary burden from airline operators, the main polluters, to consumers and their ethical decisions[53]. Moreover, the system's lack of centralisation and profit-driven nature can undermine environmental efforts.[54] Without regulatory oversight, consumers lack assurance that their contributions genuinely support carbon offsetting and legitimate projects.

Airline operators' green claims regarding voluntary carbon-offset payments may face scrutiny under the proposed Green Claims Directive.[55] Operators asserting the legitimacy and effectiveness of offsetting payments will need to substantiate their claims as outlined in Article 10 of the directive. Verifying these green claims related to carbon-offset payments could lead to a gradual regulatory shift toward a more comprehensive framework.

3 Air-Polluting Substances

Unlike GHG, polluting substances directly affect human health. During an aircraft's flight, two zones are impacted by these pollutants, where the substances are dispersed. One zone experiences impact during take-off, taxiing, and landing, relating to local air

[52] Limb (2023).

[53] Broadhead and Placani (2021), p. 413.

[54] Franki (2022), pp. 181-182.

[55] COM/2023/166 final, Proposal for a Directive of the European Parliament and of the Council on substantiation and com-munication of explicit environmental claims (Green Claims Directive).

quality. The other zone is affected during flight, where the aircraft emits pollutants from its engines over vast areas, allowing for easier dispersion of these substances.

The zone affecting local air quality is particularly problematic. Populations living near airports suffer the most from pollutants emitted by aircraft engines. The ICAO has addressed this issue in Annex 16 Vol II, setting emission standards for smoke (to be superseded by the nvPM Standard), hydrocarbons (HC), oxides of nitrogen (NOx), and carbon monoxide (CO).[56] The ICAO acknowledges that emissions of NOx and particulate matter (PM) from aircraft will increase in the future due to rising air traffic. Future scenarios up to 2050 depend on technological advancements to reduce pollutants.[57] However, despite these advances, aircraft emissions continue to rise. The ICAO also offers the Airport Air Quality Manual, attempting to shift focus from aircraft emissions to pollutants from other urban sources, such as road traffic, industry, and the energy sector.[58]

Furthermore, the Manual examines air quality standards worldwide, highlighting their diversity and, once again, shifting focus from aircraft engines to local authorities and air quality standards.

On the other hand, it's fair to say that poor air quality is not solely attributable to airports, aircraft, or air traffic in general. It must also be acknowledged that local authorities play a crucial role in overseeing local air quality and implementing specific measures. Areas around airports should be considered buffer zones where engine emissions are dispersed harmlessly, achievable through spatial planning and targeted measures.

This regulatory area remains underexploited in the EU. The main legal regulation on air quality, Directive 2008/50[59], does not address airports. This Directive focuses solely on road traffic within the transport sector, leaving aviation emissions outside its scope.

However, a new Directive on Ambient Air Quality does partially address aviation emissions.[60] Annex VII of the Directive mandates the monitoring of ultrafine particles (UFP) at locations prone to high UFP concentrations, such as airports or ports. The expansion of the monitoring network promises a comprehensive informational overview of air quality in specific areas.

Additionally, the local air quality and impact on human health could be in some cases subject to environmental impact assessment.

[56] Annex 16 – Environmental Protection, Volume II (Engine emissions) to the Convention on International Civil Aviation.

[57] Trends in local air quality. (n.d.). https://www.icao.int/environmental-protection/Pages/LAQ_Trends.aspx. Accessed 20 Aug 2025.

[58] Guidance on airport air quality. (n.d.). https://www.icao.int/environmental-protection/Pages/LAQ_GuidanceMaterial.aspx. Accessed 20 Aug 2025

[59] Directive 2008/50/EC of the European Parliament and of the Council of 21 May 2008 on ambient air quality and cleaner air for Europe, OJ L 152, 11.6.2008.

[60] Directive (EU) 2024/2881 of the European Parliament and of the Council of 23 October 2024 on ambient air quality and cleaner air for Europe, OJ L, 2024 /2881, 20.11.2024.

4 Conclusion

Aviation plays a crucial role in our modern world, connecting remote areas and driving globalisation. Since its inception in the early 20th century, it has become a popular mode of transport, significantly lowering travel costs for the general population and fostering further development. Despite challenges like the 1973 oil crisis and the 2019 COVID-19 pandemic, the sector has demonstrated resilience.

However, the aviation industry's economic growth is accompanied by an increase in negative environmental impacts. These two factors are intertwined, often complementing each other unless mitigated by authoritative measures (either by states or the international community), primarily through legal instruments.

This chapter aimed to explore the key aspects of the EU's regulatory framework for addressing air pollution and GHG emissions from aviation, highlighting relevant legal instruments under the Green Deal.

Initially, the chapter examined the regulatory landscape for reducing aviation sector GHG, considering the aircraft's life cycle. It discussed opportunities for lowering GHG emissions in areas such as aircraft design, sustainable aviation fuels, operators' obligations, and consumer choices.

Aircraft design offers significant potential for carbon emission reduction, with the ICAO setting binding emission standards. However, ICAO's cautious approach and the need for international consensus make rapid progress challenging in our urgent climate context.

SAF present a promising avenue. The EU's efforts, particularly through initiatives like RefuelEU, aim to make SAF available at major airports. Despite potential for substantial impact, immediate SAF shortages, infrastructure, and cost remain barriers.

A significant portion of the chapter analysed the evolution of the EU ETS and CORSIA. The EU ETS has seen considerable development, gradually applying similar provisions to those for stationary installations to aircraft operators. This includes not only a cap on aviation allowances but also their progressive reduction, aiming to auction all allowances eventually. Moreover, the inclusion of non-CO_2 emissions represents a pivotal shift, potentially integrating these pollutants into the EU ETS in the future.

CORSIA, while an international counterpart to the EU ETS, has notable differences. Its voluntary nature and unconvincing offsetting results highlight the challenges of achieving international consensus. The chapter pointed out key issues with CORSIA, including its offsetting requirements baseline and the nature of offsets (and their efficiencies).

The EU's strategy combines CORSIA for international flights with the ETS for intra-EEA flights and those to Switzerland and the United Kingdom. Should CORSIA prove ineffective, the EU may extend the ETS to cover all outbound flights from the EEA.

The discussion on GHG shifted focus to consumers, who drive demand and set trends, holding the key to potential aviation sector carbon reductions. Identified measures to influence consumer behaviour included financial incentives for alternative transport and bans on short-haul flights. The appropriateness of shifting carbon reduction focus from emitters to consumers and the impact on low-income households warrant consideration.

The latter part of the chapter addressed pollutants affecting local air quality, problematic mainly during ground operations and take-off/landing phases. While the ICAO sets standards for these pollutants, the responsibility largely falls to local authorities for air quality protection and enforcement. This legislative area remains underexplored. The (old) Directive 2008/50 focuses broadly on air quality, offering limited traffic restrictions. Recently adopted new Ambient Air Quality Directive (2024/2881) targets ultrafine particle monitoring at airports, highlighting the potential impact on local communities. The impact on local air quality and inhabitants could be subject to environmental impact assessment.

This chapter scrutinised a sector with undeniable climate impact, showcasing the EU's pioneering efforts and potential for serving as a global model. Newly proposed and adopted legislation focusing on novel technologies and comprehensive ETS inclusion holds promise, yet one must ponder whether these initiatives should have been introduced sooner in light of the current climate crisis.

References

Andrejiová, M., Grincova, A., Marasová, D.: Study of the percentage of greenhouse gas emissions from aviation in the EU-27 countries by applying multiple-criteria statistical methods. Int. J. Environ. Res. Public Health **17**(11), 3759 (2020). https://doi.org/10.3390/ijerph17113759

Balounová, E.: Climate litigation: targeting the aviation sector. Chin. J. Environ. Law **7**(2), 288–300 (2023). https://doi.org/10.1163/24686042-12340111

Broadhead, S., Placani, A.: The morality of carbon offsets for luxury emissions. World Futures **77**(6), 405–417 (2021). https://doi.org/10.1080/02604027.2021.1969876

Dechezleprêtre, A., Nachtigall, D., Venmans, F.: The joint impact of the European Union emissions trading system on carbon emissions and economic performance. J. Environ. Econ. Manag. **118**, 102758 (2023). https://doi.org/10.1016/j.jeem.2022.102758

European Commission: Directorate-General for Climate Action, Air Transportation Analytics, Cambridge Econometrics, HFW, ICF, NewClimate Institute & Sven Starckx. Assessment of ICAO's global market-based measure (CORSIA) pursuant to Article 28b and for studying cost pass-through pursuant to Article 3d of the EU ETS Directive. Publications Office of the European Union (2022). https://data.europa.eu/doi/10.2834/71485

Fichert, F., Forsyth, P., Niemeier, H.: Air transport and the challenge of climate change – how aviation climate change policies work. In: Fichert, et al (eds.) Aviation and Climate Change Economic Perspectives on Greenhouse Gas Reduction Policies, 1st edn., pp. 47–78. Routledge (2020). https://doi.org/10.4324/9781315572406-4

Franki, N.: Regulation of the voluntary carbon offset market. Columbia J. Environ. Law **48**(1), 39 (2022). https://doi.org/10.52214/cjel.v48i1.10442

Grewe, V.: Aviation emissions and climate impacts. In: Fichert, et al. (eds.) Aviation and Climate Change Economic Perspectives on Greenhouse Gas Reduction Policies, 1st edn., pp. 4–15. Routledge (2020). https://doi.org/10.4324/9781315572406-2

Limb, L.: It's official: France bans short-haul domestic flights in favour of train travel. Euronews (2023). https://www.euronews.com/green/2022/12/02/is-france-banning-private-jets-everything-we-know-from-a-week-of-green-transport-proposals. Accessed 20 Aug 2025

Maertens, S., Grimme, W., Scheelhaase, J.: ICAO's new CORSIA scheme at a glance – a milestone towards greener aviation? In: Fichert, et al. (eds.) Aviation and Climate Change Economic Perspectives on Greenhouse Gas Reduction Policies, pp. 117–129 (2020). https://doi.org/10.4324/9781315572406-7

Niles, R.: Airbus planning open rotor engine for A320 replacement - AVWeB. AVweb: premier Aviation News and Insights for Pilots and Professionals (2025). https://avweb.com/aviation-news/airbus-planning-open-rotor-engine-for-a320-replacement/. Accessed 20 Aug 2025

Overton, J.: NextGen: upgrading air traffic management for greater efficiency. EESI (2025). https://www.eesi.org/articles/view/nextgen-upgrading-air-traffic-management-for-greater-efficiency. Accessed 20 Aug 2025
Shehab, M., Moshammer, K., Franke, M., Zondervan, E.: Analysis of the potential of meeting the EU's sustainable aviation fuel targets in 2030 and 2050. Sustainability **15**(12), 9266 (2023). https://doi.org/10.3390/su15129266
Scheelhaase, J., Maertens, S.: How to improve the global 'Carbon Offsetting and Reduction Scheme for International Aviation' (CORSIA)? Transp. Res. Procedia **51**, 108–117 (2020). https://doi.org/10.1016/j.trpro.2020.11.013
Schmidt, N.M., Tobin, P., Moore, B.: Brace for turbulence: EU member States' climate strategies in the aviation sector. Clim. Action **1**(1) (2022). https://doi.org/10.1007/s44168-022-00018-1
van Velzen, A.: Environmental and economic impacts of EU ETS and CORSIA policy scenarios for European aviation. T&E (2022). https://www.transportenvironment.org/wp-content/uploads/2022/05/20220523-Environmental-and-economic-impacts-of-EU-ETS-and-CORSIA-policy-scenarios-for-European-aviation-Final-report-1.pdf. Accessed 20 Aug 2025
Wozny, F., Grimme, W., Maertens, S., Scheelhaase, J.: CORSIA—a feasible second best solution? Appl. Sci. **12**(14), 7054 (2022). https://doi.org/10.3390/app12147054

Others

COM/2020/747 final, Report from the Commission to the European Parliament and the Council Updated analysis of the non-CO2 climate impacts of aviation and potential policy measures pursuant to EU Emissions Trading System Directive Article 30(4), 23.11.2020
COM/2023/166 final, Proposal for a Directive of the European Parliament and of the Council on substantiation and communication of explicit environmental claims (Green Claims Directive), 22.3.2023
COM/2024/63 final, Communication from the commission to the European parliament, the council, the European economic and social committee and the committee of the regions: Securing our future Europe's 2040 climate target and path to climate neutrality by 2050 building a sustainable, just and prosperous society, 6.2.2024

Managing Intersections and Trade-Offs

Will European Biodiversity be Sacrificed on the Green Transition Altar...?: Perspectives on Habitats and Species Protection in Times of Energy Crises

Jan Darpö(✉)

Faculty of Law, Uppsala Universitet, Uppsala, Sweden
jan.darpo@jur.uu.se

Abstract. The EU's push for renewable energy, accelerated by the REPowerEU plan and the RED III Directive, risks undermining its own biodiversity safeguards. This analysis examines the legal tension between new fast-track mechanisms, like "renewable acceleration areas" and the "overriding public interest" presumption, and core EU nature conservation laws. While planning is essential, the current emphasis on speed threatens to weaken environmental assessments, public participation, and the precautionary principle. Without careful implementation, the green transition may come at the expense of European biodiversity.

1 Introduction

This contribution concerns the new legislation on energy efficiency and deployment of renewables, and its presumed consequences for biodiversity issues in Europe. The overriding question is how key components in the coming legislation will function together with some of the basic requirements for good governance in decision-making in the field of EU environmental law. The point of departure is the revised version of the *EU Renewables Directive (2018/2001),* the so-called *RED III*[1] from 2023. The discussion will also include some comparisons with other coming pieces of legislation on renewables under the Green Transition.[2] As for the encounter with environmental law, the focus of this paper is on the obligations regarding nature conservation and species protection under

This manuscript was originally published in the Nordic Environmental Law Journal 24:2.

[1] I use the term "RED III" for the revised Directive (2018/2001) on the promotion of the use of energy from renewable sources, as amended by Regulation (EU) 2022/759 of December 2021 and Directive 2023/2413 of October 2023. For the consolidated version, see: Directive (EU) 2018/2001 of the European Parliament and of the Council of 11 December 2018 on the promotion of the use of energy from renewable sources, OJ L 328, p. 82, 21.12.2018. https://eur-lex.europa.eu/legal-content/EN/TXT/?uri=CELEX%3A02018L2001-20240716. Accessed 25 Aug 2025.

[2] European Commission, Green Transition, https://reform-support.ec.europa.eu/what-we-do/green-transition_en. Accessed 25 Aug 2025.

M. Reese et al. (Eds.): EELF 2023, *Legal Implementation and Impacts of the European Green Deal*, pp. 135–158, 2026.
https://doi.org/10.1007/978-3-032-17197-9_6

the Birds Directive (2009/147) and the Habitats Directive (92/43).[3] Although existing permitting procedures for wind farms will be used as illustrative examples, drawing from the Swedish experience, the discussion will be held at a general level for the European reader.[4]

2 REPowerEU Plan

The REPowerEU Plan was launched in May 2022 in response to Russia's invasion of Ukraine and the resulting energy crises in Europe.[5] The aim of the plan is to save energy, to accelerate the transition towards a fossil-free society, and to diversify EUs energy supplies. The first step in lawmaking of relevance for environmental permitting procedures came with the so-called Emergency Regulation (EU) 2022/2577.[6] In order to mitigate the effects of the energy crisis, this legislation established temporary rules to accelerate the permit-granting processes for the production of energy from renewable energy sources, as well as for grid and infrastructure projects that are needed to integrate renewable energy into the electricity system. The Emergency Regulation introduced most of the key components recurring in RED III, such as acceleration areas for renewables, timelines for the permitting processes, positive silence rules[7] and a presumption that

[3] Valuable contributions to the discussion about RED III and EUs biodiversity obligations can be found in Anker and Olsen (2023); Malafry (2022); Jendroska and Anapyaova (2023) and Montini (2024). Further, there are also quite a few scholarly contributions on RED III within the discourse of Energy law, out of which Hardiman (2022a) and Hardiman (2022b) can be mentioned. Even though legal scholars within this discourse tackle the true conflict between climate and biodiversity, it is challenging to discuss these matters from their perspective, as the opposing interests to renewables commonly are described as "barriers" only, according to which the permit bodies and courts take excessive account to "local flora and fauna" as well to the interests of nearby communities. As for the environmental issues, I have never come across a case where such local impacts on flora and fauna have been decisive, at least when it comes to the application of the EU Nature Directives. Concerning the opposition from local communities, the overarching theme in the Energy law discourse seems to be the need for lessening of the requirements for public participation and access to justice according to Aarhus. Strangely enough, these ideas seem only to apply to the public concerned, never the operators. Here, I draw my line for discussion as I regard the principle of judicial protection as one of the key pillars of environmental democracy within the EU which may not be questioned.

[4] Those who are interested in environmental permitting procedures in the Nordic countries may find some information in Darpö (2023).

[5] European Commission, REPowerEU. https://commission.europa.eu/topics/energy/repowereu_en. Accessed 25 Aug 2025.

[6] Council Regulation (EU) 2022/2577 of 22 December 2022 laying down a framework to accelerate the deployment of renewable energy, OJ L 335, p. 36, 29.12.2022.

[7] Or "tacit agreements" or "deemed approval". The opposite is "negative silence" rules – also called "implied dismissals" or "deemed refusals" – which can be found in Article 10(6) of the Council Regulation (EC) No 139/2004 of 20 January 2004 on the control of concentrations between undertakings (the EC Merger Regulation), OJ L 24, 29.1.2004. In the field of environmental law, Article 8(3) of Regulation (EC) No 1049/2001 of the European Parliament and of the Council of 30 May 2001 regarding public access to European Parliament, Council and

renewable energy projects are of "overriding public interest". Becoming directly applicable in the Member States from 30 December 2022, it was meant to expire on 30 June 2024 when it was supposed to be replaced by RED III. However, after a short evaluation by the Commission,[8] most articles were prolonged for an additional year to make the transition seamless and more structured for the Member States.[9]

The revision of the Renewables Directive (2018/2001, RED) was finally decided in October 2023 (Directive 2023/2413). In it, the scope of Directive 2018/2001 is expanded, and the demand sectors are covered more comprehensively. Targets for the share of renewables are set for industry, transport, heating and cooling, as well as for buildings. The mandatory sustainability criteria concerning forest biomass are further specified in line with the principle of sustainable forest management. RED III includes provisions to streamline procedures for the permitting of renewable energy projects through spatial planning, simplification and shortening of time frames. Parts of the new provisions were to be implemented in the Member States by 1 July 2024, while another 18 months may be used for others. An important step in the implementation of RED III is the requirement for the Member States to set up and report to the Commission National Energy and Climate Plans (NECP). In the NECP, each Member State is obliged to show its proposals on how to contribute to the fulfilment of the 42,5% target for the share of renewable energy in the EUs overall energy consumption by 2030.

There are obviously many more initiatives from the EU to further the Green Transition that may have an impact on environmental issues raised in different permit regimes under EU law. The *Critical Raw Materials Act* (CRMA) aims at ensuring access to a secure, diversified, affordable and sustainable supply of critical raw materials in the EU.[10] In addition, the Net Zero Industry Act (NZIA) sets up the goal to make the EU home to clean technologies and to facilitate progress towards a strong domestic manufacturing capacity of those technologies.[11] Both these Regulations contain solutions similar to the

Commission documents, OJ L 145, p. 43, 31.5.2001, states that the failure of the institution to reply within the prescribed time limit shall be considered as a negative reply and entitle the applicant to institute court proceedings and/or make a complaint to the Ombudsman. Such negative silence rules have also taken root in Member State laws and are today quite common (see opinion by Advocate General Wahl in C-58/13 and C-59/13, Torresi v Consiglio dell'Ordine degli Avvocati di Macerata (2014), at para 70.

[8] COM(2023) 764 final, Report from the Commission to the Council on the review of Council Regulation (EU) 2022/2577 of 22 December 2022 laying down a framework to accelerate the deployment of renewable energy.

[9] Council Regulation (EU) 2024/223 of 22 December 2023 amending Regulation (EU) 2022/2577 laying down a framework to accelerate the deployment of renewable energy, OJ L, 2024/223, 10.1.2024.

[10] Regulation (EU) 2024/1252 of the European Parliament and of the Council of 11 April 2024 establishing a framework for ensuring a secure and sustainable supply of critical raw materials and amending Regulations (EU) No 168/2013, (EU) 2018/858, (EU) 2018/1724 and (EU) 2019/1020, OJ L, 2024/1252, 3.5.2024.

[11] Regulation (EU) 2024/1735 of the European Parliament and of the Council of 13 June 2024 on establishing a framework of measures for strengthening Europe's net-zero technology manufacturing ecosystem and amending Regulation (EU) 2018/1724, OJ L, 2024/1735, 28.6.2024.

Emergency Regulation and RED III, such as designating strategic projects, planning, and setting time limits for the permit-granting procedure. It is also worth mentioning the *European Wind Power Action Plan*, launched by the Commission in October 2023.[12] Although the proposals here align with the general trends in the above-mentioned legislation, they are mostly of a "softer" nature, such as guidelines, common digital tools, initiatives for the exchange of "best practices", recommendations on how to improve auction designs, and financial measures. Even so, they are helpful in understanding the direction of the EU's commitment to the achievement of climate neutrality and to the fulfilment of its international obligation to maintain and improve biodiversity in nature.

3 The Rules for Permit-Granting Procedures in RED III

3.1 An Overview of the New Regime

To begin with, RED III gives a more comprehensive definition of "renewable energy" compared with its predecessors. According to Article 2(1), the definition covers energy from renewable non-fossil sources, that is, wind, solar and geothermal energy, osmotic energy, ambient energy, tidal, wave and other ocean energy, hydropower, biomass, landfill gas, sewage treatment plant gas, and biogas.[13] New concepts introduced with the 2023 reform are defined, such as "renewables acceleration area", meaning a specific area on land, inland waters or sea designated as particularly suitable for the installation of renewable energy plants (Article 1(9a)). Interestingly, a definition of "permit-granting procedures" is lacking from the catalogue in Article 2. Instead, it is given in Article 16(1):[14]

> The permit-granting procedure shall cover all relevant administrative permits to build, repower and operate renewable energy plants, including those combining different renewable energy sources, heat pumps, and co-located energy storage, including power and thermal facilities, as well as assets necessary for the connection of such plants, heat pumps and storage to the grid, and to integrate renewable energy into heating and cooling networks, including grid-connection permits and, where required, environmental assessments. The permit-granting procedure shall comprise all administrative stages from the acknowledgment of the completeness of the permit application in accordance with paragraph 2 to the notification of the final decision on the outcome of the permit-granting procedure by the relevant competent authority or authorities.

---

[12] COM(2023) 669 final, Communication from the Commission to the European Parliament, the Council, the European Economic and Social Committee and the Committee of the Regions: European Wind Power Action Plan.

[13] One may note that nuclear power is not covered in this definition, although it is still mentioned as a net-zero technology in the NZIA.

[14] The wording of Article 16(1) of RED III mirrors the definition in Article 2(1) of the Emergency Regulation Council Regulation (EU) 2022/2577 of 22 December 2022 laying down a framework to accelerate the deployment of renewable energy, OJ L 335, p. 36, 29.12.2022.

Article 3(4a) of RED III requires Member States to establish a framework enabling the deployment of renewable electricity to a level that is consistent with the set national contribution and the indicative trajectories referred to in RED III. That framework is intended in particular to tackle remaining barriers to a high level of renewable electricity supply, including those related to permit-granting procedures, and the development of the necessary transmission, distribution and storage infrastructure.

Rules on administrative procedures and environmental permitting are given in twelve new provisions in Articles 15, 15b-15e and 16-16f. First, it is stated that the Member States shall ensure that the national rules concerning the authorisation, certification and licensing procedures applied to plants and transmission for renewables are proportionate and necessary and contribute to the implementation of the energy efficiency first principle. Administrative procedures shall be streamlined and expedited at the appropriate level and given predictable time frames. Rules on the procedure are required to be objective, transparent, proportionate, and non-discriminatory (Article 15).

According to Article 15b, by 21 May 2025, Member States shall carry out a coordinated mapping for the deployment of renewable energy in their territory to identify the potential of land and water areas for the installation of renewable energy plants and their infrastructures necessary to meet their national contributions towards the overall EU renewable energy target for 2030.

3.2 Renewable Acceleration Areas and Dedicated Infrastructure Areas

Renewable Acceleration Areas are regulated in Article 15c, which requires Member States to adopt one or more plans for renewable energy sources where the deployment is not expected to cause significant environmental impact. Biomass and hydropower may be excluded. Priority is to be given to artificial and built surfaces and their direct surroundings, whereas Natura 2000 sites, national nature reserves and major migratory routes for birds and mammals must be avoided. Appropriate rules on effective mitigation measures to avoid adverse environmental impacts are required to be adopted for the installations and their connection to the electric grid. When this is not possible, measures to reduce such impact are required to be prescribed to ensure compliance with Articles 6(2) and 12(1) of the Habitats Directive (92/43), Article 5 of the Birds Directive (2009/147) and Article 4(1), point (a)(i) of the Framework Water Directive (2000/60).

These rules for mitigation must be targeted to the specificities of each renewable acceleration area and type of renewables. Compliance with the prescribed measures creates a presumption that the projects in the acceleration areas are not in breach of the nature conservation or species protection obligations in those directives. New mitigation technologies and measures may be tested for a limited period if closely monitored, and appropriate steps have to be taken if those measures prove to be ineffective. Before the adoption of a renewable acceleration area, a Strategic Impact Assessment is required to be undertaken according to Directive 2001/42, and, if the plan is likely to have a significant effect on a Natura 2000 site, an Appropriate Impact Assessment (AIA) must be undertaken according to Article 6(3) of the Habitats Directive (92/43). The acceleration areas must undergo periodic review, particularly in the context of the updating of the National Energy and Climate Plans (NECP) every ten years (Article 15c). Similar provisions are given in Article 15e for areas with grid and storage infrastructure necessary to integrate renewables into the electric system ("dedicated infrastructure areas"), which aim to support and complement the renewable acceleration areas. Finally, according to Article 15d, public participation must be ensured in line with Article 6 in the SEA Directive (2001/42).

3.3 Main Principles and Organisation of the Procedure

Article 16 of RED III contains rules on the organisation and main principles of the permit-granting procedure. These provisions apply both inside and outside the renewable acceleration areas. As noted, the procedure is intended to cover all relevant administrative permits to build and operate renewable energy plants and their connection to the grid, including environmental assessments. The procedure must comprise all administrative stages from the acknowledgement of a complete application to the final decision. A decision on whether an application is complete or not shall be issued by the competent authority within 30 days if the project will be performed in a acceleration area, or within 45 days in other cases. When an application is not complete, the competent authority must request the applicant to submit the missing information without undue delay.

Member States are also required to appoint one or more contact points whose task is to inform and guide the applicant throughout the procedure and ensure that the deadlines are met. Applications may be submitted in digital form. An applicant shall not be required to contact more than one contact point during the entire procedure. Further, Member States shall ensure that those concerned in a permit procedure have easy access to alternative dispute resolution mechanisms. All appeals are to be handled in the most expeditious manner possible.

Still another provision of general applicability is given in Article 16f, which states that, from 21 February 2024 until climate neutrality is achieved, Member States shall ensure that, in the permit-granting procedure, renewables shall be presumed to have overriding public interest and to serve public health and safety when balancing different interests according to Article 9(1) of the Birds Directive (2009/147), Articles 6(4) and 16(1) of the Habitats Directive (92/43), as well as Article 4(7) of the Framework Water Directive (2000/60).

3.4 Permit-Granting Procedure within Renewable Acceleration Areas

The permit procedure for projects within renewable acceleration areas is regulated in Article 16a. To begin with, time limits are stated: the procedure as a whole for the permitting of renewables on land may not exceed 12 months, and may not exceed 24 months for off-shore projects. Under extraordinary circumstances those deadlines may be extended by up to 6 additional months. For the repowering of renewable energy plants and their grid connection, the time limit is six months.

As already noted, projects within acceleration areas are presumed to not cause any significant effect to the environment according to Article 4(2) in the EIA Directive (2011/92) or Article 6(3) of the Habitats Directive (92/43). Therefore, if the project complies with the requirement for mitigation measures in Article 15c, it is exempted from carrying out an Environmental Impact Assessment (EIA) and an Appropriate Impact Assessment (AIA) according to those directives. Even so, the competent authority must undertake a screening process to clarify if the project is likely to give rise to significant unforeseen adverse effects that were not identified in the SEA for the plan. For this evaluation, the project developer is to provide information about the mitigation measures for the project, and the screening process must be concluded within 45 days. If the competent authority has not decided on the matter within that deadline, the project is authorized from the environmental perspective without any express decision (a so-called "positive silence rule"). In contrast, if the authority finds that the project may give rise to significant unforeseen adverse effects to the environment that cannot be mitigated with the measures prescribed in the renewable acceleration area, an EIA/AIA is required to be performed within 6 months. However, Member States may exempt wind and solar projects from such assessments under the condition that the operator adopts proportionate mitigation measures, or alternatively, undertakes or pays for compensating programs.

3.5 Permit-granting Procedure Outside Renewable Acceleration Areas

The rules of procedure are somewhat different outside the renewable acceleration areas (Article 16b). First, different time limits apply: 2 years for the granting of a permit for renewables on land, 3 years for off-shore projects. When an EIA is required, it is to be carried out in a single procedure in which all relevant assessments are combined. The competent authority must issue an opinion on the scope and detail of the EIA, and the scope may not be subsequently extended. If the permit conditions for the project contain necessary mitigation measures, any killing or disturbances of the species protected under Article 5 of the Birds Directive (2009/147) and Article 16(1) of the Habitats Directive (92/43) shall be treated as not being deliberate.

3.6 Repowering

"Repowering" is defined in Article 2(10) as

> "renewing power plants that produce renewable energy, including the full or partial replacement of installations or operation systems and equipment for the purposes of replacing capacity or increasing the efficiency or capacity of the installation".

Shorter time-limits apply to those projects. In addition, there is also a limitation to the requirements under the EIA Directive (2011/92) for the repowering of a renewable energy plant. Both the screening and the assessment are limited to the potential impacts from the change or extension, compared with those of the original project (Article 16c).

4 Analysis and Discussion

4.1 Introduction

In this section, I will analyse and discuss the main issues in RED III concerning the environmental permitting procedure. However, this analysis is a preliminary one, limited to highlighting some points for further discussion, as we are only in the beginning stage of the implementation of RED III in the Member States.

4.2 The General Discourse

For obvious reasons, the preambles of the Emergency Regulation (EU) 2022/2577 and the Directive 2023/2413 are largely coloured by the energy crises in Europe after Russia's invasion of Ukraine and the subsequent shortage in energy supply. In addition, comes the general drive in the EU for green transition towards climate neutrality by 2050. Thus, the discourse is in line with many of the legislative initiatives from the EU institutions since the beginning of 2022. On top of this comes the fact that growing concerns about the high dependency of countries outside of the EU on vital resources have created a kind of "green nationalism", especially pointing at unfair competition from China. From a Scandinavian perspective, it is important to understand this emergency context, as most of our countries do not have any shortage of energy supply. This is especially true when it comes to Sweden and Norway. We are in the lead concerning the share of renewables in the energy mix, with Sweden in the top of EU27 with 66%, while both Iceland and Norway are above 70%.[15] Sweden is also the leading exporter of electricity to Europe at a level of over 33 terawatt-hours per year.[16] Against this backdrop, the analysis in this text may suffer from a certain lack of understanding of the European energy crises, as the public debate on these issues in Sweden has mainly focused on the high electricity prices resulting from the improved connection with the European continent through the Baltic cables (we are thus "importing their prices"). But even with this caveat, some remarks may be noted on the discourse in the preambles of the Emergency Regulation and RED III.

To begin with, there can be no doubt that the text is formulated mainly by the DG Energy and that the general direction here is "full speed ahead" for industrial development. Electrification and the increase of energy production is the overarching theme, and very little text is spent on energy saving. This is somewhat surprising, as the revised Energy Efficiency Directive (2023/1791) significantly raises the EUs ambition in this respect, including a binding goal to which the Member States are expected to contribute.[17] How each country will fulfil this duty is expected to be clarified in the Member

[15] European Environment Agency (2024), Share of energy from renewable sources, by country. https://www.eea.europa.eu/en/analysis/maps-and-charts/countries-breakdown-actual-res-progress-15. Accessed 25 Aug 2025.

[16] Net amount of electricity exported from Europe in 2022, by country. https://www.statista.com/statistics/1405405/net-electricity-exports-europe-by-country/. Accessed 25 Aug 2025.

[17] European Commission, Energy Efficiency Directive. https://energy.ec.europa.eu/topics/energy-efficiency/energy-efficiency-targets-directive-and-rules/energy-efficiency-directive_en. Accessed 25 Aug 2025.

States' reports of their final updated National Energy and Climate Plan (NECP), which were due on 30 June 2024. So far, it is too early to draw clear conclusions from this reporting.[18]

Surely, the new legislation on renewables brings some welcome news, such as requirements for integrated permit procedures, contact points in order to advise applicants and decision-making bodies, and time limits for different stages of the permit-granting process. At the same time, however, the package is based on a quite one-sided approach where only energy concerns are visible and regulations are characterized as "administrative burdens". When environmental protection concerns are mentioned, it is merely done by a general reference to the "no-harm principle". The general point of departure seems to be the assumption that the Union, simply by reducing greenhouse gas emissions by way of renewable energy, also can tackle challenges related to the environment, such as the loss of biodiversity. There is little thought on how this will be performed, while at the same time it is repeatedly emphasised in the preamble that environmental assessments must be made simpler and faster. Consequently, the precautionary principle is not mentioned at all in the preambles of the Emergency Regulation or Directive 2023/2413.

Another point of departure for the legislation is that permit procedures must be made swifter. This is repeated many times in the argumentation and made clear in preambular point 20 of Directive 2023/2413 (italics added):

Lengthy administrative permit-granting procedures are *one of the key barriers to investment* in renewable energy projects and their related infrastructure. Those barriers include the complexity of the applicable rules for site selection and administrative authorisations for such projects, the complexity and duration of the assessment of the environmental impact of such projects, and related energy networks, grid-connection problems, constraints on adapting technology specifications during the permit-granting procedure, and staffing problems of the permit-granting authorities or grid operators. In order to accelerate the pace of deployment of such projects it is necessary to adopt rules which would simplify and shorten permit-granting procedures, taking into account the broad public acceptance of the deployment of renewable energy.

Even though I have a general knowledge about environmental protection systems in the EU, I really cannot say if this is a valid description of the permit-granting procedures in the Member States of the EU. However, statements like this are often based on different consultants' reports and, in my experience, such reports differ quite substantially in quality. For example, in a report from the RES Simplify project in 2023, it was reported that Sweden was one of the Member States where bureaucratic barriers pose major challenges to wind power development, that permits are granted at a very low rate and

[18] On that date, only four Member States had reported their NCP. As of December 2024, the number has risen to 14 Member States, but – according to the Swedish expert Magnus Nilsson – the reports are too vague to say anything without thorough analysis; European Commission, National energy and climate plans. https://commission.europa.eu/energy-climate-change-environment/implementation-eu-countries/energy-and-climate-governance-and-reporting/national-energy-and-climate-plans_en#national-energy-and-climate-plans-2021-2030. Accessed 25 Aug 2025.

that permit procedures may take as long as ten years, both on land and at sea.[19] These statements are quite surprising and one may wonder why the authors did not undertake basic fact checking. In reality, the Swedish wind power industry is a success story with few comparisons; in 2023, wind power production amounted to 34 terawatt-hours and 20% of the total electricity production. This is an increase of more than 20% per year every year since 2021. For two years in a row, Swedish wind farms stand for 2% of the world's electricity production from wind power. According to the official statistics, the permit-granting time in the Swedish Regional Licensing Boards is 349 days (median value). Moreover, the granting rate is about 80%.[20] According to our research, the permitting procedure as such does not pose any barrier, as the main obstacle has been local resistance and the so-called "municipal veto".[21] It is true, however, that the development of wind energy located in the sea has been very slow in Swedish waters as compared with our neighbours. However, this cannot be explained by so-called "bureaucratic barriers", as resistance from the Armed Forces is the major reason for denying permits at sea. On closer scrutiny, the "facts" presented in the RES Simplify report were provided by the Swedish wind industry, well-known for its relentless campaigning and imaginative use of statistics. Thus, if industry is the main provider of facts to these reports, I suggest caution concerning any general statement about slow environmental procedures as a barrier to the Green Transition.

4.3 Renewable Acceleration Areas

RED III introduces a system with binding plans on the regional or national level by way of "renewable acceleration areas". As noted, the Member States are obliged to designate at least one such plan for one or more renewable energy techniques and their connection systems on land and/or sea. The acceleration area is required to be "sufficiently homogenous" and the deployment of renewables here are expected not to entail significant environmental impact. The plans for the adoption of an acceleration area is subject to an environmental assessment according to the SEA Directive (2001/42), and, if they are likely to have a significant impact on Natura 2000 sites, to an appropriate assessment according to Article 6(3) of the Habitats Directive (92/43). Appropriate rules must be established for effective mitigation measures that will be adopted as parts of the permits for the renewable plants and their connection facilities in order to avoid or reduce such impact. Only when the installation is "highly likely" to give rise to significant unforeseen adverse effects that were not identified in the SEA, may additional investigations, assessments or mitigation measures be required. If the permit body in this situation decides that an EIA or an AIA is required, this assessment and procedure must be undertaken within six months.

[19] COM(2023) 627 final, Commission Staff working document, 2023 Country Report - Sweden Accompanying the document Recommendation for a COUNCIL RECOMMENDATION on the 2023 National Reform Programme of Sweden and delivering a Council opinion on the 2023 Convergence Programme of Sweden.

[20] See SOU (2022) Om prövning och omprövning – en del av den gröna omställningen, 2022:33, part 3 about "myths and trues", also the Government's Proposition (2024), Prop. 2023/24:152, part 4.2. Both documents are unfortunately available only in Swedish.

[21] See Darpö (2020), pp. 59-79.

First, a general remark on this. Modern wind farms and their connection to the grid are major industrial installations, commonly covering hundreds of hectares of land or sea. Like all widespread and "area-consuming" activities, they are best regulated by means of planning ahead for the solving of conflicts between different interests. From a nature conservation perspective, planning may also provide for a population-based approach to species protection on a larger scale. Thus, if properly performed and detailed, an early environmental assessment and consultation with the public concerned according to the SEA Directive may well be a suitable tool for a proactive handling of the conflict between wind energy and biodiversity. There are lessons to be learned about such good examples from planning for wind farming from different places in Europe, for example, in Flanders.[22]

4.4 Planning, SEA and EIA

Against this backdrop, I do not think that one can object to a planning instrument such as renewable acceleration areas as a matter of principle. Instead, concerns can be raised about the lofty legislation and the weak quality control in RED III. The most important question here concerns the safeguarding of a thorough investigation in line with the precautionary principle as regards the impacts on Natura 2000 and strictly protected species and their habitats. These worries are fortified by the arguments in the preamble that the legislation allows for "simplified assessments". The regulation seems to make it possible for a Member State to introduce one single acceleration area for the whole country or a large region, covering all kinds of renewables and their connections to the grid. Surely, such an application would be considered quite extreme, as the RED III states that the acceleration areas should be homogeneous, and the projects should not be expected to have significant effects on the environment. But even so, we know little today about how this instrument will play out in practical terms. There is, however, reason to believe that a SEA for a vast area with a variety of activities cannot serve as an effective means for fulfilling the EUs biodiversity obligations. In practical terms, it may not be feasible to prescribe effective mitigation measures as early as in the planning phase of such an all-compassing renewable acceleration area.

Further, the "highly likely" formula places the burden of proof on the authorities and the public to show the necessity of further investigations and environmental assessments when an application for a project permit is submitted within an acceleration area. There is no exception to this rule, so that it will apply even if the project is applied for years after the initial SEA was performed. Learning from the experience of environmental cases in courts, this standard may be a trigger point for conflict. In virtually all environmental cases there are objections about the need for, the quality and the scope of the EIA. It is no wonder that EIA Directive (2011/92) is the single piece of legislation – together with the Habitats Directive (92/43) and the Birds Directive (2009/147) – that has created the

[22] See Backes and Ackerboom (2018).

biggest part of today's great body of case-law in environmental matters from the EU Court of Justice (CJEU).[23] In situations in which the permit-granting authority ignores objections from the public about the inadequacy of an SEA, this may even prove to be something that complicates and delays the procedure, if the appeal body or court finds the objections to be well-founded and remands the application to be considered anew. Not least, the tight time frames for the procedure and the existence of a positive silence rule in this context may prove to be counter-productive, as the authority's attitude on the matter will not be known at the outset. In this context, it also may be noted that it is only when the permit authority posits that an additional EIA is needed that the decision is required to be published.

4.5 Exemption Possibilities

Another concern may be raised about the exemption possibilities. According to Article 16(a)(5), the Member States may exclude wind projects from "such assessments", in my understanding referring to an updated EIA in the above-described situation. The only precondition for this is that the exclusion is based on "justified circumstances", including those needed for achieving the climate and energy targets. This may of course be interpreted by governments where the industry has a strong voice as the main way to escape the otherwise-applicable biodiversity obligations. If an exemption applies, the operator is admittedly obliged to undertake proportionate mitigation measures or to contribute financially to a protection programme in order to ensure the conservation status of the species affected. However, this kind of legal construct is full of pitfalls, of which a few can be mentioned here. To begin with, the assessment of what are "justified circumstances" leaves it open for the national governments to include just about anything. And how can "proportionate mitigation measures" be evaluated when no investigation or assessment has been undertaken of the protected interest that is at risk. The same can be said about the effectiveness of any compensation schemes, which according to experience can be complicated enough to establish even if one knows what kinds of risks have to be dealt with. How will it be possible to design such programmes when knowledge about the damage to be avoided is meagre?[24]

---

[23] European Commission, Focus on Environmental Impact Assessment, Further case-law on EIA (selection). https://www.era-comm.eu/EU_Legislation_on_Environmental_Assessments/part_2/part_2_13.html. Accessed 25 Aug 2025. If I am not mistaken about the Eurlex statistics, both the EIA Directive (85/337 and 2011/92) and the Habitats Directive (92/43) count for more than 160 cases each in the CJEU, while the Birds Directive (79/409 and 2009/147) counts for almost 150.

[24] In this context it should be noted that the CJEU repeatedly has stated that a precondition for making derogations according to Article 6(4) of the Habitats Directive is that an AIA has been performed showing what risks are at hand and how they can be dealt with, see C-239/04, Commission v Portugal (2006), para 35; C-182/10, Solvay and others v Région wallonne (2012), para 73-74; C-521/12, T.C. Briels and others v Minister van Infrastructuur en Milieu (2014), para 35; joined cases C-387/15 and C-388/15, Hilde Orleans and others v Vlaams Gewest (2016), para 61; C-258/11, Sweetman and others v An Bord Pleanála (2013), para 35; see also Managing Natura 2000 sites. The provisions of Article 6 of the 'Habitats' Directive 92/43/EEC, OJ C 33, 25.1.2019, section 5.2.

4.6 Decision-Making Outside Renewable Acceleration Areas

Another peculiarity in RED III concerns the processing of EIAs for projects outside acceleration areas. According to Article 16(b)(2), if an EIA is required, it is to be carried out in a single procedure that combines all relevant assessments for the project. Further, before the investigations are begun, the competent authority is obliged to issue an opinion on the scope and the level of detail of the information to be included in the EIA report. This opinion is binding in that the scope of the report cannot be extended subsequently. In my view, such a "preclusion" raises questions. Even though the provision reflects a common critique from industry about "excessive demands on investigations", the authors clearly have not considered the effects on environmental procedure. First, the provision is unclear as the preclusion only limits "the scope" of the report, and not its "level of detail". Second and more important, it is common knowledge that EIAs are normally substantially amended during the consultation phase of the permit procedure. Other branches of administration, as well as the concerned public, often have valuable comments on the investigations and assessments to be performed. If the scoping decision must be taken before that phase and perhaps even when there is not a draft report, we will see a lot of deficient EIAs. The effect of that on the protection of biodiversity is obvious. Also, the preclusion cannot be upheld during the appeal procedure as the EIA Directive (2011/92) has not been changed as regards the demands on the report.[25] In this context, one must remember that most – if not nearly all – permit decisions on renewables are challenged by way of appeal. This in turn means that at the end of the day, many permits will either be quashed or the cases remanded by the appeal body or court back to the administration with instructions on how the EIA must be amended. In this way, the RED III preclusion provision may be a recipe for delaying and prolonging the permit procedures, which is quite the opposite of the intent of the reform.

4.7 Repowering

The new rules on "repowering" are scattered in several provisions. Different time frames are given for repowering projects in renewable acceleration areas, outside those areas, and for those which do not result in an increase of the capacity of the power plants by more than 15%. The most important rule about application for the repowering of a renewable energy plant is given in Article 16c(2), stating that if the project is subject to a screening process according to Article 16a(4), the determination of the need for a new EIA shall be limited to the potential impacts of only the change or extension as such.

In my view, this statement is not easy to understand or implement. The definition of "repowering" is very broad in RED III. For example, it seems to cover the total replacement of all wind turbines in a given area. As the first wind parks in Europe have operated for 20 years and their production capacity is rather limited, we are dealing with a rapid development in technology. In those days, wind turbines on land commonly did not exceed 150 meters in total height, as compared with today's installations at almost 300 meters. In this situation, it is not easy to say what is the "change or expansion". The new location of wind turbines in a development area may also be quite different, as the modern

[25] Articles 3 and 5 together with Annex IV of the EIA Directive (2011/92).

parks contain fewer but larger turbines. In consequence, the environmental impact is different, and can be higher depending upon the area's sensitivity. Even so, Article 16a(4) may be interpreted so as to allow in a renewable acceleration area the expansion of the projects therein, including the "highly likely" criteria for an EIA. This provision in turn can be understood in two contrasting ways. The first one restricts the use of acceleration areas, as such a plan may only cover homogenous areas where no significant impact is expected to arise, not only for the foreseeable projects, but also for their expansion through repowering. The other interpretation makes room for an even more expansive application with acceleration areas covering vast areas with different renewable energy plants and their connections, where even a total new design of the installations is allowed without an EIA. This latter understanding is of course rather extreme, but in my view, it is not unrealistic in the current discourse of "green nationalism". It may also find some support in the statements about "simplified assessments" in the preamble of Directive 2023/2413.[26]

One final serious concern should be noted about repowering. The underlying idea behind limiting the assessment of environmental impacts from the repowering of an installation is that the operator and the supervisory authorities have been informed and updated on the impacts from the existing source. The monitoring and reporting requirements may differ from one country to another, but as for Sweden, it is simply not happening. Public schemes for the control and monitoring of the state of the environment covering larger areas rarely include impacts to specific species. As for the operator's responsibility to monitor the environmental effects of the permitted activity, it covers subsequent effects to the species investigated in the EIA report only when that reporting requirement has been clearly stated in the conditions. Such conditions in permits for wind farms are rare, at least when it comes to long-term effects. Consequently, when a permit-holder applies for an expansion or change in an activity, there is little or no knowledge about what has happened since the first permit application and EIA were discussed. However, this is not a phenomenon restricted to renewable energy installations, but is an issue for all activities with such an impact. Further, it goes without saying that knowledge about the cumulative effects on the environment from renewables and their connections to the grid, forestry, roads, mines, and other such operations is non-existing. If the situation is similar in other countries, this is something that needs to be considered when discussing "administrative barriers" to the repowering of renewables. In this context, it may be noted that this relaxed attitude to the following up of long-term effects on protected habitats and species is not in line with EU nature protection directives.

4.8 Time Limits

RED III introduces strict time frames for permit procedures. As a general rule, an application must be confirmed or dismissed by the permit authority within 30 days if the project is located in a renewable acceleration area, and within 45 days in other cases. The time frame for the permit procedure within an acceleration area is 12 months if the project is on land, 24 months at sea, and 6 months for repowering. Outside those areas, it is 24 months on land, 36 months at sea and 12 months for repowering. In all cases,

[26] See for example preambular points 39, 40 and 44.

the time frame for the permit procedure may be extended by 6 more months if this can be duly justified on the grounds of "extraordinary circumstances".

To begin with, these time frames may seem short as the permit procedure includes all relevant assessments and evaluations for the project (Article 16(1)). However, as the counting of time starts when the application is complete and ends when the permit authority issues the final decision, the time frames will probably not pose a great challenge to most Member States, at least not for those with an integrated environmental procedure. As for the systems where many separate permits are required for a renewable energy project, the time frames may seem tight and will probably require a certain integration. In my view, this is a positive development from an environmental perspective. On the other hand, it should also be noted that a developer is not always willing – and sometimes is not even able – to apply at the outset for all permits for a project. This may for example be the case concerning the building of a wind park and its subsequent connection to the electric grid. It is reasonable to believe that in those cases, the attitude of the developer remains decisive. However, the time limit for accepting the application may prove counterproductive. It is a common feature in environmental procedure that the project developer – intentionally or not – submits an application which has some or even many flaws. The idea behind this is to cause the permit authority to issue an order for amendments to the application, which of course is very informative and has a guiding effect on the proceedings to follow. A tight time frame for confirming an application may therefore encourage the authority to dismiss the application right away without any such order. Alternatively, it may lead the permit authority to accept an inadequate application which is ultimately quashed on appeal. It is hard to see how any of these results would be beneficial, either for the project developer or for the deployment of renewables. In addition, some of the other time frames seem very short. It goes beyond my understanding how an EIA or an AIA covering the impacts on species during different seasons of the year could possibly be performed with investigations and hearings concluding within six months, which is the rule if the authority finds the "highly likely" criterion to apply in a renewable acceleration area.

Tight time frames may therefore trigger another adaptation of the national permit systems that may not have been foreseen by the EU legislator, at least in those legal systems where the EIA procedure is integrated into the permit procedure. As the time frames cover all stages of the decision-making, they may create a certain incentive for the Member States to separate the EIA procedure – which often is very time-consuming when it comes to larger and more controversial activities – from the actual permit procedure. There is nothing in the legislation that prohibits such a "Finnish solution", namely, that there is a general requirement for an EIA for all major activities in a certain area – say a harbour – which is evaluated and confirmed by a competent body of administration separate from the permit authority.[27] Using this "confirmed" EIA, the project developer may thereafter apply for all permits needed for the operation, at which time the permit authority is able to restrict its evaluation of the EIA to the question of whether it suffices for the project at stake. Most importantly, this evaluation may be limited to whether there is a need for an updating of the original EIA or not. Also in this respect, there are

[27] See Darpö (2023), section 2.3 and 3.

pros and cons with the tight time frames for the environmental procedure, so that the effectiveness of this solution remains debatable.

Still another question on time frames concerns the role of the courts. According to Article 16(8), the time frames in RED III do not apply to "judicial appeals and remedies" or to any "other proceedings before a court or tribunal". In Sweden however, it is the environmental courts which issue integrated environmental permits for large scale industrial installations and water operations. This solution is unusual within the EU and quite odd, as seen in the case *Djurgården-Lilla Värtan* from 2009 (C-263/08). Here, the CJEU struggled to understand that Swedish environmental courts are permit-issuing bodies in the first instance, finally stating that they did so "exercising administrative powers".[28] It remains to be seen whether this system will survive the demands for time frames in the environmental procedure and other requirements of EU law. Even though Sweden is alone in the EU having courts with jurisdiction to issue environmental permits in the first instance, other national courts may have similar functions for parts of what are regarded as "all relevant permits" according to Article 16(1). Especially concerning access to land and water, compensation and similar matters, this may be a more common solution in several Member States. As courts cannot be ordered by the administration to undertake a certain action in individual cases, such decision-making must be removed from the permitting procedure time frames. Alternatively, all such decision-making and its associated time frames would have to be transferred to the administrative level.

4.9 Overriding Public Interest Presumption and the "Deliberate" Killings/Disturbances Criterion

Two of the main features of RED III directly target the interpretation of the nature directives of EU law. Both have general applicability, covering projects inside and outside renewable acceleration areas. First, according to Article 16f, renewables are presumed to have overriding public interest in serving public health and safety when balancing different interests under the Birds Directive (2009/147), the Habitats Directive (92/43), and the Water Framework Directive (2000/60). Further, when appropriate mitigation measures have been prescribed for a renewable energy project, killings and disturbances of species resulting from the permitted activity are regarded as not being "deliberate". In this respect, the provisions differ somewhat for permits inside (Article 15c) and outside (Article 16b) the acceleration areas, but the essence is the same. Such killings and disturbances will consequently not be in breach of either Article 5 of the Birds Directive (2009/147) or Article 12 of the Habitats Directive (92/43). Also, when mitigation measures have not been widely tested, they may be used in pilot projects for a limited period of time. In any event, according to both Articles under RED III, the Member States are obliged to undertake appropriate monitoring of the effects on the species and must prescribe further measures if required.

These features of the reformed RED III have been welcomed with enthusiasm and great expectations from the wind industry and other elements of the renewable business

[28] C-263/08, Djurgården-Lilla Värtan v Stockholms kommun genom dess marknämnd (2009), para 37.

sector.[29] However, I am not convinced that new rules will have any substantial effect on the application of the species protection provisions in the three directives. To begin with, it is worth noticing that none of the three directives has been changed. Concerning the overriding public interest rule, it is admittedly difficult to assess how it will play out in the water regime, as Article 4(7) of the Water Framework Directive (2000/60) is a rule about the balancing of different interests. However, as for the derogation rules in the EU nature directives, it certainly does not suffice that an activity is of overriding public interest, as both Article 9(1) of the Birds Directive (2009/147) and Articles 6(4) and 16(1) of the Habitats Directive (92/43) combine this criterion with a requirement that there be no alternatives. As for the Habitats Directive, the derogation ground is applicable only when there are "imperative reasons" of overriding public interest, an additional requirement lacking in Article 16f. Further, Article 16(1) of RED III adds that the derogation may not be detrimental to the maintenance of the population's favourable conservation status, something that also is implicit in the two other derogation grounds. As noted, many renewable energy projects, and especially wind farms, are widespread activities, where alternative locations often are available. In national case-law, windfarms therefore are rarely approved in areas where they cause any substantial harm to species, even if there is an important public interest such as energy supply in the region. One can expect that the courts will be even more sceptical in situations in which the environmental impacts of the project have been poorly investigated. An exception may however be made for certain locations at sea which are hard to replace with others; the overriding public interest rule for renewables may therefore be more decisive in those areas. Further, Article 16f states that all renewables are presumed to be of overriding public interest. Even though the provision thus is applicable to all such installations – even very small ones without any real consequence – we may assume that the courts will in many cases simply rebut the presumption in line with existing case-law on the matter. This remains however to be seen.[30]

Something similar can be said about the "deliberate" criterion, at least concerning wind energy projects. In my view, the rules in Article 15c and 16b align with how most Member States handle this criterion in the permitting of wind farms.[31] As for the protection of birds, certain locations of wind turbines are not accepted due to their proximity to the nests, flight routes or foraging areas of those species that are regarded as sensitive in this respect, such as birds of prey, other slow-flying species, forest hens and certain waterfowl. In some parts of Europe, instruments such as DT Bird are used to detect nearby birds and activate warning sounds or the stoppage of the turbine in case of a collision risk.[32] For the protection of bats, a common condition is to prescribe the use of Batmode techniques, that is to close down the turbine during sunset and sunrise

[29] WindEurope (2022), Overriding public interest is essential to the expansion of renewables. https://windeurope.org/newsroom/news/overriding-public-interest-is-essential-to-the-expansion-of-renewables/. Accessed 25 Aug 2025.

[30] Malafry (2022) gives a thorough analysis of the issues related to the application of this provision in relation to the nature directives, see section 5.3.3, p. 176 et seq.

[31] According to the study performed by Backes and Ackerboom (2018) this technique was applied everywhere except for The Netherlands.

[32] Rydell et al. (2017).

during the summer and at certain wind conditions and temperatures. The idea of using these mitigation measures is to avoid coming into a derogation scenario, as the rules on this in the EU nature directives are strict and not really relevant for widespread activities such as wind energy projects. Against this backdrop, I would argue that the rules on deliberate killings and disturbances of species merely codify what is already in place in most Member States.

It must also be mentioned that there are also aspects of RED III which are positive for species protection. Most importantly, in several places it is emphasised that the control and monitoring of the effects of the renewable installations are crucial for the application of the new rules. In sum therefore, one may argue that the provisions about overriding public interest and deliberate killings/disturbances will not be detrimental to the protection of European biodiversity.

4.10 Public Participation and Access to Justice

The new system of renewable acceleration areas in RED III also raises important questions concerning public participation and the principle of legal protection under EU law. Point 30 in the Preamble of Directive 2023/2413 states that Member States should take appropriate steps to promote participation in order to increase the public acceptance of renewable energy projects. The Preamble also notes that the Aarhus Convention remains applicable in the EU. Preamble point 20 of RED III states that broad public acceptance of the deployment of renewable energy should be taken into account when adopting rules for simplifying and shortening permit-granting procedures. This is developed in Article 15d of RED III, where it is made clear that public participation regarding the plans designating acceleration areas shall be both direct and indirect in line with the consultation order in Article 6 of the SEA Directive (2011/42). This requires that a draft of the plan to be adopted and the environmental report shall be made available for the public at an early stage in the decision-making process in order to afford an effective opportunity within appropriate time frames for the public to express opinions. The public is defined in line with the Aarhus Convention and the Public Participation Directive (2003/35), namely those who are affected by or have an interest in the decision-making, including their organizations, such as environmental NGOs.

All this seems to be fine from a public participation aspect, but how will it play out in practice? To begin with, individuals who might be affected by projects within a renewable acceleration area will have the opportunity to participate in the decision-making process by way of making addresses to the authorities and taking part in hearings and other proceedings. In this context, it should be emphasised that the case-law of the CJEU remains relevant regarding the requirements for such participation to be effective.[33] However, access to justice to challenge an adopted plan will rarely be afforded, as those

[33] See for example C-826/18, LB and others v. College van burgemeester en wethouders van de gemeente Echt-Susteren (2021), para 43 and C-280/18, Flausch and others v. Ypourgos Perivallontos kai Energeias and others (2019), para 45–54 about the information duty towards the public concerned, and C-474/10, Department of the Environment for Northern Ireland v. Seaport (NI) Ltd and others (2011), para 46 about the requirement that sufficient time to evaluate the envisaged plan or programme and the environmental report shall be affored.

having an interest or enjoying a right seldom can be defined as early as this stage. They will instead be left to appeal the permit for the project after a process where the time frames have been short and most important parameters such as the location of the project have already been set. This may prove challenging.[34]

The situation for the ENGOs is different. To begin with, the organizations will have the same opportunities as individuals to participate in the decision-making procedure. As for access to justice, they are in a better position. A decision to adopt an acceleration area clearly concerns environmental matters and will be regarded as appealable under the principle of legal protection in EU law, as the plan has a binding effect on subsequent permits.[35] But even if standing most likely is not a problem in the Member States, the question arises about what can actually be challenged in this stage of the decision-making. Clear conflicts with other interests will of course be justiciable, as well as grossly insufficient conditions on mitigation measures and very poor investigations and assessments. But many parameters need to be seen in their actual context in order to evaluate the project's impact on protected interests such as those of species. It remains to be seen what the substantive outcome of such a legal action would be.

And yet, there is an "elephant in the room" and that is the Sami people, being the only indigenous people on the European continent.[36] Their land-and cultural rights are protected by an array of international and European instruments, such as the UN Convention on Civil and Political Rights (ICCPR), the UN Convention on anti-discrimination (ICERD), and the European Convention on Human Rights and Freedoms (ECHR). The Sami reside in the northern parts of Scandinavia and Karelia, that is in Norway,[37] Sweden, Finland and Russia, all countries bound by these international obligations. The Sami's traditional enterprise of reindeer herding is heavily impacted by modern developments such as mining, roads and railroads, forestry, tourism, and – not least – wind farms. In recent years the treatment of the Sami people has raised international attention, and criticism from different committees under such agreements has been common.[38] Several Sami villages have also been successful in their actions in courts, at least in Sweden and Norway. The Norwegian Supreme Court in 2021 quashed the permits for Europe's two

---

[34] For an illustrating example, see the case Karin Andersson v. Sweden in the European Court of Human Rights, App No. 29878/09 (ECtHR 25th of September 2014).

[35] In order to illustrate the development in EU law on the principle of legal protection in environmental matters, compare the old case C-236/92, Comitato di Coordinamento per la Difesa della Cava and others v Regione Lombardia and others, on waste plans and the newly decided C-873/19 Umwelthilfe v Bundesrepublik Deutschland (2022), and the case-law mentioned therein, see also Darpö (2021), section 4;

[36] Of course, indigenous peoples reside in other places subject to some level of European governance, such as Greenland and the French "départements d'outremer", for example, French Guiana in South America.

[37] As noted, Norway is a party to the joint European energy market and bound to the EU legislation through the EEA agreement.

[38] In the beginning of 2024, the Advisory Committee under the Framework Convention for the Protection of National Minorities issued its 5th report on Sweden, criticizing the Government for its failure to afford the Sami people influence over industrial developments in the reindeer herding areas; Council of Europe (2023) Advisory Committee on the Framework Convention for the protection of national minorities.

largest wind farms (already in operation) with reference to breaches of Sami cultural rights under Article 27 ICCPR.[39] In Sweden, the Supreme Court declared that certain legislation on hunting infringes upon the Sami land-use rights and therefore is illegal. The court further declared that the Indigenous and Tribal Peoples' Convention from 1989 (the so-called ILO 169) is an international standard to be respected by Sweden, even though the country has not ratified this instrument.[40]

Very little of this is visible in the EU legislation under the Green Transition. In RED III, the Sami people are not even mentioned. The Critical Raw Materials Act (Regulation 2024/1252, CRMA) contains an obligation about meaningful consultation with local communities – including indigenous peoples – in line with Union legislation and international standards (Preambular points 17 and 20, Articles 6 and 7)). To that end, a plan for such consultation must be provided, including proposed measures dedicated to the prevention and minimisation of adverse effects on these interests. These are rather vague requirements and it remains to be seen if they have impact on the national permit decision-making processes. The EU Parliament voted for a strengthening of that requirement to include the principle of Free Prior and Informed Consent, but this reference disappeared during the trilogue. Apparently, the Swedish and Finnish governments have not been too keen on defending Sami rights in the EU negotiations. Unfortunately, this is typical of the political attitude towards the solving of conflicts of interest concerning the Green Transition. Another apparent example concerns local opposition to wind farms – quite strong in many Member States – which is equally invisible in the new legislation. Experiences from both Norway and Sweden show that one cannot neglect the role of the municipalities when it comes to local acceptance of this type of development.[41] This political abdication is worrying as it leaves it to the courts to step in to resolve such conflicts on a case-by-case basis. This in turn, is a sure recipe for the fuelling of the conflicts, which is what we need the least in times of energy crises. Or to phrase it more eloquently in Franz Timmermann's words: "If the transition will not be just, there will be no transition".

4.11 Systemic Issues

Finally, the European energy crises have triggered quite a few questions of a more systemic nature on the encounter between the interests of green transition and those of environmental protection. One obvious example is the sharply increased use of the derogation ground for "exceptional cases" in Article 2(4) of the EIA Directive (2011/92).[42] The strong drive for centralisation and streamlining of national permit procedures is another. The increased use in recent years of EU regulations instead of directives in

[39] Supreme Court of Norway, judgment 11 Oct 2021, HR-2021-1975-S (case no. 20-143891SIV-HRET, case no. 20-143892-SIV-HRET and case no. 20-143893SIV-HRET).

[40] Supreme Court of Sweden, The "Girjas" case – press release, 4.9.2020. https://www.domstol.se/en/supreme-court/news-archive/a-decision-on-cancellation-of-real-estate-sales-agreements/. Accessed 25 Aug 2025.

[41] See Darpö (2020), also Gulbrandsen et al. (2021).

[42] Between May 2017 and November 2021, one such notification was made to the Commission. Thereafter, between August 2022 and August 2024, 41 notifications have been made from different Member States, mostly covering LNG terminals and pipelines, natural gas

this field of law also raises interesting questions. On the one hand, EU regulations are directly applicable and therefore are a more efficient means for the introduction of new legislation in the Member States. On the other, there is also a tendency to formulate provisions in new regulations more vaguely than in directives, leaving it open for Member States to apply a national understanding of the common rules. The Emergency Regulation (EU) 2022/2577 is a showcase in this respect. Also, there is an ongoing debate on competence concerning the adoption of the Regulation. It is questioned whether Article 122 TFEU can be used as legal basis for this kind of regulation, but also whether the legislation is not in breach of Articles 191 and 194 TFEU.[43] As the legal basis for Directive 2023/2413 is Articles 114, 192 and 194, these issues are not directly applicable to RED III. But as for the content of the reformed directive and its relation to the requirements in existing environmental law, such as the nature directives, several questions remain. Can one really introduce a refreshed understanding of existing legislation and new provisions in EU law without also changing those provisions that are impacted, and how does this harmonise with the existing understanding in the case-law of the CJEU? This is a valid question concerning some provisions in RED III, such as the preclusion provision compared with Article 5(2) of the EIA Directive (2011/92). How this conflict plays out will be interesting to follow, but as I said in the introduction, for now we have to wait until we have seen more of the implementation of RED III in the Member States and the subsequent case-law from the national courts and the CJEU.

5 Concluding Remarks

As almost always, there are pros and cons to the introduction of any new regulation on environmental issues. On the one hand, planning is an instrument well suited for widespread land-use activities such as renewable energy installations. In this respect, RED III is a step in the right direction towards an effective resolution of the conflicts of interest that come with the development of renewable energy sources. Planning may also provide for a more comprehensive approach to biodiversity issues in this context. Some of the new provisions for streamlining the permit procedures are also welcome and will contribute to the Green Transition in Europe. On the other hand, RED III is to a certain extent coloured by haste and a too close relationship between the legislator and those who are expected to be regulated. Simply by taking for granted the background description provided by industry, the approach of the reform in some aspects has become one sided. This is the background to why some of the provisions will function less well within the national permit regimes on renewables, not only concerning biodiversity issues but also in relation to the effectiveness of the procedure as such. These problems are not confined to the renewable acceleration areas, but will certainly also occur in the ordinary permit procedure. The combination of short limits counted from when

pipelines and irrigation projects, EIA - Notification of exemptions to the European Commission. https://circabc.europa.eu/ui/group/26370f9e-245c-4c09-8a75-68655a74875b/library/7da90f54-cc36-44b4-8c78-d2435f1d44c8/details. Accessed 25 Aug 2025.

43 T-534/23 Föreningen Svenskt Landskapsskydd and Others v Council, OJ C, C/2023/220, 23.10.2023 and T-535/23 CEE Bankwatch Network and Ökobüro v Council, OJ C, C/2023/221, 23.10.2023 for a general introduction to this discussion, see Anker (2023).

the application is regarded by the permit bodies to be "complete" and the requirement to give the public concerned "early and effective opportunities to participate" in the environmental decision-making procedures according to the EIA Directive may show especially challenging. Also, the level of detail of the new rules show problematic when the new rules are to be implemented into existing procedural orders in the Member States. In my view, a little more systematic and procedural analysis and a little less superficial policymaking would have made a difference in this respect. Even so, I am not overly concerned about the outcome of RED III in those Member States with legislators loyal to the EU system as a whole, including our international obligations to biodiversity and access to justice. More troublesome is how this new package will play out in the Member States where what one may call "green nationalism" has a strong voice. One may reasonably fear that the focus in the implementation in those countries will be on "full speed ahead" with any kind of development and the lessening of any kind of administrative burdens. If that will be the case, the reform may be characterised as the sacrificing of biodiversity on the Green Transition altar.

Acknowledgments. Special thanks for valuable clarifying comments and language editing to Merideth Wright, former judge of the Vermont Environmental Court and distinguished judicial scholar at the Environmental Law Institute (Washington DC, USA).

References

Anker, H.T., Olsen, B.E.: EU species protection law and wind energy: current challenges and Danish experiences. Eur. Energ. Environ. Law Rev. **32**(1), 36–46 (2023)

Backes, C., Ackerboom, S.: Renewable energy projects and species protection. A comparison into the application of the EU species protection regulation with respect to renewable energy projects in the Netherlands, United Kingdom, BELGIUM, Denmark and Germany, Utrecht Centre for Water, Oceans and Sustainability Law (2018)

Darpö, J.: Should locals have a say when it's blowing? The influence of municipalities in permit procedures for windpower installations in Sweden and Norway. NELJ **1**, 59–79 (2020)

Darpö, J.: Nordic environmental permitting processes – results from a comparative study of environmental law and processes in Denmark, Norway, Iceland, Sweden, and Finland. Nordic Council of Ministers (Nordiska rådet) (2023)

Gulbrandsen, L., Jackson Inderberg, T.H., Jevnaker, T.: Is political steering gone with the wind? Administrative power and wind energy licensing practises in Norway. ERSS **74**, 101963 (2021)

Hardimann, A.: Seeking to deliver renewable energy infrastructure within a 'incomplete and vague' legal framework. CCLR **16**(3), 192–204 (2022a)

Hardimann, A.: Climate, energy – and environment? Reconciliation of EU environmental law with the implementation realities of EU climate law. CLAW **12**(3-4), 242–272 (2022b)

Jendroska, J., Anapyaova, A.: Towards a green energy transition: REPower directive vs environmental acqis? ELNI **23**, 1–5 (2023)

Malafry, M.: Renewable energy activities – overriding the interests of biodiversity? In: Hållbarhet ur ett rättsligt perspektiv, de Lege, Yearbook 2022 of the Faculty of Law, Uppsala Universitet (2023)

Montini, M.: Addressing the conflicts between climate-related renewable energy goals and environmental protection interests under the RED directive. ELO **3**(1), 209–219 (2024)

Rydell, J., Ottvall, R., Pettersson, S., Green, M.: The effects of wind power on birds and bats– an updated synthesis report 2017. Vindval report 6791 (2017)

Cases

C-236/92, Comitato di Coordinamento per la Difesa della Cava and others v Regione Lombardia and others (1994), ECR 1994 I-00483

C-239/04, Commission v Portugal (2006), ECLI:EU:C:2006:665

C-263/08, Djurgården-Lilla Värtan v Stockholms kommun genom dess marknämnd (2009), ECLI:EU:C:2009:631

C-474/10, Department of the Environment for Northern Ireland v. Seaport (NI) Ltd and others (2011), ECLI:EU:C:2011:681

C-182/10, Solvay and others v Région wallonne (2012), ECLI:EU:C:2012:82

C-258/11, Sweetman and others v An Bord Pleanála (2013), ECLI:EU:C:2013:220 C-521/12, T.C. Briels and others v Minister van Infrastructuur en Milieu (2014), ECLI:EU:C:2014:330

C-58/13 and C-59/13, Torresi v Consiglio dell'Ordine degli Avvocati di Macerata (2014), ECLI:EU:C:2014:2088

C-387/15 and C-388/15 Hilde Orleans and others v Vlaams Gewest (2016), ECLI:EU:C:2016:583

C-280/18, Flausch and others v. Ypourgos Perivallontos kai Energeias and others (2019), ECLI:EU:C:2019:928

C-826/18, LB and others v. College van burgemeester en wethouders van de gemeente Echt-Susteren (2021), ECLI:EU:C:2021:7

C-873/19 Umwelthilfe v Bundesrepublik Deutschland (2022), ECLI:EU:C:2022:857

Karin Andersson v. Sweden in the European Court of Human Rights, App No. 29878/09 (ECtHR 25th of September 2014)

Supreme Court of Norway, judgment 11 October 2021, HR-2021-1975-S (case no. 20-143891SIV-HRET, case no. 20-143892-SIV-HRET and case no. 20-143893SIV-HRET)

T-534/23 Föreningen Svenskt Landskapsskydd and Others v Council, OJ C, C/2023/220, 23.10.2023

T-535/23 CEE Bankwatch Network and Ökobüro v Council, OJ C, C/2023/221, 23.10.2023

Others

Anker HT (2023) EU competence and the energy crises. Environmental Law Lectures Series, Maastricht University, 19.7.2023. https://www.youtube.com/watch?v=_0XPUhGzUqo. Accessed 25 Aug 2025

Darpö J (2021) Can nature get it right? A Study on the Rights of Nature in the European context. Report to the European Parliament's Policy Department for Citizens' Rights and Constitutional Affairs at the request of the JURI Committee. https://www.europarl.europa.eu/RegData/etudes/STUD/2021/689328/IPOL_STU(2021)689328_EN.pdf. Accessed 25 Aug 2025

COM (2023) 627 final, Commission Staff working document, 2023 Country Report – Sweden Accompanying the document Recommendation for a COUNCIL RECOMMENDATION on the 2023 National Reform Programme of Sweden and delivering a Council opinion on the 2023 Convergence Programme of Sweden, 25.5.2023

COM (2023) 669 final, Communication from the Commission to the European Parliament, the Council, the European Economic and Social Committee and the Committee of the Regions: European Wind Power Action Plan, 24.10.2023

COM (2023) 764 final, Report from the Commission to the Council on the review of Council Regulation (EU) 2022/2577 of 22 December 2022 laying down a framework to accelerate the deployment of renewable energy, 28.11.2023

Council of Europe (2023) Advisory Committee on the Framework Convention for the protection of national minorities, fifth report in Sweden, 11.10.2023. https://rm.coe.int/5th-op-sweden-en/1680ae851a. Accessed 25 Aug 2025

Klimat- och näringslivsdepartementet Om prövning och omprövning – en del av den gröna omställningen, 2022: 33, https://www.regeringen.se/rattsliga-dokument/statens-offentliga-utredningar/2022/06/sou-202233/. Accessed 25 Aug 2025

Government's Proposition (2024) Steg på vägen mot en mer effektiv miljöprövning, Prop. 2023/24:152. https://www.regeringen.se/rattsliga-dokument/proposition/2024/05/prop.-202324152. Accessed 25 Aug 2025

SOU (2022) Om prövning och omprövning – en del av den gröna omställningen, 2022:33. https://www.regeringen.se/rattsliga-dokument/statens-offentliga-utredningar/2022/06/sou-202233/. Accessed 25 Aug 2025

Legal Instruments to Ensure Circularity in Construction: A Focus on Products, Procurement and the Process

Stéphanie van Gulijk[1(✉)] and Jonas Voorter[2]

[1] Tilburg University, Tilburg, The Netherlands
S.vanGulijk@tilburguniversity.edu
[2] Hasselt University, Hasselt, Belgium
Jonas.voorter@uhasselt.be

Abstract. Public policy objectives highlighting the circular economy transition in construction are clear and ambitious. Now, regulatory instruments and frameworks are needed to embrace and support these objectives. We argue that regulatory frameworks should be (re-)considered using three equally important perspectives to achieve circularity: circular products, procurement and the process. With this paper, we highlight three legal instruments (one for each P) that have the potential to contribute to the establishment of a more circular construction sector in Belgium and the Netherlands. We'll explore the introduction of an extended producer responsibility for construction and demolition waste (products & process); the use of life cycle costing as an award criterion in circular public tenders (procurement) and the need for legal frameworks that enhance cooperation between both public and private construction actors (process).

1 Introduction

Efforts in making our society more sustainable are gaining traction. The European Commission is on the forefront of this transition with policy initiatives such as the European Green Deal[1] and the Fit for 55-package.[2] These policy initiatives have already led to various regulatory initiatives, e.g. the European Climate Law.[3]

One of the tools capable of enabling a more sustainable society is the transition towards a circular economy.[4] A circular economy can be defined as an economic system that represents a change of paradigm in the way human society (business models and

[1] COM(2019) 640 final, Communication from the European Commission on the European Grean Deal, 11.12. 2019.

[2] COM(2021) 550 final, Communication from the European Commission on 'Fit for 55': delivering the EU's 2030 Climate Target on the way to climate neutrality, 14.7.2021.

[3] Regulation (EU) 2021/1119 of the European Parliament of 30 June 2021 on the establishment of a framework for achieving climate neutrality and amending Regulations (EC) No 401/2009 and (EU) 2018/1999 (European Climate Law), OJ L 243, 9.7.2021.

[4] COM(2020) 98 final, Communication from the European Commission on a new circular economy action plan: For a cleaner and more competitive Europe.

M. Reese et al. (Eds.): EELF 2023, *Legal Implementation and Impacts of the European Green Deal*, pp. 159–176, 2026.
https://doi.org/10.1007/978-3-032-17197-9_7

consumer behaviour) is interrelated with nature and aims to replace the 'end-of-life' concept with reducing, alternatively reusing, recycling and recovering resources, energy and materials in order to accomplish sustainable development.[5] A circular economy is the opposite of our current linear economic system (*take – make – waste*), a system focusing on the extraction of virgin raw materials while, simultaneously, not being interested in adequate waste management practices. Although recycling efforts have been implemented in the linear paradigm, a circular system moves beyond recycling, prioritizing the reduction and reuse of materials and products.

This transition to a more circular society requires – as the definition suggests - a paradigm shift. Therefore, all societal actors and sectors must embrace circularity and adapt their current consumption and production processes. Nonetheless, some sectors are deemed to be pivotal in boosting the transition. The construction sector is one of them as it uses a significant amount of resources and generates various waste streams.[6] Several policy initiatives, both on the European and national/regional level, focus on making this sector more sustainable and circular. In previous research, we provided an overview of these initiatives on a European level and in the member states Belgium, the Netherlands, Luxemburg, and France.[7] Then, we tried to establish a potential link between these policy initiatives and tangible statutory legislation on circularity and construction.[8] Our main conclusion was that interest in circularity in construction legislation has just started to gain traction and most national legislation can be traced back to the implementation of the revised European Waste Framework Directive (2018 onwards). New regulatory initiatives have started to appear though, e.g. the eco-design regulation and the construction products regulation.[9]

Our previous analysis shows that legislators and policymakers currently emphasize the *product*-aspect of the circular transition. However, adequate attention should also be given to *process* and *procurement*. These three P's towards circularity (Product, Procurement & the Process) equally contribute to the development of a sustainable society. Products with circular potential are crucial but without demand, supply will not follow. Public authorities must raise the demand for those products by using public contracts (procurement). Public procurement alone will unfortunately not suffice to create a circular construction system as public authorities are not the only actor bearing the (financial) responsibilities and risks associated with the use of innovative circular materials and methods. Therefore, the various construction actors must truly cooperate in construction

[5] Voorter et al. (2021), p. 26.

[6] COM(2019) 640 final, p. 11; Van Gulijk (2021).

[7] For an overview of initiatives in various Member States: Van Gulijk and Voorter (2023).

[8] Ibid.

[9] Regulation (EU) 2024/1781 of the European Parliament of the Council of 13 June 2024 establishing a framework for the setting of ecodesign requirements for sustainable products, amending Directive (EU) 2020/1828 and Regulation (EU) 2023/1542 and repealing Directive 2009/125/EC, OJ L, 2024/1781, 28.6.2024; Regulation (EU) 2024/3110 of the European Parliament and of the Council of 27 November 2024 laying down harmonised rules for the marketing of construction products and repealing Regulation (EU) No 305/2011, OJ L, 2024/3110, 18.12.2024.

practices to incorporate circularity into the whole value chain, making sure the next generation of buildings reaches its full circular potential (process).[10]

With this paper, we will expand on our 'Three P's for circularity' model by introducing a possible research pathway for each of the three P's. We will discuss 1) one research item from a Belgian perspective (par. 2) as a case study; 2) one research item that has a link with the European perspective, adding some Belgian and Dutch accents (par. 3) and 3) one research item with a Dutch perspective as a case study (par. 4). We will end this paper with a conclusion in par. 5.

2 Product: An Extended Producer Responsibility for Construction and Demolition Waste (Belgian/Flemish Regional Perspective)

2.1 Extended Producer Responsibility (EPR) in the European Union

The European Waste Framework Directive (WFD)[11] regulates the use of extended producer responsibility schemes. Article 3(21) WFD defines an extended producer responsibility scheme as "a set of measures taken by Member States to ensure that producers of products bear financial responsibility or financial and organizational responsibility for the management of the waste stage of a product's life cycle."[12] The European legislator expands upon the idea of an extended producer responsibility in article 8 WFD. EU Member States get the opportunity to take measures to ensure that natural or legal persons who professionally develop, manufacture, process, treat, sell or import products have an extended producer responsibility to further promote prevention, reuse, recycling and other recovery operations of waste. Such measures may entail an acceptance of returned products or measures considering the management of waste and the attribution of the associated financial responsibilities. If an extended producer responsibility scheme is created, the general requirements for such schemes – laid down in article 8a WFD – have to be applied by the involved Member State.[13]

2.2 The Lack of EPR for Construction and Demolition Waste in Belgium

The European provisions mentioned above were transposed at the regional level (Flanders, Wallonia, Brussels) of the Belgian federal state.[14] The provisions on extended producer responsibility schemes can, in Flanders, be found in article 21 and following

[10] Voorter and Van Vliet (2025).

[11] Directive 2008/98/EC of the European Parliament and of the Council of 19 November 2008 on waste and repealing certain directives, OJ L 312, p. 3, 22.11.2008. This Directive was amended in 2018: Directive (EU) 2018/851 of the European Parliament and of the Council of 30 May 2018 amending Directive 2008/98/EC on waste, OJ L 150, p. 109, 14.6.2018.

[12] The Flemish (Dutch speaking region Belgium) has implemented this definition from the WFD in article 25°/1 of the Flemish (Dutch speaking region of Belgium) waste legislation (Materials decree).

[13] If Member States create EPR-schemes that violate those general requirements, the scheme in question could be annulled by a court.

[14] Environmental competences are largely allocated to the regions in Belgium.

of the Flemish Materials Decree.[15] Article 21 Materials Decree was further implemented by the Flemish government through Sect. 3 of the Flemish executive order considering the sustainable management of material loops and waste streams (VLAREMA).[16]

Initially, the Flemish materials and waste legislation established an extended producer responsibility for the following materials and products: printing waste, discarded vehicles, waste tyres, waste electrical and electronic equipment, waste batteries and accumulators, waste oil, old and expired medicines, waste mattresses, plastic fishing gear waste, litter and used disposable nappies.[17] In 2024 a reference to 'used fibre cement building materials' as a product category covered by an extended producer responsibility scheme was added in Flemish legislation with no further context or legal guidance. Yet, an overarching extended producer responsibility scheme for construction and demolition waste in general is still lacking.[18] Several reasons might explain this loophole.

1. Heterogeneity of Waste Streams and Construction Layers

At a European level, 'construction and demolition waste' is defined as waste generated by construction and demolition activities.[19] This waste type is difficult to manage, as it involves several waste streams (e.g. stony, flat glass, wood, metal, etc.) in various quantities and each with their own characteristics. Setting up a joint and overall extended producer responsibility scheme for all these waste streams may be practically unfeasible and even undesirable.

Moreover, the various materials and waste streams are also part of different layers of a building, each with their own specific qualities and lifespan.[20] Materials belonging to the structure (e.g. concrete foundation) of a building have a significantly longer lifespan than materials belonging to the techniques of a building. Consequently, it seems more complex to subject construction and demolition waste originating from the structure layer to an extended producer responsibility scheme. The structure layer also contains various (stony) material types that are already (able to be) dealt with in a fairly good way within the 4R-framework (reduce – reuse – recycle – recover).[21] Consequently, at first glance, it is not necessary to create a (legal) extended producer responsibility for such

[15] This article is the implementation of article 8 WFD. This responsibility can be attributed to more actors than the producer of the products alone: Van Hoorick (2012), pp. 5-64

[16] Flemish Executive Order of 17 February 2012 considering the sustainable management of material loops and waste streams, Belgian Official Gazette 23 May 2012, 29.590.

[17] Article 3.1.1. VLAREMA.

[18] This is also the case in other European countries, such as the Netherlands. France, on the other hand, already has an extended producer responsibility for construction and demolition waste in place: Décret nr. 2021-1941 du 31 décembre 2021 relatif à la responsabilité élargie des producteurs pour les produits et les matériaux de construction du secteur du bâtiment. https://www.legifrance.gouv.fr/jorf/id/JORFTEXT000044806344. Accessed 20 Aug 2025

[19] Article 3, 2c WFD.

[20] Farouk and Abdelsabour (2019), p. 4.

[21] For several examples see: Vrijders J and Romnee A (2018), Circulair bouwen – naar een circulaire economie in de bouw, p. 14.

materials/waste streams.[22] For other materials (e.g. flat glass, glass wool) from other layers, the value chain is not so well aligned yet, making it appropriate to consider a form of extended producer responsibility scheme for these materials.[23]

2. The Substantial Amount of Construction Actors

The responsibility for managing and further processing construction or demolition waste does not lie solely with the producers of the various building materials concerned (e.g. flat glass). They do have an important role, of course, as they can design materials that can be easily disassembled and thus dismantled in a cost-efficient way, thereby promoting reuse or high-quality recycling. Nevertheless, the other actors[24] in the construction chain also have a responsibility in realising a circular construction sector. For instance, the demolition contractor should also be able to dismantle and logistically process the various materials.[25] If the demolition contractor is, because of time constraints or high (labour) costs, unable to adequately deal with the released materials, high-quality processing options can still be impeded. Additionally, the architect, an actor with a privileged position in Belgian construction, has to design buildings which embrace circular ambitions, e.g. by including reused materials or materials with recycled content; designing the building in such a way that makes it easy to dismantle when it has reached the end of its life cycle or; to focus on flexible or modular use of buildings. Because of his/her important position within the Belgian construction process, the architect has the means/possibility to align the various actors within the project from its conceptualization to the use or occupation of the building by the client, facilitating circular thinking throughout the value chain.[26]

The question thus arises whether more actors than solely the 'producer' can be given an (extended) responsibility for closing the chain of (some) waste streams within the framework of 'construction or demolition waste'? The preparatory documents of the Flemish material legislation indicate that, under Article 8 WFD, any actor in the supply chain that starts at the extraction or recovery of a raw material and ends upon receipt by the end user of a complete and finished product can be included in an extended producer responsibility scheme.[27] In that way, responsibilities and (financial) risks can be more equally shared between all the actors involved.

---

[22] Market players have the opportunity to organize their own system of 'extended producer responsibility'. In that case, Article 8,1 fourth paragraph WFD indicates hat Member States can decide that they should apply some or all of the general requirements laid down in article 8a WFD.

[23] Proeftuin Circulair Bouwen (2021), p. 87. There is no legal requirement specifying for which materials a government can decide to create an EPR-scheme. Since the use of EPR-schemes can be far-reaching, we think it would be good to be cautious and not just opt for an EPR-scheme even if it is possible to close the value chain for such materials with less intrusive measures.

[24] For example: the owner, the contractor, the architect, the engineer(s), the user, the demolition contractor, the investor, etc. For an overview of the various construction phases and its key actors: European Commission (2023).

[25] Proeftuin Circulair Bouwen (2021), p. 85.

[26] Infra paragraph 4.

[27] Draft decree on sustainable management of material cycles and waste, nr. 1, p. 27. https://www.vlaamsparlement.be/nl/parlementaire-documenten/parlementaire-initiatieven/641021, Accessed 20 Aug 2025.

2.3 Legal Tools to Establish an EPR for Construction and Demolition Waste in Belgium?

In the regional laws and regulations of Flanders (the Dutch speaking part of Belgium)[28], currently three possible legal instruments exist to establish an EPR. Within this subsection, we want to indicate - on a general level - if these instruments could be used to further establish EPR schemes for construction and demolition waste.

First, there is an option to impose an obligation on the construction sector to draft a collective plan.[29] It is a broad instrument that can go beyond a mere 'acceptance obligation' (*infra*). The plan can focus on the way specific waste streams are treated or can encompass more general aspects, such as providing information or financial efforts of producers and/or the sector.[30] Waste streams that are already fairly well monitored and treated in construction (e.g. stony rubble) could also be included in a collective plan for construction and demolition wase, ensuring a holistic view. The disadvantage, however, is that a lot of interests and visions (material producers, demolition contractors, etc.) will have to be reconciled in such a collective plan.[31]

As mentioned before, next to the collective plan, a more specific instrument exists as well: the 'acceptance obligation'. With an 'acceptance obligation', specific waste streams within construction and demolition waste can be targeted.[32] The obligation entails that if a consumer buys a specific product, the seller[33] is obliged to accept, without any costs, the similar product the consumer wants to discard. For those streams that are currently difficult to valorise (e.g. flat glass), an acceptance obligation could ensure that the chain is more adequately closed for these streams.

In both cases (acceptance obligation or collective plan), a link with (digital) traceability procedures or product passports should be considered. Such procedure and passports try to ensure that the various materials/waste streams are (or can be) processed at the highest possible quality.[34] The use of traceability procedures will be more time-consuming (and costly) than the business-as-usual scenario, yet we believe that they are necessary to make further progress towards a circular construction sector in which the value chain is fully closed for different material flows by ensuring its quality and giving verifiable information on the origin of materials.

The last possibility includes the entire construction or demolition waste stream in a so-called 'take-back obligation'[35], a specific obligation for packaging waste included in the Belgian Cooperation Agreement of 4 November 2008 on the prevention and

[28] Belgium is a federal state in which the competence for waste legislation is attributed to the regions (subnational level).

[29] Article 3.3.1 and following VLAREMA.

[30] Report to the Government with regard to VLAREMA, article 3.3.1.

[31] E.g.: EMIS (2017).

[32] Article 3.2.1.1 VLAREMA.

[33] Article 3.2.1.1 VLAREMA mentions other actors and interactions.

[34] For an overview: Voorter and Koolen (2021).

[35] This is a specific regime and is not the same as the above-mentioned acceptance obligation.

management of packaging waste.[36] After all, packaging waste is also a very diverse stream that is nevertheless dealt with in its entirety.[37]

In all cases, the ultimate financial contribution(s) of all actors involved is an important issue. Producers, demolition contractors, processors, etc. that innovate and are making an effort to close the circular construction loop should be rewarded, for example in the form of lower financial contributions to the extended producer responsibility schemes.[38] Other financial instruments could be explored as well, such as tax breaks, subsidies, easier access to credits for companies with sustainable/circular practices, etc. More research on this topic is encouraged.

3 Procurement: Life Cycle Costing (LCC) as the Only Viable Award Criterion in Circular Public Tenders? (European Perspective with Belgian and Dutch Accents)

Article 67 Directive 2014/24/EU expressly states that the contracting authority must base the award of public contracts on the most economically advantageous tender. To designate this tender, it must use award criteria allowing for a comparative assessment of the level of performance of each tender in relation to the subject matter of the contract.[39] The contracting authority has several substantive options. It can award a contract on the basis of 1) price; 2) costs (e.g. life cycle costs) or 3) the best price-quality ratio.[40] If the third method is chosen, it is possible to choose qualitative criteria with an environmental or social angle (or better: circular criteria). This was initially confirmed by the European Court of Justice in the *Concordia Bus Finland*-judgment[41] but is now also explicitly mentioned in European and national legislation.[42] However, the legislation does not include any obligations on the weight to be given to certain award criteria. Consequently, as *Petitat* rightly states, the strength of the circular ambitions included in the subject matter of the public contract will depend entirely on the environmental awareness, political will and knowledge of the contracting authority.[43]

[36] It is derived from the European packaging waste directive: Directive 94/62/EC of 20 December 1994 on packaging and packaging waste, OJ L 365, 31.12.1994.

[37] This cooperation agreement was amended in 2020. Cooperation agreement of 4 November 2008 on the prevention and the management of packaging waste, Belgian Official Gazette 29 December 2008, p. 68.366.

[38] Spaans 2017, p. 160; Vermassen (2014), p. 122.

[39] Directive (EU) 2014/24 of the European Parliament and of the Council of 26 February 2014 on public procurement and repealing Directive 2004/18/EC, OJ L 95, p. 65, 28.3.2014, recital 92. Also: Teerlinck et al. (2023), p. 555 et seq.

[40] See for more information: C(2021) 4320, Commission Notice: Guidance on innovation procurement, 18.6.2021, 41 et seq. Also: Meylemans and Schutyser (2023).

[41] Concordia Bus Finland, European Court of Justice C-513/99 EC, Judgment September 2002, para. 55.

[42] Nowadays, considerations 92 and 97 Directive (EU) 2014/24, make explicit reference to the possibility to integrate social and environmental considerations in the award criteria. This possibility is also mentioned in article 81, §2, 3° Belgian law on public procurement.

[43] Petitat (2011), p. 584. However, the possibility to impose mandatory sustainable requirements is under investigation: Janssen and Caranta (2023).

The European Directive has been implemented in the different EU Member States. Within the scope of this section, we focus on the use of LCC in European public tenders but refer to Belgian or Dutch public procurement legislation and scholars whenever this is needed or can provide some interesting insights. In general, public procurement legislation in both Belgium and the Netherlands is not that different, although the European legislator has given Member States the possibility to differentiate on specific topics. For example, the Belgian legislator has not expressed any preference regarding the method used to select the most economically advantageous tender, notwithstanding the fact the European legislator explicitly allowed this: "In order to promote a greater reliance on quality in procurement, Member States should be able, if they deem it necessary, to prohibit or restrict the determination of the most economically advantageous tender on the basis of price alone or cost alone."[44] The Dutch government, on the other hand, did choose to make use of this possibility. Currently, article 2.114(4) Dutch Procurement Act 2012 stipulates that the public contracting authority must explicitly motivate the choice to award a contract based on the lowest cost or lowest price in the tender documents. The choice to subject the cost-element to a justification obligation is criticised by *Versteeg*.[45] After all, a focus on (life cycle) costs can also lead to desirable (read: circular) results. However, an obligation to justify the mere use of a price element is, in our opinion, a good thing in a circular society as the use of the price criterion does not include the costs that will occur during the life cycle of a product or project.

The concept of 'life cycle costs' is more or less addressed in articles 68 and 2, 20° Directive 2014/24/EU.[46] Article 2, 20° defines a 'life cycle' as "all consecutive and/or interlinked stages, including research and development to be carried out, production, trading and its conditions, transport, use and maintenance, throughout the existence of the product or the works or the provision of the service, from raw material acquisition or generation of resources to disposal, clearance and end of service of utilization". Article 68 states that costs related to the life cycle consist of 1) the costs borne by the contracting authority or other users and 2) costs attributed to external environmental impacts associated with the product, service or works during its life cycle. The costs borne by the contracting authority may cover, *inter alia*[47]: 1) costs related to acquisition; 2) operating costs, such as costs for energy and other resource consumption; 3) maintenance costs and 4) costs following from the end-of-life cycle, such as collection and recycling costs. The costs of environmental externalities should be related to the product, service or works over its life cycle, provided their monetary value can be determined and verified. They may include the cost of greenhouse gas emissions and other pollutant emissions as well as other climate change abatement costs.[48] The methodology for calculating costs for environmental externalities should (1) be based on objective and non-discriminatory

44 Directive (EU) 2014/24, recital 90 and article 67, 2. Also: D'Hooghe and Kiekens (2015), p. 185.

45 Versteeg (2018), p. 158 et seq.

46 Also, in Directive (EU) 2014/24, consideration 96. For more information on this concept: Yasar and Van Garsse (2023).

47 The list of elements mentioned in article 68 of Directive (EU) 2014/24 is not exhaustive.

48 Directive (EU) 2014/24, Article 68, 1, (b).

criteria; (2) be accessible to all parties and (3) allow a normally diligent operator to provide the requested data with reasonable effort.[49]

Awarding a contract on the basis of (life cycle) costs is a step in the right (read: circular) direction when compared to mere awarding on price.[50] When making use of life cycle costing, many more elements can be considered compared to a sole focus on price and the contracting authority gets a better picture of the total cost of the project, both for himself and for the environment.[51] Furthermore, 'price' refers to the amount effectively paid to the successful bidder, while 'cost' also takes into account the expenses the contracting authority has to bear after awarding the contract.[52] The life cycle cost criterion can be used as a main award criterion and as a cost criterion to assess the best price/cost-quality ratio of bids with additional qualitative criteria.[53] However, the method(s) to calculate these life cycle costs is/are labor-intensive and complex[54] for public contracting authorities and also not always up to date.[55] Life cycle costing is, consequently, not yet widely used in practice.[56] Indeed, public contracting authorities do not yet have an overview of possible workable methods and the existing uncertainty today will not persuade contracting authorities to make the required change.[57] Concrete tips and practical guidelines are necessities in this respect.[58] In the meantime, alternative forms - for example, the use of a fixed budget or ceiling budget - are a possible way out to further – be it qualitatively - engage circularity.[59]

Versteeg indicates that, in the circular narrative, we should eventually even move away from awarding contracts on the best price/cost-quality ratio and, in the long run[60], solely focus on the life cycle cost criterion when awarding public contracts, both on the European and national level.[61] This argument is very convincing at first glance. It reduces the award phase to a score that can be determined objectively, thereby minimizing problems around (too) subjective assessments. Yet, such approach seems to focus too much on the acquired product/project and too little on the process. By awarding purely on the basis of 'cost', the contracting authority no longer has the opportunity to allow interested construction actors to really distinguish themselves on the basis of criteria rewarding a

[49] Directive (EU) 2014/24, Article 68, 2.

[50] Pilcer and Bouzekri (2020), p. 245.

[51] Mortier (2019), p. 853; De Hornois (2019), p. 64; Moras et al. (2018), p. 101.

[52] Mortier (2019), p. 854.

[53] Article 81 Belgian law on public procurement. Also: C(2021) 4320, p. 41 et seq.

[54] Article 82 Belgian law on public procurement.

[55] Versteeg (2018), p. 141 et seq.

[56] Confirmed in: Iraldo et al. (2016), p. 10.

[57] Bruyninckx (2018), p. 557; Van Garsse (2011), p. 235.

[58] E.g.: De Hornois (2019), p. 64; Wouters and Lenders (2018), p. 81; De Koninck and Flamey (2016), p. 303.

[59] This was used in a circular pioneer case in Flanders: Kamp C, 't Centrum: https://www.kampc.be/projecten/t-centrum.

[60] He mentions "in the long run" because he is also aware of the difficulties public contracting authorities experience today when applying LCC.

[61] Versteeg (2018), pp. 165-166.

good understanding of the transition to a circular economy or higher cooperation potential.[62] After all, *Versteeg* too argued that award criteria can be a stronger incentive than e.g. technical specifications.[63] Therefore, we believe that qualitative award criteria (e.g. focus on cooperation and risk allocation) remain relevant, especially in the construction sector where many construction actors are (or may be) involved in a project. Practice shows that the use of qualitative criteria in European and national public tenders can certainly lead to circular results and to a high potential for collaboration.[64] Awarding a contract based on the best price/cost-quality ratio, including qualitative criteria, thus remains a valid path as far as we are concerned although it will depend on the client itself whether and how it integrates circularity into its contract documents.[65] This is a point of attention.

Awarding a contract based on life cycle costs or the best price/cost-quality ratio are both future-proof. A contract awarded solely on the basis of 'price' certainly is not. It would therefore be a strong signal to introduce an European obligation to justify awarding a contract purely on the price-criterion, as is already the case in the Netherlands - the Belgian legislator has not taken up the choice provided by the European legislator.[66] That way, public contracting authorities would be discouraged from taking this 'easy' route any time soon. The real trade-off then only takes place between an award on (life cycle) costs or the best price/cost-quality ratio. This should be considered on a case-by-case basis.

4 Process: Enhancing Cooperation Throughout the Construction Value Chain with Stimulating Legal Frameworks (Dutch Perspective)

On the road to circularity in construction, we argue that the construction *process* is a game changer as well. We see the construction process as a continuous cycle from the first initiative taken by the client to the maintenance works by the (sub)contractor after delivery and the actors responsible for giving the building a second life.[67] Although one easily emphasizes the professional (governmental) client, public authorities or real estate developers to boost circular construction activities - usually due to the fact that these parties have enough financial resources to enable circular construction -, other participants in the construction supply chain have an important role to take up as well. As

[62] E.g. giving their vision on cooperation and risk management within the project; give an overview of potential risks they encountered when preparing an offer for this project; providing statements on several circular indicators (amount of reused materials they can incorporate) with fines they would be willing to face if they're unable to deliver. Inspiration drawn from a specific circular project in Flanders (Kamp C – 't Centrum: https://www.kampc.be/projecten/t-centrum).

[63] Versteeg (2018), p. 118.

[64] See for example the case of Kamp C ('t Centrum) in Flanders (Dutch speaking region Belgium): https://www.kampc.be/tcentrum/circulair-bouwen-t-centrum.

[65] Petitat (2011), p. 584.

[66] The duty to motivate awarding a contract on the basis of life cycle costing is, as mentioned earlier, not a good idea.

[67] European Commission (2023), p. 4.

was set out in 2017, in the Dutch Building Agenda, speeding up the circular movement in construction practice requires a social and economic system in which building partners flourish and where *roles, tasks, and responsibilities are clear*.[68] The transition to a circular building sector will, obviously, change traditional roles of building actors and create new roles.[69]

In particular, for *architects,* moving towards a circular construction sector brings on new design challenges in an ever-changing environment of ageing, mobility and urbanization.[70] The circular design is about the alternative functions of buildings, renewable materials, the costs of using the building,[71] and monitoring systems[72] regarding the building's sustainability. Developments like modular and replaceable structures, flexible building structures, adaptability of materials, disassembly and reconstruction prove to be central design principles to reach sustainability goals. According to the European Commission, the design sector is a key driver of a circular construction industry. It sees the architect as a key figure in a circular construction process and it sees circular design as a game changer for the construction industry. The European Commission has set up a working group to present a set of principles for sustainable building design as part of the implementation of the Green Deal. The principles were presented in February 2020 as "European Commission Circular Economy Principles for Buildings Design". The working group clearly pointed to the importance of sustainable design. This should ensure a reduction of waste in the longer term. More flexible use of buildings and sustainable design should make the life cycle costs of buildings cheaper.[73]

One would suspect that this will lead to architects increasingly being contracted to supervise the construction process including demolition, reusing and recycling aspects. After all, architects can easily be(come) key players in circular building processes, as the sustainable design is the basis for circular building.[74] Consequently, the designer's legal position and responsibilities need adjustment. It may be surprising then, that in the Netherlands recent legislation (January 2024)[75] has introduced a new actor in the building process, the independent 'kwaliteitsborger' (quality assessor) who has the obligation to control whether a building meets the legal technical requirements. Notwithstanding the importance of improving quality assurance in Dutch construction practice, it would have been obvious to attribute such important task to the architect who is in the best place to oversee whether the design's (circular) prerequisites are well implemented during the construction process.[76] In fact, in Belgium architects have been attributed this duty; there architects have a far more centralized position in the construction process compared to Dutch architects. This mainly has to do with the fact that Belgian architect have a legal

---

68 Dutch Building Agenda 2017, p. 24.

69 As we argued before in: Van Gulijk (2019).

70 Nysten et al. (2018); EBU (2018), p. 20.

71 TNO (2018), p. 14; Economisch Instituut voor de Bouw (2014), pp. 19-20.

72 Like BREEAM.

73 European Commission (2020), p. 8.

74 One Future Play (2018), p. 84; BNA (2020).

75 Wet kwaliteitsborging voor het bouwen (2024), accessible via wetten.nl - Regeling - Wet kwaliteitsborging voor het bouwen - BWBR0042732 (overheid.nl).

76 Also see Van Gulijk (2021).

monopoly for drawing up plans and monitoring the works.[77] As a result, to Belgian architects a rather stringent ten-years liability system applies which has been fiercely debated for several years now with the aim to reform Belgian architect law.[78] Under Dutch law too, the current liability and insurance system that applies to architects is under pressure, though. In 2018, the Dutch Architects Association issued a manifesto to draw attention to the current irresponsible risk management and liabilities of Dutch architects.[79] This manifesto becomes even more important in a circular building sector.[80]

We argue that if the greatest positive environmental impact in the construction process can indeed be achieved in the design phase, architects will get increasingly important to take their share in the transition towards a circular construction sector.[81] They are expected to participate in interdisciplinary design teams in which they work intensively with the other partners to achieve a circular building sector.[82] New design challenges include mapping the alternative functions of buildings, renewable materials, operating costs, climate systems and sustainable measurement systems. Themes such as flexible and modular construction, adaptability of materials, disassembly and reconstruction are increasingly important design principles.[83] If architects are required to play such a central role in the future construction process, this also requires a stimulating legal framework, as we argued before.[84] It requires explicit attention to cooperation, tasks and responsibilities of all building actors.[85] Construction practitioners themselves also indicated that the real breakthrough in circular construction will only come when the government creates legal frameworks.[86] Since 2023, all public governments must put out circular tenders, which is expected to give an enormous boost to circular design and construction.[87] In 2019, obstacles in laws and regulations were mapped.[88] And in the field of public law, *Van Dam* and *Neerhof* showed that the *Omgevingswet* (in force since January 1st 2024) well enables that more rules on circular building, including rules on

77 Article 4 Wet van 20 februari 1939 op de bescherming van de titel en van het beroep van architect.

78 See for instance Uytterhoeven (2013); Uytterhoeven (2017).

79 See https://www.bna.nl/wp-content/uploads/2018/01/manifest-wij-gaancirculair.pdf; Van Gulijk (2008).

80 Van Gulijk (2019).

81 See Van Gulijk (2022); Transitiebureau Circulaire Bouweconomie (2019), pp. 10-11.

82 Sociaal Economische Raad (2016), p. 15.

83 De Architect (2018); TNO (2018), p. 14; Economisch Instituut voor de Bouw (2014), pp. 19-20; See: https://bna.nl/nieuws/in-energieneutraal-bouwen-ligt-een-architectonische-opgave-besloten. Accessed 20 Aug 2025.

84 See 'Uitvoeringsprogramma Circulaire Economie' 2020-2023, par 4.2 en 4.3. https://openresearch.amsterdam/nl/page/68671/uitvoeringsprogramma-circulaire-economie-2020-2023. Accessed 20 Aug 2025.

85 Bouwagenda 2017, p. 24.

86 Cobouw (2019), see https://www.cobouw.nl/aanbesteden/artikel/2021/10/verlaag-drempel-circulaire-bouw-maak-regelgeving-dwingend-101299665, 19 Oct 2021. Accessed 20 Aug 2025

87 See 'Uitvoeringsprogramma Circulaire Economie' 2020-2023, par. 4.4.

88 Kamerstukken II 32852, nr. 97.

reuse of existing structures and building materials, can be included in the environmental plan.[89]

To further elaborate on this stimulating legal framework that is required for a circular building process, it should be noted that in the Netherlands applicable rules for design and construction works are rather fragmented. Most design and construction activities are ruled by numerous general conditions and other self-regulation which have been created by governmental organizations and private parties.[90] On the one hand, these self-regulatory mechanisms provide construction parties flexibility and ownership to develop and adapt rules for construction parties they need. Recently, for instance, a new set of rules to govern early contractor involvement were introduced, referred to as 'Modelovereenkomst Bouwteam Duurzaam Gebouwd 2020.[91] This set primarily provides rules for the collaboration between designer and contractor during the design phase of the construction project. One of the most interesting elements of the model is its attention to risk management and the life cycle approach.[92] With these kinds of newly developed self-regulatory mechanisms, the Dutch construction sector appears to be quickly agile in order to anticipate changes in society. Furthermore, initiatives like this to further improve collaboration in the construction supply chain correspond to the call for a network approach in construction contracts instead of the mere traditional, fragmented way to rule rights and obligations.[93]

Such network-based cooperation in construction projects can also be well witnessed in integrated model contracts such as Design-Build-Finance-Maintain-Operate (DBFMO), which recently have been expanded with so-called circular modules like 'recycle', 're-use', 'deconstruct', or 'refurbish.[94] The conceptual basis of these types of contracts is the project and long-term cooperation itself, not one of the bilateral legal relationships in that project. This fits well with a circular construction practice where clients, designers and contractors make commitments throughout the lifespan of a building. Partnership in consortia flourishes in these projects, which leads to the possibility of others than the mere traditional construction parties (client, architect, contractor) to

[89] Van Dam and Neerhof (2021). Nevertheless, the possibilities to promote reuse of structures and building materials are still limited. Authors argue that including ambitious circular customization in the environmental plan will not yield many circular gains. Building regulations offer more opportunities to do so, such as adjusting the environmental performance requirements, but follow-up steps are needed to actually enforce circularity in building regulations.

[90] Most commonly used are: 'The New Regulation (DNR) 2011. Legal relationship client - architect, engineer and consultant', the 'Uniform administrative conditions for the execution of works and of technical installation works (UAV) 2012' and the 'Uniform administrative conditions for the execution of integrated contracts (UAV-gc) 2005'.

[91] See: https://www.duurzaamgebouwd.nl/artikel/20200525-warme-ontvangst-voor-nieuwe-modelovereenkomst-bouwteam-dg-2020. Accessed 20 Aug 2025.

[92] In 2025, a second edition of this model is expected, in which there will be more attention to circular aspects of the design and building.

[93] See Teubner (1998), p. 413; Van Gulijk, (2017); Tjong Tjin Tai (2017).

[94] For example: DBMR, DBFMO-D. An interesting case study is the temporary Court of Justice that was built in Amsterdam for a period of 5 years and recently has been deconstructed and rebuilt as a school building.

participate in the construction contract too. After all, in a circular building sector, suppliers, sustainable producers, people who search for and select circular building materials, and even flying gardeners[95] grow more important.

The position of clients also changes, as instead of owning – and operating – a building, the client can (also) become a customer of a circular service project. He might be mainly interested in the use and performance of the structure instead of its ownership.[96] Circular construction may require that the circular product, such as a removable façade or rooftop, remains the property of the supplier or producer. In that case, traditional builders turn into circular service providers. Accordingly, the service provider remains responsible for maintenance and his final objective is to take back the product for recycling. Obviously, one should avoid problems with ownership of certain parts of a circular structure.[97] Clients and producers need appropriate, flexible property law rules on ownership in circular projects.[98]

On a process level, for each of the participants in a building process the transition towards a circular building sector will bring new challenges and opportunities. One of the biggest challenges we see is implementing, monitoring and assuring circularity from design to operation of the building. The architect seems to be in best place for this, but national legal requirements regarding the scope of the architect's obligations and his liability during the construction process differ per Member State and therefore may significantly impede in the transition described. It is therefore important to allow leeway to a certain extent to construction contracting parties to initiate appropriate legal and operational frameworks for circular construction. Dutch construction practice shows constructive developments in this regard.

5 Conclusions

The circular transition requires a paradigm shift. Within this shift, the construction sector is an essential sector that has to act. Evolving towards a circular construction sector will have an impact on the way we interpret and create regulatory frameworks, as a more holistic approach is needed with a more profound focus on synergies and creating opportunities for cooperation and solidarity. Existing legal instruments have to be reconsidered with the circular perspective in mind, while sufficient room should be given to new legal initiatives, if needed.

In previous research, we highlighted the need to approach the legal transition towards a circular economy in construction from three different, but equally important, perspectives (the so-called 3 P-perspective): product, process and procurement. Construction

[95] For an impression, see: The Flying Gardeners (Short 2015) - IMDb.

[96] Backes et al. (2018).

[97] This may cause problems when the property (the building) is sold to a third party. Van der Veen et al. (2014); Mes et al. (2016), p. 160 et seq.

[98] For instance, the 'lease roof', which after a certain period is being replaced and returned to the producer.

products with circular potential should be able to flow easily throughout the construction value chain, strengthened by cooperative efforts from all construction actors. Procurement should be used to stimulate innovation and increase the demand for circular solutions.

Within each context (process, product, procurement), there are various new and existing legal instruments that can have a beneficial impact on the realization of our circular policy goals. Within the scope of this article, we focused on three legal instruments from a European, Belgian and/or Dutch perspective: the introduction of an extended producer responsibility in Belgium; the use of life cycle costing in European circular public tenders and the creation and use of regulatory frameworks for the different construction actors to promote cooperation throughout the whole construction value chain.

All the legal instruments considered can contribute to the realization of a circular economy in the construction sector. Nevertheless, they need to be a part of a holistic approach that links regulatory frameworks affecting the construction value chain with the P-perspectives mentioned above to create a smooth and well-functioning legal basis for a circular construction sector to flourish.

References

Backes, C.W., Boeve, M.N., Koolhoven, R., et al.: Circulair Bouwen, nr. 46. Instituut voor Bouwrecht, Den Haag (2018)

Bruyninckx, T.: Gunningscriteria gebaseerd op levenscycluskosten: valstrik of opportuniteit? In: De Koninck, C., Flamey, P., Thiel, P. et al. (eds.) Jaarboek Overheidsopdrachten 2017–2018. EBP Consulting, Brussels (2018)

De Hornois, K.: Van lineair naar circulair: overheidsaankopen als hefboom voor de circulaire economie en de uitdagingen voor de overheidsinkoper. Een aantal inleidende beschouwingen. MER (1), 53–65 (2019)

De Koninck C, Flamey P (2016) De Wet Overheidsopdrachten van 17 juni 2016 – A lawyer's paradise? RW 80(8):294–295

D'Hooghe, D., Kiekens, N.: Het gunningscriterium of gunningscriteria: de geheimtaal van de overheidsopdrachtenrichtlijn 2014/24. MCP OOO **2**, 179–194 (2015)

Farouk, H., Abdelsabour, I.: Design for disassembly framework: an approach to enhance the design construction process. J. Eng. Sci. **47**(6), 883–898 (2019)

Iraldo, F., Nucci, B., De Giacomo, M.R.: The relevance of life cycle costing in green public procurement. Econ. Pol. Energ. Environ. **1**, 91–109 (2016)

Janssen, W., Caranta, R. (eds.): Mandatory Sustainability Requirements in EU Public Procurement Law. Bloomsbury, New York (2023)

Mes, A.J., Ploeger, H.D., Jansen, B.: Preadvies KNB: Boek 5 van de toekomst. SDU, Den Haag (2016)

Meylemans, R., Schutyser, B.: Beoordeling, gunning en niet gunning. Het bepalen van de economisch meest voordelige offerte. In: Schutyser, B. (ed.) De aanbesteding van overheidsopdrachten en concessies. Een interpretatieve benadering. Kluwer, Mechelen, pp. 1355–1369 (2023)

Moras, S., Ooms, J., Zegers, E., et al.: De openbare en niet-openbare plaatsingsprocedures: de voornaamste wolfijzers en schietgeweren in de nieuwe regelgeving. TBO **2**, 85–109 (2018)

Mortier, T.: Prijs en kost als gunningscriteria. Mogelijkheden, risico's en beperkingen. In: De Koninck, C., Flamey, P., Thiel, P., et al. (eds.) Jaarboek Overheidsopdrachten 2018–2019. EBP Consulting, Brussels (2019)

Nysten, S., Pauwels, S., Van Zimmeren, E.: Architect 2.0 – Juridische knelpunten in het Belgisch wettelijk kader voor architecten. TBO **16**(4), 272–285 (2018)

Petitat, V.: Groene overheidsopdrachten: stand van zaken en praktijk. In: De Koninck, C., Flamey, P., Thiel, P. et al. (eds.) Jaarboek overheidsopdrachten 2010–2011. EBP Publishing, Brussels (2011)

Pilcer, M., Bouzekri, H.: Levenscycluskost. MCP OOO **2**, 245–246 (2020)

Spaans, J.: Circulaire economie: meer dan minder afval alleen. In: Backes, C., Tieman, J., Teesing, N. (eds.) Met recht naar een circulaire economie. Boom juridisch, Den Haag, pp 151–165 (2017)

Teerlinck, P., De Koninck, C., Galot, L., et al. (eds.) Compendium overheidsopdrachtenrecht. Intersentia, Brussels (2023)

Tjong Tjin Tai, T.: Networks and informal contract law. In: Brownsword, R., Van Gestel, R., Micklitz, H. (eds.) Contract and Regulation. Edward Elgar, Cheltenham, pp 235–256 (2017)

Uytterhoeven, K.: Tien jaar de tienjarige aansprakelijkheid. Een kritische reflectie over de stevigheid van de artikelen 1792 en 2270 BW. TBO **6**, 225–232 (2012)

Uytterhoeven, K.: De wet van 31 mei 2017 betreffende de verplichte verzekering van de tienjarige burgerlijke aansprakelijkheid van aannemers, architecten en andere dienstverleners in de bouwsector van werken in onroerende staat. Een eerste aanzet naar een algemene verzekeringsplicht in de bouwsector? TBO pp. 369–374 (2017)

Van Dam, R., Neerhof, A.R.: Circulair bestemmen onder de Omgevingswet. De juridische mogelijkheden van het omgevingsplan om hoogwaardig hergebruik van bestaande bouwwerken en bouwmaterialen te bevorderen. TBR **103**, 810–819 (2021)

Van der Veen, M., Hulshof, M., Ploeger, H.D.: Cascokoop: wenkend perspectief binnen een circulaire economie. WPNR **7033**, 857–859 (2014)

Van, G.: Enkele beschouwingen bij "life cycle costing" en overheidsopdrachten. In: De Koninck, C., Flamey, P., Thiel, P. et al. (eds.) Jaarboek Overheidsopdrachten 2010–2011. EBP Consulting, Brussels (2011)

Van Gulijk, S.: European Architect Law. Towards a New Design. Maklu Uitgevers, Antwerp/Apeldoorn (2008)

Van Gulijk, S.: Contractual networks in construction services: a Dutch building block? Eur. Rev. Priv. Law **5**, 859–880 (2017)

Van Gulijk, S.: Circular and safe building: responsibility is not a relay race. Prisma Print, Tilburg (2019)

Van Gulijk, S.: The circular economy: adaptive law for Dutch circular and safe building. Int. Construct Law Rev **38**(1), 132–144 (2021)

Van Gulijk, S.: De nieuwe kleren van de architect: over de (her)waardering van zijn positie in het toekomstige bouwproces. TBR (24) (2022)

Van Gulijk, S., Voorter, J.: Systematic review of Western-European public and private policies and (proposed) legislation to implement a circular built environment. Int. Construct. Law Rev. **3**, 284–298 (2023)

Van Hoorick, G.: Sectoraal Milieurecht in X (2012) Onroerend goed in de praktijk (247) Vibis.A.5–64 (2012)

Vermassen, M.: E-waste: internationale handel en duurzaam materialenbeheer. Beoordeling van de huidige praktijken in het licht van de wetgeving. TMR **2**, 112–140 (2014)

Versteeg, D.R.: Levenscycluskosten. De sleutel naar circulair werk? In: Backes, C.W., Boeve, M.N., Koolhoven, R. et al. (eds.) Circulair Bouwen, nr. 46. Instituut voor Bouwrecht, Den Haag, pp. 113–183 (2018)

Voorter, J., Iurascu, A., van Garsse, S.: The concept 'circular economy': towards a more universal definition. Ius. Pub. Net. Rev. **2**, 1–28 (2021)

Voorter, J., Koolen, C.: The traceability of construction and demolition waste in Flanders via blockchain technology: a match made in heaven? J. Eur. Env. Plan Law **4**, 347–369 (2021)

Voorter, J., van Vliet, J.: Durkheim, individualism, human flourishing and the law: an appraisal of social solidarity and circularity in the construction sector. J. Circ. Econ. **3**(1), 1–14 (2025)
Wouters, J., Lenders, C.: De voorbereidende fase: keuze van de plaatsingsprocedure – opstellen van bestek – e-procurement – bekendmaking. TBO **2**, 77–84 (2018)
Yasar, B., Van Garsse, S.: Het concept "life-cycle costing" bij overheidsopdrachten: een blik vanuit het Europese aanbestedingsrecht. TBO **1**, 2–8 (2023)

Cases

Concordia Bus Finland, European Court of Justice C-513/99 EC, Judgment September 2002

Legislation

Flemish Executive Order of 17 February 2012 considering the sustainable management of material loops and waste streams, Belgian Official Gazette 23 May 2012, 29.590

Others

BNA, Wij gaan circulair (2020). https://s3.eu-central-1.amazonaws.com/bna-downloads/documents/manifest-wij-gaan-circulair.pdf. Accessed 20 Aug 2025
Cobouw, Overheid, stel circulair bouwen verplicht (2019). https://www.cobouw.nl/269983/bouwopdrachtgevers-overheid-stel-circulair-bouwen-verplicht. Accessed 25 Aug 2019
COM, 640 final, Communication from the European Commission on the European Grean Deal (2019)
COM, 98 final, Communication from the European Commission on a new circular economy action plan: For a cleaner and more competitive Europe (2020)
COM, 550 final, Communication from the European Commission on 'Fit for 55': delivering the EU's 2030 Climate Target on the way to climate neutrality (2021)
Cooperation agreement of 4 November 2008 on the prevention and the management of packaging waste, Belgian Official Gazette 29 December 2008
De Architect, Circulariteit biedt ruimte voor architectuur (2018). https://www.dearchitect.nl/architectuur/blog/2018/09/circulariteit-biedt-ruimte-voor-architectuur-101200916. Accessed 20 Aug 2025
Economisch Instituut voor de Bouw, Eindgebruiker en opdrachtgever in de bouw: lessen uit het buitenland. Conferentie, toetsing en implementatie (2014). https://www.eib.nl/pdf/eindgebruiker_en_opdrachtgever_in_de_bouw.pdf. Accessed 20 Aug 2025
EMIS, Keten ondertekent collectief plan voor duurzame wegwerpluiers, 13 Sep 2017 (2017). https://emis.vito.be/nl/node/40437. Accessed 20 Aug 2025
European Commission, Study on measuring the application of circular approaches in the construction industry ecosystem (2023). https://op.europa.eu/en/publication-detail/-/publication/2f3b2373-1173-11ee-b12e-01aa75ed71a1/language-en. Accessed 20 Aug 2025
European Commission, Circular Economy Principles for Buildings Design (2020). https://ec.europa.eu/docsroom/documents/39984. Accessed 20 Aug 2025
One Future Play, Samen circulair ontwerpen. Circulaire architectuur en bouw, behoeftenonderzoek in opdracht van BNA (2018). https://bna.nl/wp-content/uploads/2019/12/BNA_OFP_Onderzoeksrapport_2018.pdf. Accessed 20 Aug 2025

Proeftuin Circulair Bouwen, Urban mining van gebouwen. Het creëren van waarde via het sluiten van materiaalstromen (2021). https://bouwen.vlaanderen-circulair.be/src/Frontend/Files/userfiles/files/FINAL%20Eindrapport%20Urban%20Mining%20van%20gebouwen.pdf. Accessed 20 Aug 2025

Sociaal Economische Raad, Werken aan een circulaire economie: geen tijd te verliezen (2016). https://test.nutrientplatform.org/wp-content/uploads/2016/09/SER-rapport-circulaire-economie.pdf. Accessed 20 Aug 2025

TNO, Circulair bouwen in perspectief (2018). https://resolver.tno.nl/uuid:de7cb3d0-646c-4c5e-8f03-b1bbe240bcb0. Accessed 20 Aug 2025

Transitiebureau Circulaire Bouweconomie, Naar een circulaire bouweconomie. Uitvoeringsprogramma 2019 (2019). Accessed 20 Aug 2025

Vrijders, J., Romnee, A.: Circulair bouwen – naar een circulaire economie in de bouw (2018). https://www.buildwise.be/nl/publicaties/innovation-papers/28/. Accessed 20 Aug 2025

Sea and Forests: The Ecological Frontiers of the Green Deal

Diving into the Marine Dimension of the European Green Deal: Something Old, Something Borrowed, but How New and Blue?

Nikolaos Giannopoulos[1(✉)] and Mathilde Hoarau[2]

[1] Utrecht Centre for Water, Oceans and Sustainability Law, Utrecht University, Utrecht, The Netherlands
n.giannopoulos@uu.nl

[2] Paris Bar Association Legal Training Centre, Paris, France

Abstract. Initially marginalising the ocean's pivotal role for the EU's sustainability transformation, the European Green Deal (EGD) gradually recognized its significance in climate mitigation, adaptation, and economic growth. Yet, its level of ambition in marine ecosystem conservation and restoration has proven relatively poor. This chapter evaluates the EGD's targets and implementation instruments in terms of marine sustainability across key sectors -climate/energy, biodiversity and fisheries- highlighting challenges and opportunities in reconciling competing objectives for achieving healthy EU seas.

1 Introduction

Identified as *"this generation's defining task"* by the European Commission,[1] the fight against climate change appears to be the most pervasive objective pursued by the European Green Deal (EGD). This unprecedented set of ambitious policy initiatives, launched by the Commission in 2019, aims, *inter alia*, at achieving climate neutrality by 2050 while reversing biodiversity loss and promoting sustainable and resource-efficient development of the Union.[2]

Considered as a historic breakthrough,[3] this comprehensive instrument acknowledges the necessity of *"reconciling our economy with our planet, reconciling the way we produce, the way we consume with our planet and respecting the environment we*

The research for this paper was funded by the European Union under the Grant Agreement Grant Agreement ID 101060958. Views and opinions expressed are however those of the author(s) only and do not necessarily reflect those of the European Union. Neither the European Union nor the granting authority can be held responsible for them.

[1] COM (2019) 640 final, Communication from the Commission to the European Parliament, the Council, the European Economic and Social Committee and the Committee of the Regions, The European Green Deal.

[2] COM (2019) 640 final.

[3] Sachs (2019) Europe's Green Deal. Available via Project Syndicate. https://www.project-syndicate.org/commentary/europe-green-deal-is-global-beacon-by-jeffrey-d-sachs-2019-12. Accessed 25 Aug 2025.

M. Reese et al. (Eds.): EELF 2023, *Legal Implementation and Impacts of the European Green Deal*, pp. 179–218, 2026.
https://doi.org/10.1007/978-3-032-17197-9_8

live in."[4] Consequently, it introduces a new growth strategy that redesigns the European Union (EU) economic model into a sustainable and resilient one. This path to sustainability is paved by a set of deeply transformative policies spanning various sectors, including maritime activities. Initially, the EGD overlooked the crucial role of the ocean in this unprecedented transition. However, it has gradually integrated elements of blue economic sustainability into climate action.[5] Thus, after being the *'Cinderella'* of the climate change discourse for years, the ocean is no longer merely a victim of climate change but a *sine qua non* condition in tackling the vexed climate crisis due to its pivotal role in climate mitigation, adaptation, and sustainable economic growth.[6]

The EGD appropriately acknowledges that achieving climate neutrality necessitates nature-based solutions, such as restoring a healthy and resilient ocean. In the words of the Commissioner for the Environment, Oceans and Fisheries: *"to be truly green, we must also think blue"*.[7] While the need to *think blue* in this transition has been emphasised,[8] subsequent strategies concretizing the vision of the 2019 EGD Communication still appear to sideline the intrinsic values of the ocean and the need to refine the ecosystem-based approach for conserving n and restoring marine ecosystems.[9] The few splashes of blue fail to address the urgent need for robust ocean-focused actions to face the simultaneous biodiversity, climate and energy crises. With marine-related biodiversity targets lacking concreteness and lacking support from specific implementation measures, questions arise regarding the adequacy of the EGD and its strategies to drive the necessary radical transformation of the Blue Economy and align the targets of its various sectors. Similarly, while the EGD construes a socially fair and inclusive transition as a *leitmotiv*, doubts remain about whether it provides the necessary framework to guarantee that the social implications of the rapid economic transformation *"leave no one behind."*[10]

Focusing on three significant marine sectors – climate-energy, fisheries and marine biodiversity protection – Sect. 2 of the chapter first outlines the marine-related policy objectives to assess the 'added value' of the EGD in terms of objectives and targets. Section 3 then enquires whether these targets are accompanied by delivery mechanisms, i.e., whether the identified objectives have been translated into new or revised legislative

---

[4] Von der Leyen (2019) Speech at the Debate on the European Green Deal, https://multimedia.europarl.europa.eu/en/video/debate-on-the-european-green-deal-opening-statement-by-ursula-von-der-leyen-president-of-the-ec_I181467. Accessed 25 Aug 2025.

[5] COM (2020) 380 final, Communication from the Commission to the European Parliament, the Council, the European Economic and Social Committee and the Committee of the Regions, EU Biodiversity Strategy for 2030 Bringing nature back into our lives; COM(2021) 240 final, Communication from the Commission to the European Parliament, the Council, the European Economic and Social Committee and the Committee of the Regions, on a new approach for a sustainable blue economy in the EU Transforming the EU's Blue Economy for a Sustainable Future..

[6] COM (2021) 240 final.

[7] EU (2021) Putting the blue into the green – Sustainable Blue Economy. https://oceans-and-fisheries.ec.europa.eu/system/files/2021-05/2021-05-17-sustainable-blue-economy-factsheet_en.pdf. Accessed 25 Aug 2025.

[8] Sinkevičius, European Commissioner for Environment, Oceans and Fisheries.

[9] Sander (2023), p. 421.

[10] Von der Leyen (2019) Speech at the Debate on the European Green Deal.

and regulatory instruments.[11] Indeed, a notable array of legal instruments concerning climate and energy has been adopted, transforming the respective EGD objectives into legally binding commitments. However, these new instruments do not operate in a legal vacuum; rather, they enter into an already intricate legal framework, particularly within the marine domain, which is marked by sectoral and geographical fragmentation in its regulation.[12] Considering the ensuing potential conflicts and opportunities, Sect. 4 investigates a selection of the legislative instruments that are operationalized to achieve the EGD's Blue Economy objectives, specifically the expansion of marine renewables. It aims to identify their potential for fostering synergies and mitigating frictions between relevant sectoral EU legal instruments. The paper emphasises that maintaining a fair balance and coherence among climate-energy and biodiversity legal instruments is crucial, considering the inherent interconnectedness of the EGD's economic, social and environmental objectives.

2 Mapping Out of the EGD's Marine-Related Objectives: What's Blue and New?

The EGD has articulated a series of strategies directly or indirectly related to the marine environment, covering areas such as biodiversity conservation, climate change mitigation and adaptation, renewable energy, sustainable mobility, fisheries and zero pollution.[13] Although a European success story heavily depends on a healthy ocean and its services,[14] its contribution to the EU's broader sustainability vision was only marginally acknowledged 2019 EGD Communication (2.1). However, the recognition of the ocean's key role and the Blue Economy has gradually been integrated in the subsequent EGD strategies.

[11] The Commission referred to the need to harness 'all policy levers', including novel instruments in order to reach the EGD's ambitious targets, COM/2019/640 final, p. 4.

[12] Trevisanut et al. (2023) Scoping: Concretising the policy targets and developing key scenarios, p. 11. https://crossgov.eu/wp-content/uploads/2023/08/CrossGov_D1.1.-Green-Deal-Objectives-and-Scenarios192855226f323a3f738b788cd50d8fb95d4d8f1f801da614a9a7943f653785ed.pdf. Accessed 25 Aug 2025.

[13] See, i.e., COM (2020) 741 final, Communication from the Commission to the European Parliament, the Council, the European Economic and Social Committee and the Committee of the Regions. An EU Strategy to harness the potential of offshore renewable energy for a climate neutral future; COM (2020) 562 final, Communication from the Commission to the European Parliament, the Council, the European Economic and Social Committee and the Committee of the Regions. Stepping up Europe's 2030 climate ambition – Investing in a climate-neutral future for the benefit of our people; COM (2020) 789 final, Communication from the Commission to the European Parliament, the Council, the European Economic and Social Committee and the Committee of the Regions. Sustainable and Smart Mobility Strategy – putting European transport on track for the future; COM (2021) 82 final, Communication from the Commission to the European Parliament, the Council, the European Economic and Social Committee and the Committee of the Regions. Forging a climate-resilient Europe – the new EU Strategy on Adaptation to Climate Change.

[14] European Commission (2021) The EU Blue Economy Report. https://maritime-spatial-planning.ec.europa.eu/sites/default/files/the-eu-blue-economy-report-2021_en.pdf. Accessed 25 Aug 2025.

This section examines the EGD's marine-related objectives with a particular focus on the protection of marine biodiversity, fisheries and climate-energy. It assesses whether these targets demonstrate a higher level of ambition compared to the pre-existing EU legal and policy framework and whether there is a balance between the objectives across various interconnected policy streams (2.2–2.3).

2.1 The Scarcity of Marine-Related Actions in the 2019 EGD Communication

Despite the catalytic role of the planet's 'blue lungs' in regulating our climate and the alarming decline in marine biodiversity in Europe,[15] the 2019 EGD Communication entailed very few concrete actions and targets related to the protection of EU seas. Concerning the protection and conservation of marine biodiversity, the Communication solely advocated for the designation of more marine protected areas (MPAs) with specific measures to be spelled out in the Biodiversity Strategy 2030.[16] In terms of fisheries, the EGD acknowledges the key role of fishermen in managing the sustainability transition and pledges to continue working within the Common Fisheries Policy framework to reduce the adverse impacts of fishing on marine ecosystems.[17]

While nature and biodiversity appear to take a backseat, the primary focus lies on achieving climate neutrality, which requires transforming all economic sectors, while recognizing the pivotal role of the projected energy transition.[18] In this context, the Communication, particularly under its dedicated biodiversity section, emphasises plans to bolster the sustainable blue economy and expand aquaculture and offshore renewable energy (ORE), which can bring considerable climate and economic benefits for the Union. The shipping sector also falls within its purview. The proposal commits to reviewing current tax exemptions, including those for maritime fuels, and extending European emissions trading (Directive 2003/87) to the maritime sector to address EU shipping's climate footprint.[19] However, the Communication remains silent on reasonable questions about the potential environmental effects of its plans to boost the blue economy (and similarly other resource-intensive economic sectors on land contributing to marine biodiversity loss) and their alignment with the biodiversity objectives[20] pledged as a contracting party to the Convention on Biological Diversity (CBD).[21] For instance, it does not acknowledge the high dependence of (offshore) renewable infrastructure on rare metals and the environmental impacts of their extraction, nor does it address the

[15] IPCC (2019) Summary for Policymakers. In: Portner H.O et al. (eds) IPCC Special Report on the Ocean and the Cryosphere in a Changing Climate. https://www.ipcc.ch/srocc/chapter/summary-for-policymakers/. Accessed 25 Aug 2025; European Environmental Agency (2019) The European Environment - state and outlook 2020. https://www.eea.europa.eu/en/analysis/publications/soer-2020. Accessed on 25 Aug 2025.

[16] COM (2019) 640 final, p. 13.

[17] COM (2019) 640 final, p. 12.

[18] COM (2019) 640 final, p. 4: 'The Commission has already set out a clear vision of how to achieve climate neutrality by 2050'.

[19] COM (2019) 640 final, pp. 10–11.

[20] Hereu-Morales et al. (2023), p. 655.

[21] The EU has become a party to the CBD through Decision 93/626, OJ 1992, L 309, 1.

challenge of their geographic distribution,[22] or propose measures to handle potential trade-offs.

Overall, the 2019 Communication appears primarily concerned with restoring the health of the ocean, as indicated by the passing reference to the findings of the IPCC's report on oceans,[23] albeit only to the extent that the ocean's resilience is indispensable to achieve climate neutrality without jeopardising the economic development of the Union. Interestingly, it pledges that all policies adopted in its implementation shall adhere to a green oath to 'do no harm'.[24] Nonetheless, the ocean is still perceived as an underutilised resource,[25] at least in terms of renewable energy, which renders the plan reminiscent of the 'green growth' narrative of the 1990s. This narrative increases efficiency through technology and innovation to reconcile economic growth with environmental targets.[26] The EGD's lack of emphasis on biodiversity protection plans is compounded by its failure to address how its growth vision can mitigate the impact on biodiversity.[27] Notably, the European Environmental Agency cautioned that pursuing a green growth trajectory will not enable Europe to succeed in "living well within the limits of the planet".[28]

2.2 The Gradual but Unequal Integration of Marine-Related Objectives in the EGD's Strategies

Since its adoption in 2019, the EGD has undergone significant developments due to the publication of over 30 strategic documents and numerous legislative proposals. These documents flesh out and concretize the EGD's overarching sustainability vision by delineating specific objectives and designing a roadmap with a broad number of implementation instruments to achieve them.[29] This all-encompassing set of policies is grounded in the recognition that environment, economy and societal wellbeing are intrinsically connected.[30] Consequently, the EGD promised to enhance cross-sectoral policy coordination, a challenge that the EU has repeatedly struggled with.[31] The waves of its development progressively covered the EU seas, with the Sustainable Blue Economy Strategy aiming to integrate the blue elements of the EGD strategies cohesively (2.2.1–2.2.3). However, there appears to be some discrepancy between the EGD's environmental and economic sustainability vision for the ocean (2.2.4).

---

[22] Hereu-Morales et al. (2023), p. 654.

[23] COM (2019) 640 final, p. 12.

[24] COM (2019) 640 final, p. 19, subsequently clarified as an oath to do no 'significant' harm, see art 17 of the Taxonomy Regulation. See also, Sikora (2021), pp. 689–690.

[25] Marine ecosystem restoration can 'form part of an economic sector in its own right, while 'all potential impacts must be addressed in a holistic way for them to be truly sustainable', with no further elaboration, COM (2021) 240 final, pp. 6–7.

[26] European Environmental Bureau, Decoupling Debunked, Report 8.7.2019.

[27] Ossewaarde and Ossewaarde-Lowtoo (2020); Vezzoni (2023).

[28] European Environmental Agency (2019) The European Environment - state and outlook 2020. https://www.eea.europa.eu/en/analysis/publications/soer-2020. Accessed on 25 Aug 2025.

[29] Eckert (2021), p. 81.

[30] COM (2020) 380 final, p. 2.

[31] Paleari (2024), p. 2.

2.2.1 Marine Biodiversity

The majority of the EGD's marine biodiversity-related objectives are outlined in the Biodiversity Strategy 2030, purporting to ensure that all of the world's ecosystems are restored, resilient and adequately protected by 2050, while setting Europe's biodiversity on the path to recovery by 2030.[32] Within the marine domain, the Strategy sets a target that by 2030, 30% of the EU seas should be legally protected, compared to the current coverage of 11% by Natura 2000 MPAs and 3% under other national measures.[33] These areas are envisioned to be connected through ecological corridors, with at least one-third of the EU's MPAs of *"very high biodiversity value"* receiving strict protection.[34] Despite obligations under the Habitats Directive (HD) and the Marine Strategy Framework Directive (MSFD),[35] the current network of MPAs lacks ecological representation.[36] Strengthening the connectivity of MPAs can enhance the overall resilience of the EU seas and their adaptive capacity to natural disasters. However, there is a risk that expanding the network may prioritise areas solely for their residual commercial value and their compatibility with boosting of the Blue Economy.[37]

Relevantly, these policy objectives include quantitative targets for expanding MPAs and specific deadlines for compliance. Nonetheless, these objectives largely entail Member States' action in compliance with existing obligations under EU environmental law and do not demonstrate a higher level of ambition at EU level. They merely align with targets established under the CBD post-2020 Global Biodiversity Framework.[38]

Similarly, the Strategy provides that by 2030, the Commission will 'request' Member States to ensure that Natura 2000 sites receive adequate protection, protected species show no deterioration in their conservation status and that 30% of protected species and habitats reach a favourable conservation status or show a 'strong positive trend' in that direction.[39] These targets bring nothing new to the table; rather, they serve as a reminder that Member States have not duly fulfilled their duties under the Nature Directives, which require them to implement measures to improve the conservation status

[32] COM (2020) 380 final, p. 3. Similar objectives to halt biodiversity loss had been set by the previous biodiversity strategies for 2010 and to 2020, yet to no avail, as the Strategy acknowledges the failure of the existing EU legal and policy framework in achieving the Aichi biodiversity targets and acknowledges the poor state of biodiversity in Europe, which keeps declining.

[33] Latest EU Statistics European database of nationally designated protected areas, https://ec.europa.eu/eurostat/web/products-eurostat-news/-/edn-20220521-1. Accessed 25 Aug 2025.

[34] COM (2020) 380 final, p. 4. See also COM(2021) 240 final, p. 6.

[35] Art 10 Council Directive 92/43/EEC of 21 May 1992 on the conservation of natural habitats and of wild fauna and flora, OJ L 206, 22.7.1992, pp. 7–50; Art 13(4) Directive 2008/56/EC of the European Parliament and of the Council of 17 June 2008 establishing a framework for community action in the field of marine environmental policy (Marine Strategy Framework Directive), OJ L 164, 25.6.2008, pp. 19–40.

[36] EU Court of Auditors (2018) Special Report 1/2017: More efforts are needed to implement the Natura 2000 network to its full potential, EEA: 'Marine Protected Areas'.

[37] Lennan et al. (2020), pp. 4–5.

[38] (2020) Zero draft of the post-2020 global biodiversity framework. CBD/WG2020/2/3. https://www.cbd.int/doc/c/efb0/1f84/a892b98d2982a829962b6371/wg2020-02-03-en.pdf. Accessed 25 Aug 2025.

[39] COM (2020) 380 final pp. 6–7.

of habitats and species.[40] Recognising the shortcomings of the voluntary approach taken in by previous Biodiversity Strategies, the Biodiversity Strategy 2030 suggests a potential legally binding biodiversity governance framework in 2023, although there is no progress in that direction.[41] It, furthermore, pledged to enhance the public's role as a 'compliance watchdog' by improving access to justice for individuals and NGOs, and by expanding the standing for the latter through a revision of the Aarhus Regulation.[42] The only new ambition of the Biodiversity Strategy for 2030 appears to be the commitment to adopt legally binding EU nature restoration targets aimed at restoring degraded ecosystems, including important fish spawning and nursery areas, with a focus on those contributing to climate change mitigation and adaptation![43]

On paper, the Strategy employs strong language regarding the imperative to reverse biodiversity loss. However, upon closer examination, there is a clear emphasis on the ecosystem services provided by nature, namely the economic benefits and financial requirements of nature protection measures.[44] For instance, it underscores that investing one euro in MPAs would yield a return of at least three euro,[45] while the failure to implement existing nature conservation legislation was estimated to cost around 50 billion euro per year.[46] Arguably, the strategy seeks to establish a business case to promote measures in favour of biodiversity protection,[47] by stressing the devastating financial repercussions of inaction against biodiversity loss.[48]

2.2.2 Fisheries

Fishing poses one of the most significant pressures on marine ecosystems, affecting resource extraction, by-catch of sensitive species and seabed damage. Therefore, taking action in this sector is an imperative for achieving a healthy ocean.[49] The implementation of the ecosystem-based approach is expected to play a key role in reducing adverse

[40] Art 6 and 12 Council Directive 92/43/EEC, pp. 7–50.

[41] The Commission has set up a monitoring and review mechanism, which on the basis of agreed indicators is keeping track of the progress in achieving the goals of the BD. https://dopa.jrc.ec.europa.eu/kcbd/actions-tracker/. Accessed on 25 Aug 2025.

[42] COM(2020) 380 final, p. 16.

[43] COM(2020) 380 final, p. 6. The need to restore marine ecosystems due to their role in climate change resilience is similarly highlighted in COM (2021) 82 final.

[44] COM (2020) 380 final, pp. 4, 15.

[45] COM (2021) 240 final, p. 6.

[46] COM (2021) 240 final, p. 8.

[47] Kramer (2020), pp. 293–294, see also COM (2020) 380 final, p.16.

[48] Biodiversity loss and ecosystem collapse are one of the biggest threats facing humanity in the next decade. They also threaten the foundations of our economy and the costs of inaction are high and are anticipated to increase', COM (2020) 380 final, p. 2.

[49] European Environmental Agency (2019), Marine Messages II, Navigating the Course towards clean, healthy and productive seas through implementation of an ecosystem-based approach. https://www.eea.europa.eu/en/analysis/publications/marine-messages-2. Accessed on 25 Aug 2025.

impacts of fishing on sensitive species and seabed habitats.[50] For instance, urgent action is needed to address the negative effects of bottom trawling.[51] In this context, the Biodiversity Strategy pledges a significant reduction in the impact of fishing and other extraction activities on sensitive species and habitats to achieve a good environmental status (GES) of EU seas by 2030. Additionally, it mandates halting harmful fisheries subsidies and eliminating or minimising by-catch to a level that facilitates species recovery and conservation.[52] While these targets do not echo any groundbreaking ambition, they essentially extend the original deadline for reaching the overarching objective of the MSFD by 2020.[53]

To specify the actions necessary for protecting sensitive species and habitats, the Commission released a dedicated Action Plan in February 2023.[54] Building on the commitment to legally protect 30% of EU seas, the Action Plan centres on MPAs[55] and promoting more sustainable fishing practices.[56] The Plan aspires to enhance the effectiveness of marine biodiversity protection and restoration, thus contributing to the objectives outlined in the proposal for the Nature Restoration Law.[57] Specifically, it provides for the phasing out of mobile bottom fishing in all MPAs by 2030 at the latest to reduce the impact of fisheries on the seabed.[58] Moreover, it calls on Member States to implement more ambitious measures to increase the selectivity of fishing methods and minimise by-catch.[59] Notably, the actions primarily require Member States to implement national measures, or where appropriate, propose joint recommendation to the regional

---

[50] COM (2023) 103 final, Communication from the Commission to the European Parliament and the Council: The common fisheries policy today and tomorrow: a Fisheries and Oceans Pact towards sustainable, science-based, innovative and inclusive fisheries management,, p. 103.

[51] Hiddink et al. (2017).

[52] COM (2021) 240 final, pp. 6–7.

[53] Art 1(1) Directive 2008/56/EC, pp. 19–40.

[54] COM (2023) 102 final, Communication from the Commission to the European Parliament, the Council, the European Economic and Social Committee and the Committee of the Regions. EU Action Plan: Protecting and restoring marine ecosystems for sustainable and resilient fisheries.

[55] This illustrates a lower level of ambition compared to the calls by the EU Parliament to prohibit all environmentally damaging extracting activities in MPA, European Parliament (2022) Resolution toward a sustainable blue economy in the EU: the role of the fisheries and aquaculture sectors (2021/2188(INI)), para. 119.

[56] ECA Special Report 26/2020, Marine Environment: EU protection is wide but not deep, which highlighted that EU tools for tackling overfishing under the CFP do not contribute towards achieving a GES under the MSFD. European Court of Auditors (2020) Special Report 26/2020, Marine Environment: EU protection is wide but not deep, https://eca.europa.eu/en/publications?did=57066. Accessed 25 Aug 2025.

[57] Regulation (EU) 2024/1991 of the European Parliament and of the Council of 24 June 2024 on nature restoration and amending Regulation. EU/2022/869, OJL, 2024/1991, 29.7.2024.

[58] COM (2023) 102 final, pp. 8–12. Fishing has been found to be the most disturbing human activity for the seafloor across all European seas, see also COM(2020) 259 final, Report from the Commission to the European Parliament and the Council on the implementation of the Marine Strategy Framework Directive.

[59] COM (2023)102 final, pp. 6–7.

groups to prohibit bottom fishing in Natura 2000 sites,[60] which will be monitored by the EU Commission.[61]

2.2.3 Climate-Energy

The EGD's climate goals and their level of ambition must be considered in light of the unprecedented momentum surrounding the climate crisis, driven by the scientific warnings that the world must reach net zero emissions by 2050 to avert catastrophe.[62] The overarching objective of attaining climate neutrality by 2050 and reducing GHG emissions by 55% by 2030 below 1990 levels appears notably more ambitious than the pre-existing targets.[63] As a party to the Paris Agreement, the EU has already pledged to achieve carbon neutrality by 2050, with some of its Members, like France, explicitly including that target in their national climate strategies.[64]

Meeting the ambitious climate objectives demands a profound transformation of the energy system, driven in part by increased targets for the production and consumption of renewable energy. This was deemed particularly crucial given that the energy sector contributes over 75%of total GHG emissions.[65] Building upon the ambitious 2030 climate and energy targets, the RePowerEU Plan sought to further accelerate the energy transition to simultaneously achieve economic and 'green' objectives. It seeks to advance the energy transition not only for the sake of decarbonization but also to ensure energy supply security and reduce dependence on Russian fuel imports.[66] With ORE offering a higher average output than land-based installations, they are projected to become a core component of Europe's energy system by 2050 and substantially contribute to carbon neutrality. To that end, the 2020 Offshore Renewable Energy Strategy initially proposed specific actions and milestones to increase the installed capacity of ORE five-fold by 2030 and 30-fold by 2050.[67] By quantifying these targets and setting time frames, the Commission can monitor the progress and intervene when necessary.

---

[60] COM (2023) 102 final, pp. 11–12.

[61] The plan further provides that in order to assist Member States, 30% of the European Maritime and Fisheries Fund should contribute to support the transition to more selective and less damaging fishing techniques, COM (2023) 102 final, pp. 12–15.

[62] IPCC (2018) Summary for Policymakers Special Report on Global Warming of 1.5C. https://www.ipcc.ch/sr15/chapter/spm/. Accessed on 25 Aug 2025.

[63] COM (2020) 562 final; European Council (2014) Conclusions on 2030 Climate and Energy Policy Framework. EUCO 169/14.

[64] Laurent (2020), p. 3.

[65] COM (2021) 557 final, Proposal for a Directive of the European Parliament and of the Council Amending Directive (EU) 2018/2001 of the European Parliament and of the Council, Regulation (EU) 2018/1999 of the European Parliament and of the Council and Directive 98/70/EC of the European Parliament and of the Council as regards the promotion of energy from renewable sources, and repealing Council Directive (EU) 2015/652.

[66] COM (2022) 108 final, Communication from the Commission to the European Parliament, the Council, the European Economic and Social Committee and the Committee of the Regions. Communication from the European Commission on REPowerEU: Join European Action for more affordable, secure and sustainable energy.

[67] COM (2020) 741 final.

Since then, Member States have raised their ambitions to achieve 111 GW of ORE by 2030, nearly doubling the goal set by the 2020 Strategy.[68] Additionally, increasing targets have been set for 2040 and 2050 for each EU's sea basin. The Commission estimates that to bridge the gap between the existing capacity and the 2030 target, almost 12 GW/year on average will need to be installed – a figure 10 times higher than the 1.2 GW installed in 2022.[69] Despite the progress made so far, the disparity between the ambitious goals and actual installations underscores the urgent need to rapidly increase the existing capacity by 2030, while also overcoming existing economic, regulatory and technical obstacles.

Recognizing the financial and technological challenges the European offshore wind industry is facing, the European Wind Action Plan set out further urgent measures to support the EU offshore wind sector.[70] Strategies to boost ORE are complemented by various opportunities for financial support, including the Innovation Fund, the Recovery and Resilience Facility, InvestEU, and the Just Transition Fund.[71] Nonetheless, the main responsibility still rests on the Member States for realising these targets, despite action being taken at the EU level.[72]

Other core sectors of the Blue Economy must also contribute to the overarching climate goal, yet without discussing their potential trade-offs for marine biodiversity. In that regard, transport via short sea shipping is projected to increase by 25 percent by 2030, with zero-emission vessels expected to be market-ready by 2030, alongside a series of measures to decarbonize maritime transport.[73] This aligns with the target of reducing emissions from the transport sector by 90 per cent below 1990 levels by 2050,[74] representing a considerable increase compared to the previous policy goal of 60 percent reduction.[75]

2.3 Interim Conclusion

The EGD has introduced a comprehensive climate neutrality lens to all its policies, representing a paradigm shift compared to the priorities of the 2014–2019 Commission.[76] Despite their indivisibility,[77] there appears to be a dichotomy between climate-energy

[68] COM (2023) 688 final, Communication from the Commission to the European Parliament, the Council, the European Economic and Social Committee and the Committee of the Regions. Delivering on the EU offshore renewable energy ambitions, pp. 2–3.

[69] Press release (2023) Commission sets out immediate actions to support the European wind power industry', https://ec.europa.eu/commission/presscorner/api/files/document/print/en/ip_23_5185/IP_23_5185_EN.pdf. Accessed on 25 Aug 2025.

[70] COM (2023) 669 final, Communication from the Commission to the European Parliament, the Council, the European Economic and Social Committee and the Committee of the Regions. European Wind Power Action Plan.

[71] COM/2023/669 final, pp. 6–7.

[72] Van der Sluis (2023), p. 233.

[73] COM (2020) 789 final; Sustainable Blue Economy Strategy.

[74] COM (2020) 789 final; Sustainable Blue Economy Strategy.

[75] COM (2011) 144 final, White paper roadmap to a single European Transport Area - towards a competitive and resource efficient transport system.

[76] Bongardt and Torres (2021), p. 172.

[77] Charveriat and Holme (2021).

objectives and those concerning marine biodiversity conservation. The policy targets under these two streams do not exhibit the same level of ambition.[78] Climate neutrality emerges as the predominant goal across the majority of the EGD strategies, emphasising the anticipated contribution of other policies, such as the ones on biodiversity conservation, to climate mitigation and adaptation, albeit partially addressing potential negative impacts on biodiversity goals resulting from climate-related measures.[79]

Targets for the sustainable blue economy, including initiatives to boost offshore energy, increase short sea shipping, and exploited fisheries to safeguard food security may not align seamlessly with commitments to expand and strengthen the protection of MPAs while reducing adverse impact of economic activities on sensitive marine ecosystems. Although maritime spatial plans, the strict application of environmental legislation and the improvement of stakeholders' involvement are briefly mentioned as mechanisms to address potential trade-offs, specific action on translating these measures into detailed implementation measures are lacking. However, achieving a truly sustainable Blue Economy necessitates decoupling the utilisation of marine natural capital from the impacts on marine ecosystem capital.[80]

3 The Imbalanced Transformation of the EGD's Marine-Related Objectives into Implementation Instruments

The crux of the matter, however, lies in whether all the EGD's promises are accompanied by concrete legislative and regulatory initiatives to ensure their fulfilment. Policy objectives without efficient legal enforcement mechanisms risk remaining empty promises, unable to catalyse the envisioned sustainability transformation.[81] The dichotomy between climate-energy and biodiversity objectives is similarly evident at this stage of the EGD's policy implementation cycle, as the objectives under these two streams lack equal support from legislative instruments.

Regarding marine biodiversity conservation, the scarcity of proposals for revising existing legislation and adopting new legal commitments does not appear to align with the level of ambition of the biodiversity-related strategies (3.1). Conversely, the EU legislative machinery has already generated a broad package of legislative proposals in the field of climate and energy law to achieve the 55% GHG reduction by 2030, attesting to their centrality to the EGD's objective of establishing a sustainable Union (3.2). These instruments translate the overarching climate neutrality objective into legally binding targets and establish implementation mechanisms firmly rooted in the transformation of critical economic sectors, including energy and transport.[82]

78 Paleari (2022), pp. 214–215.

79 Paleari (2024), p. 6.

80 European Environmental Agency (2019) Marine Messages II, Navigating the Course towards clean, healthy and productive seas through implementation of an ecosystem-based approach, p. 6. https://www.eea.europa.eu/en/analysis/publications/marine-messages-2. Accessed 25 Aug 2025.

81 Sikora (2021), p. 684.

82 Romppanen and Huhta (2023), p. 53.

3.1 The Dea(r)th of Legislative Proposals Implementing Marine Biodiversity Objectives

The EU Biodiversity Strategy suggests that expanding and strengthening the protection of marine areas can be accomplished through the implementation of existing EU rules.[83] For instance, article 10 of the HD, imposes a weakened obligation on Member States to endeavour, where they consider it necessary, to improve the ecological coherence of Natura 2000. This flexible duty is supplemented by article 13(4) of the MSFD, which requires States to contribute to coherent and representative networks of MPAs, adequately covering the diversity of constituent ecosystems as part of the measures required to achieve GES.

However, these instruments have significant shortcomings.[84] Despite being the cornerstone of EU nature conservation law, the implementation of the Nature Directives alone cannot successfully achieve the Biodiversity Strategy's marine environmental protection targets. This is due to several factors, including the limited coverage of marine habitats and species,[85] as well as the incomplete and fragmented network of MPAs, which fails to address the interconnected challenges the ocean faces.[86]

Although the Commission has recognized that the implementation of the existing EU environmental rules has been incomplete, that the restoration of marine areas has taken place on a small scale and that enforcement is insufficient,[87] it has not proposed any revisions of the Nature Directives.[88] Instead, it has limited its 'intervention' in releasing a guidance on the designation of additional protected areas.[89] It is worth noting that the Annexes to the Nature Directives, adopted more than 25 years ago, do not incorporate recent scientific knowledge, as the procedures for updating those lists have never been applied.[90] The Commission reiterates that Member States bear the responsibility for designating additional protected areas and taking action to enhance implementation.[91]

---

83 The MSFD is the only existing environmental directive currently under review since 2021, pursuant to its article 23.

84 Puharinen (2023); Giannopoulos (2023), pp. 165–168.

85 Significant aspects of the marine ecosystem are excluded, such as marine fish (commercially exploited species), invertebrate species (mussels and sea stars) and marine offshore habitats (sandbanks below 20m or soft bottom habitats) and their associated communities of fauna and flora. Some threatened species, such as sharks benefit only from catch restrictions under the CFP, COM (2009) 40 final, Communication from the Commission on a European Action Plan for the Conservation and Management of Sharks.

86 European Court of Auditors (2020).

87 COM (2020) 380 final, p. 3.

88 COM (2020) 380 final, p. 5: the Commission has pledged to assess if the combined efforts of the Member States are sufficient to reach EU-wide targets or whether stronger actions, including EU legislation, are needed.

89 European Commission (2022) Criteria and guidance for protected areas designations. SWD/2022/23 final. https://environment.ec.europa.eu/system/files/2022-01/SWD_guidance_protected_areas.pdf. Accessed 25 Aug 2025.

90 European Environmental Agency (2015) Report 3/2015: Marine protected areas in Europe's seas. https://www.eea.europa.eu/en/analysis/publications/marine-protected-areas-in-europes. Accessed 25 Aug 2025.

91 COM (2020) 380 final, pp. 4–5.

However, experience has shown that relying solely on Member States to take action is not effective unless the EU provides for financial or other sanctions for non-compliance.[92]

The Commission has further promised to strengthen the enforcement of EU environmental legislation by improving public participation and access to justice.[93] In its communication on improving access to justice, the Commission explicitly acknowledged the public's role as a driving force in the green transition, noting that individuals and NGOS *"play a crucial role in identifying potential breaches of EU law by submitting complaints to administrations and taking cases to courts."*[94] As a result, it advocated for the inclusion of provisions on access to justice in EU legislative proposals or revised EU law concerning environmental matters.[95] After lengthy negotiations, a revision of the Aarhus Regulation was adopted in 2021.[96]

Furthermore, on 22 June 2022, the Commission published a proposal for a Regulation on Nature Restoration, a key instrument for implementing the new restoration objectives outlined in the Biodiversity Strategy 2030. The proposed Regulation aimed at establishing *"a framework within which Member States shall put in place, without delay, effective and area-based restoration measures which together shall cover, by 2030, at least 20% of the Union's land and sea areas and, by 2050, all ecosystems in need of restoration."*[97] Hinting at the indivisibility of biodiversity and the climate mitigation and adaptation objectives, it emphasises that restoring nature not only facilitates long-term recovery but also enhances resilience, aligning with the EU's climate commitments and international obligations.[98]

Supplementing existing EU environmental legislation, the Nature Restoration Regulation purports to facilitate the recovery of ecosystems both within and outside protected areas. Its broad scope of application makes it a rather unique environmental law instrument. The new Regulation adopted on 24 June 2024 operationalises the EGD's restoration targets into legally binding commitments with specific deadlines, and is applicable to marine ecosystems, which are not covered by the Nature Directives. Article 5, dedicated to marine ecosystems, requires Member States to put in place restoration measures covering 30% of certain marine habitat types, 60% by 2040 and 90% by 2050.[99] It entails obligations for the restoration of certain habitat types included in its Annexes but also for specific ecosystems. Continuous improvement of the environmental status of

---

92 Kramer (2020), p. 292.

93 COM (2019) 640 final, p. 23.

94 COM (2020) 643 final, Communication from the Commission to the European Parliament, the Council, the European Economic and Social Committee and the Committee of the Regions. Improving access to justice in environmental matters in the EU and its Member States, p. 9.

95 COM (2020) 643 final, p. 33.

96 Regulation (EU) 2021/1767 of the European Parliament and of the Council of 6 October 2021 amending Regulation (EC) 1367/2006 on the application of the provisions of the Aarhus Convention on Access to Information, Public Participation in Decision-Making and Access to Justice in Environmental Matters to Community Institutions and Bodies, OJ L 356, 8.10.2021.

97 EU (2022) Proposal for a Regulation of the European Parliament and the Council on Nature Restoration, COM(2022) 204 final, art 1(2).

98 See also Explanatory Memorandum to COM/2022/304 – Nature Restoration.

99 Regulation (EU) 2024/1991, Article 5(1).

these habitats/ecosystems until reaching a good condition[100] and prevention of deterioration are also required.[101] These duties and targets must be further pursued by Member States through the adoption of national restoration plans, which need to be periodically reviewed.[102]

Despite its broader scope, the proposal's restoration measures are limited to specific habitats,[103] overlooking the ecosystem-based approach of the MSFD. Unfortunately, political resistance to the proposal led to a Provisional Agreement text between the Parliament and the Council, featuring significantly weakened provisions.[104] Following the significant decrease in ambition by the Council in June 2023, the Parliament introduced more than 100 amendments which severely weakened the initial proposal by lowering its overall ambition, granting Member States greater discretion in implementation, shifting its core priorities.[105] In November 2023, after several rounds of negotiations, a political compromise was reached between the Commission, Parliament, and Council during the Trilogue. The European Parliament approved this compromise in February 2024, but the final Council vote, initially scheduled for March, was postponed due to a lack of majority support, largely influenced by shifting Member State positions in response to farmer protests and upcoming elections.[106]

The main weakness of the final text of the Nature Restoration Regulation lies in its significant weakening of the non-deterioration obligations, which are crucial for ensuring long-term ecosystem recovery.[107] Originally, the regulation included two strong non-deterioration clauses—one for restored habitats and another for all Annex I and II habitat types. However, the final text limits protection to only *"significant"* deterioration, introducing legal ambiguity and reducing enforceability.[108] Additionally, the regulation reinforces the primacy of climate objectives over biodiversity protection, particularly by granting renewable energy projects an overriding public interest status without a temporal limit.[109] This legal framework allows exemptions from restoration obligations, prioritising the rapid expansion of renewables even when less damaging alternatives exist. As a result, the Nature Restoration Law paradoxically undermines

[100] Regulation (EU) 2024/1991, Article 5(9).

[101] Regulation (EU) 2024/1991, Article 5(9). These non-deterioration provisions have been significantly weakened from obligations of result into obligations of conduct in the final text of the Regulation. On the provisions on non- deterioration, De Leeuw and Backes (2024).

[102] Regulation (EU) 2024/1991, Articles 11–15.

[103] Art 5(1) referring only to habitats included under its Annex II.

[104] Cliquet et al. (2024).

[105] Society for Ecological Restoration Europe Legal Working Group (2023) The EU Nature Restoration Law: avoiding legal pitfalls in further negotiations.https://chapter.ser.org/europe/. Accessed 25 Aug 2025.

[106] Cagney (2024) Nature Restoration Law fails to Secure Support at Critical Member States Meeting. Euractiv, https://www.euractiv.com/section/biodiversity/news/breaking-nature-restoration-law-fails-to-secure-support-at-critical-member-states-meeting/. Accessed 25 Aug 2025.

[107] De Leeuw and Backes (2024).

[108] Regulation (EU) 2024/1991, Article5(9).

[109] Regulation (EU) 2024/1991, Article 6.

its core goal—biodiversity recovery—by making it legally subordinate to climate and energy policies.[110]

3.2 The Elaborate Package of Legislative Measures at the Service of Climate Neutrality

In the climate-energy domain, there have been remarkable legislative developments both in terms of quantity and complexity.[111] The proposals aimed at delivering the overall climate neutrality target have followed a trend of adopting comprehensive packages of legislative initiatives to meet increasingly ambitious objectives.[112] Achieving these objectives involves a convoluted normative process, where various legal instruments intersect, subject to varying EU competences and involving diverse institutions with potentially competing interests.

The first significant step in that direction was taken with the adoption of EU Climate Law, in 2021, which serves as the cornerstone of the EGD.[113] It is, however, noteworthy, that while the EU Climate Law enshrined climate objectives into binding law for the EU and its Member States, it did not clarify how the burden must be shared among them.[114] Demonstrating a clear prioritisation of the EGD's climate objectives, it mandates the Commission to *"assess the consistency of any draft measure or legislative proposal with the climate neutrality objective"* as well as the interim targets established for 2030 and 2040.[115] Additionally, it requires periodic reviews of all Union measures to ensure their alignment with the climate-neutrality objective every five years.[116] Climate neutrality also becomes a new additional criterion for reporting and evaluating the National Energy and Climate Plans under the EU Governance Regulation.[117] These measures appear to operationalise the environmental integration principle under article 11 TFEU, stipulating that all Union measures must integrate the EGD's climate targets.

To ensure that all EU policies contribute to the net zero objective and that every sector plays its part, the Commission devised a plan to review all relevant instruments and propose revisions, where necessary.[118] In July 2021, the Commission unveiled the

---

[110] Devis (2024) Change of paradigm in EU environmental law: does the climate crisis now override the biodiversity crisis?, European Law Blog. https://www.europeanlawblog.eu/pub/l74pacq5/release/4, Accessed 25 Aug 2025.

[111] Peeters and Misonne (2022), p. 60.

[112] Birger Skjaerseth (2021), p. 25.

[113] Regulation (EU) 2021/1119 of the European Parliament and of the Council of 30 June 2021 establishing the framework for achieving climate neutrality and amending Regulations (EC) No 401/2009 and (EU) 2018/1999 ('European Climate Law'), OJ L 243, 9.7.2021.

[114] Regulation (EU) 2021/1119, art 44(1).

[115] Regulation (EU) 2021/1119, art 6(4).

[116] Regulation (EU) 2021/1119 establishing the framework for achieving climate neutrality and amending Regulations (EC) No 401/2009 and (EU) 2018/1999, art 6(2).

[117] Regulation (EU) 2021/1119, art 13.

[118] COM/2019/640 final, p. 6 'Further decarbonizing the energy system is critical to reach climate objectives in 2030 and 2050. The production and use of energy across economic sectors account for more than 75% of the EU's green gas emissions. … A power sector must be developed that is based largely on renewable energy sources, complemented by the rapid phasing out of coal

package of legislative proposals to deliver the EU's 2030 target, known as 'Fit-for-55'. This package includes reforms to all major pillars of the EU's energy and climate legal landscape, encompassing the ETS Directive, the RED II, the EED and the ETD.[119] While discussing the full series of instruments under the Fit for 55 package exceeds the scope of this chapter,[120] some notable changes concerning ocean governance include the expansion of the EU ETS scope to cover all intra-EU and, partly extra-EU maritime transport, signalling to the sector to sail away from fossil fuels.[121] In addition, the revised Renewable Energy Directive requires MS to collectively ensure that at least 42,5% of all gross energy consumed in the EU comes from renewable sources by 2030, with an aspiration to reach 45%.[122]

The revised Trans-European Networks for Energy (TEN-E) Regulation also streamlines permitting provisions, including the establishment of a single point of contact for offshore projects of common interest, such as offshore hybrid interconnectors and cross-border energy islands, to prevent delays impeding the energy transition.[123] In an effort to expedite the deployment of renewable energy projects,[124] the Council adopted an emergency regulation as part of the RepowerEU Plan, which simplified and shortened

---

and decarbonizing gas... The regulatory framework for energy infrastructure, including the TEN-E Regulation will need to be reviewed to ensure consistency with the climate neutrality objective'.

[119] COM (2021) 550 final, Communication from the Commission to the European Parliament, the Council, the European Economic and Social Committee and the Committee of the Regions. Fit for 55: Delivering the EU's 2030 Climate Target on the way to climate neutrality.

[120] Schlacke et al. (2022).

[121] SWD/2021/601 final, Commission Staff Working Document. Impact Assessment Report Accompanying the document Directive of the European Parliament and of the Council amending Directive 2003/87/EC establishing a system for greenhouse gas emission allowance trading within the Union, Decision (EU) 2015/1814 concerning the establishment and operation of a market stability reserve for the Union greenhouse gas emission trading scheme and Regulation (EU) 2015/757, 14.7.2021.

[122] The Directive also covers renewable energy produced by wind farms at sea, Directive (EU) 2023/2413 of the European Parliament and of the Council of 18 October 2023 amending Directive (EU) 2018/2001, Regulation (EU) 2018/1999 and Directive 98/70/EC as regards the promotion of energy from renewable sources, and repealing Council Directive (EU) 2015/652, OJ L, 2023/2413, 31.10.2023, art 2.

[123] Regulation (EU) 2022/869 of the European Parliament and of the Council of 30 May 2022 on guidelines for trans-European energy infrastructure, amending Regulations (EC) No 715/2009, (EU) 2019/942 and (EU) 2019/943 and Directives 2009/73/EC and (EU) 2019/944, and repealing Regulation (EU) No 347/2013, OJ L 152, p. 45, 3.6.2022.

[124] To further support the implementation of these legislative measures, the EU has issued a Recommendation on speeding up the permit process, which includes best practice examples to support the expansion of offshore renewable energy, such as multi-use platforms and environmental pre-assessment of designated sites: SWD/2022/149 final, Commission Staff Working Document. Guidance to Member States on good practices to speed up permit-granting procedures for renewable energy projects and on facilitating Power Purchase Agreements Accompanying the document Commission Recommendation on speeding up permit-granting procedures for renewable energy projects and facilitating Power Purchase Agreements, 18.5.2022. As a

permitting procedures.[125] Despite divergences in domestic implementation, the emergency regulation has yielded results, with a record volume of new permits issued in 2023.[126] Additionally, several other legislative proposals, such as the Net Zero Industry Act and the Critical Raw Materials Act, aim to support the development of net-zero technologies crucial for expanding the rollout of renewables by accelerating permitting for manufacturing facilities.[127]

When evaluating the abundance and diversity of legislative proposals pertaining to the EU's climate neutrality objective, it is crucial to acknowledge that time is a luxury in short supply. Some obligations, such as those concerning the decarbonization of the maritime transport sector under the Refuel Maritime are only triggered after 2030.[128] Therefore, achieving a *"transformational change ... across our economy, society and industry"* within less than a decade is remarkably ambitious,[129] especially considering that many of these instruments entail a lengthy transposition period, which could delay their domestic implementation.[130] However, the legality of adopting the emergency regulation under the special legislative process of article 122 TFEU may raise concerns from a rule of law perspective, as it might be seen as a means to circumvent Parliamentary scrutiny while introducing significant amendments to existing EU environmental rules, even if only temporarily.[131] The rule of law appears to face challenges, when democratic procedures for law-making are viewed as impediments. Framing the issue as a matter of security not only legitimises any measures – portrayed as exceptional and temporary – but also expands the power of the executive, relegating the Parliament to a secondary role. This reduction in transparency in the law-making process and the diminished ability of judges to hold the executive accountable are consequential outcomes of this approach.[132]

These legislative proposals indicate a departure from the EU's previous regulatory strategies, which relied on an 'open method of coordination' of national measures to promote the energy transition. This method set overarching targets to increase the overall consumption of renewable energy at EU level, granting Member States considerable

follow-up an informal expert group has been created to discuss the implementation of recommendations and exchange good practices on, *inter alia,* the permit-granting process for offshore renewables.

125 Council Regulation (EU) 2022/2577 laying down a framework to accelerate the deployment of renewable energy. ST/14787/2022/INIT. OJ L 335. pp. 36–44.

126 COM(2023) 669 final, p. 5.

127 COM(2023) 161, Proposal for a regulation of the European Parliament and of the Council on establishing a framework of measures for strengthening Europe's net-zero technology products manufacturing ecosystem (Net Zero Industry Act); COM(2023) 160 final, Proposal for a regulation of the European Parliament and of the Council establishing a framework for ensuring a secure and sustainable supply of critical raw materials and amending Regulations (EU) 168/2013, (EU) 2018/858, 2018/1724 and (EU) 2019/1020..

128 EU (2023) Regulation of the European Parliament and of the Council on the use of renewable and low-carbon fuels in maritime transport, and amending Directive 2009/16/EC. PE-CONS 26/23. OJ L 234, 22.9.2023, pp. 48–100.

129 COM(2021) 550 final.

130 Scheuing and Kamm (2022), p. 16.

131 Javier Dura-Aleman et al. (2023), p. 2.

132 Van Zeben et al. (2022), p. 2.

freedom to choose the sources in their national energy mix.[133] This transformation of EU energy rules to implement the EGD appears to be catalysed by the securitization of the objective of climate neutrality.[134] This shift has recently prompted the CJEU to adopt a more restrictive interpretation of Member States' sovereignty over their energy mix.[135] Their freedom to select their energy sources cannot be unlimited, but the EU should be empowered, given its role in environmental protection and climate change mitigation, to make decisions promoting certain renewable energy sources as long this does not *significantly* impinge on Member States' choices.[136] However, Member States are still not subject to binding requirements concerning their individual contributions to the overall climate and energy targets.[137] Instead, each of them must pledge a specific amount to be delivered within the set deadlines and periodically report on the measures adopted to meet their targets.[138]

3.3 Interim Conclusions

This brief analysis highlights disparities in the support provided by legislative implementation instruments for the various EGD's policy streams, with significant discrepancies between progress made in the climate-energy domain compared to biodiversity.[139] While the Commission has identified deficiencies in the implementation of existing EU environmental law, its proposals to remedy this situation are notably poor.[140] In the words of the European Environmental Agency "*the partial successes seem barely to register against the observed continued degradation and the expected increased use of the sea, as well as the observed and forecast worsening of climate change impacts on Europe's seas*".[141] It is, therefore, evident that achieving the biodiversity objectives requires the adaptation and development of the EU legal framework, specifically sectoral, legislation regulating resource-intensive activities that accentuate marine biodiversity loss.[142]

---

133 Hardiman (2022), p. 195.

134 Van Zeben et al. (2022), p. 14.

135 Case C-5/16, Poland v European Parliament and Council of the European Union (2018), ECLI:EU:C:2018:483, p. 23–24. Para. 43.

136 Case C-5/16, Poland v Parliament and Council (2018), p. 23–24. Para. 46.

137 Peeters and Athanasiadou (2020).

138 See also Regulation (EU) 2018/1999 of the European Parliament and of the Council on the Governance of the Energy Union and Climate Action, amending Regulations (EC) No 663/2009 and (EC) No 715/2009 of the European Parliament and of the Council, Directives 94/22/EC, 98/70/EC, 2009/31/EC, 2009/73/EC, 2010/31/EU, 2012/27/EU and 2013/30/EU of the European Parliament and of the Council, Council Directives 2009/119/EC and (EU) 2015/652 and repealing Regulation (EU) No 525/2013 of the European Parliament and of the Council, OJ L 328, 21.12.2018.

139 Charveriat and Holme (2021), p. 17.

140 Kramer (2020), pp. 293–294.

141 European Environmental Agency (2019) The European Environment - state and outlook 2020. https://www.eea.europa.eu/en/analysis/publications/soer-2020. Accessed on 25 Aug 2025.

142 Paleari (2022), pp. 214–215.

4 The Interaction of the EU Legal Instruments Concerning Marine Environmental Protection and the Blue Energy Transition

These novel EGD implementation instruments, primarily focusing on swiftly realising its time-sensitive climate-energy targets, have entered an already convoluted EU legal framework, raising concerns about potential normative conflicts. The following section examines the potential synergies and frictions among the legal instruments implementing the EGD, particularly focusing on the interactions between measures designed to expand ORE while addressing the loss of marine biodiversity. The Commission has thus far adopted a narrative that downplays potential trade-offs and instead emphasises the positive interplay of these activities (4.1). Although it recommends the use of Maritime Spatial Planning (MSP) to alleviate possible tensions by allocating marine space according to the carrying capacity of marine ecosystems, the implementation of this tool presents weaknesses (4.2). Moreover, recent normative developments, aiming at accelerating the energy transition, in light of the failure to successfully revise or adopt new binding rules on biodiversity restoration and conservation, appear to disrupt the necessary balance between climate-energy action and marine environmental protection (4.3).

4.1 The Commission's Optimistic Discourse on the Potential Synergies

Aligned with its clear prioritisation of climate goals, the EGD relies on the ocean for the decarbonisation of the EU. Besides its key contribution as a natural carbon sink, the ocean is projected to play a key role in the energy transition from fossil fuels to ORE.[143] The Commission acknowledges that the objectives relating to the energy transition will inevitably interact and possibly clash with those of marine biodiversity protection.[144] In its proposal for the Nature Restoration Regulation, it emphasised the need to ensure the *"sound coexistence"* between offshore installations and the marine environment,[145] where *"restoration of biodiversity should take into account the deployment of renewable energy and vice versa."*[146]

The Commission, however, underestimates the environmental impact of ORE. According to its 2020 Offshore Renewable Energy Strategy, the expansion of offshore installations required to meet the 2030 climate and renewable energy targets occupies less than 3% of the European Maritime Space, suggesting a marginal impact on marine biodiversity.[147] This assumption appears overly simplistic since it overlooks the interconnectedness of the marine environment and the potentially varying carrying capacity and sensitivity of the marine basins surrounding the EU.[148] It is not solely a matter

143 COM (2020) 741 final.

144 COM(2020/380 final; Regulation (EU) 2024/1991.

145 COM (2020) 741 final.

146 Regulation (EU) 2024/1991, Recital 68.

147 COM (2020) 741 final.

148 European Environmental Agency (2019) Marine Messages II, Navigating the Course towards clean, healthy and productive seas through implementation of an ecosystem-based approach. https://www.eea.europa.eu/en/analysis/publications/marine-messages-2. Accessed on 25 Aug 2025.

of spatial requirements but also whether the cumulative, long-term pressures from the proliferation of new installations might surpass the ecological limits of different marine regions, potentially jeopardising the attainment of good environmental status.[149]

In its recent report, the European Court of Auditors highlights that the EU has left the impact of ORE installations beyond their immediate surroundings and their potential cumulative effects unaddressed.[150] The Commission's silence on the spatial requirements to achieve the 2050 targets is also notable. As early as 2020, meeting these targets necessitated an increase in the installed capacity of ORE.[151] However, the ambitious targets of both the EU and its Member States have surged even further by 2023.[152] The potential for trade-offs is significant, especially considering the objectives to transform 30% of European marine space into MPAs, including a third of them under strict protection.[153] Consequently, the Commission's perspective downplays the extent of the potential conflict between the projected proliferation of ORE installations and the protection of the marine environment.[154]

Moreover, the Commission's techno-solutionist approach, which portrays untested future technologies as a primary means of mitigating the impact of ORE on marine ecosystems,[155] is significantly undermined by the dearth of scientific knowledge regarding the effects of mitigating measures.[156]

4.2 MSP, a Flawed Solution to Reconcile the Conflicting Objectives of the Marine-Related Strategies

To alleviate conflicts between ORE and marine biodiversity, the EGD relies on an existing framework, namely the Maritime Spatial Planning (MSP) Directive.[157] Several marine-related EGD strategies make cross-references to MSP[158] portraying it as a key enabler for the sustainable blue economy.[159] MSP aims to *"ensur[e] that potential negative impacts on the natural environment are identified and avoided at a very early stage in the planning process."*[160] This instrument is therefore crafted to improve compatibility

149 European Court of Auditors (2020).

150 European Court of Auditors (2023) Special Report Offshore Renewable Energy in the EU, Ambitious Plans for Growth but Sustainability Remains a Challenge, paras. 98 and 101.

151 COM (2020) 741 final.

152 COM (2023) 668 final.

153 Galparsoro et al. (2022), p. 63.

154 COM (2023) 668 final, para. 96.

155 COM (2020) 741 final.

156 Haugen et al. (2024).

157 European Council (2019) Presidency Conclusions, p. 4; Directive 2014/89/EU of the European Parliament and of the Council of 23 July 2014 establishing a framework for maritime spatial planning, OJ L, p. 135, 28.8.2014.

158 E.g., COM(2020) 741 final; COM(2020) 380 final; COM(2021) 240 final; Directive (EU) 2023/2413.

159 COM (2021) 240 final, p. 15.

160 COM (2021) 240 final, p.15.

between potentially competing uses of the sea, including *"designated sea spaces for offshore energy exploitation"* and *"biodiversity protection"*.[161]

As a strategic planning tool which intended to contribute towards the achievement of GES of EU seas,[162] MSP holds, at first sight, significant potential for improving EU ocean governance.[163] This horizontal and cross-sectoral policy tool can seemingly foster positive interactions between the different uses of the ocean in the European region.[164] It promotes multi-use of maritime space, which is particularly relevant in crowded marine areas.[165] This function of MSP becomes even more crucial given that the objective of reaching climate neutrality demands the expansive use of maritime space for renewable energy production. Therefore, MSP appears essential to realise the blue energy transition. However, due to the EU's lack of competence in this field, the MSPD only lays down minimum requirements about the content of national MSPs, allowing Member States broad discretion in allocating marine space to different ocean uses.[166]

According to the MSPD, the ecosystem-based approach is a fundamental principle underpinning this planning tool.[167] Ecosystem-based management has emerged as a reply to the predominantly sectoral, piecemeal management of the environment under environmental law and is defined by the OSPAR Commission as the *"comprehensive integrated management of human activities in the marine environment based upon the best available scientific knowledge about the ecosystem and its dynamics"*.[168] The underlying rationale is that adopting such a management approach can prevent irreversible damage caused by the long-term accumulation of anthropogenic stressors on interconnected marine ecosystems.[169] While scientists have differing views on its practical implementation, there is a consensus that this approach should involve integrated management solutions for various offshore sectoral activities (such as fishing, transport, energy, and aquaculture).[170] Additionally, it should prioritise mitigating risks to marine ecosystems to maintain their resilience and ensure the continued provision of essential goods and services for present and future generations. Therefore, this integrated and

161 COM (2020) 741 final; COM(2020) 562 final.

162 Directive 2014/89/EU, para. 22. See also, Frank (2008), pp. 789- 798.

163 Galparsoro et al. (2022), p. 62.

164 COM/2007/575, Communication from the Commission to the European Parliament, the Council, the European Economic and Social Committee and the Committee of the Regions, An Integrated Maritime Policy for the European Union. See also, COM(2012) 0494, Communication from the Commission to the European Parliament, the Council, the European Economic and Social Committee and the Committee of the Regions, Blue growth opportunities for marine and maritime sustainable growth.

165 The Offshore Renewable Energy Strategy and the Sustainable Blue Economy Strategy promote a more multi-use and multi-sectoral approach to MSP.

166 Art 2, 4 and 5 Directive 2014/89/EU, pp. 135–145.

167 Directive 2014/89/EU, pp. 135–145, recital 3.

168 See, OSPAR Commission. https://www.ospar.org/convention/principles/ecosystem-approach#:~:text=For%20the%20purpose%20of%20the,to%20the%20health%20of%20marine. Accessed 25 Aug 2025.

169 Directive 2008/56/EC, pp. 19–40. Recital 44.

170 Long (2011), p. 12.

holistic approach can, in principle, help reconcile the environmental impacts of the projected expansion of ORE as it requires the consideration and inclusion of all dimensions of sustainability into a single management scheme.[171] This approach can, thus, enable the harmonious coexistence of natural processes and human activities in the same maritime space.[172] Moreover, as a *"continuing, iterative process that learns and adapts over time,"* its dynamic nature allows for its adaptation to the evolving scientific knowledge of the natural processes of the marine environment as well as the implications of the activities increasingly carried out at sea, such as offshore wind energy generation.[173] However, despite these apparent qualities of MSP, its ability to balance conservation with development is not guaranteed.

MSP can play a central role in expediting the permitting process for new ORE installations. Specifically, the MSPD requires Member States to design their national MSPs with the aim of facilitating the co-location of several marine activities, including ORE generation.[174] The Directive explicitly purports to promote economic growth in the maritime sector,[175] yet is not a facilitator of sustainable ocean development *per se.*[176] Its effectiveness in contributing to marine environmental protection depends on the degree to which environmental considerations are incorporated in national MSP.[177] Where MSP primarily aims at promoting the expansion of offshore economic activities for the sake of growth, for instance, by advancing the development of offshore projects, without sufficient safeguards for the conservation and restoration of marine ecosystems,[178] it risks undermining marine environmental protection.[179]

Paradoxically, the cross-cutting nature of MSP poses a challenge to implementing its ecosystem-based approach to ocean management, as outlined in the MSPD.[180] In its first implementation report, the Commission acknowledges that applying such an approach has been the main challenge in the designation of MSP.[181] Relevantly, the Commission has issued *Guidelines for implementing an ecosystem-based approach in Maritime*

171 Langlet and Rayfuse (2019), pp. 1, 446.

172 (2021) Guidelines for implementing an Ecosystem-based Approach in Maritime Spatial Planning Including a method for the evaluation, monitoring and review of EBA. In: MSP, European Climate, Infrastructure and Environment Executive Agency, pp. 1, 19.

173 (2021) Guidelines for implementing an Ecosystem-based Approach in Maritime Spatial Planning Including a method for the evaluation, monitoring and review of EBA. In: MSP, European Climate, Infrastructure and Environment Executive Agency, p. 17, referring to the IOC-UNESCO 2009 guidance.

174 Directive 2014/89/EU, pp. 135–145. Art 4 and 5.

175 Directive 2014/89/EU, pp. 135–145. Art 5.

176 Yen-Chiang (2021), pp. 12, 24.

177 Yen-Chiang (2021), p. 23.

178 Yen-Chiang (2021), p. 24.

179 Santos et al. (2014), pp. 61–63.

180 COM (2022) 185 final, Report from the Commission to the European Parliament and the Council outlining the progress made in implementing Directive 2014/89/EU establishing a framework for maritime spatial planning, point 4.4.

181 COM (2022) 185 final, point 4.4.

Spatial Planning.[182] However, their influence remains limited, since they were issued after the environmental assessment of most national MSPs had been completed.[183] They also cannot alter the fact that the success of an ecosystem-based approach depends on the political will and the resources committed by Member States to ensure the coordination of their national plans at a regional or sub-regional basis taking into account the ecological carrying capacity.[184] All the more so in semi-enclosed seas such as the Mediterranean, where the success of such a holistic approach relies on the effective cooperation of Member States with third countries and the regional sea institutional mechanisms mandated with the protection of the marine environment.[185]

In addition, the Commission's guidelines confine the ecosystem-based approach to a strong sustainability model.[186] According to that model, *"economic goals can only be pursued if the basic societal needs are fulfilled which, in turn, can only be achieved within the limits of a healthy environment."*[187] Besides assuming the prevalence of environmental goals over social and economic goals, this sustainability model is also based on the misconception that all environmental goals are necessarily compatible. As such, it fails to address the scenario where climate goals, notably the objective of climate neutrality and the ensuing time-bound energy transition, conflict with those of marine biodiversity protection.

As highlighted in the RepowerEU Plan, the rapid transformation of the European energy sector is a matter of utter urgency not only in terms of climate but also from a political and economic perspective.[188] Thus, this imperative of boosting ORE production for the sake of climate and energy security tends to tip the balance in favour of prioritising climate-energy objectives at the detriment of marine environmental protection. This is confirmed by the exemptions contained in recent legislative developments, including the RepowerEU Emergency Regulation, the RED III, revised TEN-E Regulation as well as the watered-down final text of the Nature Restoration Regulation.[189]

182 (2021) Guidelines for implementing an Ecosystem-based Approach in Maritime Spatial Planning Including a method for the evaluation, monitoring and review of EBA. In MSP, European Climate, Infrastructure and Environment Executive Agency, p. 1, 39.

183 COM (2022) 185 final, point 5.1.

184 Hatcher and Bradbury (2006), p. 208.

185 Long (2011), p. 43.

186 (2021) Guidelines for implementing an Ecosystem-based Approach in Maritime Spatial Planning Including a method for the evaluation, monitoring and review of EBA. In MSP, European Climate, Infrastructure and Environment Executive Agency, p.1.

187 (2021) Guidelines for implementing an Ecosystem-based Approach in Maritime Spatial Planning Including a method for the evaluation, monitoring and review of EBA. In MSP, European Climate, Infrastructure and Environment Executive Agency, p. 1.

188 COM (2022)108 final.

189 See Sect. 4.3.

4.3 The Recent Legislative Implementation Instruments: A Light in the Abyss of the EGD to Balance Marine Biodiversity Protection and the Acceleration of the Blue Energy Transition?

The Commission has stressed the urgency of expediting the permitting procedures for renewables to meet the time-sensitive climate-energy goals.[190] In its view, environmental procedural obligations hinder the energy transition by significantly delaying renewable energy projects. Therefore, it was deemed necessary to streamline certain environmental-related aspects of the permitting procedures through a series of new normative developments.[191] To cut on the duration of these processes, the new instruments have introduced two regulatory measures: a) the designation of RAAs, which allow for the simplification of environmental assessments required under EU and domestic law (4.3.1), b) the legislative recognition that renewable energy projects constitute an overriding public interest, justifying their exceptional authorization even when they have significant impacts on legally protected elements of marine biodiversity (4.3.2).

4.3.1 The Designation of RAAs and the Simplification of EU Environmental Rules

A regulatory strategy that could reconcile the proliferation of marine renewables with biodiversity conservation is the designation of dedicated *"renewables go-to areas,"*[192] recently renamed *"renewables acceleration areas" (RAA).*[193] They refer to *"a specific location or area, whether on land, sea or inland waters, which a Member State designated as particularly suitable for the installation of renewable energy plants."*[194] The underlying rationale is that ORE installations will preferably be deployed in areas where their environmental impacts are expected to be limited.[195]

Following the example of the provisions of the Emergency Regulation,[196] the RED III provides that the designation of RAAs entails a duty to carry out a Strategic Environmental Assessment (SEA),[197] to assess the potential impact of each type of renewable energy technology in the relevant RAA and identify necessary rules and mitigation measures.[198] Although a strategic assessment of the potential impacts of such plans allows

---

[190] SWD/2022/149 final, Recitals 7 and 8.

[191] COM (2022) 222 final, Proposal for a Directive of the European Parliament and of the Council amending Directive (EU) 2018/2001 on the promotion of the use of energy from renewable sources, Directive 2010/31/EU on the energy performance of buildings and Directive 2012/27/EU on energy efficiency, recital 7.

[192] COM (2022) 230 final, Communication from the Commission to the European Parliament, the Council, the European Economic and Social Committee and the Committee of the Regions, REPowerEU Plan.

[193] Directive (EU) 2023/2413, Art 15c.

[194] Directive (EU) 2023/2413, Art 1(1)(c).

[195] See, COM (2022) 108 final, explanatory memorandum.

[196] Council Regulation (EU) 2022/2577 laying down a framework to accelerate the deployment of renewable energy. ST/14787/2022/INIT, OJ L 335, p. 36–44, Art 4(1) and recital 6.

[197] See, Directive 2001/42/EC of the European Parliament and of the Council on the assessment of the effects of certain plans and programmes on the environment, OJ L 197, 21.7.2001, pp. 30–37.

[198] Directive (EU) 2023/2413, recital 28 and Art 15c(2).

each Member State to have a more integrated approach to planning and take environmental considerations at a strategic level,[199] it appears to fall short of its purpose for a number of reasons. First, the duty to carry out a SEA is imposed on Member States, without any requirement to assess the cumulative environmental impact of RAAs in the marine areas of EU Member States bordering the same marine region. This lack of a comprehensive assessment is not in conformity with the EU's duty to carry out cumulative SEAs as a contracting party to the Kiev Protocol of the Espoo Convention.[200] Second, the absence of cumulative strategic assessments at the regional level can undermine the overarching duty of EU Member States to achieve a GES of EU seas at the regional level, as required by the MSFD.[201] In particular, the MSFD and its ecosystem-based approach demand an analysis of the sum of negative effects to the overall ecosystem conditions within an entire EU marine region.[202] Meeting that goal requires close cooperation and coordination of the plans for designation of RAAs among Member States. RED III seems to consider this, but only as part of the need to coordinate national Maritime Spatial Plans which include the location of marine renewables.[203]

In addition, the reliability of SEAs to foresee the impact of the planned expansion of ORE projects, especially in the marine environment, is questionable.[204] These assessments are often conducted at a high level of abstraction and defer the quantitative examination of various environmental stressors to the project-level EIAs. Studies have evidenced a gap between perceived and actual risks due to lack of data about the real environmental impacts of these technologies.[205] Similarly, multiple interactions between human activities and ecosystem elements remain understudied. Such considerations are critical especially considering that future ORE projects will add to the cumulative impacts resulting from already existing activities and climate change.[206] This lack of baseline data about the ecological status of the EU seas further undermines the effectiveness of SEA.[207] Equally importantly, there can be no certainty about the physical nature of the individual projects,[208] since technology in the sector, notably offshore wind farms, is rapidly developing.[209]

---

199 The proposal for the Directive provided also for a duty to subject the plans for the designation of RAAs to an appropriate assessment pursuant to article 6(3) HD, proposal article 15c(2), but this requirement has been eliminated from the text of RED III.

200 Jendroska and Anapyanova (2023), p. 4.

201 Art 1(1) Directive 2008/56/EC, pp. 19–40.

202 Art 8(1)(b)(ii) Directive 2008/56/EC, pp. 19–40.

203 Directive (EU) 2023/2413, recital 14.

204 WWF (2022) Position on the legislative proposal to amend the Renewable Energy Directive as part of 'REPowerEU', 'Go-To Areas' for Renewables: Making the Puzzle Fit, https://www.wwf.eu/?7526366/repowereu-RED-revision-position-paper; Caine (2020), p. 84.

205 Galparsoro et al. (2022), p. 1.

206 Galparsoro et al. (2022), p. 2.

207 European Court of Auditors (2020).

208 Pursuant article 3 and 4 the developer of a project bears an obligation to identify all the effects of his project and submit extensive information about the specific characteristics of the project that could harm the environment.

209 Hardiman (2022), p. 199.

ORE projects located within RAAs are presumed as not having significant effects to the environment. They are therefore exempted from the obligation to carry out an environmental impact assessment (EIA) under Directive 2011/92/EU.[210] According to the recital of RED III, *"[i]t is appropriate to allow Member States to introduce derogations from the obligation to carry out [EIA] for wind and solar photovoltaic projects in justified circumstances, because such projects are expected to provide a vast majority of the renewable electricity by 2030."*[211] Although RED III aims to mitigate this gap by requiring Member States to monitor the effects of the implementation of their plans for the designation of RAAs[212] and, when needed, undertake remedial action,[213] this exemption seems inconsistent with prior case law.[214] The CJEU has stressed the complementarity of SEAs and EIAs and the fact that they are not meant to substitute each other.[215] In particular, ORE projects fall under the scope of Annex II of the EIA Directive, meaning that Member States retain some discretion in determining whether in each case an EIA is due in light of their potential impacts.[216] Moreover, despite[217] its obvious benefits in terms of speeding up the permit-granting process for these climate-friendly projects, this derogation appears diametrically opposed to the CJEU's case law, which has upheld that Member States are not allowed to adopt a blanket exception from the duty to carry out an EIA for whole categories of activities listed in Annex II of the EIA Directive, since it would contradict the object and purpose of article 2 of the EIA directive.[218] Needless to say, the duty to conduct EIA is a fundamental expression of the prevention and precaution principles and is therefore indispensable to safeguard a high level of environmental protection,[219] as enshrined in article 191 TFEU.

Going a step further than the Emergency Regulation, RED III also exempts all ORE projects from an appropriate assessment under the HD,[220] despite the EGD's promises to strengthen EU environmental law's implementation to expand the marine Natura 2000 network, increase marine ecosystems protection and strictly protect at least one third of the EU's MPAs.[221] This also suggests that, although RAAs are not allowed within Natura

[210] Directive (EU) 2023/2413, recital 33.

[211] Directive (EU) 2023/2413, recital 35.

[212] Art 8(4) of the EIA Directive provides for mandatory monitoring during the whole life-cycle of projects that are likely to have significant adverse environmental impacts. Directive 2011/92/EU of the European Parliament and of the Council on the assessment of the effects of certain public and private projects on the environment (codification), OJ L 26, 28.1.2012.

[213] Directive (EU) 2023/2413, recital 29.

[214] RED III provides that a renewable energy project which complies with the rules and measures identified in the plans establishing RAAs is presumed as not having significant effects on the environment: Directive (EU) 2023/2413, recital 33.

[215] Case C-9/22, NJ and OZ v. An Bord Pleanála and Others (2023); Case C-671/16, Inter-Environnement Bruxelles ASBL and Others v Région de Bruxelles-Capitale (2018), para. 65.

[216] Directive 2011/92/EU, Art 4(2).

[217] See Sect. 1.

[218] Case C-66/06, Commission of the European Communities v Ireland (2008), para 95.

[219] Directive 2011/92/EU, recitals 2 and 4.

[220] Directive (EU) 2023/2413, Art16a(3).

[221] See Sect. 1.2.1.

2000 sites,[222] the EU legislator is aware and accepts the possibility that ORE installations may cause adverse impacts to such sites in their vicinity.[223] Thus, RED III requires Member States to adopt *"effective mitigation measures"* to ensure compliance with the non-deterioration duties for these sites and the rules on species protection under the Nature Directives.[224] It remains, however, obscure how Member States can select these effective mitigation measures to be applied in a *"proportionate and timely manner"* in the absence of an appropriate assessment both when designating an RAA and authorising individual projects, which would precisely identify the risks posed by each new ORE project.[225] Admittedly, the Emergency Regulation contained an even more controversial provision required the *"appropriate and proportionate mitigation measures"* to be based on *"existing data"*,[226] largely unavailable for ORE.[227] As a remedy, *"the operator pays a monetary compensation for species protection programmes in order to secure or improve the conservation status of the species affected"*. Coupled with the weakening of the non-deterioration obligation under the Nature Restoration Regulation,[228] such derogations can seriously undermine the goal of adequate protection of vulnerable elements of marine ecosystems even within MPAs, which can remain *"paper tigers."*[229]

These derogations from the duty to carry out EIA at the project level can further deprive the public from the possibility to participate and challenge the authorization based on their right of access to justice,[230] which is not aligned with the EGD's pledge to improve the enforcement of EU environmental law.[231] This shortcoming concerning the right of access to justice[232] cannot be remedied by the new article 15d of the RED III on public participation nor by the application of the Aarhus Convention and the revised Aarhus Regulation, because the simplified authorisation process impairs any effective exercise of such right by the public. In recognition of the potential blindspots of a SEA, RED III stipulates that projects are subject to a screening to identify possible *"significant unforeseen adverse effects"* that were not identified during the strategic assessment.[233] Projects shall be authorised with a tacit decision within 45 days unless the competent authority, within 45 days, adopts an express decision *"setting out due reasons on the*

---

222 With the exception of artificial and built surfaces built in those areas, art 15c (1)(a)(ii) Directive (EU) 2023/2413.

223 This also seems inconsistent with the so far strict interpretation of the precautionary principle under the HD, see CJEU Judgment, Case C-127/02, Landelijke Vereniging tot Behoud van de Waddenzee and Nederlandse Vereniging.

224 Directive (EU) 2023/2413, Art 15c(1)(b).

225 Anker and Olsen (2023), p. 45.

226 Council Regulation (EU) 2022/2577 laying down a framework to accelerate the deployment of renewable energy, OJ L 335, p. 36–44, Art 6.

227 The derogations from the duties to carry out EIAs and appropriate assessments for ORE projects in RAAs does not seem to assist in the collection of such data either.

228 Regulation (EU) 2024/1991, Articles 5(9) and 6.

229 European Court of Auditors (2020).

230 Directive 2011/92/EU, Art 11; Art 6 and 9.2 of the Aarhus Convention.

231 Jendroska and Anapyanova (2023), p. 4.

232 Unlike the EIA Directive that explicitly provides for a right of access to justice under its article 11, the SEA Directive does not contain any provision on the right of access to justice.

233 Directive (EU) 2023/2413, Art 16a (4).

basis of clear evidence to the effect that a specific project is highly likely to give rise to significant unforeseen effects."[234] That considerably high evidentiary threshold required within a short-time limit before the submission of a project to an EIA does not seem to be consistent with the precautionary principle.[235] The tacit authorization from an environmental perspective without the need of any express decision[236] and the lack of publicity of the findings of the screening unless the outcome is positive, undercuts the transparency of the process and hampers the effective exercise of the right of access to justice. Even when the administrative law of Member States enables the public to challenge tacit decisions, the lack of transparency not only hinders access to crucial environmental information which reduces the potential legal grounds to challenge it but also puts a heavier burden on potential applicants to calculate the deadlines for appropriately filing any claim.

Despite the legal possibility for Member States to adopt more stringent measures when transposing the RED III,[237] for instance, requiring an EIA under their domestic law for ORE projects, it does not seem really viable in practice. Besides the fact that a more ambitious approach is contingent on their discretion to go beyond gold-plating,[238] there is an evident heightened EU interest in the rapid transposition of the provisions regarding the speeding up of permit-granting processes, which need to exceptionally be transposed by 1 July 2024 when the Emergency Regulation ceases to apply. The urgency for the adoption of these legislative measures, which have been almost elevated to an issue of national security trumping all other considerations, is confirmed by their duty to *"immediately inform the Commission of these measures"*.[239] States shall ensure that they *"contribute to the achievement of the objectives set out in this Directive,"*[240] that is increasing the share of renewable energy in the EU's overall energy consumption to 42.5% by 2030, with a further indicative target of 2.5%.[241] The discretion to adopt stricter measures appears therefore probably restrained given Europe's energy needs.

4.3.2 The Legislative Crystallisation of the Predominance of the Climate-Energy Targets: The Presumption of Overriding Public Interest

Despite the expected potential of RAAs to host ORE projects in marine areas, where they are presumed not likely to have significant adverse environmental impacts, meeting the skyrocketing renewable energy targets will inevitably require some installations to be located elsewhere. Thus, another regulatory tool employed to accelerate the energy transition was the legislative introduction of a rebuttable presumption that all renewable

[234] (2023) Directive (EU) 2023/2413, Art 16a (5).

[235] Case C–157/14, Société Neptune Distribution v Minister for Economic Affairs and Finance (2015, para. 82; Afton Chemical Limited v Secretary of State for Transport (2010), para. 76.

[236] To the contrary, the Emergency Regulation required all authorization decisions to be made public, see articles 4(5) and 5(5).

[237] Art 193 TFEU.

[238] Directive (EU) 2023/2413, recital 33.

[239] (2023) Directive (EU) 2023/2413, Art 5(1).

[240] (2023) Directive (EU) 2023/2413, Art15c(3).

[241] (2023) Directive (EU) 2023/2413, Art 3(1).

energy projects qualify as overriding public interest.[242] This does not only translate the primacy of climate-energy targets over biodiversity into a clear legal commitment, but it is also one of the key conditions for exceptionally authorising projects, which have or are likely to have significant impacts on meeting the conservation objectives or can lead to the deterioration of the ecological status of Natura 2000 sites.[243] The presumption can similarly have legal implications for the application of the derogations under the MSFD, which provides that Member States can justify not meeting the goal of GES due to projects qualifying as being in the overriding public interest.[244]

The Regulation further stipulates that these projects should be given priority by the competent national authorities when balancing legal interests in individual cases to eliminate bottlenecks in the permit-granting process.[245] This far-reaching measure can undermine fundamental nature conservation obligations under the Nature Directives[246] by transforming the exceptional authorization of environmentally harmful projects into a rule, especially given its applicability to all renewable energy projects irrespective of their location, size and impacts[247] Initially, portrayed as a *"temporary measure"*[248] adopted through the emergency legislative process[249] due to the urgent and exceptional energy situation, the incorporation of these measures in the RED III[250] proved that nothing is more permanent than temporary measures.

Just a few months prior to the entry into force of the emergency regulation, the revised TEN-E regulation provided that projects of common interest, such as offshore interconnectors, should be considered by competent authorities as being of public interest. Therefore, even when their adverse environmental impact is uncertain they can be authorised as long as the other conditions laid out in the Water Framework Directive and the HD are met.[251] The regulation did not introduce a presumption about the existence of an overriding public interest, but explicitly enabled the competent national authorities, and in cases of sensitive protected areas, the Commission and the national authorities, to examine whether each project could be exceptionally authorised upon the satisfaction of all the conditions under these instruments.[252] Emphasising the strategic importance of developing an EU-wide renewable energy network, it provides that projects of common interest shall be granted the status of "*the highest national significance possible*" and be

242 Council Regulation (EU) 2022/2577, Art 3.

243 Art 6(4) Council Directive 92/43/EEC, p. 7–50.

244 Art 14 Directive 2008/56/EC, pp. 19–40.

245 Council Regulation (EU) 2022/2577, pp. 36–44, Recital 9.

246 Art 6(4), 16(1)(c) Council Directive 92/43/EEC, pp. 7–50; Art 9(1)(c) Directive 2009/147/EC of the European Parliament and of the Council of 30 November 2009 on the conservation of wild birds, OJ L 20, 26.1.2010, p. 7.

247 Jendroska and Anapyanova (2023), p. 4.

248 Council Regulation (EU) 2022/2577, p. 36–44, recital 8.

249 Art 122 TFEU.

250 Directive (EU) 2023/2413, Art 16f which provides that this presumption shall be applicable 'until climate neutrality is achieved', which is a goal expected to be met by 2050.

251 Regulation (EU) 2022/869, recital 37, Art 7(8).

252 Regulation (EU) 2022/869, Art 7(8).

treated with urgency in the permit granting process, including processes relating to environmental assessments.[253] That priority status is also granted to ensure rapid treatment in all judicial and dispute resolution procedures relating to them.[254]

Compared to the revised TEN-E regulation, the subsequent provisions of the Emergency Regulation and the RED III, which automatically qualify all ORE projects as being in the overriding public interest, crystallise the predominance of the EGD's climate-energy objectives over biodiversity considerations.[255] Arguably, the presumption would also apply in case of Natura 2000 sites hosting *"a priority natural habitat type and/or a priority species"*, where in principle, economic justifications are subject to the opinion of the EU Commission.[256] The provisions remain ambiguous and further clarifications by the Commission appear necessary, for instance, to shed light on the practical assessment and application of the additional condition relating to the absence of feasible alternatives.[257] One could argue that the competent authority would put more focus on that condition, since ORE projects outside RAAs can still be subject to an EIA[258] and, in that case, project developers would have to provide information about all reasonable alternatives.[259] In some cases, however, no alternative locations are examined at the project level, because these have been definitely determined at the planning level.[260] Although Member States may restrict the application of the presumption of overriding public interest to some areas of their territory and certain types of technologies, their discretion is subjected to a duty to inform the Commission of such restrictions with the reasons thereof.[261] This provision could, however, be operationalized to simply exclude some environmentally sensitive areas or disruptive technologies from the application of such presumption.

A similar provision reinforcing the presumption of overriding public interest for ORE projects made its way also into article 6 of the Nature Restoration Regulation, which did not initially feature in the original Commission's text but got introduced in the watered down provisional agreement.[262] According to this article, Member States cannot only authorise ORE projects despite them causing the deterioration of areas within or outside Natura 2000 sites, but they are also released from the duty to assess

[253] Regulation (EU) 2022/869, Art 7(3).

[254] Regulation (EU) 2022/869, recital 37.

[255] Directive (EU) 2023/2413, recital 44, art 16(f).

[256] Art 6(4) Council Directive 92/43/EEC, p. 7–50.

[257] See below the clearer provision of article 5(a) of Regulation (EU) 2024/1991.

[258] Directive (EU) 2023/2413, Art 16b(2).

[259] Directive 2011/92/EU, Art 5(1)(d).

[260] See the example of the Netherlands, where article 3(1) of the Offshore Wind Energy Act provides that wind farms can only be authorized in locations previously designated in the Dutch maritime spatial plan.

[261] Directive (EU) 2023/2413, Art 16f. Note that this duty to notify the Commission of any exceptions to the presumption did not exist under the Emergency Regulation. Council Regulation (EU) 2022/2577, Art 3(1).

[262] Regulation (EU) 2024/1991.

the existence of less damaging alternative solutions in the permit-granting process, subject to the condition that either a SEA or EIA was carried out.[263] At first sight, that simplification would seem partly rational, given that project developers must assess all reasonable alternatives during the EIA,[264] but could be problematic in case the project causing the deterioration of protected marine habitats was authorised solely based on a SEA that does not entail an equivalent assessment of alternatives. The weakened final text of the Regulation also included a provision requiring Member States to coordinate their national restoration plans with their plans of areas that are required to meet their national contributions towards the 2030 renewable energy targets and with the designation of renewable acceleration areas.[265] Highlighting the prevalence of the plans for the acceleration of renewables, the proposal stipulated that Member States shall ensure that these plans remain unchanged, therefore, restoration plans should not interfere in any way with meeting the climate-energy targets.

The recognition that all ORE projects meet the condition of an overriding public interest seems to reverse the rationale of the derogation under article 6(4) of the HD, which requires a casuistic examination of projects likely to have significant adverse impacts on the achievement of the conservation objectives of Natura 2000 sites. The CJEU has stressed in its case law that the conditions of this derogation shall be interpreted restrictively.[266] A presumption appears to be useful in the case of small projects, for which the competent authority could face challenges in justifying that their long-term and uncertain contribution to climate neutrality overrides the direct local effects on protected Natura 2000 sites.[267] Similarly, it would be relevant in the case of a project with so significant adverse impacts on a strictly protected MPA[268] – which cannot be prevented or minimised through mitigation measures that can be considered in the appropriate assessment under article 6(3) of the HD – making it difficult to argue that its long-term contribution to climate-energy objectives overrides the interest in marine biodiversity conservation. In any case, such a presumption reverses the burden of proof in case the authorization of such a project is challenged before domestic courts, as the applicants would have to prove that the presumption should have been rebutted in that particular case.

This absolute prioritisation of ORE further paves the way for an extensive use of derogations to the rules on species protection under the Nature Directives.[269] That is crucial, since the construction and operation of ORE installations can result in the killing or disturbances of birds and other species falling under the scope of protection.[270]

---

263 Regulation (EU) 2024/1991, Article 6.

264 Directive 2011/92/EU, art 5(1)(d).

265 Regulation (EU) 2024/1991, Article 14(13).

266 Case C-182/10, Marie-Noëlle Solvay and others v Région Wallonne (2012), para. 73.

267 See for instance ABRvS, 18 February 2015, ECLI:NL:RVS:2015:438 (Sabinapolder), regarding whether a smaller wind farm consisting of 3 wind turbines could be considered as an overriding public interest.

268 See above, one third of the MPAs should be strictly protected according to the promises of the Biodiversity Strategy for 2030.

269 Anker and Olsen (2023), p. 45.

270 Directive (EU) 2023/2413, recital 37.

The Emergency Regulation provides that when balancing with species protection, such projects – regardless of their location – should enjoy priority insofar *"appropriate species conservation measures contributing to the maintenance or restoration of the populations of the species at a favourable conservation status are undertaken and sufficient financial resources as we as areas are made available for this purpose"*.[271] To the extent that this provision refers to conservation measures aimed at the population level of the species,[272] it seems to disregard the ruling of the CJEU in the Skydda Skogen case, which clarified that the prohibitions under article 12 of the HD apply at the specimens level and do not depend on the conservation status of the species concerned.[273] Building on that exception to the strict rules on species protection, RED III provides that *"when a renewable energy project has adopted necessary mitigation measures, any killing or disturbance of the species ... shall not be considered to be deliberate"*.[274] The provisions do not clarify which mitigation measures might be appropriate or necessary to justify an exception from the strict prohibition on the deliberate killing or disturbance of species.[275] Although the wording suggests that the effectiveness of these measures should be based on solid evidence, it enables Member States to take an adaptive approach and test novel mitigation measures,[276] whose effectiveness has not yet been widely tested, on condition that their effects are closely monitored and appropriate steps are taken immediately if they do not prove to be effective.[277] Despite the pragmatic reasons for this adaptive approach, its compatibility with the precautionary principle, as interpreted by the CJUE remains debatable.[278]

Overall, the far-reaching derogations from fundamental EU environmental legislation within and beyond RAAs showcases that the EGD's implementation instruments construes climate-energy action and a high level of biodiversity protection as mutually exclusive,[279] despite its promises for win-win situations. This could have significant implications on the health of European seas and more broadly on the ocean. Additionally, the possibility to enjoy the rights to information and access to justice vanishes along with the obligation to carry out an EIA. This fast-paced energy transition consequently raises questions concerning its democratic nature.

---

[271] Council Regulation (EU) 2022/2577, p. 36–44, Art 3(2).

[272] See also Directive (EU) 2023/2413, recital 37: '*such killing or disturbance should not be considered to be deliberate if the project provides for appropriate mitigation measures to ... take further measures required to ensure that there are no significant adverse impacts on the population of the species concerned*'.

[273] Joined cases C-473/19, C-474/19, Föreningen Skydda Skogen and Others v Länsstyrelsen i Västra Götalands län and Others (2021), para 54.

[274] Directive (EU) 2023/2413, Art 16(2).

[275] Ruge (2022), pp. 260, 263.

[276] Le Lièvre (2019).

[277] Directive (EU) 2023/2413, Art 16b(2).

[278] CJEU Judgment (2019) Case C-674/17, Luonnonsuojeluyhdistys Tapiola Pohjois-Savo – Kainuury v Risto Mustonen and Others, para 66.

[279] Directive (EU) 2023/2413, recital 28.

5 Concluding Remarks

Growing concerns have been expressed that the promoted as groundbreaking EGD falls short of the revolutionary change necessary to tackle the intertwined climate, energy and biodiversity crises.[280] Despite gradually incorporating ocean-related objectives into EGD strategies, its targets and actions remain insufficiently transformative to restore marine ecosystem health effectively. Allowing the bulk of the responsibility for the implementation of environmental actions on Member States, the EGD's promises in terms of marine biodiversity protection are rather "business as usual" for the EU. The intense political pressures surrounding the Nature Restoration proposal triggered a rollercoaster of negotiations between EU institutions, ultimately leading to a significant weakening of its obligations. This back-and-forth exemplifies how the adoption of truly transformative policies, especially those impacting key economic sectors, has become increasingly difficult in today's political landscape.[281] As the EGD elevates the climate crisis to an almost Machiavellian priority, a risk at the level of national security, and sees the ocean as a significant ally in this fight, its blue shade remains rather dull. Regardless of the attempts to embed environmental sustainability within its social market paradigm by underlining the economic value of ecosystem services and the cost of inaction for the protection and restoration of marine biodiversity,[282] no equally convincing business case for marine biodiversity conservation has been framed. It therefore fails to reinvent marine environmental protection while putting the ocean in the spotlight of the EU's energy transition. This lack of balance becomes even more evident when examining the recent legislative instruments adopted to pursue the EGD's time-sensitive climate-energy goals, such as the RepowerEU Emergency Regulation and RED III.

The urgency to accelerate the energy transition, become independent from fossil fuel imports, and catalyse rapid climate mitigation, appears to justify the undercutting of environmental safeguards, or rather what the EU considers as obstacles to ORE projects. Although facilitating a blue energy transition constitutes a welcome breakthrough to speeding up the permit-granting process, including rules on strict time limits for decision-making processes, measures that introduced blanket exceptions from core EU law environmental obligations – especially ones that have been vehemently supported as fundamental for biodiversity conservation by the CJEU – can seriously undermine the balance between the EGD's climate-energy objectives and the ones on the conservation and restoration of marine biodiversity. Indeed, these objectives are only as good as their effective implementation, which the EU Commission promised to sharpen in order to reach a GES of EU seas. Additionally, some of the novel regulatory strategies seriously impact the transparency, accountability and the effective exercise of the public's rights of access to information and justice. Indispensable safeguards to ensure social inclusion and control of new EGD policies do not cause significant harm, their absence risks undermining the rapid blue energy transition's legitimacy.

Ultimately, the EGD's anthropocentric ocean management questions the effectiveness of the EU's response to the challenge of competing ocean uses. The proposed

280 Van der Sluis (2023), pp. 231–235; European Court of Auditors (2023), pp. 43–46.
281 Van Gaal (2024).
282 Monti (2021), p. 1326.

rationale does not truly depart from the unlimited growth narratives that led to the climate and ecological crises in the first place, namely the commodification of nature.[283] The Biodiversity Strategy refers to elements of the environment as *"natural capital"* and focuses on the economic value of *"ecosystem services"* reinforcing a business-oriented agenda in an attempt to establish a business case for biodiversity conservation. That confirms that the EGD still operates within a framework that treats humans and nature as two separate entities.[284] It systematically opposes human growth with nature protection. Their interactions are perceived through an economic lens, where the marine environment is an untapped resource to be exploited. Consequently, any references to the ecosystem-based approach are somewhat obscured by the rather anthropocentric concept of ecosystem services.[285] A genuine implementation of the ecosystem-based approach would go beyond the anthropo-/eco-centric dichotomy,[286] based on the premise that humans should not be considered apart from, but a part of nature.[287] In line with traditional environmental law, the EGD focuses on the piecemeal regulation of environmental pressures in order to protect humans from the consequences of climate change rather than ecosystem health *per se.*[288] It therefore perpetuates the anthropocentric view that nature is worthy of protection only to the extent that it serves human interests, and not for its intrinsic value. Yet, the rationale behind environmental/climate action is primordial,[289] since the ways in which humans construe and value nature influence its state.[290] The rules on the acceleration of the energy transition exemplify this distorted view.

However, scientists have warned that the race to green energy cannot be allowed at any cost. It would indeed be highly paradoxical to address climate change by further endangering nature, including the ocean. The EGD's goal is still to serve short-term human interests when a viable and effective transition requires a more holistic vision embracing nature's intrinsic values.[291] While this chapter does not argue against the deployment of the ORE, it highlights the necessity for a more robust understanding of this process and its environmental impacts and a more democratic involvement of EU citizens. Relevantly, the EU Biodiversity Strategy underlines that *"protecting and restoring biodiversity is the only way to preserve the quality and continuity of human life on Earth."*[292] Consequently, EGD's implementation measures must strike a better balance to prevent problem-shifting,[293] as the energy transition at sea risks becoming yet another driver of biodiversity loss. Hopefully, their full potential in marine biodiversity protection remains to unfold. However, with the closing window to save the ocean and the planet, time is critical.

283 Windmer and Heron (2017), p. 7.
284 Lennan et al. (2020), pp. 4–5.
285 De Lucia (2015), pp. 94–95.
286 De Lucia (2017), p. 191.
287 Sander (2023), p. 425.
288 Richardson (2018), p. 277; Ban and Bax N, Gjerde K (2017) p. 41.
289 Unai et al. (2022), pp. 1, 6.
290 Unai et al. (2022), p. 4.
291 Unai et al. (2022), p. 6.
292 COM (2020) 380 final, p. 22.
293 Kim and Van Asselt (2016).

References

Anker, H.T., Olsen, B.E.: EU species protection law and wind energy: current challenges and Danish experiences. Eur. Energy Env. Law Rev. **32**(1), 36–46 (2023). https://doi.org/10.54648/eelr2023002

Skjærseth, J.B.: Towards a European green deal: the evolution of EU climate and energy policy mixes. Int. Environ. Agreements: Polit. Law Econ. **21**(1), 25–41 (2021). https://doi.org/10.1007/s10784-021-09529-4

Bongardt, A., Torres, F.: The European green deal: more than an exit strategy to the pandemic crisis, a building block for a sustainable European Economic model. JCMS **60**, 170–185 (2021). https://doi.org/10.1111/jcms.13264

Caine, C.A.: The race to the water for offshore renewable energy: assessing cumulative and in-combination impacts for offshore energy developments. J. Environ. Law **32**(1), 83–109 (2020). https://doi.org/10.1093/jel/eqz031

Cliquet, A., et al.: The negotiation process of the EU nature restoration law proposal: brining nature back in Europe against the backdrop of political turmoil? Restor. Ecol. **32**(5), 1–7 (2024). https://doi.org/10.1111/rec.14158

De Leeuw, B., Backes, C.: The non-deterioration obligation in the nature restoration regulation – a necessary and proportionate addition to the habitats directive or a monstrosity with disastrous consequences for society? J. Eur. Environ. Plan. Law 22–40 (2024). https://doi.org/10.1163/18760104-21010004

De Lucia, V.: Competing narratives and complex genealogies: the ecosystem approach in international environmental law. J. Environ. Law **27**(1), 91–117 (2015). https://doi.org/10.1093/jel/equ031

De Lucia, V.: Beyond anthropocentrism and ecocentrism: a biopolitical reading of environmental law. J. Hum. Rights Env. **8**(2), 181–202 (2017). https://doi.org/10.4337/jhre.2017.02.01

Devis, A.: Change of paradigm in EU environmental law: does the climate crisis now override the biodiversity crisis? European Law Blog (2024). https://doi.org/10.21428/9885764c.eaa4248f

Eckert, S.: The European green deal and the EU's regulatory power in times of crisis. JCMS **59**, 81–91 (2021). https://doi.org/10.1111/jcms.13241

Frank, M.: The international legal framework for marine spatial planning. Marine Policy **32** (2008). https://doi.org/10.1016/j.marpol.2008.03.013

Galparsoro, I., et al.: Mapping potential environmental impacts of offshore renewable energy. ETC/ICM Report 2/2022. European Topic Centre on Inland, Coastal and Marine Waters (2022)

Giannopoulos, N.: The proliferation of offshore renewable energy in European seas: the regulatory challenges of emerging technologies for EU environmental law. In: Weishaar, S., De Graaf, K. (eds.) The Future of Environmental Law: Ambition and Reality. Edward Elgar, pp. 165–168 (2023). https://doi.org/10.4337/9781035314645.00020

Hatcher, B.G., Bradbury, R.H.: Marine ecosystem management: is the whole greater than the sum of the parts. In: Rothwell, D., VanderZwaag, D. (eds.) Towards Principled Oceans Governance. Routledge (2006)

Haugen, J.B., et al.: Marine ecosystem-based management: challenges remain, yet solutions exist, and progress is occurring. Ocean Sustain. **3** (2024). https://doi.org/10.1038/s44183-024-00041-1

Hardiman, A.: Seeking to deliver renewable energy infrastructure within an incomplete and vague legal framework. CCLR **16**, 192–204 (2022). https://doi.org/10.21552/cclr/2022/3/6

Hereu-Morales, J., et al.: The European (green?) deal: a systematic analysis of environmental sustainability. Sustainability Dev. **32**, 647–661 (2023). https://doi.org/10.1002/sd.2671

Hiddink, J.G., et al.: Global analysis of depletion and recovery of seabed biota after bottom trawling disturbance. Proc. Natl. Aca Sci. USA (2017). https://doi.org/10.1073/pnas.1618858114

Jendroska, J., Anapyanova, A.: Towards a green energy transition: RePowerEU directive vs environmental acquis?. Elni Rev. **23**, 1–5 (2023). https://doi.org/10.46850/elni.2023.001

Javier Dura-Aleman, C., et al.: Climate change and energy crisis drive an unprecedented EU environmental law regression, Conserv. Lett. **16**(3) (2023). https://doi.org/10.1111/conl.12958

Kim, R., Van Asselt, H.: Global governance: problem shifting in the Anthropocene and the limits of international law. In: Morgera, E., Kulovesi, K. (eds.) Research Handbook on International Law and Natural Resources, pp. 473–495. Edward Elgar Publishing (2016). https://doi.org/10.4337/9781783478330.00039

Kramer, L.: Planning for climate and the environment: the EU green deal. J. Eur. Environ. Plan Law. **17**(3), 267–306 (2020). https://doi.org/10.1163/18760104-01703003

Long, R.: The marine strategy framework directive: a new European approach to the regulation of the marine environment, marine natural resources and marine ecological services. J Energy Nat. Res. Law **29**, 1–44 (2011). https://doi.org/10.1080/02646811.2011.11435256

Langlet, D., Rayfuse, R.: Challenges in implementing the ecosystem approach: lessons learned. In: Langlet, D., Rayfuse, R. (eds.) The Ecosystem Approach in Ocean Planning and Governance – Perspectives from Europe and Beyond. Brill (2019). https://doi.org/10.31230/osf.io/8xqjt

Laurent, E.: The European green deal: bring back the new. OFCE Policy Brief (2020)

Le Lièvre, C.: Sustainably reconciling offshore renewable energy with Natura 2000 sites: an interim adaptive management framework. Energy Policy **129**, 491–501 (2019). https://doi.org/10.1016/j.enpol.2019.02.007

Lennan, M., et al.: 2030 for the EU: real steps of change? SCELG Policy Brief (2020)

Monti, G.: The European climate law: Making the social market economy fit for 55? Common Mark. Law Rev. **58**(5), 1321–1340 (2021)

Ossewaarde, M., Ossewaarde-Lowtoo, R.: The EU's green deal: a third alternative to green growth and degrowth?. Sustainability **12** (2020). https://doi.org/10.3390/su12239825

Paleari, S.: The Impact of the European Green Deal on EU environmental policy. J. Environ. Dev. **31** (2022). https://doi.org/10.1177/10704965221082222

Paleari, S.: The EU policy on climate change, biodiversity and circular economy: moving towards a Nexus approach. Env. Sci. Pol. **151** (2024). https://doi.org/10.1016/j.envsci.2023.103603

Peeters, M., Athanasiadou, N.: The continued effort sharing approach in EU climate law: binding targets, challenging enforcement? RECIEL **29**, 201–211 (2020). https://doi.org/10.1111/reel.12356

Peeters, M., Misonne, D.: The European Union and its rule-creating force on the European continent for moving to climate neutrality by 2050 at the latest. In: Reins, L., Verschuuren (eds.) Research Handbook on Climate Change Mitigation Law, 2nd edn., pp. 59–102. Edward Elgar Publishing (2022). https://doi.org/10.4337/9781839101595.00010

Puharinen, S.-T.: Achieving good environmental status in the EU – implications of the marine strategy framework directive for member states and blue economic activities. Mar. Policy **155** (2023). https://doi.org/10.1016/j.marpol.2023.105712

Richardson, B.: The emerging age of ecological restoration law. Rev. Eur. Comp. Int. Environ. Law **25**, 277–290 (2018). https://doi.org/10.1111/reel.12165

Romppanen, S., Huhta, K.: The Interface between EU climate and energy law. Maastricht J. Eur. Comp. Law **30**(1), 45–62 (2023). https://doi.org/10.1177/1023263X231159976

Ruge, R.: The Reality Gap: Simplification of environmental law as key for the acceleration of permit procedures for Europe's Green Deal. Eur. Energy Env. Law Rev. 260–263 (2022). https://doi.org/10.54648/EELR2022018

Sander, G.: European approaches support an essential definition of ecosystem-based management and demonstrate its implementation for the oceans. Ocean Dev. Int. Law **54**(4), 421–447 (2023). https://doi.org/10.1080/00908320.2023.2301105

Santos, C., et al.: How sustainable is sustainable marine spatial planning? Part I: linking the concepts. Mar. Policy **49**, 59–65 (2014). https://doi.org/10.1016/j.marpol.2014.04.004

Sikora, A.: European green deal – legal and financial challenges of the climate change. ERA Forum **21**, 681–697 (2021). https://doi.org/10.1007/s12027-020-00637-3

Scheuing, H., Kamm, J.: The EU on the road to climate neutrality - is the 'Fit for 55' package fit for purpose? Renew. Energy Law Pol. **10**(3), 4–18 (2022). https://doi.org/10.4337/relp.2022.03-04.01

Schlacke, S., Wentzien, H., Thierjung, E.-M., Köster, M.: Implementing the EU climate law via the 'Fit for 55' package. Oxford Open Energy 1–13 (2022). https://doi.org/10.1093/ooenergy/oiab002

Van der Sluis, M.: The European green deal paradox – remarkably successful, but falling short? Maastricht J. Eur. Comp. Law **30**, 231–235 (2023). https://doi.org/10.1177/1023263X231216860

Van Zeben, J., et al.: Stress testing the european green deal: the 'securisation or energy, food and climate. EU Law Live **106**, 2–14 (2022)

Vezzoni, R.: Green growth for whom, how and why? The REPowerEU plan and the inconsistencies of European Union energy policy. Energy Res. Soc. Sci. **101** (2023). https://doi.org/10.1016/j.erss.2023.103134

Windmer, G.M., Heron, L.R.: Assembling a blue economy moment? Geographic engagement with globalizing biological-economic relations and multi-use marine environments. Dialogues Hum. Geogr. **7**(1), 3–26 (2017). https://doi.org/10.1177/2043820617691643

Yen-Chiang, C.: Legal Issues concerning marine spatial planning – a note. China Oceans Law Rev. **17**(2), 12–24 (2021)

Cases

Case C-66/06, Commission of the European Communities v Ireland (2008), ECLI:EU:C:2008:637

Case C–343/09, Afton Chemical Limited v Secretary of State for Transport (2010), ECLI:EU:C:2010:419

Case C-182/10, Marie-Noëlle Solvay and others v Région Wallonne (2012), ECLI:EU:C:2012:82

Case C–157/14, Société Neptune Distribution v Minister for Economic Affairs and Finance (2015), ECLI:EU:C:2015:823

Case C-5/16, Poland v European Parliament and Council of the European Union (2018), ECLI:EU:C:2018:483

Case C-671/16, Inter-Environnement Bruxelles ASBL and Others v Région de Bruxelles-Capitale (2018), ECLI:EU:C:2018:403

Case C-674/17, Luonnonsuojeluyhdistys Tapiola Pohjois-Savo – Kainuu ry v Risto Mustonen and Others (2019), ECLI:EU:C:2019:851

Cases C-473/19 und C-474/19, Föreningen Skydda Skogen and Others v Länsstyrelsen i Västra Götalands län and Others (2021), ECLI:EU:C:2021:166

Case C-9/22, NJ and OZ v. An Bord Pleanála and Others (2023), ECLI:EU:C:2023:176

Others

COM (2007) 575, Communication from the Commission to the European Parliament, the Council, the European Economic and Social Committee and the Committee of the Regions, An Integrated Maritime Policy for the European Union, 10.10.2007

COM (2009) 40 final, Communication from the Commission on a European Action Plan for the Conservation and Management of Sharks, 5.2.2009

COM (2011) 144 final, White paper roadmap to a single European Transport Area - towards a competitive and resource efficient transport system, 28.3.2011

COM (2012) 0494, Communication from the Commission to the European Parliament, the Council, the European Economic and Social Committee and the Committee of the Regions, Blue growth opportunities for marine and maritime sustainable growth, 13.9.2012

COM (2019) 640 final, Communication from the Commission to the European Parliament, the European Council, the Council, the European Economic and Social Committee and the Committee of the Regions – The European Green Deal, 11.12.2019

COM (2020) 380 final, Communication from the Commission to the European Parliament, the Council, the European Economic and Social Committee and the Committee of the Regions, EU Biodiversity Strategy for 2030 Bringing nature back into our lives, 20.5.2020

COM (2020) 259 final, Report from the Commission to the European Parliament and the Council on the implementation of the Marine Strategy Framework Directive, 25.6.2020

COM (2020) 562 final, Communication from the Commission to the European Parliament, the Council, the European Economic and Social Committee and the Committee of the Regions. Stepping up Europe's 2030 climate ambition – Investing in a climate-neutral future for the benefit of our people, 17.9.2020COM(2020) 643 final, Communication from the Commission to the European Parliament, the Council, the European Economic and Social Committee and the Committee of the Regions. Improving access to justice in environmental matters in the EU and its Member States, 14.10.2020

COM (2020) 741 final, Communication from the Commission to the European Parliament, the Council, the European Economic and Social Committee and the Committee of the Regions. An EU Strategy to harness the potential of offshore renewable energy for a climate neutral future, 19.11.2020

COM (2020) 789 final, Communication from the Commission to the European Parliament, the Council, the European Economic and Social Committee and the Committee of the Regions. Sustainable and Smart Mobility Strategy – putting European transport on track for the future, 9.12.2020

COM (2021) 82 final, Communication from the Commission to the European Parliament, the Council, the European Economic and Social Committee and the Committee of the Regions. Forging a climate-resilient Europe – the new EU Strategy on Adaptation to Climate Change, 24.2.2021

COM (2021) 240 final, Communication from the Commission to the European Parliament, the Council, the European Economic and Social Committee and the Committee of the Regions, on a new approach for a sustainable blue economy in the EU Transforming the EU's Blue Economy for a Sustainable Future, 17.5.2021

COM (2021)550 final, Communication from the Commission to the European Parliament, the Council, the European Economic and Social Committee and the Committee of the Regions. Fit for 55: Delivering the EU's 2030 Climate Target on the way to climate neutrality, 14.7.2021

COM (2021) 557 final, Proposal for a Directive of the European Parliament and of the Council Amending Directive (EU) 2018/2001 of the European Parliament and of the Council, Regulation (EU) 2018/1999 of the European Parliament and of the Council and Directive 98/70/EC of the European Parliament and of the Council as regards the promotion of energy from renewable sources, and repealing Council Directive (EU) 2015/652, 14.7.2021

COM (2022) 108 final, Communication from the Commission to the European Parliament, the Council, the European Economic and Social Committee and the Committee of the Regions. Communication from the European Commission on REPowerEU: Join European Action for more affordable, secure and sustainable energy, 8.3.2022

COM (2022) 185 final, Report from the Commission to the European Parliament and the Council outlining the progress made in implementing Directive 2014/89/EU establishing a framework for maritime spatial planning, 3.5.2022

COM (2022) 222 final, Proposal for a Directive of the European Parliament and of the Council amending Directive (EU) 2018/2001 on the promotion of the use of energy from renewable sources, Directive 2010/31/EU on the energy performance of buildings and Directive 2012/27/EU on energy efficiency, 18.5.2022
COM (2022) 230 final, Communication from the Commission to the European Parliament, the Council, the European Economic and Social Committee and the Committee of the Regions. REPowerEU Plan,18.5.2022
COM (2023) 102 final, Communication from the Commission to the European Parliament, the Council, the European Economic and Social Committee and the Committee of the Regions. EU Action Plan: Protecting and restoring marine ecosystems for sustainable and resilient fisheries, 21.2.2023
COM (2023) 103 final, Communication from the Commission to the European Parliament and the Council: The common fisheries policy today and tomorrow: a Fisheries and Oceans Pact towards sustainable, science-based, innovative and inclusive fisheries management, 21.2.2023
COM/2023/160 final, Proposal for a regulation of the European Parliament and of the Council establishing a framework for ensuring a secure and sustainable supply of critical raw materials and amending Regulations (EU) 168/2013, (EU) 2018/858, 2018/1724 and (EU) 2019/1020, 16.3.2023
COM (2023) 161, Proposal for a regulation of the European Parliament and of the Council on establishing a framework of measures for strengthening Europe's net-zero technology products manufacturing ecosystem (Net Zero Industry Act), 16.3.2023
COM (2023) 669 final, Communication from the Commission to the European Parliament, the Council, the European Economic and Social Committee and the Committee of the Regions. European Wind Power Action Plan, 24.10.2023
COM (2023) 688 final, Communication from the Commission to the European Parliament, the Council, the European Economic and Social Committee and the Committee of the Regions. Delivering on the EU offshore renewable energy ambitions, 24.10.2023
SWD (2021) 601 final, Commission Staff Working Document. Impact Assessment Report Accompanying the document Directive of the European Parliament and of the Council amending Directive 2003/87/EC establishing a system for greenhouse gas emission allowance trading within the Union, Decision (EU) 2015/1814 concerning the establishment and operation of a market stability reserve for the Union greenhouse gas emission trading scheme and Regulation (EU) 2015/757, 14.7.2021
SWD (2022) 149 final, EU (2022) Commission Staff Working Document. Guidance to Member States on good practices to speed up permit-granting procedures for renewable energy projects and on facilitating Power Purchase Agreements Accompanying the document Commission Recommendation on speeding up permit-granting procedures for renewable energy projects and facilitating Power Purchase Agreements, 18.5.2022

Caring for Forests Here and Abroad: The EU's Strategies for Sustainable Forest Ecosystems Around the World

Gauthier Martens(✉)

UCLouvain Saint-Louis Bruxelles, Brussels, Belgium
gauthier.martens@uclouvain.be

Abstract. International efforts to address deforestation have proven unable to efficiently tackle the issue, global rates remaining high. For two decades now, the EU has put in place a framework whose objective is to reduce its contribution to illegal logging. However, its prime objective was not the fight against deforestation and, all in all, it was not entirely successful either. The Union thus adopted Regulation 2023/1115 as the centrepiece of a new EU forest protection framework, the legislation building on existing ones but expanding the scope and objectives.

1 Introduction

Among the various elements of the European Green Deal (EGD)[1] is the objective to preserve and restore ecosystems and biodiversity. Considering that the former "provide essential services such as food, fresh water, clean air, and shelter, [...] mitigate natural disasters, pests and diseases, and help regulate the climate",[2] the EU has adopted, in the wake of the EGD, several plans and legislations whose aim is to protect said ecosystems and the biodiversity they contain, and to address the main causes to the latter's erosion.

Forests are an important part of the biological diversity component of the Green Deal as "emissions from land-use and land-use change, *mostly due to deforestation*, are the second biggest cause of climate change after burning fossil fuels".[3] The Commission

The present contribution is part of the research project (PDR) Regulating the Cocoa Global Value Chain in Order to Avoid Deforestation: Towards Securing the Planetary Boundaries in the EU, for which it received the support of the Fonds de la Recherche Scientifique – FNRS (Belgium). The author would like to thank Prof. Nicolas de Sadeleer for his comments and advice.

[1] COM (2019) 640 final, Communication from the Commission to the European Parliament, the European Council, the Council, the European Economic and Social Committee and the Committee of the Regions – The European Green Deal.

[2] Ibid, p. 13.

[3] COM (2019) 352 final, Communication from the Commission to the European Parliament, the Council, the European Economic and Social Committee and the Committee of the Regions – Stepping up EU Action to Protect and Restore the World's Forests, , emphasis added.

M. Reese et al. (Eds.): EELF 2023, *Legal Implementation and Impacts of the European Green Deal*, pp. 219–243, 2026.
https://doi.org/10.1007/978-3-032-17197-9_9

thus rightly considers that both the quality and quantity of forested areas need improvement if the Union wants to attain climate neutrality and a healthy environment.[4] Consequently, those areas are the object of a dedicated Forest Strategy for 2030,[5] established in 2021. Together with another Commission Communication dedicated to "Stepping up EU Action to Protect and Restore the World's Forests",[6] and put forth a few months prior to the EGD, they culminated in Regulation 2023/1115 (hereinafter also addressed as the EU Deforestation Regulation, or EUDR) whose aim is, in a nutshell, to reduce deforestation and forest degradation through controls on the trade, including imports and exports, of a select list of commodities and their derived products,[7] and Regulation 2024/1991 (known as the nature restoration law) which requires Member States to adopt measures for the recovery and enhancement of, *inter alia*, forest ecosystems situated within their territory.[8] Complementing the well-established Birds and Habitats directives,[9] those Communications and Regulations thus constitute the core the Union's forest policies.

This contribution consists of four sections. First, the context surrounding this EU framework for forest protection will be succinctly explained (2), as well as the legislations' scope and general principles (3). Then, it shall highlight how Regulation 2023/1115 builds on and develops further Regulation 995/2010 (4), focusing in particular on its extraterritorial ambit and on the way it relegates a "legality criterion" in favour of a "sustainability criterion". Then, in order to paint a complete picture, it reviews subsequent EU legislations and proposals (5).

2 Context of the EU Instruments

The aforementioned communications and regulations have not emerged in a vacuum. As fundamental providers of ecosystem services, the role of forests in the global environment and for the preservation or provision of health, shelter and revenue have long been recognised. Hence, many political and legislative initiatives have targeted woodland ecosystems. Their ecological, cultural and economic importance shall first be succinctly

[4] COM (2019) 640 final, p. 13.

[5] COM (2021) 572 final, Communication from the Commission to the European Parliament, the Council, the European Economic and Social Committee and the Committee of the Regions – New EU Forest Strategy for 2030.

[6] COM (2019) 352 final.

[7] Regulation (EU) 2023/1115 of the European Parliament and of the Council of 31 May 2023 on the making available on the Union market and the export from the Union of certain commodities and products associated with deforestation and forest degradation and repealing Regulation (EU) N° 995/2010, OJ L 150, p. 206, 09.6.2023, art. 2(1) and (2).

[8] Regulation (EU) 2024/1991 of the European Parliament and of the Council of 24 June 2024 on nature restoration and amending Regulation (EU) 2022/869, OJ L, 2024/1991, 29.7.2024, art. 12, 13 and 2(a).

[9] Directive 2009/147/EC of the European Parliament and of the Council of 30 November 2009 on the conservation of wild birds, OJ L 20, p. 7, 26.01.2010; Council Directive 92/43/EEC of 21 May 1992 on the conservation of natural habitats and of wild fauna and flora, OJ L 206, 22.7.1992.

outlined (2.1), then the prior (European) political and legal texts regarding these specific ecosystems will be addressed (2.2).

2.1 The Ecological, Cultural and Economic Context, in Short

Forests are one of the most important providers of ecosystem services, a notion which *inter alia* "include[s] the *provisioning services* that supply the goods we harvest and extract (food, water, fibres, timber, medicines) and *cultural services*, such as the gardens, parks and coastlines we visit for pleasure, even emotional sustenance and recuperation".[10] In addition, and although this part is often overlooked because it doesn't directly relate to humans, the notion also comprises services *for* ecosystems, although they also benefit humans, namely, in the Millenium Ecosystem Assessment classification,[11] *supporting* and *regulating* services,[12] e.g., the maintaining of genetic libraries, the formation and preservation of soils, the assimilation of waste or the regulation of climate. Covering respectively 43% and 30% of the EU and the world's land area, woodland ecosystems in particular provide significant services like carbon capture and oxygen production, habitat for both *fauna* and *flora*, water flow regulation, protection of soil from erosion, and "resilience to disasters and to climate change".[13]

Their cultural, social and economic roles are of course of particular interests to human populations, as many rely on the large diversity of woodlands, and notably forests, for their subsistence: both within and beyond the EU, they are "an important resource for employment and economic development, especially within rural areas"..[14] This is all the truer for indigenous peoples, for whom the degradation of those ecosystems thus often implies a deterioration of living conditions. Yet, more than 4.2 million km^2 of forest area have been lost between 1990 and 2020 and this trend continues at the rate of approximately 100,000 km^2 a year.[15] To a large extent, this loss is due to land-use change as it "has had the largest relative negative impact on nature since 1970, followed by the direct exploitation, in particular overexploitation, of animals, plants and other organisms, mainly via harvesting, logging, hunting and fishing […]". Among the detrimental forms of land-use, agriculture is an important cause of change as its widespread expansion has led to more than a third of the Earth's land surface being dedicated to farming under its many forms. Old-growth and tropical forests have been among the main victims of this conversion, along with wetlands and grasslands.[16]

---

[10] Dasgupta (2021), p. 16.

[11] Millenium Ecosystem Assessment (2005), pp. vi and vii.

[12] In the Common International Classification of Ecosystem Services (CICES), those two are considered together, under the name of *regulation and maintenance services* (see Haines-Young R [2023] Common International Classification of Ecosystem Services (CICES) V5.2: Guidance on the Application of the Revised Structure, p. 19).

[13] COM (2019) 352 final, p. 5.

[14] Eurostat (2020), p. 84.

[15] Regulation (EU) 2023/1115, recital 2.

[16] Intergovernmental Science-Policy Platform on Biodiversity and Ecosystem Services (2019), p. XVI.

Quantity-wise, the EU fares better than other regions of the world as its forest cover has increased by 6% between 1990 and 2020.[17] Two caveats must however be raised in that regard.

First, this does not tell us anything about the quality of those forests. As Regulation 2023/1115 rightly points out, "plantation forests and planted forests have a different biodiversity composition and provide different ecosystem services compared to primary and naturally regenerating forests".[18] While data regarding the repartition between types, quality of, and pressures on forests within the EU as a whole is not available,[19] a rough evaluation can be made from data available for the States with the largest woodland cover: taken together, Sweden, Spain, Finland, France, Italy and Germany have more than two thirds of the EU's woodland area. Based on the Food and Agriculture Organisation (FAO)'s data,[20] Table 1 shows how their cover is distributed between different types of woodlands.[21]

Table 1. Types of forests and wooded land in the six EU States with the most woodland areas in 2020 (in millions of hectares) according to the FAO's Global Forest Resources Assessment

	Sweden	Spain	Finland	France	Italy	Germany
Forests and other wooded land	30.34	27.95	23.2	18.09	11.43	11.42
- Forests	27.98	18.57	22.41	17.25	9.57	11.42
• Naturally regenerating forests	14.07	15.92	15.04	14.82	8.92	5.71
o Primary forest	2.25	*No data*	0.20	*No data*	0.09	0.00
• Planted forests	13.91	2.59	7.37	2.43	0.64	5.71
o Plantation forests	0.38	1.00	0.03	0.00	0.13	0.00
- Other wooded land	2.36	9.38	0.75	0.84	1.87	0.00

The share of forests and other wooded land in the total land area is 74.50% for Sweden, 55.94% for Spain, 76.19% for Finland, 33.05% for France, 38.87% for Italy, and

[17] Eurostat (2020), p. 87.

[18] Regulation (EU) 2023/1115, recital 15. The different types of forests are defined in art. 2.

[19] COM (2023) 728 final, Proposal for a Regulation of the European Parliament and of the Council on a monitoring framework for resilient European forests, p. 1 and 2.

[20] We fully acknowledge how "[t]he FAO's data and methods are criticised because these are dependent on voluntary country reporting and built upon the concept of 'forest area net change', which allows natural forest loss to be compensated for by forest plantations, for example, and which considers clear-cut areas that are supposed to be replanted as 'forest areas' too" (Arts [2021], p. 10).

[21] Data adapted from the *FAO*'s "Global Forest Resources Assessment 2020" Reports for Sweden (https://www.fao.org/3/cb0063en/cb0063en.pdf), Spain (https://www.fao.org/3/cb0103es/cb0103es.pdf, only available in Spanish), Finland (https://www.fao.org/3/ca9995en/ca9995en.pdf), France (https://www.fao.org/3/cb0131fr/cb0131fr.pdf, only available in French), Italy (https://www.fao.org/3/cb0012en/cb0012en.pdf) and Germany (https://www.fao.org/3/ca9997en/ca9997en.pdf).

32.73% for Germany.[22] While naturally regenerating forests account for, in the represented countries, the majority of the wooded land, only a small part of them are primary forests. Although quite variable between the six States, planted forests do most often than not compose a non-negligible share of forest cover: only in Italy and Spain is it below 10%, while it is at almost 46% in Sweden. Germany's forests are split 50/50 between naturally regenerated and planted. More globally, the state of EU forests is, according to the European Environment Agency (EEA), "a mixed picture of improvement and deterioration [as] some indicators, such as structural indicators, biomass volume and productivity, suggest improving forest conditions [while] others, such as defoliation, tree canopy mortality and deadwood, suggest critical conditions".[23] In other words, the health of EU forests is at best contrasted, with both positive and negative developments occurring simultaneously. In that regard, Regulation 2023/1115 itself explains that.

> "As regards the situation of forests within the Union, the State of Europe's Forests 2020 report states that, between 1990 and 2020, the area of forests in Europe has increased by 9 %, carbon stored in the biomass has grown by 50 % and wood supply has risen by 40 %. Primary and naturally regenerating forests are at risk, inter alia, from intensive management, and their unique biodiversity and structural features are in danger. Furthermore, the European Environment Agency has noted that less than 5 % of European forest areas are now considered to be undisturbed or natural, whereas 10 % of European forest areas have been classified as intensively managed. Forest ecosystems have to cope with multiple pressures caused by climate change, ranging from extreme weather patterns to pests, and with human-related activities that negatively affect ecosystems and habitats. In particular, intensively managed even-aged forests through clear-cutting and deadwood removal can have a severe impact on whole habitats."[24]

Second caveat, although the Union is back to being a net exporter of goods after the perturbations caused by covid, a lot of the EU's consumption is still produced in third countries and thus has environmental consequences in other parts of the world. Following that logic, the Union's increase in forest cover has significantly "been offset by deforestation occurring elsewhere in order to produce commodities for consumption in Europe".[25] The progress of the EU is thus more the consequence of an outsourcing of its production externalities than of its efforts to preserve its biodiversity. This is not to say that the Union has not made any such effort or that those have been meaningless. Afforestation initiatives have effectively contributed to the increase in forest cover within the Union.[26] Broadly speaking, its legislation regarding the protection, preservation and restoration of biodiversity is among the most ambitious in the world. Nevertheless, this ambition is to a somewhat large extent rendered possible by its externalisation of adverse environmental impacts.

[22] For comparison, the EU States with the smallest percentage of forest cover are Malta with 1.5%, the Netherlands with 9.9% and Ireland with 11.4% (Rossi R (Rossi, 2025)).

[23] European Environment Agency (2023).

[24] Regulation (EU) 2023/1115, recital 9.

[25] Marín Durán and Scott (2022), p. 247.

[26] Eurostat (2020), p. 87.

2.2 The Political and Legal Context, at Length

In the last thirty years, concerns with regards to "the disappearance and degradation of forests" have been an important aspect of international environmental policies.[27] Indeed, the 1992 UN Conference on Environment and Development (a.k.a. the Earth Summit) resulted in both the Convention on Biological Diversity (CBD)[28] and the more specific Non-Legally Binding Authoritative Statement of Principles for a Global Consensus on the Management, Conservation and Sustainable Development of All Types of Forests (a.k.a. the Rio Forest Principles).[29] Since then, a flurry of international (2.2.1) and European (2.2.2) initiatives has addressed the preservation of biodiversity or even, more precisely, the protection and restoration of forests.

2.2.1 International Non-binding Instruments

First and foremost, the aforementioned Rio Forest Principles emerged from the failure to attain a global convention against deforestation – akin to the CBD or the UN Convention to Combat Desertification[30] – during the Earth Summit negotiations. So-called developed and developing States indeed disagreed on the financing of costly required efforts. The principles were thus a (soft law) compromise specifying in the preamble that "[t]he subject of forests is related to the entire range of environmental and development issues and opportunities, including the right to socio-economic development on a sustainable basis",[31] inducing that questions pertaining to these ecosystems should be addressed holistically, by taking into account for all types of forests the economic, traditional/social and ecological stresses and opportunities of constraining forestry practices or of their sustainable management.[32] Concretely, the Rio Forest Principles reaffirmed States' sovereign right to exploit their forest resources[33] but insisted on the necessity for them to provide a sustainable and comprehensive framework for the management of forests in order to meet the many needs of their populations.[34] Following elements relate *inter alia* to the consideration and participation of women and indigenous peoples,[35] the necessity for "non-discriminatory and multilaterally agreed rules and procedures" regarding trade in forest products,[36] as well as for a "supportive international economic

[27] Marín Durán and Scott (2022), p. 248.

[28] Done in Rio de Janeiro on 5 June 1992, UNTS, 1993, vol. 1760.

[29] UN Doc/A/CONF.151/26 (Vol. III), Annex III.

[30] United Nations Convention to Combat Desertification in those Countries Experiencing Serious Drought and/or Desertification, particularly in Africa, done in Paris on 14 October 1994, UNTS, 1996, vol. 1954: While not adopted at the Summit but two years later, so also after the Forest Principles, the Convention is the culmination of Chapter 12 (Managing Fragile Ecosystems: Combating Desertification and Drought) of the Earth Summit's Agenda 21. Conversely, chapter 11 (Combating Deforestation) did not *per se* lead to another legal instrument.

[31] Rio Forest Principles, recital (a).

[32] Ibid, recitals (c), (e) and (f).

[33] Ibid, principles 1(a) and 2(a).

[34] Ibid, principles 1(b), 2(b) and 3(a) and (c).

[35] Ibid, principle 5.

[36] Ibid, principle 13.

climate conducive to sustained and environmentally sound development of forests in all countries",[37] including the provision of financial resources, technologies and know-how/knowledge to developing countries.[38] The broad character of those requirements has made them a basis for the forest-protecting initiatives that followed.

A few years after the Earth Summit, the UN Economic and Social Council (ECOSOC) established, first, an ad hoc open-ended Intergovernmental Panel on Forests (the IPF) – with the role to "pursue consensus and to formulate coordinated proposals for action towards the management, conservation and sustainable development of all types of forests"[39] – and, second, a similarly ad hoc and open-ended Intergovernmental *Forum* on Forests (the IFF) supposed to "continue the intergovernmental policy dialogue on forests and to promote and facilitate the implementation of the proposals for action" of the IPF.[40] Then, in 2000, the same council agreed on the creation of an international arrangement on forests (IAF) "based on the Rio Declaration on Environment and Development, the [Rio Forest Principles], chapter 11 of Agenda 21 and the outcomes of the [IPF/IFF] process".[41] This arrangement comprises *inter alia* the UN Forum on Forests (UNFF) and the Collaborative Partnership on Forests (CPF).[42]

In the context of the CBD, the COP10 held in Nagoya in 2010 resulted in the adoption, along the Nagoya Protocol,[43] of the Aichi Biodiversity Targets for 2020, twenty in total divided into five Strategic Goals. Of particular interest are Target 5 ("By 2020, the rate of loss of all natural habitats, including forests, is at least halved and where feasible brought close to zero, and degradation and fragmentation is significantly reduced") and Target 7 ("By 2020 areas under agriculture, aquaculture and forestry are managed sustainably, ensuring conservation of biodiversity") under the Strategic Goal B ("Reduce the direct pressures on biodiversity and promote sustainable use"). Although there has been improvement with regards to some of the Aichi objectives – including Target 5 as "[t]he rate of deforestation has fallen globally by about a third compared to the previous decade" – *none* has been fully achieved.[44] Its follow-up, the 2022 Kunming-Montreal Global Biodiversity Framework, consisting of four long-term goals and 23 targets, only contains one mention of forestry, Target 10 calling for its sustainable management "including through a substantial increase of the application of biodiversity friendly practices, such as sustainable intensification, agroecological and other innovative approaches

---

[37] Ibid, principle 7(a).

[38] Ibid, principles 10, 11 and 12.

[39] ECOSOC, Decision 1995/226, 1.6.1995.

[40] ECOSOC, Resolution 1997/65, 25.7.1997.

[41] ECOSOC, Resolution 2000/35, 18.10.2000 – Report on the fourth session of the Intergovernmental Forum on Forests.

[42] For their current iterations, see ECOSOC, Resolution 2015/33, 22.7.2015 – International arrangement on forests beyond 2015, UN Doc/E/RES/2015/33.

[43] Nagoya Protocol on Access to Genetic Resources and the Fair and Equitable Sharing of Benefits Arising from their Utilization to the Convention on Biological Diversity, done in Nagoya on 29 October 2010, UNTS, 2014, vol. 3008.

[44] Secretariat of the Convention on Biological Diversity and United Nations Environment Programme (2020), p. 10.

contributing to the resilience and long-term efficiency and productivity of these production systems and to food security".[45] The lack of consideration for forests can probably be explained by their incorporation into the 2015 UN Sustainable Development Goals (SDGs) for 2030[46] and, to an even larger extent, by the adoption of the 2017 UN Strategic Plan for Forests, also with a timeframe to 2030.[47]

Among the SDGs, two in particular are relevant here: First, SDG 15's aim is to "protect, restore and promote sustainable use of terrestrial ecosystems, sustainably manage forests, combat desertification, and halt and reverse land degradation and halt biodiversity loss". More precisely, target 15.2's objective is to, "by 2020, promote the implementation of sustainable management of all types of forests, halt deforestation, restore degraded forests and substantially increase afforestation and reforestation globally". Second, SDG 12 does not relate directly to forests but is especially pertinent for the EUDR (see *infra*) insofar as its objective is to "ensure sustainable consumption and production patterns", with target 12.2 aiming to "achieve the sustainable management and efficient use of natural resources", using material footprint as an indicator, and target 12.6 to "encourage companies, especially large and transnational companies, to adopt sustainable practices and to integrate sustainability information into their reporting cycle".[48]

Another important political initiative then came in 2017 when the UN General Assembly adopted the UNFF's strategic plan for forests 2017–2030, which contains six Global Forest Goals tackling the various aspects of forest management (enhancing economic, social and environmental benefits; increasing cover of (protected) forest area; mobilizing financial resources and political cooperation; promote governance frameworks and cooperation; etc.). All in all, these goals remain quite broad, non-binding declarations of intent with little added value besides putting the issue of the health of forests back in the limelight. In that regard, one can also mention the November 2021 Glasgow Leaders' Declaration on Forests and Land Use.[49]

2.2.2 Europe's Variety of Instruments

At EU level, the first Communication specifically dedicated to tackling deforestation came in 2008[50] and underlined that "one of the main drivers for deforestation is economic

---

[45] CBD/COP/15/L.25, Target 10.

[46] Adopted by UNGA Resolution 70/1, 25.9.2015 – Transforming our world: the 2030 Agenda for Sustainable Development, UN Doc/A/RES/70/1.

[47] UNGA Resolution 71/285 of 27.4.2017, UN Doc/A/RES/71/285.

[48] Global indicator framework for the Sustainable Development Goals and targets of the 2030 Agenda for Sustainable Development, Annex to UNGA Resolution 71/313, 6.7.2017 – Work of the Statistical Commission pertaining to the 2030 Agenda for Sustainable Development, UN Doc/A/RES/71/313.

[49] Glasgow Leaders (2021) Glasgow Leaders' Declaration on Forests and Land Use. For a more exhaustive vision of the international legal and political framework applicable to forests, see Arts (2021); Marín Durán and Scott (2022), pp. 248–250; Savaresi (2012), pp. 149–173.

[50] COM(2008) 645 final, Communication from the Commission to the European Parliament, the Council, the European Economic and Social Committee and the Committee of the Regions – Addressing the challenges of deforestation and forest degradation to tackle climate change and biodiversity loss.

[as] forests are destroyed because it is more profitable in the short run to use land for other purposes than to keep them standing", concluding that "an effective policy has to reward the value of the services provided by forests".[51] Prior to that communication, the 2003 Forest Law Enforcement, Governance and Trade (FLEGT) action plan targeted illegal logging but environmental consideration, although part of it, where somewhat secondary.[52] Indeed, the Commission presented the FLEGT Communication as follows:

> "The Action Plan is the start of a process which places particular emphasis on governance reforms and capacity building, supported by actions aimed at developing multilateral cooperation and complementary demand-side measures designed to reduce the consumption of illegally harvested timber in the EU (and ultimately major consumer markets elsewhere in the world)."[53]

These communications would be followed by the 2011 EU Biodiversity Strategy to 2020,[54] the 2013 strategy "for forests and the forest-based sector",[55] the 7th Environment Action Programme,[56] and the 2018 "A Clean Planet for all" strategic long-term vision.[57]

More concretely, as Regulation 2023/1115 explains, prior to its adoption, "the existing Union legal framework focuse[d] on tackling illegal logging and associated trade and [did] not address deforestation directly".[58] In effect, this was pursued by two offshoots of the aforementioned FLEGT action plan: Council Regulation 2173/2005 of 20 December 2005 on the establishment of a FLEGT licensing scheme for imports of timber into the European Community (FLEGT Regulation)[59] and Regulation 995/2010 of 20 October 2010 laying down the obligations of operators who place timber and timber products on the market (EUTR).[60]

---

[51] Ibid, p. 6.

[52] COM (2003) 251 final, Communication from the Commission to the Council and the European Parliament – Forest Law Enforcement, Governance and Trade (FLEGT): Proposal for an EU Action Plan.

[53] Ibid, p. 3, emphasis added.

[54] COM (2011) 244 final, Communication from the Commission to the European Parliament, the Council, the European Economic and Social Committee and the Committee of the Regions – Our life insurance, our natural capital: an EU biodiversity strategy to 2020.

[55] COM (2013) 659 final, Communication from the Commission to the European Parliament, the Council, the European Economic and Social Committee and the Committee of the Regions – A new EU Forest Strategy: for forests and the forest-based sector.

[56] Decision 1386/2013/EU of the European Parliament and of the Council of 20 November 2013 on a General Union Environment Action Programme to 2020 'Living well, within the limits of our planet', OJ L 354, p. 171, 28.12.2013.

[57] COM(2018) 773 final, Communication from the Commission to the European Parliament, the European Council, the Council, the European Economic and Social Committee, the Committee of the Regions and the European Investment Bank – A Clean Planet for all: A European strategic long-term vision for a prosperous, modern, competitive and climate neutral economy.

[58] Regulation (EU) 2023/1115, recital 32.

[59] OJ L 347, 30.12.2005.

[60] OJ L 295, 12.11.2010.

In practice, the 2005 FLEGT Regulation provides for the establishment of Voluntary Partnership Agreements (VPAs) whereby "FLEGT licenses" would be issued by partner countries "for timber products for export to the Community"[61] in order to ensure that EU wood consumption has been harvested in compliance with the country of production's legislation. As of May 2025, ten countries have concluded such agreements with the Union: the Republic of Ghana[62] in November 2009, the Republic of the Congo[63] and the Republic of Cameroon[64] in May and October 2010, the Republic of Liberia[65] and the Central African Republic[66] in July and November 2011, the Republic of Indonesia[67] in September 2013, the Socialist Republic of Viet Nam[68] in October 2018, the Republic of Honduras[69] in February 2021, the Co-operative Republic of Guyana[70] in December 2022, and the Republic of Côte d'Ivoire[71] in February 2024. Yet, Indonesia remains the only country effectively issuing FLEGT licenses[72] (soon to be joined, however, by

[61] Council Regulation (EC) 2173/2005, art. 2(1).

[62] Voluntary Partnership Agreement between the European Community and the Republic of Ghana on forest law enforcement, governance and trade in timber products into the Community, OJ L 70, 19.3.2010.

[63] Voluntary Partnership Agreement between the European Union and the Republic of the Congo on forest law enforcement, governance and trade in timber and derived products to the European Union (FLEGT), OJ L 92, 06.4.2011.

[64] Voluntary Partnership Agreement between the European Union and the Republic of Cameroon on forest law enforcement, governance and trade in timber and derived products to the European Union (FLEGT), OJ L 92, 06.4.2011.

[65] Voluntary Partnership Agreement between the European Union and the Republic of Liberia on forest law enforcement, governance and trade in timber products to the European Union, OJ L 191, 19.7.2012.

[66] Voluntary Partnership Agreement between the European Union and the Central African Republic on forest law enforcement, governance and trade in timber and derived products to the European Union (FLEGT), OJ L 191, 19/07.2012.

[67] Voluntary Partnership Agreement between the European Union and the Republic of Indonesia on forest law enforcement, governance and trade in timber products into the European Union, OJ L 150, 20.5.2014.

[68] Voluntary Partnership Agreement between the European Union and the Socialist Republic of Viet Nam on forest law enforcement, governance and trade, OJ L 147, 05.6.2019.

[69] Voluntary Partnership Agreement between the European Union and the Republic of Honduras on Forest Law Enforcement, Governance and Trade in Timber Products to the European Union, OJ L 217, 18.6.2021.

[70] Voluntary Partnership Agreement between the European Union and the Cooperative Republic of Guyana on Forest Law Enforcement, Governance and Trade in Timber Products to the European Union, OJ L 121, 05.5.2023.

[71] Voluntary Partnership Agreement between the European Union and the Republic of Côte d'Ivoire on forest law enforcement, governance and trade in timber and derived products to the European Union (FLEGT), OJ L, 2024/1414, 27.5.2024.

[72] Commission Delegated Regulation (EU) 2016/1387 of 9 June 2016 amending Annexes I and III to Council Regulation (EC) No 2173/2005 following a Voluntary Partnership Agreement with Indonesia for a FLEGT licensing scheme for imports of timber into the European Union, OJ L 223, 18.08.2016.

Ghana),[73] leading the Commission's experts to consider, in a fitness check made in 2021 in preparation for the most recent regulation, that "the VPAs have only had a limited impact on preventing illegal timber from being placed on the EU market, and/or reducing illegal logging globally", adding that "many important exporters to the EU, which are considered to be high-risk countries regarding illegal logging, have never shown interest in engaging in the VPA process".[74]

As for the 2010 EUTR, in response to the "institutional and governance deficiencies that are present in the forest sector in a number of timber-producing countries"[75], it more unilaterally imposes due diligence obligations on operators that want to place timber and timber products on the Union market.[76] The due diligence aspect is composed of three elements related to the question of risk management: "access to *information*, risk *assessment* and *mitigation* of the risk identified".[77] So, whereas the FLEGT Regulation had set a supply-side mechanism, the licenses being issued by the producing countries, the EUTR established demand-side measures whereby illegally harvested timber is prohibited from entering the common market through control by (and in turn of) the operators. Yet, according to the aforementioned fitness check, here too the picture is contrasted: although the regulation is considered to have reduced anywhere between 12 and 29% of illegally harvested timber imports, the due diligence obligation has had "no significant effect on the volume of timber from known high-risk sources" while presenting "too complex and resource-intensive" challenges for micro, small and medium-sized enterprises.[78] Furthermore, inasmuch as the definition and implementation of sanctions is left to EU member States, operators have an incentive to import timber from high-risk third States through member States with less stringent implementation and/or slacker controls.[79] This EUTR is repealed by the EUDR,[80] in contrast to the FLEGT Regulation.

Very briefly, in addition to this FLEGT framework, and more indirectly, Directive 2018/2001, which "establishes a common framework for the promotion of energy from renewable sources", contains provision restricting the possibility to use biofuels, bioliquids and biomass fuels "made from raw material obtained from land with a high biodiversity value", chiefly primary or highly biodiverse forests and wooded land.[81] The same

[73] Commission Delegated Regulation (EU) 2025/530 of 30 October 2024 amending Annexes I and III to Council Regulation (EC) No 2173/2005 following a Voluntary Partnership Agreement with the Republic of Ghana for a Forest Law Enforcement, Governance and Trade (FLEGT) licensing scheme for imports of timber into the European Union, OJ L, 20.3.2025, art. 3 in particular.

[74] SWD (2021) 328 final, Commission Staff Working Document, 17.11.2021, p. 25 and 26.

[75] Regulation (EU) No 995/2010 of the European Parliament and of the Council of 20 October 2010 laying down the obligations of operators who place timber and timber products on the market, OJ L 295, p. 23, 12.11.2010, recital 2.

[76] Ibid, recital 15 and art. 1.

[77] Ibid, recital 17 and art. 6, emphasis added.

[78] SWD (2021) 328 final, p. 21 and 22.

[79] Ibid, p. 23.

[80] Regulation (EU) 2023/1115, art. 37.

[81] Directive (EU) 2018/2001 of the European Parliament and of the Council of 11 December 2018 on the promotion of the use of energy from renewable sources (recast), OJ L 328, p. 82, 21.12.2018, art. 1 and 29(3).

year, several provisions relating to forest land were contained in Regulation 2018/841, which overall "sets out the commitments of Member States for the land use, land use change and forestry ('LULUCF') sector that contribute to achieving the objectives of the Paris Agreement and meeting the greenhouse gas emission reduction target of the Union for the period from 2021 to 2030".[82] A few weeks before the adaption of the EUDR, Regulation 2018/841 was amended by Regulation 2023/839 on the basis that "[t]he accounting rules set out in Articles 6, 7, 8 and 10 of Regulation (EU) 2018/841 were designed to determine the extent to which mitigation performance in the LULUCF sector could contribute to the 2030 Union target for reduction of greenhouse gas net emissions of 40%, which did not include the LULUCF sector [and, in] order to simplify the regulatory framework for that sector, the current accounting rules should not apply after 2025, and the compliance with national targets of the Member States should be verified on the basis of reported greenhouse gas emissions and removals[, which] would provide methodological consistency with Directive 2003/87/EC of the European Parliament and of the Council, with Regulation (EU) 2018/842 of the European Parliament and of the Council, and with the new target for reduction of greenhouse gas net emissions of at least 55%, which includes the LULUCF sector".[83]

3 Scope and Principles of the Contemporary EU Framework for Forest Protection

Around the EGD, three EU instruments were put forth and addressed deforestation specifically, both within and beyond the frontiers of the Union. Before tackling the EUDR which tries to limit deforestation and forest degradation through the control of both exports and imports of a several commodities and derived products (4), the July 2019 Commission communication relating to the protection of the world's forests – i.e., beyond its Member States' territory – (3.1) and the 2021 communication targeting forests situated within the EU (3.2) shall be developed.

3.1 Outside EU Frontiers: The Communication on Stepping up EU Action to Protect and Restore the World's Forests

The aim of this communication is to "propose ways to step-up EU action to protect the world's forests, in particular primary forests, and restore forests in a sustainable and responsible way [in order to] improve people's health and livelihoods and ensure

[82] Regulation (EU) 2018/841 of the European Parliament and of the Council of 30 May 2018 on the inclusion of greenhouse gas emissions and removals from land use, land use change and forestry in the 2030 climate and energy framework, and amending Regulation (EU) No 525/2013 and Decision No 529/2013/EU, OJ L 156, 19.6.2018, art. 1, 6, 8, 9 and 13, and Annexes IV, V and VII.

[83] Regulation (EU) 2023/839 of the European Parliament and of the Council of 19 April 2023 amending Regulation (EU) 2018/841 as regards the scope, simplifying the reporting and compliance rules, and setting out the targets of the Member States for 2030, and Regulation (EU) 2018/1999 as regards improvement in monitoring, reporting, tracking of progress and review, OJ L 107, 21.4.2023, recital 10.

a healthy planet for our children and grandchildren".[84] To do so, it establishes five priorities,[85] each being supplemented by "actions to be implemented by the European Commission" documented in its first annex[86] (in Table 2, only the broad guidelines of those actions are indicated).

Table 2. Priorities and Actions Guidelines in Commission Communication on Stepping up EU Action to Protect and Restore the World's Forests and its First Annex

Priorities		Key actions
1	Reduce the EU consumption footprint on land and encourage the consumption of products from deforestation-free supply chains in the EU	Promote transparent supply chains
		Promote deforestation-free consumption
2	Work in partnership with producing countries to reduce pressures on forests and to 'deforest–proof' EU development cooperation	Support sustainable land and forest use practices and forest protection
		Support national efforts in partner countries to reduce pressure on forests
3	Strengthen international cooperation to halt deforestation and forest degradation and encourage forest restoration	Push for strong commitments
		Address deforestation and forest degradation in the trade policy
4	Redirect finance to support more sustainable land-use practices	Support producing countries to mobilise public and private financing and ensure its effectiveness
		Step up consideration as part of the Sustainable Finance Action Plan
5	Support the availability of, quality of, and access to information on forests and commodity supply chains. Support research and innovation	Improve monitoring and provision of reliable information
		Mobilise and better coordinate research and innovation

A second annex specifies "actions recommended to Member States' authorities, industries and civil society". Those are not differentiated by priority and encourage, *inter alia,* support and cooperation between countries, voluntary commitments by industries to improve supply chains by taking into account forest degradation and the rights of indigenous peoples, or, for civil society, creating networks to raise awareness on those issues.[87]

As for the Communication itself, in a nutshell, and in light of how "forest goods and services" are put in jeopardy by the consequences of deforestation,[88] it calls for

[84] COM (2019) 352 final, p. 6.
[85] Ibid, pp. 7 to 16.
[86] Annex 1 to COM (2019) 352 final.
[87] Annex 2 to COM (2019) 352 final.
[88] COM (2019) 352 final, pp. 2 and 3, figures 1 and 2.

the EU to promote solutions specific for each country and/or region and which rely on cooperative and financially supportive means. The initiative is therefore based on partnership, between "producer and consumer countries as well as business and civil society",[89] in particular with a view to improving information and the transparency of supply chains.

3.2 Inside the Union's Territories: The New EU Forest Strategy for 2030

The forest strategy contains "measures for strengthening forest protection and restoration, enhancing sustainable forest management, and improving the monitoring and effective decentralised planning on forests in the EU with a view to ensuring resilient forest ecosystems and enabling forests to deliver on their multifunctional role".[90] Established in 2021, it replaces the previous strategy for forests and the forest-based sector.[91] Even though it is explicitly focused on EU forests, the strategy for 2030 does reaffirm early on the Commission's "full commitment to deliver on" the World's Forests communication.[92] Nevertheless, the ambit of the Forest Strategy is very much internal, hinging on six axes:

- Supporting the socio-economic functions of forests for thriving rural areas and boosting forest-based bio-economy within sustainability boundaries;
- Protecting, restoring and enlarging EU's forests to combat climate change, reverse biodiversity loss and ensure resilient and multifunctional forest ecosystems;
- Strategic forest monitoring, reporting and data collection;
- A strong research and innovation agenda to improve our knowledge on forests;
- Inclusive and coherent EU forest governance framework;
- Stepping up implementation and enforcement of existing EU *acquis*.

More concretely, seven milestones have been established as part of a "roadmap of the Commission's action to implement the pledge to plant 3 billion trees by 2030 in the EU".[93] It essentially planned the creation of guidelines on biodiversity-friendly afforestation and reforestation, the development of a website (the Forest Information System for Europe),[94] a monitoring platform and a tree counter,[95] and the conduct of a study establishing a panorama of the pledges and their state of progress.

4 Addressing Both Intra-EU and International Trade: Regulation 2023/1115

Finally, in May 2023, the EU adopted Regulation 2023/1115 (the EUDR) on the making available on the Union market and the export therefrom of commodities and products embodying EU-caused deforestation and forest degradation. Its objective is twofold:

89 Ibid, p. 6.
90 COM (2021) 572 final, p. 3.
91 COM (2013) 659 final.
92 COM (2021) 572 final, p. 3.
93 Annex to COM (2021) 572 final.
94 https://forest.eea.europa.eu/.
95 https://forest.eea.europa.eu/3-billion-trees/introduction.

"minimis[e] the Union's contribution to deforestation and forest degradation worldwide" and "reduc[e] the Union's contribution to greenhouse gas emissions and global biodiversity loss".[96] To this end, it prohibits the trade to, within or from the EU of a select list of commodities, and their derived products, if they are not "deforestation-free", "produced in accordance with the relevant legislation of the country of production" and "covered by a due diligence statement".[97]

As a major consumer of commodities associated with deforestation and forest degradation (so-called "Forest-risk commodities"),[98] the EU has indeed a responsibility, although an indirect and partial one, regarding the unprecedented loss of woodland ecosystems, both within and beyond its frontiers. This "environmental footprint" relates to six commodities in particular: cattle, cocoa, oil palm, soya and wood. In its adopted version, the scope of the regulation concerns these commodities plus rubber (the "relevant commodities") and all products listed in the legislation's first annex, which "contain, have been fed with or have been made using said commodities" (the "relevant products").[99]

In a way, the EUDR marks a step forward from the FLEGT framework, and in particular it constitutes an evolution of the aforementioned EUTR,[100] with which it shares its general structure. After a panorama of the main common points of the two regulations and how the EUDR builds upon the EUTR (4.1), two specific questions shall be explored further: the regulations' territorial scope (4.2) and the addition in the latest regulation of a "sustainability criterion" (the products should be deforestation-free) to the legality criterion (they should be legally harvested) that existed in the previous framework (4.3).

4.1 Building Upon EUTR

Both regulations rely on the same basic idea, i.e. that, if the EU wants to decrease its contribution to deforestation and in turn the "social, political and economic implications"[101] and CO_2 emissions arising therefrom, the trade on its single market of specified products should be regulated through a due diligence mechanism in order to ensure that, *a minima*, they have been legally harvested in their country of origin. But the latest's regulation advancements are plural.

First, the material scope is much larger: whereas the EUTR only targeted "timber and timber products",[102] the EUDR covers the seven aforementioned commodities (cattle, cocoa, coffee, oil palm, rubber, soya and wood) and their derived products.[103]

Second, while the categories of people subject to the regulations' obligations are the same (operators and traders),[104] the EUTR, considering that "[i]n order to avoid imposing

96 Regulation (EU) 2023/1115, art. 1(1).
97 Ibid, art. 3.
98 Marín Durán and Scott (2022), p. 246.
99 Regulation (EU) 2023/1115, art. 2.
100 Regulation (EU) 995/2010.
101 Regulation (EU) 2023/1115, recitals 1 and 3 to 5; Regulation (EU) 995/2010, recital 3.
102 Regulation (EU) 995/2010, art. 1.
103 Regulation (EU) 2023/1115, art. 1 and 2(1).
104 Ibid, art. 2(15) and (17); Regulation (EU) No 995/2010, art. 2(c) and (d).

any unnecessary administrative burden, only operators that place timber and timber products on the internal market for the first time should be subject to the due diligence system, while a trader in the supply chain should be required to provide basic information on its supplier and its buyer to enable the traceability of timber and timber products",[105] only provides for somewhat simple and general information keeping requirements on traders.[106] On the other hand, traders' obligations under EUDR are more detailed and thorough,[107] although they remain differentiated from operators'. As for the latter, the provisions of the EUDR are much stronger than those of the EUTR, calling for a much more robust due diligence on their part.[108]

The same goes for the due diligence statement which in EUDR is developed in no less than six articles, in contrast with the one in EUTR. Overall, the requirement can be distinguished into the three constituting components of risk management: access to information,[109] risk assessment[110] and risk mitigation.[111]

4.2 Extraterritorial Extent

One should keep in mind that "[w]hile most commodities associated with deforestation and forest degradation are consumed at local or regional level, the EU imports products such as palm oil, meat, soy, cocoa, maize, timber, rubber, including in the form of processed products or services" to the extent that the Union's total consumption accounts for approximately 10% of embodied deforestation,[112] a "disproportionally large" share.[113]

One can thus wonder what the real ambit of the regulation is. As an EU legislation, it should logically concern EU interests. In a way it does: as mentioned, the regulation's obligations fall, like for the EUTR, on operators[114] – i.e. "any natural or legal person who, in the course of a commercial activity, places relevant products on the market or export them"[115] – and traders[116] – "any person in the supply chain other than the operator who, in the course of a commercial activity, makes relevant products available on the market"[117] –, meaning that the regulated activity is the trade in the aforementioned commodities and products on the EU single market.

Yet, the ultimate objective of the regulation is not only to ensure that EU consumption does not lead to deforestation and forest degradation, as it also states that "Union policy

105 Regulation (EU) 995/2010, recital 15.
106 Bid, art. 5.
107 Regulation (EU) 2023/1115, art. 5.
108 Ibid, art. 4; Regulation (EU) 995/2010, art. 4.
109 Regulation (EU) 2023/1115, art. 8(2)(a) and 9; Regulation (EU) 995/2010, art. 6(1)(a).
110 Regulation (EU) 2023/1115, art. 8(2)(b) and 10; Regulation (EU) 995/2010, art. 6(1)(b).
111 Regulation (EU) 2023/1115, art. 8(2)(c) and 11; Regulation (EU) 995/2010, art. 6(1)(c).
112 COM(2019) 352 final, p. 4.
113 Regulation (EU) 2023/1115, recital 18.
114 Ibid, art. 4.
115 Ibid, art. 2(15).
116 Ibid, art. 5.
117 Ibid, art. 2(17).

should aim at influencing the global market".[118] Moreover, it is presented as complementary to the World's Forests communication in its goal to support and foster cooperation with producer countries, notably for "addressing root causes of deforestation", and also to encourage in other major consumer States the "trade in deforestation-free products and [...] adoption of similar measures".[119]

So, the regulation clearly has a global objective and, although it theoretically targets imports, exports and intra-EU trade, the selected commodities effectively lean towards an application on imports, and thus rather extraterritorial effects. The EUTR targeted timber, or industrial roundwood, a product for which the EU produced more than 500 million square meters in 2022. It is one of the two only commodities targeted by EUDR for which EU's production is significant, as, according to FAOSTAT, it is responsible for 30% of the world's industrial roundwood production and 18% for cattle meat.[120] In contrast, the Union accounts for (virtually) 0% of the production of 4 of the EUDR's targeted commodities (cocoa, coffee, oil palm and rubber) and less than 3% for soya beans.[121]

Interestingly, Indonesia – which as a reminder is, as of writing, the only State with an effective FLEGT licensing scheme[122] for timber – is involved in the production of all commodities and among the five main players for four of them (natural rubber, palm oil fruit, coffee and cocoa). Other countries with concluded VPAs that are among the main producers for some of these commodities include Ghana and Côte d'Ivoire with regards to cocoa and Viet Nam for coffee and rubber. For industrial roundwood, none of the five most important producers is involved in a VPA,[123] but imports from all of them are of course concerned by the EUTR.

Consequently, whereas the EU promotes Regulation 2023/1115 as a complement to its collaborative endeavours to address root causes of deforestation and improve both quantity and quality of woodland ecosystems around the world, this is not how production countries have received it. In November 2022, when the EUDR was only still a proposal from the Commission, Indonesia and Brazil submitted in the World Trade Organization (WTO)'s Committee on Agriculture a joint letter signed by the ambassadors to the EU of a total of fourteen States[124] and "regret[ting] that the EU has chosen the option towards unilateral legislation instead of an international engagement to deal with these shared objectives [that are the fight against climate change and the conservation and sustainable management of forests], reflected in the Paris Agreement and the SDGs,

118 Ibid, recital 18.

119 Ibid, recitals 25 to 28, in particular 27.

120 FAOSTAT Forestry Production and Trade. In: fao.org. https://www.fao.org/faostat/en/#data/FO/visualize. Accessed 30.8.2025.

121 FAOSTAT Crops and livestock products. In: fao.org. https://www.fao.org/faostat/en/#data/QCL/visualize. Accessed 18.8.2025, Data for cattle was not available.

122 Council Regulation (EC) 2173/2005, art. 3 to 5. Ghana should become second some time in 2025.

123 Nor are there any for soya beans and cattle meat, but this is less relevant as the FLEGT scheme only concerns timber/wood.

124 Argentina, Brazil, Colombia, Ghana, Guatemala, Indonesia, Ivory Coast, Nigeria, Paraguay, Peru, Honduras, Malaysia, Ecuador and Bolivia.

to which [they] have all subscribed". In particular, the letter condemns "the country assessment criteria and benchmarking system [as] inherently discriminatory and punitive in nature".[125] Article 29 of the Regulation indeed provides for benchmarking system distinguishing (producing) countries between high, standard and low risk according to a range of criteria, including three mandatory ones (rate of deforestation and forest degradation, rate of expansion of agricultural land, and production trends of relevant commodities and products), and several criteria that *may* be taken into account.[126] This first letter also expresses the signees' concern with regards to.

> "[…] the EU's approach regarding several elements in the proposed regulation, such as the uncertain and discriminatory nature of the scope of products; definitions that are not multilaterally agreed; retroactive cut-off date; burdensome due diligence mechanism and subjective risk assessment criteria; costly and impractical traceability and geo-localization requirements; and insufficient unilaterally defined transition period, which could increase costs and have negative social and economic consequences for developing countries."[127]

In the end of September 2023, four months after the adoption of the EUDR, another such letter, this time submitted by Indonesia, Brazil, Malaysia and Thailand, and signed by seventeen countries,[128] reiterated their "deep concern regarding the recent entry into force of the European Union's regulation on deforestation-free products", especially as to how, according to them, "this legislation disregards local circumstances and capabilities, national legislations and certification mechanisms of developing producer countries, their efforts to fight deforestation, and multilateral commitments, including the principle of common but differentiated responsibilities [and] establishes a unilateral benchmarking system that is inherently discriminatory and punitive, which is potentially inconsistent with WTO obligations".[129]

4.3 The Decisive Criterion: From Legality of Sustainability

As mentioned, whereas the EUTR only relied upon a "legality criterion" accompanied by the exercise of due diligence,[130] the EUDR adds a "sustainability criterion": in order to be accepted on the EU market, products must be deforestation-free.[131] Much of the above criticism actually relates to this requirement and to its implementation. The legality

---

[125] Joint Letter – European Union Proposal for a Regulation on Deforestation-Free Products, submission by Indonesia and Brazil, 27 July 2022, G/AG/GEN/213, 29.11.2022, p. 2.

[126] Regulation (EU) 2023/1115, art. 29(1), (3) and (4).

[127] Joint Letter, G/AG/GEN/213, p. 2.

[128] The fourteen signatories of the first letter joined by the Dominican Republic, Mexico and Thailand.

[129] Joint Letter – European Union's Regulation on Deforestation-Free Products (EUDR), submission by Indonesia, Brazil, Malaysia, and Thailand, 7 September 2023, G/AG/GEN/223/Rev.1, p. 2.

[130] Regulation (EU) No 995/2010, art. 4.

[131] Regulation (EU) 2023/1115, art. 3.

criterion is inherently multilateral as it refers to the legislation of the country of production and requires the respect thereof. Conversely, the sustainability criterion implies that said producing countries' legislation does not suffice to effectively reduce deforestation, and thus that external (in this case European) assessment is needed, including through a benchmarking of the countries of production.

This position has been criticised by so-called developing countries, but also by some NGOs, on the argument that "deforestation will only be eliminated when there is sufficient domestic political consensus to codify these objectives into law and implement them through effective regulations, governance and enforcement".[132] By imposing a sustainability criterion, the EU bypasses, and according to some undermines, the measures that States of production already have in place. Critics, on the assumption that "[d]emand-side regulations will work the fastest if they do not meet significant resistance from producer country governments and will ultimately have the longest impact if they support producer country governance reforms",[133] identify five interrelated reasons why the sustainability criterion is likely to fail:[134]

- The lack of empowerment of producing countries with regards to the setting end enforcement of land use legislation,
- The lack of cooperation between producer and consumer States,
- The legality criterion is more likely to be "adopted as a broadly shared global norm, […] reducing leakage",
- The sustainability criterion, because of its unilaterality, goes against "principles of equity, self-determination and mutual respect among nations",
- The imposition of a sustainability criterion is likely to be challenged at the WTO, "resulting in years of delay".

Two remarks must be made in that regard. First, the adoption of the EUDR results in part from the lack of effectiveness of the currently fragmented policies and actions at global level.[135] Yet, in order for the effort to enhance the fight against deforestation and encourage "protection, restoration, afforestation and reforestation"[136] to be more collaborative, Article 30 stipulates that "[w]ithin their respective spheres of competence, the Commission, on behalf of the Union, and interested Member States shall engage in a coordinated approach with producer countries and parts thereof that are concerned […] through existing and future partnerships, and other relevant cooperation mechanisms to jointly address the root causes of deforestation and forest degradation".[137]

132 Wolosin (2022), p. 4.
133 Ibid, p. 11.
134 Ibid, p. 12.
135 Regulation (EU) 2023/1115, recitals 11, 19 et seq.
136 ibid, recital 21.
137 Ibid, art. 30(1).

For this cooperation, the Commission developed a Strategic Framework for International Cooperation Engagement,[138] which has been criticised as "no longer 'comprehensive', and ha[ving] scrapped its partnership ambition, focusing instead on technical and development cooperation".[139]

Second, the Commission must also adopt, initially before 30 December 2024, an implementing act "classify[ing] countries or parts thereof that present a low or high risk" (the aforementioned benchmarking system).[140] The deadline was however postponed by six months by Regulation 2024/3234, as were, by up to one year, the entry into force of most of the EUDR's provisions.[141] Said implementing act was finally adopted on 22 May 2025[142] and the country classification made public: only four countries are classified as high risk (Belarus, North Korea, Myanmar and the Russian Federation), fifty as presenting a standard risk (none from the EU), and 140 as low risk.[143]

5 Subsequent Legislations Impacting Forests

So far have been exposed the EU legislations (and communications) which concern the protection of forests that existed before the adoption of the EUDR. The latter ushered a new step in the European legislative framework for forest protection, including several legislations or proposals.

First, on the heels of the proposal that led to the EUDR,[144] the Commission submitted in December 2021 another proposal, for a revision of the EU's 2008 environmental crimes directive.[145] This revision proposal notably provided that.

[138] C/2024/6604, Communication from the Commission on the Strategic Framework for International Cooperation Engagement in the context of Regulation (EU) 2023/1115 on the making available on the Union market and the export from the Union of certain commodities and products as-sociated with deforestation and forest degradation, OJ C.

[139] Van Gisbergen I (2024).

[140] Regulation (EU) 2023/1115, art. 29(2).

[141] Regulation (EU) 2024/3234 of the European Parliament and of the Council of 19 December 2024 amending Regulation (EU) 2023/1115 as regards provisions relating to the date of application, OJ L, 2024/3234, 23.12.2024, art. 1.

[142] Commission Implementing Regulation (EU) 2025/1093 of 22 May 2025 laying down rules for the application of Regulation (EU) 2023/1115 of the European Parliament and of the Council as regards a list of countries that present a low or high risk of producing relevant commodities for which the relevant products do not comply with Article 3, point (a), OJ L, 23.5.2025.

[143] For an overview of all classifications, see European Commission Country Classification List. In: green-forum.ec.europa.eu. https://green-forum.ec.europa.eu/deforestation-regulation-implementation/eudr-cooperation-and-partnerships/country-classification-list_en. Accessed 18 Aug 2025.

[144] COM(2021) 706 final, Proposal for a Regulation of the European Parliament and of the Council on the making available on the Union market as well as export from the Union of certain commodities and products associated with deforestation and forest degradation and repealing Regulation (EU) No 995/2010.

[145] See Garcia Da Silva and Milcamps (2023), p. 308.

"Member States shall ensure that the following conduct constitutes a criminal offence when it is unlawful and committed intentionally: […] (n) the placing or making available on the Union market of illegally harvested timber or of timber products that were made of illegally harvested wood, falling within the scope of Regulation (EU) No 995/2010 of the European Parliament and of the Council, except for cases where the conduct concerns a negligible quantity; [If a Regulation on the making available on the Union market as well as export from the Union of certain commodities and products associated with deforestation and forest degradation and repealing Regulation (EU) No 995/2010 is adopted before this Directive, point (n) to be replaced with a criminal offence within the scope of Article 3 of that Regulation.]"[146]

At the outset, the construction of this provision demonstrated again, if need be, that the EUDR is an evolution of the EUTR: the conduct that must be criminalized is the violation of the latter, safe for the adoption of the former, in which case it is its violation that shall be criminalized instead. In addition, considering that the EUDR repeals the EUTR, the lack of this specification would have eventually rendered the provision moot. And indeed, the revised Environmental Crimes Directive was adopted in April 2024, making any violation of the prohibition of placing relevant commodities and products on the EU market – in other words, violations of the EUDR – a criminal offence if done intentionally or with serious negligence.[147]

Second, in June 2024, the Corporate Sustainability Due Diligence Directive (CSDDD) was adopted.[148] It is less prescriptive than the EUDR, has a different scope ("actual and potential human rights adverse impacts and environmental adverse impacts" of companies that have "more than 1 000 employees on average and had a net worldwide turnover of more than EUR 450 million")[149] and, while it does not address deforestation directly, "will complement the Regulation on deforestation-free products by introducing a value chain due diligence related to activities that are not covered by the Regulation on deforestation-free products but might be directly or indirectly leading to deforestation".[150] It is in line with SDG target 12.6 but also with the 2011 UN Guiding Principles on Business and Human Rights.

Third, the aforementioned Nature Restoration Law was proposed and adopted the same months as the CSDDD, with the aim of "establish[ing] a framework within which Member States shall put in place effective and area-based restoration measures with the

[146] COM(2021) 851 final, Proposal for a Directive of the European Parliament and of the Council on the protection of the environment through criminal law and replacing Directive 2008/99/EC, art. 3(1)(n), emphasis in the original text.

[147] Directive (EU) 2024/1203 of the European Parliament and of the Council of 11 April 2024 on the protection of the environment through criminal law and replacing Directives 2008/99/EC and 2009/123/EC, OJ L, 2024/1203, 30.2024, art. 3(2)(p).

[148] Directive (EU) 2024/1760 of the European Parliament and of the Council of 13 June 2024 on corporate sustainability due diligence and amending Directive (EU) 2019/1937 and Regulation (EU) 2023/2859, OJ L, 2024/1760, 05.07.2024.

[149] Ibid, art. 1 and 2.

[150] COM (2022) 71 final, Proposal for a Directive of the European Parliament and of the Council on Corporate Sustainability Due Diligence and amending Directive (EU) 2019/1937, p. 7.

aim to jointly cover, as a Union target, throughout the areas and ecosystems within the scope of this Regulation, at least 20% of land areas and at least 20% of sea areas by 2030, and all ecosystems in need of restoration by 2050".[151] With regards to forests, the restoration measures have among their various objectives the improvement of forest biodiversity and resilience.[152]

Finally, the Commission proposed a Forest Monitoring Regulation with the objective to "(a) ensur[e] timeliness, accuracy, consistency, transparency, comparability and completeness of forest data within the Union and their public accessibility; (b) [support] the voluntary development of integrated long-term plans at the level of the Member States through an evidence-based, inclusive, cross-sectoral and adaptive approach; [and] (c) [set] up a strengthened governance between the Commission and the Member States".[153] The monitoring framework therefore created encompasses a geographical identification system as well as data collection and sharing frameworks, and requires cooperation between Member States "to improve the quality, timeliness and coverage of forest data".[154] As it was proposed in November 2023, this potential regulation is still in the early stages of the EU legislative process.[155]

6 Conclusion

Between 2010 and 2020, average annual net forest loss has been of 4.7 million hectares, but deforestation has concerned 10 million hectares per year.[156] The difference is thus the result of afforestation and reforestation efforts, and thus essentially consists of planted forests which do not have the same biodiversity composition and do not offer the same ecosystem services as primary forests. To conserve those, efforts against deforestation must be ramped up.

Due to its fragmentation and lack of mandatory instruments, the international forest governance framework, if one can even call it that, has been unable to sufficiently decrease deforestation rates. For that reason, the EU has put forth communications and developed legislations with the aim of protecting forest and woodland ecosystems not only within, but also beyond the Union's frontiers. In particular, the EUDR is the most ambitious EU legislation addressing the destruction of forests ecosystems. This ambition has however raised many concerns, leading to the postponement of its provisions' entry into force by up to one year, an all in all relatively small change considering the significant pressures exerted upon the European legislators.

Importantly, these pressures did not originate from within the EU only, far from it. Considering the unilateral nature of the EUDR, many third countries evidently think that such initiatives do not correctly take their own means and objectives, interests and

151 Regulation (EU) 2024/1991, art. 1(2).

152 Ibid., recitals 31, 61 to 64, art. 12, 13 and 14, and Annex VI.

153 COM (2023) 728 final, art. 1.

154 Ibid, art. 3 et seq. and 11 et seq.

155 Proposal for a Regulation on a Monitoring Framework for Resilient European Forests – Presentation by the Commission – Progress report, ST 16255 2024 INIT, 29 November 2024.

156 Ritchie (2021).

concrete situations into account. If the EU wants to ensure the longevity and effectiveness of its framework outside its Member States' territory, it must ensure a strong and respectful cooperation with countries of production.

References

Arts, B.: Forest Governance: Hydra or Chloris?, 1st edn. Cambridge University Press (2021)

Dasgupta, P.: The Economics of Biodiversity: The Dasgupta Review: Abridged Version, Updated: 2 February 2021. HM Treasury, London (2021)

Eurostat (2020) Agriculture, forestry and fishery statistics: 2020 edition. Publications Office of the European Union, Luxembourg

Garcia Da Silva, B., Milcamps, P.-N.: The regulation on deforestation-free products: when the EU takes on deforestation's corrupted roots. EEELR **32**, 293–310 (2023). https://doi.org/10.54648/eelr2023019

Intergovernmental Science-Policy Platform on Biodiversity and Ecosystem Services (2019) The global assessment report on biodiversity and ecosystem services: Summary for policymakers. IPBES Secretariat, Bonn

Marín Durán, G., Scott, J.: Regulating trade in forest-risk commodities: two cheers for the European Union. J. Environ. Law **34**, 245–267 (2022). https://doi.org/10.1093/jel/eqac002

Millenium Ecosystem Assessment. Ecosystems and Human Well-Being: Synthesis. Island Press, Washington, DC (2005)

Ritchie, H.: Deforestation and Forest Loss: Explore long-term changes in deforestation and deforestation rates across the world today. In: ourworldindata.org (2021). https://ourworldindata.org/deforestation. Accessed 18 Aug 2025

Rossi, R.: The European Union and forests. In: europarl.europa.eu (2025). https://www.europarl.europa.eu/factsheets/en/sheet/105/the-european-union-and-forests. Accessed 18 Aug 2025

Savaresi, A.: EU external action on forests: FLEGT and the development of international law. In: Morgera, E. (ed.) The External Environmental Policy of the European Union, 1st edn. , pp 149–173. Cambridge University Press (2012)

Secretariat of the Convention on Biological Diversity, United Nations Environment Programme (2020) Global Biodiversity Outlook 5. Secretariat of the Convention on Biological Diversity, Montreal. https://www.cbd.int/gbo5. Accessed 18 Aug 2025

Wolosin, M.: Navigating the False Dichotomy between Legality and Zero Deforestation: An International Partnership Pathway to Reducing Agro-conversion. Forest Trends, Washington, DC (2022). https://www.forest-trends.org/publications/navigating-legality-and-zero-deforestation-intl-partnership-pathway/. Accessed 18 Aug 2025

Others

C/2024/6604: Communication from the Commission on the Strategic Framework for International Co-operation Engagement in the context of Regulation (EU) 2023/1115 on the making available on the Union market and the export from the Union of certain commodities and products as-sociated with deforestation and forest degradation, OJ C, 7.1.2024 (2024)

COM: 251 final, Communication from the Commission to the Council and the European Parliament – Forest Law Enforcement, Governance and Trade (FLEGT): Proposal for an EU Action Plan, 21.5.2003(2003)

COM: 645 final, Communication from the Commission to the European Parliament, the Council, the European Economic and Social Committee and the Committee of the Regions – Addressing the challenges of deforestation and forest degradation to tackle climate change and biodiversity loss, 17.10.2008 (2008)

COM: 244 final, Communication from the Commission to the European Parliament, the Council, the Euro-pean Economic and Social Committee and the Committee of the Regions – Our life insurance, our natural capital: an EU biodiversity strategy to 2020, 3.5.2011 (2011)

COM: 659 final, Communication from the Commission to the European Parliament, the Council, the Euro-pean Economic and Social Committee and the Committee of the Regions – A new EU Forest Strategy: for forests and the forest-based sector, 20.9.2013 (2013)

COM: 773 final, Communication from the Commission to the European Parliament, the European Council, the Council, the European Economic and Social Committee, the Committee of the Regions and the European In-vestment Bank – A Clean Planet for all: A European strategic long-term vision for a prosperous, modern, competitive and climate neutral economy, 28.11.2018 (2018)

COM: 640 final, Communication from the Commission to the European Parliament, the European Council, the Council, the European Economic and Social Committee and the Committee of the Regions – The European Green Deal, 11.12.2019 (2019)

COM: 352 final, Communication from the Commission to the European Parliament, the Council, the Euro-pean Economic and Social Committee and the Committee of the Regions – Stepping up EU Action to Protect and Restore the World's Forests, 23.7.2019 (2019)

COM: 572 final, Communication from the Commission to the European Parliament, the Council, the Euro-pean Economic and Social Committee and the Committee of the Regions – New EU Forest Strategy for 2030, 16.7.2021 (2021)

COM: 706 final, Proposal for a Regulation of the European Parliament and of the Council on the making available on the Union market as well as export from the Union of certain commodities and products associated with deforestation and forest degradation and repealing Regulation (EU) No 995/2010, 17.11.2021 (2021)

COM. 851 final, Proposal for a Directive of the European Parliament and of the Council on the protection of the environment through criminal law and replacing Directive 2008/99/EC,15.12.2021(2021)

COM: 71 final, Proposal for a Directive of the European Parliament and of the Council on Corporate Sustainability Due Diligence and amending Directive (EU) 2019/1937, 23.2.2022 (2022)

COM:728 final, Proposal for a Regulation of the European Parliament and of the Council on a monitoring framework for resilient European forests, 22.11.2023 (2023)

ECOSOC, Decision 1995/226, Establishment of an open-ended Ad Hoc Intergovernmental Panel on Forests of the Commission on Sustainable Development, 1.6.1995, p. 73 (1995)

ECOSOC, Resolution 1997/65, Establishment of an open-ended Ad Hoc Intergovernmental Forum on Forests of the Commission on Sustainable Development (E/1997/l.49 and E/1997/SR.42), 25.7.1997, p. 122 (1997)

ECOSOC, Resolution 2000/35, Report on the fourth session of the Intergovernmental Forum on Forests (E/2000/29, E/2000/L.32 and E/2000/SR.46), 18.10.2000, p. 64 (2000)

ECOSOC, Resolution 2015/33, International arrangement on forests beyond 2015, 22.7.2015, UN Doc/E/RES/2015/33 (2015)

European Environment Agency (2023) How are European forest ecosystems doing? (2023). https://www.eea.europa.eu/publications/how-are-european-forest. Accessed 18 Aug 2025

Glasgow Leaders: Glasgow Leaders' Declaration on Forests and Land Use. In: nationalarchives.org.uk (2021). https://webarchive.nationalarchives.gov.uk/ukgwa/20230418175226/https://ukcop26.org/glasgow-leaders-declaration-on-forests-and-land-use/. Accessed 18 Aug 2025

SWD: 328 final, Commission Staff Working Document – Fitness Check on Regulation (EU) No 995/2010 of the European Parliament and of the Council of 20 October 2010 laying down the obligations of operators who place timber and timber products on the market (the EU Timber Regulation) and on Regulation (EC) No 2173/2005 of 20 December 2005 on the establishment of a FLEGT licensing scheme for imports of timber into the European Community (FLEGT Regulation), Accompanying the document Proposal for a Regulation of the Eu-rope-an Parliament and of the Council on the making available on the Union market as well as export from the Un-ion of certain commodities and products associated with deforestation and forest degradation and repealing Regulation (EU) No 995/2010, 17.11.2021 (2021)

UNGA Resolution 70/1, Transforming our world: the 2030 Agenda for Sustainable Development, 25.9.2015, UN Doc/A/RES/70/1 (2030)

UNGA Resolution 71/285, 27.4.2017, UN Doc/A/RES/71/285

UNGA Resolution 71/313, Work of the Statistical Commission pertaining to the 2030 Agenda for Sustainable Development, 6.7.2017, UN Doc/A/RES/71/313

UN Doc/A/CONF.151/26 (Vol. III), Annex III, https://www.un.org/esa/documents/ga/conf151/aconf15126-3.htm. Accessed 18 Aug 2025

Van Gisbergen, I.: European Commission's draft Strategic Framework for international cooperation is no longer comprehensive and skips partnerships focus. In: fern.org (2024). https://www.fern.org/publications-insight/european-commissions-draft-strategic-framework-for-international-cooperation-is-no-longer-comprehensive-and-skips-partnerships-focus/. Accessed 18 Aug 2025

Author Index

M. Reese et al. (Eds.): EELF 2023, *Legal Implementation and Impacts of the European Green Deal*, p. 245, 2026.
https://doi.org/10.1007/978-3-032-17197-9

MIX
Papier aus verantwortungsvollen Quellen
Paper from responsible sources
FSC® C105338

If you have any concerns about our products,
you can contact us on
ProductSafety@springernature.com

In case Publisher is established outside the EU,
the EU authorized representative is:
Springer Nature Customer Service Center GmbH
Europaplatz 3, 69115 Heidelberg, Germany

Printed by Libri Plureos GmbH
in Hamburg, Germany